Take the Next
in Your IT Ca

T0293703

Save
10%
on Exam Vouchers*

(up to a $35 value)

*Some restrictions apply. See web page for details.

CompTIA.

CompTIA®
DataX
Study Guide

CompTIA®
DataX
Study Guide
Exam DY0-001

Fred Nwanganga

To my darling wife, Melinda, and my A-team (Alex, Abigail, and Andrew).
Thank you for your love and support. You make it all worth it!

Acknowledgments

I would like to thank and acknowledge all those who helped directly and indirectly in the development of this book. It takes a lot of hard work and dedication from many people to bring a project like this to completion.

First and foremost, I am profoundly grateful to my family for their unwavering support throughout this demanding project. Your constant encouragement and understanding were crucial as I navigated the complexities of this work. I also wish to express my heartfelt thanks to my friend and colleague, Mike Chapple, who consistently inspires me and encourages me to explore new horizons. A special acknowledgment to Kenyon Brown, the senior acquisitions editor at Wiley. Your guidance and support during this initial collaboration was invaluable. I look forward to many more projects like this one.

To the editing and production team, Brad Jones, Ashirvad Moses, Saravanan Dakshinamurthy, Elizabeth Welch, Arielle Guy, Sara Deichman, and others who worked diligently behind the scenes, thank you for your professionalism, exceptional organizational skills, and the insightful contributions you made toward enhancing the quality of the book. I am also thankful to Dr. Scott Nestler for taking the time to review the content thoroughly and provide detailed, thoughtful technical edits. Your expertise has greatly enhanced the quality of this book, making it a more accurate and valuable resource.

Carole Jelen of Waterside Productions continues to be a great literary agent and partner. Her continued support and ability to develop new opportunities have been tremendously beneficial in bringing this project and others like it to life.

Lastly, to my wonderful student assistants, Melissa Perotin and Ricky Chapple, thank you for reading through the material to make sure that it was coherent and accessible to a broad audience. Your work on the assessment questions was invaluable. I couldn't have done it without you.

About the Author

Fred Nwanganga, PhD, is an author, teacher, and data scientist with more than 20 years of analytics and information technology experience in higher education and the private sector. Fred currently serves as an associate teaching professor in the IT, Analytics, and Operations Department at the University of Notre Dame's Mendoza College of Business. He teaches undergraduate and graduate courses in machine learning, unstructured data analytics, and Python for analytics.

Fred is the author of several LinkedIn Learning courses on machine learning, Python, and generative AI. He is also the coauthor of *Practical Machine Learning in R* (Wiley, 2020). He earned both his BS and MS in computer science from Andrews University. He also holds an MBA from Indiana University and a PhD in computer science and engineering from the University of Notre Dame.

About the Technical Editor

Scott Nestler is a business analytics "pracademic" (practitioner-academic). Previously, he was director of research & development, as well as principal data scientist and optimization lead, at SumerSports. Prior to that, he was director of statistics & modeling at Accenture Federal Services. Previously, he was the academic director of the MS in Business Analytics program and is still an adjunct associate teaching professor in the Mendoza College of Business at the University of Notre Dame.

Originally from Harrisburg, Pennsylvania, Scott is a 1989 graduate of Lehigh University (with a BS in civil engineering), where he received his commission as an officer through the U.S. Army Reserve Officer Training Corps. He earned a PhD in business and management (management science and finance) from the University of Maryland in 2007 and a Master of Science in applied mathematics and operations research from the Naval Postgraduate School in 1999. He also earned a Master of Strategic Studies from the U.S. Army War College in 2013. He retired from the U.S. Army as a Colonel in 2015. In his last Army assignment, Scott served as director of strategic analytics at the Center for Army Analysis, an internal Army think tank. Scott's other tours of duty include assignments as an assistant professor at the Naval Postgraduate School; director of the center for data analysis and statistics at West Point; chief of strategic assessments at the U.S. Embassy – Baghdad; force structure analyst in the Pentagon; and director of computer operations at West Point. Scott won the Barchi Prize from the Military Operations Research Society in 2010 and was recognized by INFORMS with the Volunteer Award (Gold Level) in 2019. He has earned and maintains the Certified Analytics Professional (CAP) and Accredited Professional Statistician (PStat) certifications. He has published numerous articles and is coauthor (with Wayne Winston and Konstantinos Pelechrinis) of the book *Mathletics* (Princeton University Press, 2022).

Contents at a Glance

Contents

Introduction

Congratulations on taking the initial step toward achieving your CompTIA DataX certification. The DataX certification, as described by CompTIA, is "the premier skills development program for highly experienced professionals seeking to validate their competency in the rapidly evolving field of data science." This study guide is tailored for data scientists who are in the early to mid-stages of their careers. It is designed to serve as a refresher for some and a source of new insights for others. No matter your level of expertise, this guide aims to solidify your understanding of essential data science tools and concepts necessary to effectively prepare for and pass the DataX certification exam.

In the following pages, you will find essential information about the CompTIA DataX exam, details on the organization and scope of this book, and a sample assessment test. This test is intended to help gauge your initial readiness for the certification exam. The answer key for the assessment questions references which chapter within the book addresses the concepts or exam objective behind the question. I encourage you to concentrate your study efforts on those chapters that cover areas where you feel you need to build your skills and confidence.

About the DataX Certification

The DataX certification is designed to be a vendor-neutral validation of expert-level data science skills. CompTIA recommends the certification for professionals with 5+ years of experience in data science or similar roles. You can find additional information about the certification at:

www.comptia.org/certifications/datax

According to CompTIA, the certification is designed to assess a candidate's ability to:

- Understand and implement data science operations and processes
- Apply mathematical and statistical methods appropriately and understand the importance of data processing and cleaning, statistical modeling, linear algebra, and calculus concepts
- Apply machine learning models and understand deep learning concepts
- Utilize appropriate analysis and modeling methods and make justified model recommendations
- Demonstrate understanding of industry trends and specialized data science applications

Certification Objectives

CompTIA goes to great lengths to ensure that its certifications accurately reflect industry best practices. It works with a team of professionals, training providers, publishers, and subject matter experts (SMEs) to establish baseline competency for each of its exams. Based on this information, CompTIA has published five major domains that the DataX certification exam covers. The following is a list of the domains and the extent to which they are represented on the certification exam:

Domain	Percentage of exam
1.0 Mathematics and Statistics	17%
2.0 Modeling, Analysis, and Outcomes	24%
3.0 Machine Learning	24%
4.0 Operations and Processes	22%
5.0 Specialized Applications of Data Science	13%

Certification Exam

The DataX exam employs what CompTIA refers to as a "performance-based assessment" format. This approach integrates traditional multiple-choice questions with a variety of interactive question types, including fill-in-the-blank, multiple-response, drag-and-drop, and image-based problems, to create a more dynamic and comprehensive evaluation of a candidate's abilities. For more details about CompTIA's performance exams, visit:

`www.comptia.org/testing/testing-options/about-comptia-performance-exams`

The exam consists of 90 questions and has a time limit of 165 minutes. The results are provided in a pass/fail format. As you prepare, keep in mind two important aspects regarding the nature of the questions you will encounter.

First, CompTIA exams are known for their occasionally ambiguous questions. You may find yourself faced with multiple answers that seem correct, requiring you to choose the "most correct" one based on your knowledge and sometimes intuition. It's important not to spend too much time on these questions. Make your best choice, and then move on to the next question.

Second, be aware that CompTIA often includes unscored questions in their exams to collect psychometric data, a process known as item seeding. These questions are used to help develop future versions of the exam. Although these questions won't affect your score, you may not be able to distinguish them from scored questions, so you should attempt to answer every question as accurately as possible. Before starting the exam, you'll be informed about the possibility of encountering unscored questions. If you come across a question that doesn't seem related to any of the stated exam objectives, it might be one of these seeded questions, but since you can't be sure, it's best to treat every question as if it counts toward your final score.

Taking the Exam

Once you are ready to take the exam, visit the CompTIA store (https://store.comptia .org) to purchase a voucher for the exam. This book also includes a coupon that you may use to save 10 percent on the exam registration. CompTIA offers two options for taking the certification exam. You can either take the exam in person at a Pearson VUE testing center or online. The online exam involves a remote exam proctoring service powered by Pearson OnVUE.

> You can find more information about CompTIA testing options at www .comptia.org/testing/testing-options/about-testing-options.

How This Book Is Organized

This study guide covers everything you need to prepare and pass the DataX exam. Each chapter includes several recurring elements to help you prepare. Here's a description of some of those elements:

Assessment Test At the conclusion of this introduction, you'll find an assessment test designed to gauge your readiness for the exam. I recommend taking this test before you begin reading the book, as it will help you identify which areas might require further review. The answers to the assessment test questions are provided at the end of the test. Each answer comes with an explanation and a note indicating the chapter where the relevant material is covered, allowing you to focus your studies more effectively.

Summary The summary at the end of each chapter provides a concise review, highlighting the key points and concepts discussed. This overview helps to reinforce your understanding and ensures you grasp the essential elements covered in the chapter.

Exam Essentials The "Exam Essentials" section located near the end of each chapter underscores topics that are likely to be included on the exam in some capacity. While it's impossible to predict the exact content of the certification exam, this section emphasizes crucial concepts that are fundamental to understanding the topics discussed in the chapter. This feature is designed to reinforce your knowledge and help you focus on the most significant aspects that could be tested.

Chapter Review Questions Each chapter includes 20 practice questions intended to assess your understanding of the key ideas discussed. After completing each chapter, take the time to answer these questions. If you find some of your responses are incorrect, it's a signal that you should revisit and spend additional time on those topics. The answers to the practice questions are located in Appendix. Please note that these questions are designed to measure your retention of the material and may not necessarily mirror the format or complexity of the questions you will encounter on the exam.

The chapters in this book are structured to facilitate a smooth flow and deepen your understanding of key concepts. They are not necessarily arranged in alignment with the sequence or structure of the certification exam objectives. To assist you in your exam preparation, the following is a high-level map that shows how the exam objectives correspond to the chapters in this study guide. This mapping will help you navigate the material more effectively and ensure that you cover all necessary topics as you prepare for the exam.

Exam objective	Chapter(s)
1.0 Mathematics and Statistics	
1.1 Given a scenario, apply the appropriate statistical method or concept.	2, 6
1.2 Explain probability and synthetic modeling concepts and their uses.	2
1.3 Explain the importance of linear algebra and basic calculus concepts.	2
1.4 Compare and contrast various types of temporal models.	6
2.0 Modeling, Analysis, and Outcomes	
2.1 Given a scenario, use the appropriate exploratory data analysis (EDA) method or process.	4
2.2 Given a scenario, analyze common issues with data.	4
2.3 Given a scenario, apply data enrichment and augmentation techniques.	5
2.4 Given a scenario, conduct a model design iteration process.	7
2.5 Given a scenario, analyze results of experiments and testing to justify final model recommendations and selection.	7
2.6 Given a scenario, translate results and communicate via appropriate methods and mediums.	7
3.0 Machine Learning	
3.1 Given a scenario, apply foundational machine learning concepts.	6, 8, 9, 10
3.2 Given a scenario, apply appropriate statistical supervised machine learning concepts.	9
3.3 Given a scenario, apply tree-based supervised machine learning concepts.	9
3.4 Explain concepts related to deep learning.	10
3.5 Explain concepts related to unsupervised machine learning.	8
4.0 Operations and Processes	
4.1 Explain the role of data science in various business functions.	1
4.2 Explain the process of and purpose for obtaining different types of data.	3

Exam objective	Chapter(s)
4.3 Explain data ingestion and storage concepts.	3
4.4 Given a scenario, implement common data-wrangling techniques.	5
4.5 Given a scenario, implement best practices throughout the data science life cycle.	1
4.6 Explain the importance of DevOps and MLOps principles in data science.	7
4.7 Compare and contrast various deployment environments.	7
5.0 Specialized Applications of Data Science	
5.1 Compare and contrast optimization concepts.	12
5.2 Explain the use and importance of natural language processing (NLP) concepts.	11
5.3 Explain the use and importance of computer vision concepts.	12
5.4 Explain the purpose of other specialized applications in data science.	1

 Exam objectives are subject to change by CompTIA at any time without prior notice. Always endeavor to visit the CompTIA website (www .comptia.org) for the most current exam objectives.

Interactive Online Learning Environment and Test Bank

This book comes with a number of interactive online learning tools to help you prepare for the certification exam. Here's a description of some of those tools:

Bonus Practice Exams   In addition to the practice questions provided for each chapter, this study guide features two practice exams. These exams are designed to test your knowledge of the material covered throughout the book, allowing you to assess your readiness for the actual exam and identify areas where you may need further study.

Sybex Test Preparation Software   Sybex's test preparation software enhances your study experience by offering electronic versions of the review questions from each chapter, along with bonus practice exams. With this software, you can customize your preparation by building and taking tests that focus on specific domains, individual chapters, or the entire range of DataX exam objectives through randomized tests. This flexibility allows you to tailor your study approach to best suit your needs and ensure comprehensive coverage of the material.

Electronic Flashcards   This study guide includes over 100 flashcards designed to reinforce your learning and facilitate last-minute test preparation before the exam. These flashcards are a valuable tool for reviewing key concepts and ensuring you are well prepared for testing day.

Go to www.wiley.com/go/sybextestprep to register and gain access to this interactive online learning environment and test bank with study tools.

Like all exams, the DataX certification from CompTIA is updated periodically and may eventually be retired or replaced. At some point after CompTIA is no longer offering this exam, the old editions of our books and online tools will be retired. If you have purchased this book after the exam was retired, or are attempting to register in the Sybex online learning environment after the exam was retired, please know that we make no guarantees that this exam's online Sybex tools will be available once the exam is no longer available.

How to Contact the Publisher

If you believe you have found a mistake in this book, please bring it to our attention. At John Wiley & Sons, we understand how important it is to provide our customers with accurate content, but even with our best efforts an error may occur.

In order to submit your possible errata, please email it to our Customer Service Team at wileysupport@wiley.com with the subject line "Possible Book Errata Submission."

Assessment Test

1. A technology firm is developing a new app that uses biometric data. To prevent the misuse of this sensitive information, which of these techniques should be prioritized to secure the data?

    A. Increasing server capacity for data storage

    B. Making sure users have strong passwords

    C. Implementing robust data anonymization processes

    D. Enhancing user interface security features

2. Ebube is analyzing a company's logistics operations to improve delivery times. In which step in the requirements-gathering process would she identify key metrics like average delivery time and percentage of on-time deliveries?

    A. Defining business objectives

    B. Understanding business processes

    C. Determining the project's budget

    D. Conducting cost-benefit analyses

3. A cybersecurity firm wants to detect unusual network traffic that could indicate a security breach. Which of these applications of data science is best suited for this?

    A. Natural language processing

    B. Recommendation systems

    C. Prediction

    D. Segmentation

4. Yucheng is conducting a study to analyze the distribution of wealth among individuals in a country. The distribution is expected to have a few individuals with extremely high wealth compared to the majority. Which of these probability distributions is most appropriate for modeling the data?

    A. Continuous uniform

    B. Student's t

    C. Power law

    D. Gaussian

5. What is a two-sample t-test used for?

    A. To compare the means of two independent groups to determine if there is a significant difference

    B. To compare the mean of a single sample to a known population mean

    C. To compare the means of two related groups or samples at two points in time

    D. To compare the means of more than two independent groups

6. Verite is examining a distribution of stock returns. The distribution has a longer tail on the left side compared to the right side. How should he characterize this distribution in terms of skewness?

   A. Positively skewed

   B. Negatively skewed

   C. Zero skewness

   D. Right skewed

7. Migdalia wants to estimate how much time customers spend on average shopping in a chain of retail stores. To do this, she tracks the shopping time for a sample of 500 customers and calculates the average. In this scenario, the average shopping time calculated from the sample is an example of:

   A. A parameter

   B. A hypothesis

   C. A confidence interval

   D. A statistic

8. Kevin wants to detect lightning strikes as soon as they occur using an array of sensors spread across a 25-mile radius from his base station. Which data ingestion approach should he use and why?

   A. Batching, because it is cost effective

   B. Batching, because the data can be ingested after a predetermined time interval has elapsed

   C. Streaming, because he can receive real-time alerts

   D. Streaming, because the data can be aggregated before storage

9. Which of the following datasets would be the most suitable candidate for compression to improve storage efficiency without significantly impacting data retrieval performance?

   A. Real-time telemetry data from an autonomous vehicle

   B. Daily atmospheric pressure readings from a weather station

   C. Instantaneous stock trade data for high-frequency trading algorithms

   D. Live video feed from a security camera

10. Which of the following formats is specifically designed for organizing and storing large quantities of structured scientific data?

    A. JSON

    B. XML

    C. YAML

    D. HD5

11. Which of the following is not an appropriate way to handle missing data?

    A. Remove the missing records.

    B. Replace the missing data with the mean of the non-missing values of the same feature.

C. Use machine learning to predict the value of the missing data.

D. Replace the missing data with random values.

12. Pete maintains a baseball database containing information and statistics on every player from the last decade. One column of Pete's database is the player's team. Which type of variable is this?

   A. Continuous

   B. Discrete

   C. Nominal

   D. Ordinal

13. Professor Held teaches a college course with over 300 students. He has two separate lists in his possession. One list is of students who received an A on the midterm exam, and the other is a list of students who received an A on the final exam. Which type of join should Professor Held use to create a list of students who received an A on both exams?

   A. A left join

   B. An inner join

   C. An anti-join

   D. A cross join

14. Which of the following techniques results in values with a mean of 0 and a standard deviation of 1?

   A. Log transformation

   B. Box-Cox transformation

   C. Binning

   D. Standardization

15. Sally converts nested data in JSON format to tabular form so she can more easily work with it. Which of the following does she do?

   A. Pivoting

   B. Flattening

   C. Ground truth labeling

   D. Binning

16. Naliba works for a travel agency and would like to predict how many flights are likely to be canceled each day over the next six months. She has access to the daily flight cancelation data for the past five years. Which of these models would be most appropriate to make this forecast?

   A. Linear regression

   B. Binary classification

   C. ARIMA

   D. Survival analysis

17. Ahmed has created a model to predict how many games a football team is likely to win in the coming season. The model performs very well on the training data but does poorly on the test data. Which of the following should Ahmed consider doing to remedy this?

    A. Introduce cross-validation to the model training process.

    B. Reduce the number of predictors in the model.

    C. Add more predictors to the model.

    D. Tune the model hyperparameters.

18. A hospital is developing a model to help classify tumors as either malignant (cancerous) or benign. Assuming that malignant is the class of interest in this model, which of these metrics should the model prioritize for maximization?

    A. Sensitivity

    B. Specificity

    C. Area under the curve (AUC)

    D. Accuracy

19. A healthcare organization has developed a machine learning model to predict the risk of readmission based on patient characteristics. They want to share the model's insights with a group of clinicians who are not familiar with machine learning concepts. Which of these visualization tools would be most appropriate?

    A. An interactive dashboard

    B. A decision tree visualization

    C. A confusion matrix

    D. A feature importance chart

20. In an MLOps workflow, which of the following best describes the purpose of continuous monitoring?

    A. To automate the deployment of new models to production

    B. To regularly update the model with new data to maintain its performance

    C. To streamline the data preprocessing and feature engineering stages

    D. To ensure the security and compliance of the deployed models

21. Which of the following represents a challenge associated with hybrid deployment?

    A. Sensitive data cannot be retained on premises.

    B. Scalability offered by the cloud cannot be leveraged.

    C. Ensuring seamless integration between cloud and on-premises environments can be complex.

    D. Hybrid deployment requires a greater investment in physical infrastructure compared to other deployment methods.

22. Sangita works for an online video streaming startup. She wants to create an algorithm that will recommend new videos to users based on their past viewing history. Which of the following techniques is best for this task?

   A. Association rules

   B. Clustering analysis

   C. Dimensionality reduction

   D. Content-based filtering

23. Which of the following is not a typical reason to conduct principal component analysis (PCA)?

   A. To minimize the dimensionality of a dataset

   B. To improve the interpretability of a model

   C. To minimize the risk of overfitting

   D. To improve the efficiency of a model

24. A grocery store is analyzing historical customer purchases to identify which items are frequently bought together. Based on their analysis, they find that customers who buy both cheese and bread are more likely to also buy lunch meat. Which type of unsupervised machine learning approach are they using?

   A. Association rules

   B. Recommender systems

   C. Clustering

   D. Dimensionality reduction

25. Tori plans to use linear regression to predict car prices. She applies the Durbin–Watson test to all the observations in her historical dataset. Which linear regression assumption is she trying to validate?

   A. Autocorrelation of residuals

   B. Homoscedasticity

   C. Independence of observations

   D. Normality of residuals

26. Fatima wants to create a linear regression model to predict the grades of students in a college course. However, she has too many predictors and wants to reduce them. Which of these techniques should she use?

   A. L2 regularization

   B. Ridge regularization

   C. L1 regularization

   D. Gradient descent

27. Sanjay wants to predict the outcome of basketball games. He builds an ensemble model that combines the results of a logistic regression model and a decision tree to make predictions. Which approach is he using?

    A. Bagging

    B. Stacking

    C. Boosting

    D. Bootstrap aggregating

28. DJ is a marketing analyst for a grocery store chain and would like to categorize shoppers into three categories: loyal customers, occasional buyers, and one-time customers. He is using a neural network for this classification problem. Which activation function should he use in the output layer?

    A. Threshold

    B. SoftMax

    C. Sigmoid

    D. Hyperbolic tangent

29. Which of these approaches should Grace use to prevent her neural network model from over-fitting against the training data?

    A. Batch normalization

    B. Learning rate schedulers

    C. Early stopping

    D. Vanishing gradients

30. Vamsi is in the process of creating a large language model to enhance the customer service chatbot on his company's website. Which deep learning architecture is most suitable for this purpose?

    A. Generative adversarial network

    B. Convolutional neural network

    C. Transformer

    D. Recurrent neural network

31. Joy is exploring a large collection of news articles to discover the underlying thematic structure. She wants to identify sets of words that frequently occur together and assign each article to one or more of these sets. Which text analysis technique is Joy using?

    A. Keyword extraction

    B. Sentiment analysis

    C. Topic modeling

    D. Semantic matching

32. Alex wants to automatically create product descriptions for an online product catalog based on specific inputs such as product features and specifications. Which of these aspects of natural language processing is most relevant to Alex's goal?

A. Language understanding

B. Language generation

C. Named entity recognition

D. Semantic analysis

33. Patrick is developing a search engine that retrieves documents that are contextually related to a user's query, even if the exact query terms are not present in the document. Which of these is most relevant to Patrick's task?

A. Semantic matching

B. Sentiment analysis

C. Topic modeling

D. String matching

34. The one-armed bandit problem is often used as a simplified model for decision-making in various fields. In which of the following scenarios can the one-armed bandit problem be applied as a model for optimization?

A. Determining the optimal mix of crops to plant on a farm

B. Allocating budget among different marketing channels

C. Scheduling flights to minimize delays

D. Selecting the best treatment option for a patient

35. A security system needs to use facial recognition to verify the identity of individuals entering a building. Which computer vision approach is primarily involved in this application?

A. Object detection and recognition

B. Image segmentation

C. Optical character recognition (OCR)

D. Motion analysis and object tracking

36. A farm wants to optimize its irrigation water usage to maximize crop yield while adhering to regulations. What type of optimization problem is this?

A. Pricing

B. Network topology

C. Scheduling

D. Resource allocation

Answers to Assessment Test

1. C. For an app using sensitive biometric data, implementing robust data anonymization processes is essential to secure the data against misuse and ensure privacy and compliance. See Chapter 1 for more information.

2. B. Ebube would identify critical metrics such as average delivery time and percentage of on-time deliveries, which are pivotal for analyzing and improving logistics operations, during the "understanding business processes" phase. See Chapter 1 for more information.

3. D. Anomaly detection based on segmentation is particularly effective in identifying unusual data points or patterns, such as those that might indicate a cybersecurity threat. This technique can help the company quickly isolate and respond to a potential security breach. See Chapter 1 for more information.

4. C. The power law distribution is characterized by a heavy tail and is used when one quantity varies as a power of another. It is suitable for modeling the distribution of wealth, where a few individuals have significantly higher wealth than the majority. See Chapter 2 for more information.

5. A. A two-sample t-test, also known as the independent samples t-test, is used to determine whether there is a significant difference between the means of two independent groups. See Chapter 2 for more information.

6. B. The distribution would be characterized as negatively skewed because the left tail is longer or heavier than the right. In a negatively skewed distribution, the majority of the data is concentrated on the right side, with a few extreme values on the left. See Chapter 2 for more information.

7. D. The average shopping time calculated from the sample is a statistic, as it is a numerical characteristic of the sample used to estimate the corresponding population parameter. See Chapter 2 for more information.

8. C. Streaming is the most appropriate method of ingestion in this scenario. Streaming would enable Kevin to capture and analyze each sensor's data instantaneously, providing the ability to react to lightning strikes as they happen. See Chapter 3 for more information.

9. B. Compression introduces a delay in the data access pipeline. Daily atmospheric pressure readings from a weather station, while valuable, do not typically require the instant access that real-time systems, like the other options in the question, demand. See Chapter 3 for more information.

10. D. Unlike JSON, XML, and YAML, which are more suited for semi-structured data, HDF5 is a binary file format that provides a versatile and efficient methodology for organizing and storing complex scientific datasets that demand a structured storage approach. See Chapter 3 for more information.

11. D. Substituting missing data with random values is not an advisable strategy, as it can inject random noise into the dataset, potentially skewing analysis and outcomes. See Chapter 4 for more information.

12. C. Variables can be broken down into two categories, quantitative and qualitative. Team name is a qualitative variable because it is not numerical. Qualitative variables can either be nominal or ordinal. Because there is no inherent order among team names, it is considered a nominal variable. See Chapter 4 for more information.

13. B. An inner join will merge the two lists based on common entries, thus displaying only those students who earned an A grade on both the midterm and the final exams. See Chapter 5 for more information.

14. D. Standardization, often referred to as Z-score normalization, is a scaling technique that transforms features to have a mean of 0 and a standard deviation of 1. See Chapter 5 for more information.

15. B. Flattening refers to the process of transforming hierarchical or multilevel structured data into a flat, tabular format. See Chapter 5 for more information.

16. C. Because Naliba is working with chronological data, she should create a time-series model. ARIMA, short for autoregressive integrated moving average, is a time-series model that factors in historical values and forecast errors. See Chapter 6 for more information.

17. B. Ahmed's model appears to be overfitting the training data. It is not generalizing well to the test data. Using feature selection to reduce the number of predictors in the model is one way to address this. See Chapter 6 for more information.

18. A. Sensitivity measures the ability of the model to correctly identify malignant tumors. High sensitivity means that the model is effective at catching malignant cases, which is crucial in a medical context where early detection of cancer can significantly impact treatment success and patient survival. See Chapter 6 for more information.

19. A. An interactive dashboard with drill-down capabilities would allow clinicians to explore not only the overall predictions of the model but also the specific relationships between multiple features and readmission risk. See Chapter 7 for more information.

20. B. Continuous monitoring and model retraining are crucial in an MLOps workflow to keep the model updated with fresh data and maintain its accuracy and relevance over time. This process helps address concept drift and data drift, ensuring the model continues to perform well on new data. See Chapter 7 for more information.

21. C. One of the primary challenges of hybrid deployment is achieving seamless integration between cloud and on-premises environments. This involves ensuring consistent data management, security protocols, and application performance across both platforms, which can be complex and requires careful planning and coordination. See Chapter 7 for more information.

22. D. Content-based filtering is the most appropriate technique for this task, as it uses the characteristics of items (in this case, videos) that users have previously interacted with to recommend similar items. See Chapter 8 for more information.

23. B. PCA is commonly used to reduce the dimensionality of a dataset, decrease the risk of overfitting, and enhance the efficiency of a model. However, improving the interpretability of a model is not a primary reason for conducting PCA, as the transformation to principal components can sometimes make the data more abstract and less directly interpretable in terms of the original features. See Chapter 8 for more information.

24. A. This is an example of the use of association rules, an unsupervised machine learning approach that describes the co-occurrence of items within a transaction set. See Chapter 8 for more information.

25. A. Tori is validating the independence of residuals assumption of linear regression, which states that the residuals from the regression should not be correlated with each other. The Durbin–Watson test is primarily used to detect the presence of autocorrelation among the residuals, a specific form of independence check. See Chapter 9 for more information.

26. C. L1 regularization (LASSO regression) modifies the loss function to include a penalty that can reduce some coefficients to zero, effectively removing them from the model. Therefore, it should be used if feature selection is a priority for Fatima. See Chapter 9 for more information.

27. B. Stacking involves combining the predictions of multiple heterogenous base models using a meta-model. In Sanjay's case, the logistic regression model and the decision tree serve as the base models, and their predictions are combined to make the final prediction. See Chapter 9 for more information.

28. B. The SoftMax activation function is particularly useful for multiclass classification. The function returns a decimal probability for each class, allowing the model to assign each item to its most probable class. See Chapter 10 for more information.

29. C. Early stopping is a regularization technique used to prevent overfitting in neural networks. It involves monitoring the model's performance on a validation set and stopping the training process when the performance starts to degrade or no longer improves significantly. This prevents the model from learning the noise in the training data, which is a common cause of overfitting. See Chapter 10 for more information.

30. C. The Transformer architecture is particularly well suited for building large language models used in natural language processing tasks, including chatbots. It excels at handling sequential data, such as text, and can process entire sentences or even paragraphs in parallel, significantly improving efficiency and effectiveness over traditional models. See Chapter 10 for more information.

31. C. Topic modeling is an unsupervised machine learning technique used to discover the underlying thematic structure in a large collection of documents by identifying topics (sets of words that frequently occur together) and assigning each document to one or more of these topics. See Chapter 11 for more information.

32. B. Language generation can be used in automated content creation to create written content for websites, reports, and articles based on specific inputs or prompts. See Chapter 11 for more information.

33. A. Semantic matching involves comparing text based on its underlying meaning rather than its surface form, which is useful in retrieving documents that are contextually related to a query. See Chapter 11 for more information.

34. B. Allocating budget among different marketing channels is a scenario where the one-armed bandit problem can be used to model the decision-making process, as it involves choosing how to distribute resources among various options (marketing channels) with unknown outcomes. See Chapter 12 for more information.

35. A. Object detection and recognition are fundamental in facial recognition applications, as they involve identifying and classifying faces into predefined categories. See Chapter 12 for more information.

36. D. This scenario represents a resource allocation problem, where the objective is to distribute limited resources (water for irrigation) among competing activities or projects while adhering to constraints. See Chapter 12 for more information.

Chapter

1

What Is Data Science?

The rapid advances in data science have changed the way we work, live, and interact with the world around us. But what exactly is data science? Is it the same thing as machine learning? What about artificial intelligence? In this chapter, we define what data science is and how it differs from other closely related but distinct disciplines. We then explore some common applications of data science to a wide variety of problems in different domains. The chapter wraps up with a spotlight on data science best practices, which include the use of standardized workflow models and toolkits.

Data Science

Data science is an interdisciplinary field that has rapidly evolved to become a cornerstone of modern business, research, and technology. It encompasses a wide range of techniques and methodologies aimed at extracting meaningful information from both structured and unstructured data. The emergence of data science as a distinct discipline can be attributed to the digital revolution of the 21st century, which has led to an exponential growth in the volume, velocity, and variety of data. This deluge of data, often referred to as "big data," presents both challenges and opportunities. The challenge lies in the ability to manage, process, and analyze vast amounts of data efficiently. The opportunity, on the other hand, is the potential to uncover hidden patterns, correlations, and insights that can inform strategic decisions, optimize processes, and create value.

At its core, data science integrates principles from statistics, mathematics, computer science, and domain-specific knowledge to unlock insights that can drive decision-making and innovation. Statistics and mathematics provide the foundational framework for data analysis, enabling data scientists to summarize data, test hypotheses, and draw inferences. Computer science, particularly in areas such as algorithms, data structures, database management, and programming, is essential for handling and processing data efficiently. Domain expertise, meanwhile, is crucial for understanding the context of the data and interpreting the results in a meaningful way.

One of the key strengths of data science is its applicability across a wide range of domains. In healthcare, data science is used to develop predictive models for disease outbreaks, personalize treatment plans, and improve patient outcomes. In finance, it is applied to detect fraudulent transactions, manage risk, and optimize investment strategies. Retailers use data science to understand customer behavior, forecast demand, and enhance the shopping experience. The applications are virtually limitless, spanning sectors such as manufacturing, education, transportation, and government.

As data continues to play an increasingly central role in society, the importance of data science cannot be overstated. It has the potential to drive innovation, improve efficiency, and solve complex problems in virtually every area of human endeavor. The field of data science is not only a fascinating area of study but also a critical driver of progress in the modern world.

Data Science, Machine Learning, and Artificial Intelligence

The term "data science" is frequently misunderstood and conflated with closely related but distinct fields such as machine learning and artificial intelligence. While these disciplines share some commonalities and often work in tandem, each has its own unique focus and scope. As shown in Figure 1.1, data science is an umbrella term that encompasses a broad range of techniques and methodologies for extracting knowledge and insights from data.

FIGURE 1.1   Data science, machine learning, and artificial intelligence

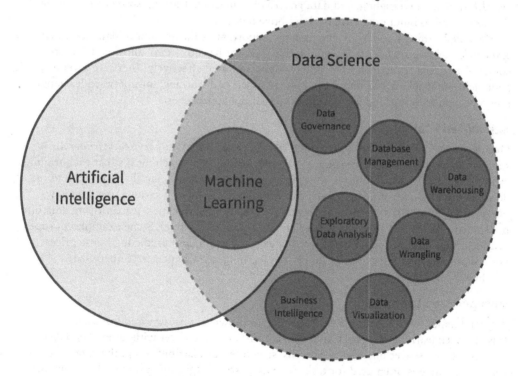

Data science encompasses the entire data processing lifecycle, including data collection, storage, cleaning, analysis, and visualization. It also involves using data analysis tools and techniques to inform business decision-making. Additionally, data science includes practices

and policies to ensure ethical data use, regulatory compliance, and the protection of data privacy and security.

Artificial Intelligence

Artificial intelligence (AI) is a broad field that aims to create systems or machines that can perform tasks that typically require human intelligence. This includes reasoning, learning, problem-solving, perception, and language understanding. AI encompasses various techniques and approaches, including rule-based systems, expert systems, and machine learning.

Machine Learning

Machine learning is a subset of AI that focuses on developing algorithms that enable computers to learn from and make predictions or decisions based on data. It is one of the key approaches behind many AI applications, such as image recognition, natural language processing, and recommendation systems.

The fields of machine learning and data science also intersect and complement each other in several ways. While data science encompasses a broader set of practices, including data visualization, data wrangling, and data governance, machine learning specifically deals with the use of data to build predictive or descriptive models.

Machine learning has become increasingly important as the amount of data generated and collected has grown, and as computational power has advanced, allowing for more complex models and algorithms to be developed and used effectively. There are several approaches to machine learning. They include supervised learning, unsupervised learning, reinforcement learning, and various other specialized approaches.

Supervised Learning

One of the major approaches to machine learning is known as *supervised learning*. In supervised learning, a model is trained on a labeled dataset, which means that each training example is paired with an output label. The algorithm learns to map the input data to the desired output. Once trained, a model can make predictions or decisions based on new, unseen data. Supervised learning is commonly used for classification (categorizing data into predefined classes) and regression (predicting a continuous value). Some examples of supervised learning tasks are spam detection, image recognition, and predicting house prices. For a more in-depth discussion of supervised learning, see Chapter 9, "Supervised Machine Learning."

Unsupervised Learning

A second major approach to machine learning is known as *unsupervised learning*. Unsupervised learning involves training an algorithm on a dataset without explicit labels. The goal is to discover underlying patterns, structures, or distributions in the data. Unsupervised learning is often used for tasks such as clustering (grouping similar data points), dimensionality reduction (reducing the number of variables in data), and association rule mining (finding rules that describe large portions of data). Unsupervised learning is introduced in Chapter 8, "Unsupervised Machine Learning."

Reinforcement Learning

Reinforcement learning is a third major approach to machine learning. In this approach, an agent learns to make decisions by interacting with an environment. The agent receives rewards or penalties for its actions and aims to maximize its cumulative reward over time. Reinforcement learning is used in scenarios where there is no fixed dataset, and the learning is based on the outcomes of the agent's actions. It is commonly applied in game playing, robotics, autonomous vehicles, and other decision-making systems.

Other Specialized Approaches

There are several specialized approaches to machine learning, some of which are semi-supervised learning, self-supervised learning, multimodal machine learning, and federated learning. Each of these approaches addresses specific challenges related to the availability, labeling, type, and location of training data.

In *semi-supervised learning*, the algorithm is trained on a dataset that is partially labeled, meaning that some of the data has outcome labels, but a significant portion of the data does not. This approach is useful when obtaining labels for the entire dataset is expensive or impractical. Semi-supervised learning algorithms leverage the structure of the unlabeled data to improve the learning process and make better predictions on new data.

Self-supervised learning is an approach in which the algorithm generates its own supervisory signal from the input data. This is often done by creating a pretext task, where the algorithm tries to predict a part of the data from other parts of the data. For example, an algorithm might try to predict the next word in a sentence or the missing part of an image. The idea is that by learning to solve these pretext tasks, the algorithm will learn useful representations of the data that can be used for other tasks, such as classification or clustering.

Multimodal machine learning is a specialized approach to machine learning that focuses on building models that can process and relate information from multiple modalities, such as text, images, and audio. It is used in applications like image captioning, speech recognition, and emotion recognition, where integrating information from different types of sources (modalities) leads to more robust and accurate models.

Another specialized approach to machine learning is *federated learning*. In this technique, a model is trained across multiple decentralized devices or servers holding local data samples, without exchanging them. This approach is beneficial for privacy-preserving applications because it allows for the development of models without requiring central access to all the training data.

Common Applications of Data Science

Data science is a multifaceted field that encompasses a variety of techniques and applications aimed at extracting insights and helping users make informed decisions based on data. Its applications are vast and varied, impacting numerous industries and aspects of business and society. Data science is commonly used in tasks such as prediction, pattern mining, segmentation, natural language processing, network analysis, recommendation systems, signal processing, and optimization.

As you prepare for the DataX exam, you should be able to explain the purposes of various specialized applications of data science. Make note of the applications mentioned in this section and think of new scenarios or problems that they could be applied to.

Prediction

Prediction involves leveraging historical data to anticipate future outcomes. By analyzing past patterns and trends, data science models can make informed predictions about the future. For instance, data science techniques can be employed to predict future sales volumes based on historical sales data, seasonal trends, and market conditions (as shown in Figure 1.2). These types of models are known as time series models and are discussed in Chapter 6, "Modeling and Evaluation." Time-series models allow companies to make informed decisions about inventory management, production planning, and marketing strategies to optimize revenue.

FIGURE 1.2   Sales forecast based on historical data

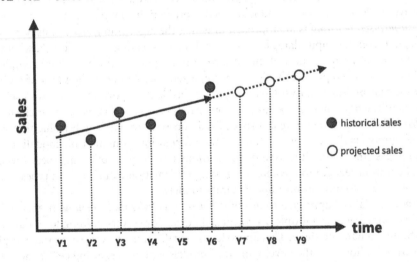

Predictive models can also help companies identify customers who are at risk of churning based on their behavior, purchase history, and engagement with the company. By recognizing these patterns early, businesses can implement targeted retention strategies, such as personalized offers or improved customer service, to prevent churn and enhance customer loyalty.

Pattern Mining

Pattern mining involves uncovering hidden patterns, correlations, or associations within large datasets. By analyzing these patterns, data scientists can gain insights into underlying trends and relationships that may not be immediately apparent.

One notable application of pattern mining is *market basket analysis*, which is used in retail to understand the relationships between products purchased together. By analyzing transaction data, retailers can identify sets of products that are frequently bought together, enabling them to optimize product placement, cross-selling strategies, and promotional offers. The use of association rules for market basket analysis is discussed in Chapter 8.

Event detection is another specific application of pattern mining that focuses on identifying significant occurrences or changes in data over time. In the finance industry, event detection algorithms can monitor stock market data to detect events such as sudden spikes or drops in stock prices, which may indicate market volatility or significant financial events. By identifying these events in real time, traders and analysts can make informed decisions to capitalize on market opportunities or mitigate risks.

Segmentation

Segmentation is a powerful data science technique that involves dividing data into distinct groups or segments based on shared characteristics. This allows organizations to better understand and target specific subsets of data for various purposes. Clustering, a popular approach to segmentation, is introduced in Chapter 8.

Anomaly detection is a key application of segmentation (and also pattern mining), where data scientists identify unusual data points that deviate significantly from the norm. This is crucial in many fields, such as cybersecurity, where detecting anomalies in network traffic can help identify potential security breaches, or in manufacturing, where unusual patterns in sensor data can indicate equipment failures. Figure 1.3 illustrates how segmentation is used to group data with shared characteristics into clusters, effectively isolating anomalous data.

FIGURE 1.3   Using segmentation to identify anomalous data

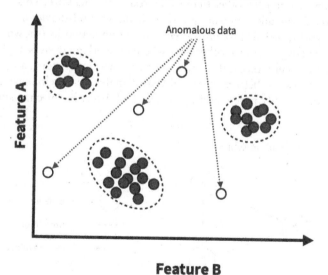

Fraud detection is another important application that combines segmentation and pattern mining. In the financial industry, data scientists use both techniques to analyze transaction patterns and detect irregularities that may indicate fraudulent activities, such as credit card

fraud or insurance fraud. By identifying these anomalies, businesses can take proactive measures to prevent unauthorized transactions and protect their customers and assets.

Natural Language Processing

Natural language processing (NLP) is the process of enabling machines to comprehend, interpret, and generate human language. One of the prominent applications of NLP is sentiment analysis, where algorithms are used to analyze text data, such as customer reviews or social media posts, to determine the underlying emotion of the author. This can help businesses gauge customer satisfaction, monitor brand reputation, and understand public opinion on certain topics.

Another significant use of NLP is in the development of chatbots. Chatbots are designed to communicate with users using natural language, enhancing interactions across various digital platforms. They can provide customer support, respond to common inquiries, and guide users through website navigation. For a more detailed discussion of the use of NLP in data science, see Chapter 11, "Natural Language Processing."

Network Analysis

Network analysis is a data science technique that involves examining the structures of networks to understand the relationships and interactions within them. By utilizing *graph analysis* and *graph theory*, data scientists can gain insights into the complexities of various types of networks.

In social networks, network analysis techniques are used to explore the connections between individuals or groups. This can involve identifying influential nodes, which are individuals or entities that have significant impact or centrality within the network. Additionally, network analysis can be used to detect communities, which are clusters of nodes that are more densely connected to each other than to the rest of the network. This can help in understanding social dynamics, information spread, and group behaviors.

Biological networks, such as protein-protein interaction networks (shown in Figure 1.4) or gene regulatory networks, are another area where network analysis is applied. In these networks, nodes represent biological entities (such as genes or proteins), and edges represent interactions or relationships between them. Network analysis can help uncover important biological processes, identify potential drug targets, and detect the mechanisms of diseases.

FIGURE 1.4   Biological network

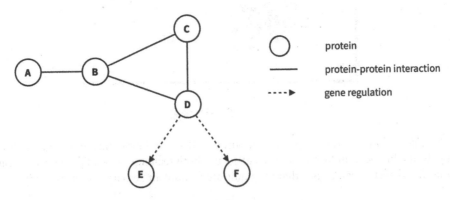

Recommendation Systems

Recommendation systems are designed to provide personalized suggestions to users based on their preferences, past behavior, and interactions. These systems, which are discussed in more detail in Chapter 8, employ various algorithms and techniques to analyze user data and predict items or content that users are likely to be interested in.

In e-commerce platforms, recommendation systems play a crucial role in enhancing the shopping experience. They analyze a customer's browsing history, purchase history, and preferences to recommend products that the customer might like to purchase. This not only helps increase customer satisfaction, but it also boosts sales by presenting relevant products that customers may not have otherwise discovered.

Streaming services, such as Netflix or Spotify, utilize recommendation systems to suggest movies, TV shows, or music to their users. By analyzing a user's viewing or listening history, ratings, and preferences, these systems can curate personalized content, keeping users engaged and encouraging them to explore new content that aligns with their tastes.

Signal Processing

The goal of *signal processing* is to analyze, manipulate, and synthesize signals such as sound, images, and scientific measurements to extract useful information. It is crucial in fields like computer vision and edge computing.

In computer vision, signal processing techniques are used in tasks such as object recognition (as shown in Figure 1.5), facial recognition, motion detection, and image enhancement, all of which rely on processing visual signals to extract meaningful insights.

FIGURE 1.5   Object recognition in computer vision

Source: zapp2photo/Adobe Systems Incorporated

In *edge computing*, data processing is performed at the edge of the network (i.e., closer to the source of the data, rather than in a centralized data center). This reduces latency and bandwidth usage, which is critical for real-time applications such as autonomous vehicles or Internet of Things (IoT) devices. Signal processing algorithms play a key role in optimizing data transmission and processing at the edge, ensuring efficient and timely delivery of information.

Optimization

Optimization is a fundamental aspect of data science that involves finding the most efficient or optimal solutions to various problems. It plays a crucial role in decision-making processes across different industries and applications. Several methods exist for solving optimization problems, including linear and nonlinear programming, both of which are discussed in Chapter 12, "Specialized Applications of Data Science."

Another common method used to solve optimization problems is the use of greedy algorithms. A *greedy algorithm* is a specific type of heuristic that makes a series of locally optimal choices, with the hope that these choices will eventually lead to a globally optimal solution. A *heuristic* is a technique that is used to find a quick, approximate solution to a complex problem when finding an exact solution is not feasible due to time or computational constraints. For example, in the classic optimization problem known as the "traveling salesman problem," the goal is to find the shortest possible route that visits each city exactly once and returns to the origin city. Instead of finding the optimal route, a greedy algorithm can be used to find a "good enough" route that satisfies most of the requirements of the problem within a reasonable amount of time.

Data Science Best Practices

The data science lifecycle covers a comprehensive range of activities, from problem understanding to the deployment and ongoing maintenance of models that meet business needs. Implementing best practices throughout this lifecycle is essential for the success, sustainability, and scalability of data science projects. In the subsequent sections, we will explore key facets of these practices, focusing on standard workflow models as well as the tools and techniques typically employed in data science projects.

As you prepare for the DataX exam, you should be able explain how to implement best practices throughout the data science lifecycle. Make note of the frameworks and tools mentioned in this section and be ready to identify which are most appropriate to use when presented with a scenario.

Data Science Workflow Models

Employing a standardized workflow model or framework is essential for effectively organizing and overseeing data science projects. Two frameworks, the *Cross-Industry Standard Process for Data Mining (CRISP-DM)* and the *Data Management Association (DAMA)* models, are notable due to their comprehensive nature. These frameworks are complementary rather than exclusive. CRISP-DM provides the process framework for carrying out data mining projects effectively, whereas DAMA focuses on the broader governance and stewardship of data. Used together, they provide a comprehensive approach to managing data science projects, ensuring not only that the insights derived are robust but also that the data is managed responsibly and ethically.

Cross-Industry Standard Process for Data Mining (CRISP-DM)

CRISP-DM is a well-established framework that provides a structured approach for data mining and analytics projects. It is highly regarded in the data science community for its adaptability and effectiveness in various industries and project types. As shown in Figure 1.6, the CRISP-DM framework is divided into six distinct phases, starting with business understanding and ending with deployment. Each phase includes specific tasks and objectives. The framework is designed to be iterative, allowing for the continuous refinement and improvement of a model based on feedback and evolving business requirements.

FIGURE 1.6   The CRISP-DM framework

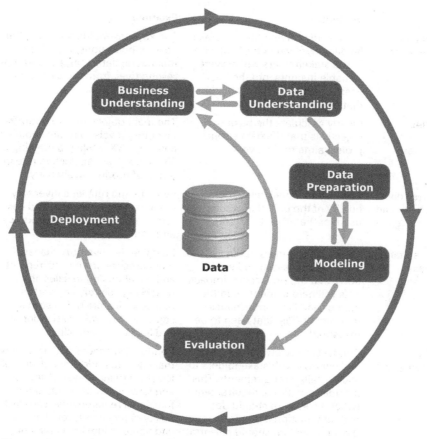

Source: Shearer, 2000 / DATA WAREHOUSING INSTITUTE

Business Understanding

The initial phase of the framework, business understanding, lays the foundation for the project. It involves working closely with stakeholders to gather the requirements that clearly define the project objectives and identify the business problems that the data science project aims to solve.

 Real World Scenario

Key Steps in Requirements Gathering

Requirements gathering is a crucial process that occurs during the business understanding phase of a data science project. It involves understanding and documenting the business needs, objectives, and constraints that a project aims to address. This process ensures that the data science solutions developed are aligned with the organization's goals and provide tangible value. Here's how to approach requirements gathering in a scenario where the objective is to optimize inventory for an online retailer:

Step	Description	Example
1. Identify stakeholders	Start by identifying the key stakeholders involved in the project. These stakeholders will provide valuable insights into the business context and the problems that need to be solved.	The key stakeholders include the head of operations, inventory managers, data analysts, and representatives from the sales and marketing teams.
2. Define business objectives	Clearly articulate the business objectives that the data science project aims to achieve.	The main objective is to optimize inventory levels to reduce holding costs by 15% while maintaining a 95% customer satisfaction rate in terms of product availability.
3. Assess data availability and quality	Evaluate the availability and quality of the data that will be used for the project.	Evaluate the retailer's inventory database, sales records, and customer feedback data for accuracy and completeness.
4. Understand business processes	Gain a deep understanding of the business processes and workflows that the project will impact. This will help in identifying the metrics and key performance indicators (KPIs) that need to be measured.	Examine the inventory management process, from procurement and warehousing to sales and restocking. Identify key performance indicators (KPIs) such as stock turnover rate, backorder rate, and lead time variability.
5. Elicit requirements	Conduct interviews, workshops, and surveys with stakeholders to elicit detailed requirements. This includes functional requirements (what the system should do) and nonfunctional requirements (how the system should perform, such as speed, scalability, and security).	Conduct workshops with inventory managers to understand their challenges in managing stock levels and forecasting demand. Gather functional requirements, such as the ability to predict seasonal demand, and nonfunctional requirements, like the system's response time for generating reports.

Step	Description	Example
6. Translate business needs into analytical solutions	Based on the gathered requirements, translate the business needs into specific analytical questions or problems that can be addressed using data science techniques.	The need to optimize inventory levels translates into the analytical problem of forecasting demand for each product and determining the optimal reorder points and quantities to minimize costs while ensuring product availability.
7. Conduct cost-benefit analyses	For each potential solution, conduct a cost-benefit analysis to evaluate the expected costs (e.g., data acquisition, technology infrastructure, and personnel) against the anticipated benefits (e.g., increased revenue, cost savings, or improved decision-making). This will help in prioritizing the solutions that offer the best return on investment.	Estimate the costs associated with implementing a new inventory management system, including data integration, software development, and training, against the anticipated benefits of reduced holding costs, decreased stock-outs, and increased sales.
8. Recommend appropriate solutions	Based on the cost-benefit analyses and the alignment with business objectives, recommend the most appropriate data science solutions. Clearly communicate the rationale behind the recommendations, including the expected outcomes and any risks or limitations.	Based on the analysis, recommend a data-driven inventory management solution that uses time-series forecasting models to predict demand and optimize reorder points and quantities.
9. Define scope and constraints	Establish the scope of the project, including the specific goals, deliverables, and timelines. Also, identify any constraints that may impact the project, such as budget limitations, regulatory requirements, or technical constraints.	Establish that the project's goal is to develop and implement the inventory management solution within nine months, with constraints such as the budget for software development, the ability to integrate with existing systems, and the need to adhere to supplier agreements.
10. Document requirements	Finally, document the requirements in a clear and concise manner, ensuring that they are agreed upon by all stakeholders. This document will serve as the foundation for the subsequent phases of the data science project.	Ensure that the head of operations, inventory managers, data analysts, and representatives from the sales and marketing teams review and agree on the detailed requirements document.

Data Understanding

Once the business objectives are clear, the focus shifts to the data. This phase involves collecting the necessary data (see Chapter 3, "Data Collection and Storage") and conducting exploratory analysis (see Chapter 4, "Data Exploration and Analysis") to better understand the data. It also includes identifying data quality issues, such as missing values or outliers, and gaining preliminary insights that can inform the subsequent phases.

Data Preparation

This phase is often the most time-consuming, as it involves transforming the raw data into a format suitable for modeling. Tasks in this phase include data cleaning, handling missing values, feature engineering, and data integration. The goal is to create a clean, high-quality dataset that can be used to build robust models. The tasks involved in this phase are covered in Chapter 5, "Data Processing and Preparation."

Modeling

In this phase, various modeling techniques are selected and applied to the prepared data. This may involve experimenting with different algorithms, tuning hyperparameters, and validating models to find the best fit for the problem at hand. The choice of model often depends on the nature of the data and the business objectives.

Evaluation

Once modeling is completed, the performance of the model must be evaluated thoroughly to ensure that it meets the business objectives set in the first phase. This phase also involves reviewing the steps taken so far to identify any potential issues or areas for improvement. See Chapter 6 for more detail on the tasks involved in the modeling and evaluation phases.

Deployment

The final phase involves putting the model into production, where it can be used to make decisions or provide insights. This may include integrating the model into existing systems, developing a user interface, or creating reports. The deployment phase also involves continuously monitoring the model's performance and adjusting it as needed to ensure it remains effective over time. See Chapter 7, "Model Validation and Deployment," for more details.

Data Management Association (DAMA)

DAMA has a defined and comprehensive framework for the skills, concepts, and best practices that data management professionals should understand, known as the Data Management Body of Knowledge (DMBoK). The framework concentrates on the governance and management of data as an asset and identifies several essential knowledge areas (see Figure 1.7) for developing effective data management strategies, policies, and procedures. The DMBoK framework serves as an essential model for organizations looking to establish a culture of data stewardship and governance.

FIGURE 1.7   The DMBoK framework

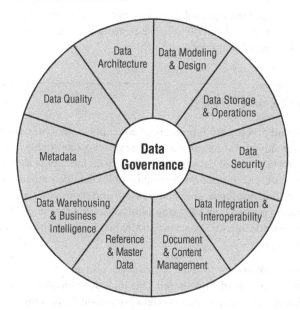

Copyright© 2017 DAMA International

Source: Earley et.al., 2017 / DAMA-DM BOK /Technics Publications

Data Governance

Data governance provides a framework for decision-making and accountability regarding data assets. It involves establishing and enforcing data management policies and standards, as well as ensuring compliance with regulations and internal guidelines.

Data Architecture

Data architecture aims to align the way data is structured with business requirements, ensuring that data is organized in a way that supports efficient operations and strategic objectives.

Data Modeling and Design

Data modeling and design involves analyzing data requirements and creating logical and physical models that represent data entities and their relationships. These models provide a blueprint for the structure and organization of data in databases and other storage systems.

Data Storage and Operations

Data storage and operations covers the processes and technologies involved in storing, securing, and managing data across various storage mediums and environments. It ensures that data is secure and available and that it performs well, regardless of the complexity of the underlying storage infrastructure.

Data Security

Data security focuses on the methods and processes used to protect data from unauthorized access, alterations, and breaches. It involves implementing measures that ensure security, maintain privacy, and enforce compliance.

Compliance, Security, and Privacy

Compliance, security, and privacy are foundational concepts in data management, particularly when handling sensitive information such as *personally identifiable information (PII)* and proprietary data. PII is a type of data that can identify an individual either on its own or when combined with other information. Examples of PII include names, Social Security numbers, addresses, phone numbers, email addresses, and biometric data. *Proprietary data* refers to information owned by a company or organization that is considered confidential or sensitive, such as trade secrets, business strategies, financial information, research data, and intellectual property.

Compliance refers to the adherence to laws, regulations, and standards governing how data is collected, stored, processed, and shared. This includes compliance with data use regulations like the European Union's General Data Protection Regulation (GDPR), the California Consumer Privacy Act (CCPA), and the Health Insurance Portability and Accountability Act (HIPAA). Compliance ensures that organizations follow legal and ethical guidelines, avoid legal penalties, and maintain public trust.

Security involves the measures and practices put in place to protect data from unauthorized access, theft, or damage. This encompasses the protection of both PII and proprietary data, critical for maintaining an individual's privacy and a company's competitive advantage. Techniques such as *data anonymization* (removing PII), *obfuscation* (concealing the original data with modified content), encryption, and masking are often employed to secure data during transit, storage, or processing.

Privacy pertains to the right of individuals to control their personal information and how it is used. Protecting privacy involves ensuring that PII is handled in a way that respects an individual's preferences and legal rights. Anonymizing sensitive data is a method commonly used to balance the utility of data for analysis with the need to protect an individual's privacy.

Data Integration and Interoperability

Data integration and interoperability includes techniques and processes for combining data from multiple sources into a cohesive and consistent view. It ensures that data can be shared and used across different systems and applications, facilitating seamless data exchange and collaboration.

Document and Content Management

Document and content management involves the strategies, methods, and tools for managing documents and other unstructured content throughout their lifecycle. It ensures that unstructured data can be efficiently stored, retrieved, shared, and integrated with structured data to support effective knowledge management and collaboration.

Reference and Master Data Management

Reference and master data management focuses on ensuring that key business data (i.e., reference and master data) is used consistently across the organization. It aims to reduce redundancy, minimize data integration costs, and ensure data consistency and accuracy.

Data Warehousing and Business Intelligence

Data warehousing and business intelligence involves designing, implementing, and managing reporting and analysis tools. It ensures that business users have access to the insights needed for informed decision-making.

Metadata Management

Metadata is data that provides information about other data. Metadata management improves the understanding and the use of data by providing context, which includes comprehensive data definitions, the lineage of data showing its origin and transformations, and usage guidelines for the data.

Data Quality

Data quality involves the processes used in monitoring and ensuring that data is accurate, complete, consistent, and reliable for its intended uses. It also involves ensuring that data is up to date and available when needed.

Common Tools and Techniques

Data science projects often rely on a robust development toolkit and best practices. This toolkit includes the use of integrated development environments, version control systems, and dependency license management tools. Additionally, techniques such as adhering to clean code principles and using application programming interfaces (APIs) to deploy models enhance the function and utility of project solutions.

Integrated Development Environment

An *integrated development environment (IDE)* is a critical tool in data science that offers a centralized platform for code development, debugging, and testing. IDEs enhance productivity by providing features like code completion, syntax highlighting, and direct integration with databases and version control systems. Popular IDEs for data science include Jupyter Notebook (shown in Figure 1.8), RStudio, PyCharm, and Visual Studio Code.

FIGURE 1.8   The Jupyter Notebook IDE

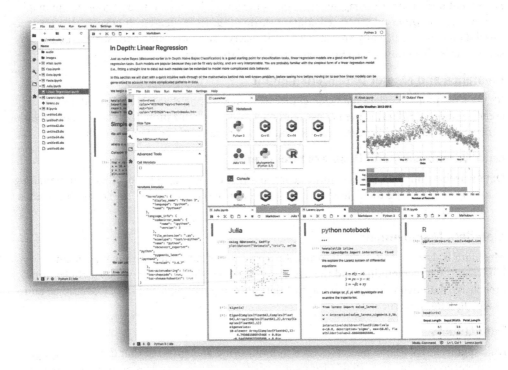

Source: www.jupyter.org

Version Control Systems

Version control systems are essential for managing changes to code, data, model hyper-parameters, and entire models throughout the project lifecycle. Tools like Git, along with platforms such as GitHub, GitLab, or Bitbucket, help teams track revisions, revert to previous versions of the project, and manage branching and merging to accommodate multiple contributors. They also facilitate the versioning of entire projects, including both code and associated data, ensuring that all elements of a project are synchronized across development environments.

Clean Code Methods

Writing *clean code* is fundamental in data science to ensure that code is easy to maintain, understandable, and error free. This involves practices such as using meaningful names for variables and functions, keeping functions short and focused on a single task, adhering to a consistent coding style, handling errors gracefully and explicitly where appropriate, and code reviews to ensure code quality and consistency across the team.

Incorporating *unit testing* is an integral part of maintaining clean code. In a unit test, individual units or components of a software application are tested. The goal is to validate that each unit of the software performs as designed. It usually has one or few inputs and a single output. By writing unit tests that cover various cases and edge conditions for each function or module, data scientists can ensure that their code performs as expected and quickly identify when a change in the codebase causes a break in functionality. Tools like `pytest` for Python and `testthat` for R are commonly used to automate unit testing in data science projects.

Effective documentation is equally crucial in the context of clean code. Well-documented code is easier to understand, maintain, and use. This includes comprehensive *docstrings* that describe the purpose and usage of functions and classes, as well as inline comments that explain complex or non-obvious parts of the code. *Markdown* files, such as READMEs, provide high-level documentation of the project, guiding new users and developers through the structure and setup of the codebase.

Dependency Licensing

Open source and proprietary software libraries often come with licenses that dictate how they can be used or distributed. Managing *dependency licenses* is crucial to ensure that the software components and libraries used in data science projects comply with legal requirements. Tools like FOSSA and Mend (formerly WhiteSource) automate the detection of license compatibility issues and security vulnerabilities within project dependencies.

Application Programming Interface (API)

In data science projects, *application programming interfaces (APIs)* play a crucial role in enabling secure and efficient data access and retrieval. APIs facilitate the automation of data pipelines. For instance, APIs can be configured to automatically capture new data as it becomes available, process it based on preset algorithms, and update systems or dashboards instantaneously.

APIs are also instrumental in deploying machine learning models by exposing them as endpoints. This capability allows data scientists to integrate their models directly into various applications or systems, effectively turning them into accessible services. It also allows multiple clients or applications to simultaneously access the same model, efficiently scaling the model without requiring each client to operate the model locally. Additionally, deploying a model using an API enhances the ease of maintenance. Central updates to models can be made without disrupting user experience, since changes can be made at the backend while the API interface remains consistent for end users.

Summary

Data science encompasses a wide range of techniques for extracting insights from data. It covers the entire data lifecycle as well as the practices and policies that ensure responsible use of data. Common applications of data science include prediction, pattern mining, segmentation, natural language processing, network analysis, recommendation systems, signal processing, and optimization.

Data science, machine learning, and AI are interconnected yet distinct fields. AI focuses on creating systems that perform tasks that mimic human intelligence. Machine learning is a subset of AI and involves building models that make decisions based on data or identify previously unknown patterns in data.

Standardized frameworks like CRISP-DM and DAMA are critical for managing data science projects. CRISP-DM provides a six-phase framework for effective data science projects. DAMA, on the other hand, focuses on data governance, offering a comprehensive framework for managing data as an asset.

Effective data science projects often leverage a comprehensive toolkit, which includes the use of IDEs, version control systems, and dependency license management tools. They also employ certain best practices, such as adhering to clean code principles and using APIs to deploy solutions.

Exam Essentials

Explain the six phases of the CRISP-DM framework.   The six phases of the CRISP-DM framework are (1) define project objectives and requirements (business understanding), (2) collect and explore data to understand it (data understanding), (3) clean and construct datasets for analysis (data preparation), (4) apply modeling techniques to discover patterns (modeling), (5) assess the model to ensure it meets business objectives (evaluation), and (6) implement the model and monitor its performance (deployment).

List some common applications of data science.   Prediction is used to forecast future events based on historical data. Pattern mining is used to identify hidden patterns and associations in data. Segmentation is used to group data into clusters based on shared characteristics. NLP enables machines to comprehend and generate human language. Signal processing is used to extract information from sensors and edge computing devices.

Explain the importance of clean code methods in data science projects.   Clean code methods ensure that code is maintainable, understandable, and efficient. It involves using meaningful variable and function names, keeping functions focused, adhering to a consistent coding style, handling bugs and errors gracefully, creating proper documentation, and unit test writing.

Understand the importance of compliance, security, and privacy to data science projects.   Compliance involves ensuring adherence to legal and regulatory standards relevant to data handling and processing. Security means protecting data from unauthorized access to maintain the integrity of the information. Privacy has to do with safeguarding data against misuse and ensuring that the rights of the data owner are respected in collection, storage, and usage.

Understand how the use of APIs enhances the deployment of data science models.   APIs enhance the deployment of data science models by exposing them as endpoints. This enables seamless integration with other applications or systems, enables multiple clients to access the same model simultaneously, facilitates the automation of data pipelines, and enhances the ease of maintenance.

Review Questions

1. A healthcare organization needs to ensure that patient data is consistently used and referenced correctly across all departments. Which aspect of the DAMA-DMBoK should they focus on?

    A. Data integration and interoperability

    B. Reference and master data management

    C. Metadata management

    D. Data warehousing and business intelligence

2. A team is evaluating the feasibility of integrating a new AI tool to enhance decision-making in financial services. What step in the requirements-gathering process directly supports making an informed recommendation for or against the project?

    A. Recommending appropriate solutions

    B. Documenting requirements

    C. Translating business needs into analytical solutions

    D. Conducting cost-benefit analyses

3. Carlos is working with a manufacturing company that is experiencing frequent equipment failures. To minimize downtime, he builds a model that detects early signs of equipment malfunction based on unusual patterns in sensor data. Which of these is Carlos most likely doing?

    A. Network analysis

    B. Segmentation

    C. Optimization

    D. Recommendation systems

4. Which of the following knowledge areas in the DAMA-DMBoK focuses on aligning how data is structured with business requirements?

    A. Data integration and interoperability

    B. Data security

    C. Data quality

    D. Data architecture

5. A healthcare provider wants to ensure that patient information is handled respectfully and according to individual preferences. Which knowledge area of the DAMA-DMBoK deals with this?

    A. Data storage and operations

    B. Data integration and interoperability

    C. Data security

    D. Data quality

6. After building several predictive models to identify potential financial fraud, Juan needs to select the best model based on its performance. Which phase of the CRISP-DM framework is Juan most likely in?

   A. Data understanding

   B. Modeling

   C. Deployment

   D. Evaluation

7. An automotive company is developing an autonomous vehicle system that learns and improves its navigation decisions based on real-time driving experiences. Which machine learning approach is best suited for this?

   A. Supervised learning

   B. Unsupervised learning

   C. Reinforcement learning

   D. Federated learning

8. Marisol is tasked with developing a system to detect unusual bank transactions that could indicate fraud. She decides to use clustering to isolate outlier transaction patterns. Which of these is she doing?

   A. Segmentation

   B. Pattern mining

   C. Prediction

   D. Network analysis

9. A financial institution is upgrading its fraud detection system to better identify and prevent unauthorized transactions. They want to leverage both labeled and unlabeled transaction data to train the model. Which machine learning approach is best suited for this?

   A. Supervised learning

   B. Unsupervised learning

   C. Semi-supervised learning

   D. Federated learning

10. Raj is managing a large data science project and needs to keep track of changes made to the codebase by members of his team. Which of these tools should he use?

   A. An automated deployment tool

   B. A version control system

   C. An integrated development environment

   D. A dependency license management tool

11. Anna's team built a model that can forecast how much inventory is needed to meet customer demand in the next quarter based on historical data. Which of the following is their model doing?

   A. Segmentation

   B. Pattern mining

   C. Prediction

   D. Optimization

12. Nathan is reviewing the steps his team took on a data science project to optimize supply chain logistics. During this process, he identifies potential improvements for future projects. Which phase of CRISP-DM is Nathan most likely in?

   A. Business understanding

   B. Evaluation

   C. Deployment

   D. Data preparation

13. Ayo is a data security officer working to protect her company's proprietary data and PII from cyberthreats. Which of these should be her primary focus?

   A. Implementing advanced password management techniques

   B. Introducing new data entry protocols

   C. Implementing data anonymization and encryption techniques

   D. Upgrading hardware systems for better performance

14. As a data scientist, Carmen is tasked with reducing operational costs for a manufacturing company. She starts by spending considerable time understanding the business processes involved. What benefit does this provide to Carmen in terms of the data science project design?

   A. It allows her to define a clear project timeline.

   B. It aids in identifying which operational aspects can be automated.

   C. It ensures compliance with international manufacturing standards.

   D. It helps her prepare for stakeholder interviews.

15. Eva is managing a data science project that utilizes numerous open source packages, raising concerns about potential compliance issues with software licensing. Which tool should she use to monitor the project and ensure that all software components are in compliance with legal and regulatory requirements?

   A. A dependency license management tool

   B. A version control system

   C. An integrated development environment

   D. An automated deployment tool

16. What is the purpose of conducting cost-benefit analyses during requirements gathering?

    A. To identify all potential stakeholders

    B. To translate business needs into analytical solutions

    C. To define the business objectives

    D. To prioritize solutions based on their return on investment

17. At the end of a project planning session, a team decides to create a comprehensive document that lists all agreed-upon expectations for the project. What is the primary purpose of this document?

    A. To serve as a contractual agreement with vendors

    B. To act as a guideline for the execution phase of the project

    C. To ensure compliance with industry standards

    D. To facilitate initial project funding

18. Lily is integrating a fraud detection model into the banking system to provide real-time alerts. She is also setting up mechanisms for ongoing adjustments to the model based on the model's performance over time. Which phase of the CRISP-DM framework is her project in?

    A. Deployment

    B. Evaluation

    C. Modeling

    D. Data understanding

19. Kazeem wants to optimize product placement and promotional strategies for a supermarket chain based on prior sales data. Which of these approaches is best suited for this?

    A. Prediction

    B. Segmentation

    C. Pattern mining

    D. Optimization

20. An AI research team is working on a system that integrates audio, visual, and textual data to improve interaction in virtual reality environments. Which of these approaches to machine learning best describes what they're doing?

    A. Multimodal machine learning

    B. Supervised learning

    C. Reinforcement learning

    D. Federated learning

Chapter

2

Mathematics and Statistical Methods

THE COMPTIA DATAX EXAM OBJECTIVES COVERED IN THIS CHAPTER INCLUDE:

✓ **Domain 1: Mathematics and Statistics**

- 1.1 Given a scenario, apply the appropriate statistical method or concept.

- 1.2 Explain probability and synthetic modeling concepts and their uses.

- 1.3 Explain the importance of linear algebra and basic calculus concepts.

Understanding essential mathematical concepts is fundamental in data science, as they form the basis for a wide range of analyses, models, and algorithms used in the field. This chapter begins with an overview of basic calculus, concentrating on the foundational concepts of differentiation and integration. Next, the chapter delves into probability distributions, which are crucial for characterizing entire populations based on sample data. The discussion then progresses to inferential statistics, a key area that focuses on estimating the parameters of a population and conducting hypothesis testing. The chapter concludes with an exploration of important linear algebra concepts with a focus on how they are used in various algorithms and processes.

Calculus

Calculus is a branch of mathematics that primarily deals with two interconnected concepts: differential calculus and integral calculus. Differential calculus focuses on quantifying rates of change, which is crucial for understanding how variables change in response to other variables. Integral calculus, on the other hand, deals with the accumulation of quantities, such as the area under a curve or cumulative growth over an interval. Calculus plays a foundational role in many machine learning algorithms and optimization problems.

As you prepare for the DataX exam, you should be able to explain the importance of basic calculus concepts in data science. Make note of how the concepts introduced in this section relate to one another and the various ways in which they are used to solve problems in data science.

Derivatives

Functions are mathematical constructs that define the relationship between a set of variables. In data science, functions are used to model the relationships between features (or inputs) and outcomes. A simple function might be $f(x) = 2x + 3$, where x is the input variable. If we input $x = 5$ to the function, then the output of the function would be 13 (i.e., $f(5) = (2 \times 5) + 3$). Functions play a fundamental role in certain supervised machine learning algorithms such as linear regression and logistic regression (both of which are introduced in Chapter 9, "Supervised Machine Learning").

The *derivative* of a function measures the rate at which the value (or output) of a function changes as its inputs change. Visually, it represents the slope of a function at any point. For example, consider the function $f(x) = x^2 + 3$, shown as a curve in Figure 2.1. The derivative of the function describes the steepness or slope of a hypothetical tangent line at any given point on the curve.

FIGURE 2.1   Curve of $f(x) = x^2 + 3$ showing hypothetical tangent line at $x = 3$

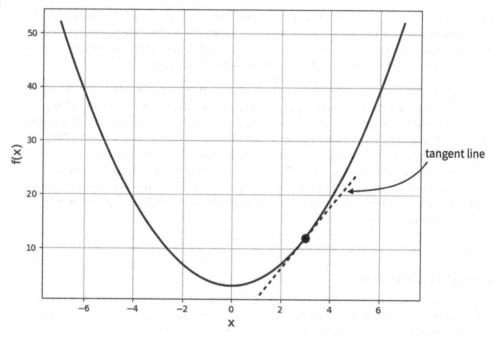

To calculate the derivative of a function, we make the exponent a multiplier and decrement the exponent by 1. For example, the derivative of $f(x) = x^2 + 3$ with respect to x is:

$$\frac{d}{dx}f(x) = \frac{d}{dx}x^2 + 3 = 2x$$

So, if we wanted to figure out the slope of the curve when $x = 3$, we simply plug in the x-value:

$$\frac{d}{dx}f(2) = 2(3) = 6$$

Notice that the derivative of a constant (that is, the 3 in $f(x) = x^2 + 3$) is 0. Imagine that every constant has an exponent of 1. If we make the exponent a multiplier and decrement it by 1 just as we did with the variable, we get $3^0 = 0$.

In data science, derivatives are crucial in optimization problems, where the goal is often to find the minimum or maximum of a function. For example, in gradient descent, a popular optimization algorithm, the derivative of the cost function with respect to the model parameters is used to find points in the function where the slope is 0. These points represent potential solutions to the optimization problem (see Chapter 12, "Specialized Applications of Data Science").

Exponents and Logarithms

Exponents are used to represent the repeated multiplication of a base number by itself. In the expression 3^2, 3 is the base number and 2 is the exponent. This means that 3 is multiplied by itself 2 times: $3^2 = 3 \times 3 = 9$. In data science, exponential functions are used in modeling phenomena such as population growth or radioactive decay.

A *logarithm* is the inverse operation of exponentiation. It answers the question: "To what exponent must the base be raised to produce a given number?" The logarithm of a number is usually written as $log_{base}number$. For example, the logarithm of 1000 to base 10 is written as $log_{10}1000$ and the answer is 3. In other words, raising 10 (the base) to 3 returns 1000. Logarithms are pivotal in data science for transforming skewed data to a more normal or uniform distribution, making it easier to analyze and model (see Chapter 5, "Data Processing and Preparation"). They also play a key role in logistic regression and in quantifying the degree of randomness (or entropy) in the recursive partitioning process of decision trees (see Chapter 9).

Partial Derivatives

In functions with multiple variables, a *partial derivative* represents the rate at which the values of the function change with respect to one of the variables, assuming the others are held constant. For example, let's take the function:

$$f(x, y) = 3x^2 + 2y^3$$

The partial derivative of the function with respect to x is:

$$\frac{d}{dx}f(x, y) = 6x$$

and the partial derivative of the function with respect to y is:

$$\frac{d}{dy}f(x, y) = 6y^2$$

Machine learning models often have multiple parameters that need to be adjusted during the training process. Partial derivatives play a key role in finding the optimal value of these parameters simultaneously.

The Chain Rule

The *chain rule* is used to calculate the derivative of a composite function. It states that if you have a function g inside another function f, the derivative of the composite function $y = f(g(x))$ with respect to x can be found by multiplying the derivative of the outer function f with respect to the inner function g by the derivative of the inner function g with respect to x. Mathematically, this is represented as:

$$\frac{dy}{dx} = \frac{df}{dg} \cdot \frac{dg}{dx}$$

To illustrate how this works, let's say we have a composite function $y = (3x^2 + 5)^4$ and we want to find the derivative of y with respect to x. To solve this, we first need to identify the inner function $g(x)$, which in this case would be $g(x) = 3x^2 + 5$. This means that the outer function, f with respect to g, would then be $f(g) = g^4$.

The derivative of the outer function with respect to the inner function is:

$$\frac{df}{dg} = 4g^3$$

The derivative of the inner function with respect to x is:

$$\frac{dg}{dx} = 6x$$

Using the chain rule, the derivative of the composite function is:

$$\frac{dy}{dx} = \frac{df}{dg} \cdot \frac{dg}{dx} = 4g^3 \cdot 6x$$

Substituting $g(x) = 3x^2 + 5$ back into the equation, we get:

$$\frac{dy}{dx} = 4(3x^2 + 5)^3 \cdot 6x = 24x(3x^2 + 5)^3$$

In summary, the derivative of the composite function $y = (3x^2 + 5)^4$ with respect to x is $24x(3x^2 + 5)^3$.

The chain rule is used extensively in *backpropagation*, which is the algorithm used for training neural networks (introduced in Chapter 10, "Neural Networks and Deep Learning"). Backpropagation involves computing the derivative of the cost function with respect to each parameter in the network. Since neural networks are composed of nested functions, the chain rule is used to calculate these derivatives efficiently by breaking down the derivative computation into a series of simpler steps.

Integrals

The opposite of a derivative is an *integral*. *Integration* is the inverse process of differentiation. It measures the total accumulation of quantities, such as the area under a curve, the volume of an object, and other quantities that add up infinitesimally small pieces. There are two main types of integration: indefinite integration and definite integration.

Indefinite Integration

Indefinite integration finds the antiderivative of a function, which is a function whose derivative is the original function. The result of indefinite integration is a function, plus a constant of integration (C), since differentiation removes constants. For example, the indefinite integral of $f(x) = x^2$ is:

$$\int x^2 dx = \frac{1}{3}x^3 + C$$

This means that the derivative of $\frac{1}{3}x^3 + C$ with respect to x is x^2.

Definite Integration

Definite integration calculates the area under the curve of a function between two points. It provides a numerical value that represents the total accumulation of the quantity represented by the function over the specified interval. For example, the definite integral of $f(x) = x^2$ from $x = 0$ to $x = 3$ is:

$$\int_0^3 x^2 dx = \left[\frac{1}{3}x^3\right]_0^3 = \frac{1}{3}(3^3) - \frac{1}{3}(0^3) = 9$$

This represents the area under the curve of the function $f(x) = x^2$ and above the x-axis, within the x range 0 and 3, as shown by the shaded area in Figure 2.2.

FIGURE 2.2   Area under the curve of $f(x) = x^2$ for x between 0 and 3

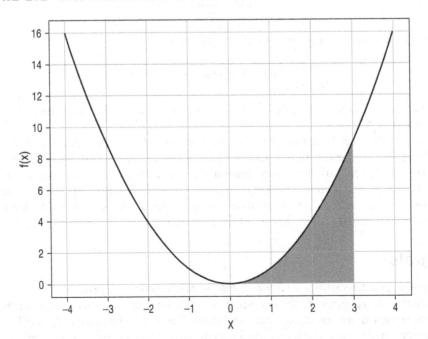

Integrals are used in data science for various purposes. They are used to calculate probabilities and cumulative distribution functions (CDFs) for continuous random variables. This is covered in the next section. When evaluating the performance of a classifier (which is introduced in Chapter 6, "Modeling and Evaluation"), integrals are also used to calculate the area under the curve (AUC).

Probability Distributions

In data science, a *population* is a group of interest that we intend to study or draw conclusions about. Because it is oftentimes infeasible to observe or gather data on an entire population, we often resort to using a few members of the group, known as a *sample*, to understand the whole. Ideally, for a sample to be representative of the population, it must be randomly selected to avoid sampling bias, which can occur when one group is overrepresented within a sample at the expense of others.

Imagine that you work in a factory that produces light bulbs and you want to monitor the lifespan of the bulbs to ensure they meet the advertised lifespan. All the bulbs manufactured by the factory form the population of interest. However, because you cannot test every light bulb, you decide to randomly test a sample of 200 light bulbs. You describe the lifespan of the bulbs you tested as a frequency distribution using a histogram like Figure 2.3.

FIGURE 2.3 Frequency distribution of the lifespan of sample light bulbs tested

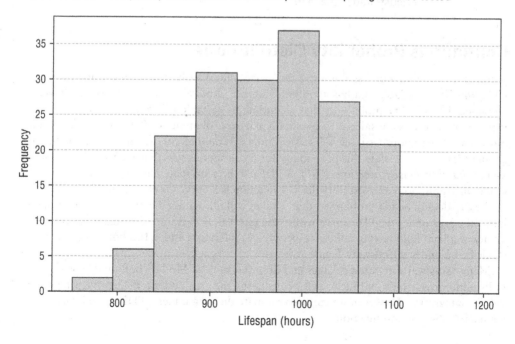

A *frequency distribution* describes the number of times a particular value for a variable occurs within a dataset. The number of times a value occurs in a sample is determined by its probability of occurrence. *Probability* is a measure of the likelihood of an event occurring. It ranges from 0 to 1, where 0 indicates an impossible event and 1 indicates a certain event.

By observing the frequency distribution in Figure 2.3, you can get a rough idea of the probability of different lifespans. For example, you can see that there's a high probability of a light bulb lasting 1,000 hours but a low probability of it lasting less than 800 hours or much more than 1,100 hours. However, what if you wanted a more precise probability estimate of the lifespan of a bulb? For example, what is the probability that a light bulb would last between 1,000 and 1,100 hours? You can determine this by using a probability distribution.

A *probability distribution* is a mathematical function that describes the probability of the possible values for a variable. Probability distributions can be thought of as idealized versions of frequency distributions that aim to describe the population a sample was drawn from. Depending on whether the variable we're trying to understand is continuous or discrete, we can use either a continuous probability distribution or a discrete probability distribution to describe the population.

As you prepare for the DataX exam, you should be able to explain probability and synthetic modeling concepts and their uses. Make note of the differences between the probability distributions listed here and consider additional scenarios of how each distribution could be used beyond what is illustrated in the text.

Continuous Probability Distributions

A continuous probability distribution is the probability distribution for a continuous variable, which is a variable that has an infinite number of possible values between its lower and upper bounds. The probability that a continuous variable will have any specific value is so minute that it is considered to essentially have a probability of 0. However, the probability that a continuous variable will fall within a certain interval of values within its range is greater than 0. To calculate this probability for a continuous variable, we use what is known as a *probability density function (PDF)*. A PDF can be represented as an equation or as a graph. In graph form, a probability density function is a curve (as shown in Figure 2.4).

We can determine the probability that a value will fall within a certain interval by calculating the area under the PDF curve within the interval. For example, to figure out the probability of a light bulb having a lifespan between 1,000 hours and 1,100 hours, we find the shaded area under the curve in Figure 2.5.

Many statistical software packages and libraries, such as MATLAB, R, and SciPy in Python, provide built-in functions for calculating the area under a PDF curve using definite integration. However, we can also estimate the area under a PDF curve by using a cumulative distribution function.

FIGURE 2.4   Probability density function (PDF)

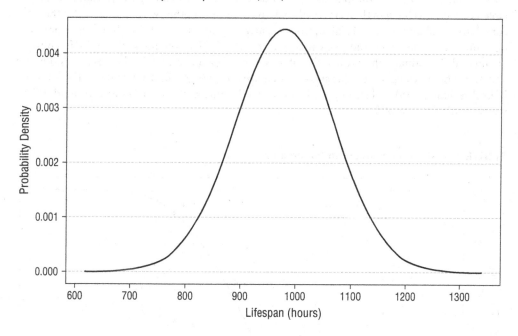

FIGURE 2.5   PDF showing interval of interest (shaded area)

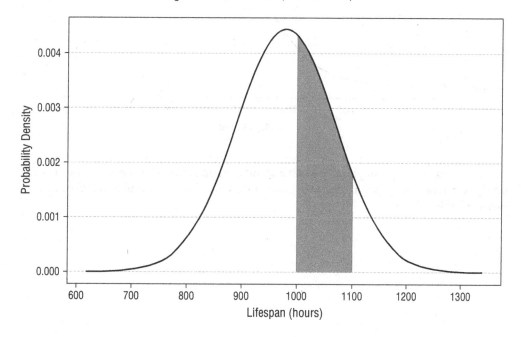

A *cumulative distribution function (CDF)* describes the probability that a random variable takes on a value less than or equal to a given point. In other words, it provides the cumulative probability of a variable, from negative infinity (in theory) or 0 (often in practice), up to a certain threshold. We can also think of a CDF as the integral of a PDF within an interval. To estimate the probability of a light bulb having a lifespan between 1,000 hours and 1,100 hours using a CDF (as shown in Figure 2.6), we get the CDF value at the 1,000-hour threshold (0.59) and subtract it from the CDF value at the 1,100-hour threshold (0.91), which yields 0.32, or 32%.

FIGURE 2.6   Cumulative distribution function (CDF)

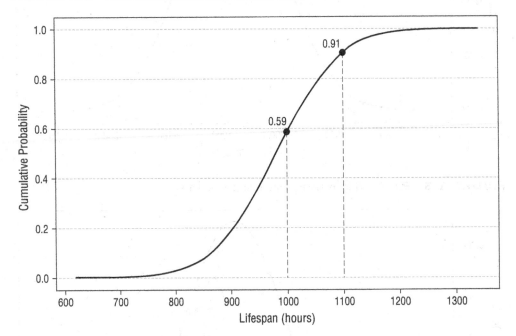

Depending on the assumptions we make about the population and the nature of the variable, we can describe a population using one of the continuous probability distributions listed in Table 2.1.

TABLE 2.1 Common continuous probability distributions

Distribution	Description	Example usage
Normal (Gaussian)	A bell-shaped curve characterized by its mean and standard deviation. It is used to model continuous data with a symmetric distribution around the mean.	Modeling the heights of people in a population
Continuous Uniform	All outcomes in a given range are equally likely. It is used when there is no preference or bias toward any interval within the range.	Generating random numbers in a fixed interval for simulations
t (Student's t)	Similar to the normal distribution but with heavier tails. Used when the sample size is small and the population standard deviation is unknown.	Estimating the mean of a small sample from a normally distributed population when the population standard deviation is unknown
Power Law (Pareto)	A distribution with a heavy tail, characterized by a scaling relationship between quantities. Used when one quantity varies as a power of another.	Modeling the distribution of wealth or city sizes

Skewness and Kurtosis

Skewness is a statistical measure that describes the asymmetry of a probability distribution. If a distribution is symmetrical, it has zero skewness.

Normal Distribution
(Symmetrical, Mesokurtic)

However, if the distribution is asymmetrical, it can be either positively skewed, where the right tail is longer or heavier than the left, or negatively skewed, where the left tail is longer or heavier than the right.

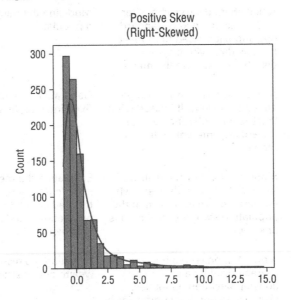

Skewness is important in statistical analysis, as it can affect hypothesis testing and the calculation of confidence intervals.

Kurtosis, on the other hand, measures the "tailedness" and "peakedness" of a distribution. A distribution with positive kurtosis, known as leptokurtic, has a sharper peak and heavier tails than a normal distribution, indicating the presence of outliers.

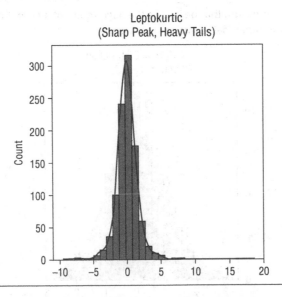

A distribution with negative kurtosis, or platykurtic, has a flatter peak and lighter tails, suggesting a lack of outliers.

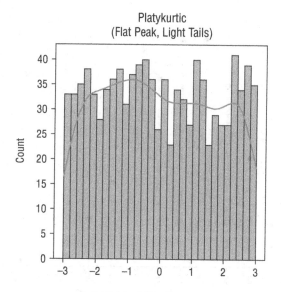

Platykurtic
(Flat Peak, Light Tails)

A distribution with zero kurtosis, known as mesokurtic, has the same kurtosis as a normal distribution. Understanding the kurtosis of a distribution helps in identifying the presence of outliers and the likelihood of extreme values in data.

Discrete Probability Distributions

A discrete probability distribution is a probability distribution for a categorical or discrete variable. This type of distribution is used when the set of possible outcomes is countable. For example, the probability distribution of a coin toss, where the outcomes can only be heads or tails, is a discrete distribution. The probability of all possible values adds up to one. In other words, there is certainty that an observation will have one of the possible values.

The probability of every possible value in a discrete probability distribution can be represented using a *probability mass function (PMF)*, which assigns a probability to each possible outcome. Like a PDF, a PMF can also be represented as an equation or as a graph. Let's consider a scenario where we use a common type of discrete probability distribution, known as a Poisson distribution, to model the number of emails a person receives in an hour. We can show the probability of receiving various quantities of emails in an hour using the PMF in Figure 2.7.

FIGURE 2.7   Probability mass function (PMF)

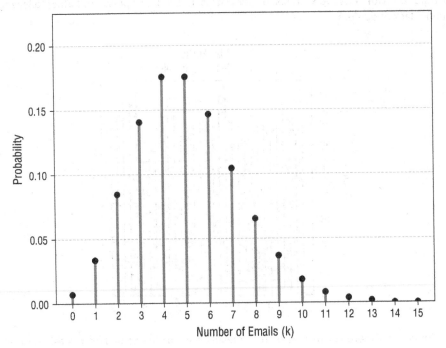

From the PMF, we can see that the probability of receiving exactly four or five emails in an hour is the highest, with a decrease in probabilities as the number of emails increases and decreases. Along with the Poisson distribution, some of the other commonly used discrete probability distributions are listed in Table 2.2.

TABLE 2.2   Common discrete probability distributions

Distribution	Description	Example usage
Discrete Uniform	Each outcome in a finite set of outcomes is equally likely. It is used when each outcome in a discrete set has the same probability.	Rolling a fair six-sided die
Poisson	Models the number of events occurring within a fixed interval of time or space, given that these events happen with a known constant mean rate and independently of the time since the last event.	Counting the number of emails received in an hour
Binomial	Models the number of successes in a fixed number of independent Bernoulli trials (i.e., trials with only two outcomes), each with the same probability of success.	Counting the number of heads in a fixed number of coin tosses

Monte Carlo Simulation

A *Monte Carlo simulation* is a mathematical technique that uses random sampling to estimate the likelihood of various outcomes. It involves simulating numerous scenarios involving random variables and using the results to approximate the properties of the system being studied. For example, to determine the probability of rolling a seven with two dice, one can simulate rolling the dice multiple times and observe the outcomes. Rolling the dice 300 times and getting a seven on 52 of those times would be the actual probability (52/300, or 17.3%), which is close to the mathematical (or theoretical) probability of 6/36, or 16.67%. Each dice roll in this simulation is an iteration, and the accuracy of the estimation will improve with more iterations. This is in line with the *law of large numbers*, which states that as the number of trials increases, the sample mean approaches the *expected value* (mean) of the population distribution.

In data science, Monte Carlo simulations are used in various ways to model and solve problems that involve uncertainty, randomness, or complex systems. In cases where it's impractical to collect data from an entire population, Monte Carlo simulations can be used to generate representative samples for statistical analysis and hypothesis testing. In those situations, *stratification* is often used to reduce variance and improve the accuracy of the simulation results. It involves dividing the domain of the random variables into distinct subgroups or strata and then sampling separately from each stratum. The key idea is to ensure that each stratum is well represented in the sample, which leads to more precise estimates.

Inferential Statistics

Inferential statistics is a branch of statistics that focuses on making predictions or inferences about a population based on a sample of data drawn from that population. A fundamental concept underpinning inferential statistics is the central limit theorem. This theorem is based on the idea of a sampling distribution, which is the distribution of a statistic over many samples drawn from a population. Before we continue, let's clarify what a statistic means in this context, as well as a related term known as a *parameter*.

A parameter is a numerical characteristic of a population. It is a fixed value that describes some aspect of the population, such as the population mean (μ) or the population standard deviation (σ). The parameters of a population are "usually unknown" because it is often impractical or impossible to examine an entire population.

A statistic is a numerical characteristic of a sample. It is calculated from the sample data and is used to estimate the corresponding population parameter. Examples include the sample mean ($\bar{x}$) or the sample standard deviation (s). Unlike parameters, statistics are known values because they are computed from the sample data.

Now, let's imagine that we draw a random sample from a population and calculate a statistic, such as the mean. Next, we repeat the same process many times and end up with a large number of means, one from each sample. The *central limit theorem* states that regardless of the probability distribution of the population, for a large enough sample size, the sampling distribution of the mean will always be normally distributed. This is saying that if, for each of the samples, we only selected one item (i.e., a sample size of 1), the distribution of the sample means would be a uniform distribution that looks like the first chart in Figure 2.8. However, as we increase the sample size, the distribution of means would gradually converge onto a normal distribution (last chart in Figure 2.8) as the sample size becomes greater than 30.

FIGURE 2.8   Sampling distributions illustrating the central limit theorem

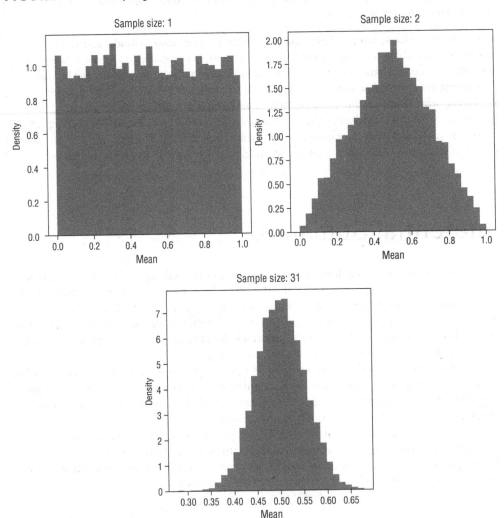

The assumptions of the central limit theorem are crucial in statistics and data science because they allow for the use of normal distribution-based statistical inference techniques, even when the population distribution is not normal. This is particularly important for estimating the characteristics of populations and for hypothesis testing.

Estimating Population Parameters

There are two important types of estimates we can make about a population based on a sample. The first is known as a *point estimate*. This is a single-value estimate of a population parameter. A sample mean is an example of a point estimate of a population mean. The other type of estimate is known as an interval estimate. An *interval estimate* is a range of values within which we expect the true value of a population parameter to lie.

The most common type of interval estimate is the *confidence interval*. Unlike point estimates, which give us a precise value for a parameter, a confidence interval factors in the variability around a statistic to come up with an estimate that takes into account the uncertainty of the point estimate.

Confidence intervals are made up of a sample statistic (point estimate), a margin of error (the amount added and subtracted from the sample statistic to create the interval), and a confidence level (the probability that the interval will contain the true population parameter). Mathematically, a confidence interval is represented as:

$$CI = \bar{x} \pm z_{\alpha/2} \left(\frac{s}{\sqrt{n}} \right)$$

where $\bar{x}$ is the sample mean, $z_{\alpha/2}$ is the critical z-value for the desired confidence level, s is the sample standard deviation, and n is the sample size. Common confidence levels are 90 percent, 95 percent, and 99 percent, which correspond to α values of 0.1, 0.05, and 0.01, respectively.

To illustrate how confidence intervals are used and interpreted, suppose a sample of 100 students have an average test score of 75 with a standard deviation of 10. To construct a 95 percent confidence interval for the population mean, we use the confidence interval formula with $z_{0.05/2}$ approximately equal to 1.96:

$$CI = 75 \pm 1.96 \left(\frac{10}{\sqrt{100}} \right) = 75 \pm 1.96 \times 1$$
$$= (73.04, 76.96)$$

There are couple of ways to interpret this result:

- Based on a sample of 100 students with a sample mean test score of 75 and sample standard deviation of 10, we are 95 percent confident that the population mean lies between 73.04 and 76.96.

- If we sample the population of students 100 times using the same approach, we expect the mean for each sample to fall between 73.04 and 76.96, 95 percent of the time.

When interpreting confidence level values, note that although we can say that our point estimate will lie within an interval a certain percentage of the time, we cannot say with certainty that the actual population parameter will. That is because we cannot know the true value of the population parameter without collecting data from the entire population.

Hypothesis Testing

Hypothesis testing is a formal statistical method used to compare populations or assess relationships between variables based on sample data. It involves formulating two competing hypotheses, conducting an appropriate statistical test, and then making a decision based on the test result.

To understand how hypothesis testing is used at a high level, suppose a school claims that its students have an average SAT score of 1100. As a data scientist, you suspect that this average might be an overestimate and decide to test the claim. To do this, you take a random sample of 50 students and find that their average SAT score is 1070, with a standard deviation of 80.

To evaluate the school's claim, you set up a hypothesis test. The *null hypothesis* (H_0) is the default hypothesis that assumes no effect, no difference, or no association between variables. In this scenario, the null hypothesis is that the average SAT score of the students is 1100. The *alternative hypothesis* (H_1) is contrary to the null hypothesis and represents the effect, difference, or association that a researcher is trying to detect. In this example, the alternative hypothesis is that the average score is less than 1100.

To accept or reject the null hypothesis, you choose a significance level (α) of 0.05, which is commonly used in hypothesis testing. After conducting a statistical test, you obtain a p-value of 0.03 (we explain *p-values* in a moment). When deciding to accept or reject the null hypothesis, the basic principle is:

- If the p-value $\leq \alpha$, reject H_0 (the result is statistically significant).

- If the p-value $> \alpha$, fail to reject H_0 (the result is not statistically significant).

Since 0.03 is less than 0.05, you would reject the null hypothesis and conclude that there is sufficient evidence to suggest that the true average SAT score of the students is likely different from (in this case, less than) the claimed average of 1100.

Understanding P-values

A *p-value* is the probability of something occurring by chance rather than because of a hypothesized explanation. Whenever we frame an experiment, we always have to account for the possibility that random luck plays a role in the occurrence of an event or an outcome. Taking the possibility of random luck into account helps us frame our null hypothesis (H_0), which suggests that the variable in question had no impact on the experiment and that any positive results are simply due to chance. So, we can think of the p-value as a gauge of how surprising our data is, assuming that the null hypothesis is true.

Imagine conducting an experiment to test whether a coin is "fair." The null hypothesis is the default assumption that there's nothing unusual going on—in this case, that the coin has an equal chance of landing heads or tails. You flip the coin multiple times to collect data. Let's say you get an unusually high number of heads. The p-value in this scenario would quantify how surprising it is to get that many heads if the coin were indeed fair. It is the probability of getting a result as extreme as, or more extreme than, the one you observed (lots of heads) if the coin is fair.

If the p-value is high (above the significance level), it means getting this many heads isn't very surprising for a fair coin. It's within the realm of normal fluctuations. However, if the p-value is low (at or below the significance level), it means getting this many heads is quite surprising for a fair coin. In other words, it's evidence that the coin might not be fair.

Several statistical tests are employed for hypothesis testing, each tailored for specific types of data and research questions. Some of them include the t-test, ANOVA (analysis of variance), chi-squared test, and several correlation tests.

t-test

A *t-test* is a statistical test used to compare the means of two groups or samples to determine if there is a statistically significant difference between them. Depending on the objective, we can opt for either a two-tailed t-test or a one-tailed t-test. A two-tailed t-test is appropriate when we're interested in determining if there's any significant difference between two population means, without specifying the direction of the difference. On the other hand, a one-tailed t-test is suitable when we aim to assess if one population mean is specifically greater than or less than the other, thereby focusing on a particular direction of the difference. The t-statistic is calculated as:

$$t = \frac{\bar{x} - \mu}{s/\sqrt{n}}$$

where $\bar{x}$ is the sample mean, μ is the population mean, s is the sample standard deviation, and n is the sample size. To ensure the validity of its results, the t-test assumes that the data is approximately normally distributed, the samples are independent (two-sample t-test), the variances of the two groups are equal (two-sample t-test), and the differences between pairs are assumed to be normally distributed (paired samples t-test).

There are different types of t-tests. When choosing which test to use, you first need to consider whether the groups being compared come from a single population or two different populations. Depending on the answer, you can conduct a one-sample t-test, a two-sample t-test, or a paired-samples t-test.

One-Sample t-test

A one-sample t-test is used to compare the mean of a single sample to a known or hypothesized population mean. This test is particularly useful when the population standard deviation is unknown and the sample size is relatively small. The SAT score example given on page 42 is an example of a one-sample t-test.

Two-Sample t-test

A two-sample t-test, also known as the independent samples t-test, is used to determine whether there is a significant difference between the means of two independent groups. This test is particularly useful when comparing two groups under different conditions or treatments to see if an intervention has a significant effect on the outcome of interest.

 Real World Scenario

Evaluating Teaching Methods

As a data scientist at an educational research organization, you're tasked with evaluating the effectiveness of two teaching methods in a local high school. Class A, with 25 students, uses a traditional method and has an average score of 78 (standard deviation of 10). Class B, with 30 students, uses an innovative method and has an average score of 82 (standard deviation of 12).

You conduct an independent samples t-test to see if the difference in average scores is significant. Setting the null hypothesis (H_0) as no difference in scores ($\mu A = \mu B$) and the alternative hypothesis (H_1) as a difference ($\mu A \neq \mu B$), you choose a significance level (α) of 0.05.

The t-test results in a t-statistic of 1.96 and a p-value of 0.04. Since the p-value is less than 0.05, you reject the null hypothesis, concluding that there is a significant difference in average scores between the two classes. This suggests that the innovative teaching method in Class B may be more effective than the traditional method in Class A.

Paired-Samples t-test

The paired samples t-test, also known as the dependent t-test, is used to compare the means of two related groups or samples between two points in time. This test is particularly useful when the same subjects are measured under two different conditions, such as before and after an intervention, or when subjects are matched in pairs that are somehow related.

Real World Scenario

Evaluating Drug Effectiveness

You are a medical researcher investigating the effectiveness of a new medication designed to lower blood pressure. To evaluate the medication's impact, you conduct a study involving 20 patients who have been diagnosed with hypertension. You measure each patient's blood pressure before administering the medication and then again after they have completed a course of treatment.

Using a paired samples t-test, you set up your hypotheses as follows: the null hypothesis (H_0) states that there is no difference in blood pressure before and after the treatment, while the alternative hypothesis (H_1) suggests that there is a difference. You choose a significance level (α) of 0.05.

The results yield a t-statistic of -1.2 and a p-value of 0.24. Given that the p-value exceeds the significance level of 0.05, you fail to reject the null hypothesis. This outcome suggests that the new medication does not have a statistically significant effect on lowering blood pressure, as there is no notable difference in blood pressure levels before and after the treatment.

Analysis of variance (ANOVA)

Analysis of variance (ANOVA) is a statistical test used to compare the means of more than two independent groups to determine if there is a significant difference among them. It is particularly useful when we want to test the effects of a categorical independent variable on a continuous dependent variable across multiple groups. Depending on the number of independent variables we're working with, we can either use the *one-way ANOVA* (for one independent variable) or the *two-way ANOVA* (for two independent variables).

The basic idea behind ANOVA is to compare variability of each group's data points around their own mean (mean square within groups or "unexplained variance") and the variability of the group means around the overall mean (mean square between groups or "explained variance"). By comparing these variances, ANOVA determines whether the differences among group means are statistically significant or likely due to chance. ANOVA uses the F-statistic for statistical significance. It is calculated as:

$$F = \frac{Mean\ Square\ Between\ Groups\ (MSB)}{Mean\ Square\ Within\ Groups\ (MSW)}$$

To ensure the validity of its results, the F-statistic assumes that the dependent variable is continuous, the independent variables are categorical, the observations are independent, the groups have similar variances (homogeneity of variances), and the values of the dependent variable are approximately normally distributed for each group.

Real World Scenario

Evaluating Marketing Strategies Across Regions

You are a data scientist working for a large retail company that wants to understand the impact of two marketing strategies, Strategy A and Strategy B, on sales performance across stores in three regions: North, South, and West. There are two independent variables in this analysis: the marketing strategy (with two levels: A and B) and the store region (with three levels: North, South, and West). The dependent variable is the sales performance, measured in terms of total sales revenue.

You decide to use a two-way ANOVA test to assess the effects of marketing strategy and store region on sales revenue. The null hypotheses suggest no significant differences in sales between marketing strategies, store regions, or their interaction. The alternative hypotheses assert that there are significant differences in these aspects.

After collecting sample sales data from the stores and conducting the statistical test, your results show that the p-value for the marketing strategy factor is more than 0.05, the p-value for the store region factor is less than 0.05, and the p-value for the interaction effect between marketing strategy and store region is less than 0.05. These results suggest that the choice of marketing strategy does not appear to have a significant impact on sales. However, the location of a store plays a significant role in determining sales performance, and the effectiveness of the marketing strategies varies depending on the store region (e.g., Strategy A might be more effective in the North region, whereas Strategy B might perform better in the South region).

Chi-Squared Test

The *chi-squared* (χ^2) *test* is a statistical test used to determine if there is a significant difference between the observed frequency distribution and expected frequency distribution of a categorical variable. The chi-squared statistic is calculated as:

$$\chi^2 = \sum \frac{(O_i - E_i)^2}{E_i}$$

where O_i is the observed frequency of the i-th category, and E_i is the expected frequency of the i-th category. To ensure its validity, the chi-squared statistic assumes that the data is categorical, the observations are independent, and there are at least a minimum of five observations in each category. There are two main types of chi-squared tests—the chi-squared test of independence and the chi-squared goodness-of-fit test.

Chi-Squared Test of Independence

The chi-squared test of independence, also known as the chi-squared test of association, is used to test if there is a significant association or relationship between two categorical variables. The null hypothesis (H_0) posits that the variables are independent, meaning there is no association between them. Conversely, the alternative hypothesis (H_1) suggests that the variables are not independent and that there is an association.

Chi-Squared Goodness-of-Fit Test

The chi-squared goodness-of-fit test is used to evaluate if a sample dataset adheres to a specific distribution or if the observed frequencies of a categorical variable match the expected frequencies. The null hypothesis (H_0) in this context asserts that the observed frequencies are consistent with the expected frequencies, implying that the sample fits the specified distribution. The alternative hypothesis (H_1), on the other hand, posits that the observed frequencies are not consistent with the expected frequencies, indicating a deviation from the expected distribution.

 Real World Scenario

Investigating Diet Preferences

You are a public health researcher investigating the diet preferences of individuals in a small town. The town is known for its diverse dietary habits, and you suspect that the distribution of these habits might differ from national trends. According to national data, the distribution of dietary preferences is as follows: 5 percent vegetarian, 91 percent non-vegetarian, and 4 percent vegan.

To test this hypothesis, you conduct a survey of 1,200 randomly selected residents of the town and ask them about their dietary preferences. The results are as follows:

- Vegetarian: 100 residents

- Non-vegetarian: 1,000 residents

- Vegan: 100 residents

To determine if the distribution of dietary preferences in the town differs significantly from the national distribution, you decide to use the chi-squared goodness-of-fit test. The null hypothesis (H_0) is that the distribution of dietary preferences in the town is the same as the national distribution. The alternative hypothesis (H_1) is that the distribution in the town is different from the national distribution.

The expected frequencies for each category, based on the national distribution, are:

- Vegetarian: 60 residents (5 percent of 1,200)

- Non-vegetarian: 1,092 residents (91 percent of 1,200)

- Vegan: 48 residents (4 percent of 1,200)

After calculating the chi-squared statistic based on the observed and expected frequencies, you get a p-value of less than 0.001. Since the p-value is less than the significance level (of 0.05), you reject the null hypothesis. This suggests that there is a significant difference between the observed distribution of dietary preferences in the town and the national distribution. Based on these results, you conclude that the dietary habits of the town's residents differ from national trends, with notably higher proportions of vegetarians and vegans in the town.

Correlation Tests

A correlation test is a statistical test used to measure the strength and direction of the relationship between two continuous variables. It helps to determine whether changes in one variable are associated with changes in another variable. The most common correlation tests are Pearson's correlation coefficient and Spearman's rank correlation coefficient.

Pearson's Correlation Coefficient

Pearson's correlation coefficient, r, measures the linear relationship between two continuous variables, ranging from -1 to $+1$. A value of $+1$ signifies a perfect positive linear correlation, whereas -1 indicates a perfect negative correlation. A value of 0 implies no linear correlation. It's important to note that r only captures linear associations and can be skewed by outliers or nonlinear relationships.

Spearman's Rank Correlation Coefficient

Spearman's rank correlation coefficient, ρ, quantifies the monotonic relationship between two variables. Unlike linear relationships where variables change at a constant rate, monotonic relationships only require the variables to change in the same direction but not necessarily at the same rate. Like Pearson's r, Spearman's ρ varies between -1 and $+1$, with -1, 0, and $+1$ indicating perfect negative monotonic, no monotonic, and perfect positive monotonic relationships, respectively. Spearman's rank correlation is particularly useful for ordinal data and for assessing correlation when the assumptions of Pearson's correlation (such as normality and linearity) are not satisfied.

Linear Algebra

Linear algebra is a branch of mathematics that deals with vectors, vector spaces, matrices, linear transformations, and systems of linear equations. In data science, data is often represented as vectors (individual data points) and matrices (collections of data points). Linear algebra provides an efficient framework for manipulating these representations.

Many machine learning algorithms, especially those related to supervised and unsupervised learning, rely heavily on linear algebra. For example, one of the most common approaches to estimating the coefficients of a linear regression model (see Chapter 9) is the *ordinary least squares (OLS)* method. OLS represents the problem as a system of linear equations, where each observation in the dataset provides one equation:

$$y_1 = \beta_0 + \beta_1 x_{11} + \beta_2 x_{12}$$

$$y_2 = \beta_0 + \beta_1 x_{21} + \beta_2 x_{22}$$

$$\ldots$$

$$y_n = \beta_0 + \beta_1 x_{n1} + \beta_2 x_{n2}$$

This system of equations can be written in matrix form as follows:

$$
\begin{bmatrix} y_1 \\ y_2 \\ \vdots \\ y_n \end{bmatrix}
=
\begin{bmatrix}
1 & x_{11} & x_{12} \\
1 & x_{21} & x_{22} \\
\vdots & \vdots & \vdots \\
1 & x_{n1} & x_{n2}
\end{bmatrix}
\times
\begin{bmatrix} \beta_0 \\ \beta_1 \\ \beta_2 \end{bmatrix}
$$

In this representation, the vector $[\beta_0, \beta_1, \beta_2]$ is analogous to the unknowns or variables in a system of linear equations (e.g., x, y, and z), the matrix with elements 1 and x_{ij} represents the variable coefficients, and the vector with elements y_i represents the constants (see the upcoming section "Solving a System of Linear Equations").

As you prepare for the DataX exam, you should be able to explain the importance of basic linear algebra concepts. Linear algebra is a vast field in mathematics, and understanding many of its concepts can be time-consuming. While going through this section, concentrate on gaining a broad understanding of how these concepts are interconnected and their importance in addressing different kinds of problems in data science.

Vectors

In mathematics, a *vector* is an object that has both magnitude and direction. It is the central building block of linear algebra. Vectors are often represented as an arrow in space with a specific direction and length. In two-dimensional space, a vector $\vec{v}$ can be represented as:

$$\vec{v} = \begin{bmatrix} x \\ y \end{bmatrix}$$

where x and y are the components of the vector along the x-axis and y-axis, respectively. Figure 2.9 illustrates a vector in two-dimensional space, where $x = 3$ and $y = 2$.

FIGURE 2.9   A vector in two-dimensional space

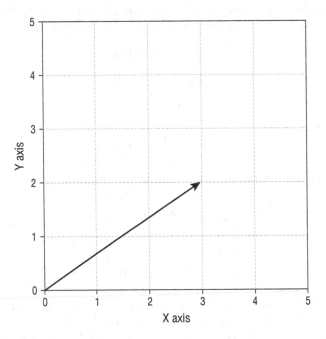

Vectors can be used to represent any piece of data. For instance, in a dataset of houses, a vector might represent a house with its components corresponding to the number of bedrooms, square footage, and price:

$$\overrightarrow{house} = \begin{bmatrix} 3 \\ 1200 \\ 80000 \end{bmatrix}$$

Vector Operations

When manipulating data, we often need to apply operations and functions to vectors. A common operation is vector addition. Suppose we have two vectors, $\vec{v}$ and $\vec{w}$, that we want to add together. The sum of these vectors is simply the sum of their components:

$$\vec{v} + \vec{w} = \begin{bmatrix} v_1 \\ v_2 \end{bmatrix} + \begin{bmatrix} w_1 \\ w_2 \end{bmatrix} = \begin{bmatrix} v_1 + w_1 \\ v_2 + w_2 \end{bmatrix}$$

We can also multiply vectors. The simplest approach is known as scalar multiplication (or scaling). Scaling involves multiplying each component of a vector by a scalar (real-valued constant):

$$c\vec{v} = c \times \vec{v} = c \times \begin{bmatrix} v_1 \\ v_2 \end{bmatrix} = \begin{bmatrix} c \times v_1 \\ c \times v_2 \end{bmatrix}$$

By scaling and adding two vectors, we can create any new vector we want. The space of possible vectors that can be created in this manner is known as the *span* of the vectors. If we have two vectors that exist in the same direction or exist on the same line, as shown in Figure 2.10, scaling and adding them will always result in a new vector on the same line. For that reason, we consider the two vectors *linearly dependent*.

FIGURE 2.10   Linearly dependent vectors

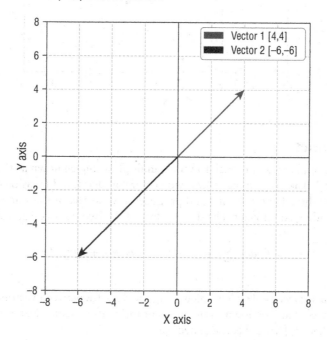

However, when we have two vectors in two different directions, like what is shown in Figure 2.11, we consider them *linearly independent*. Neither of the two vectors can be written as a linear combination of the other. These vectors have unlimited span and are known as *basis vectors*. We can combine these vectors linearly to create a new vector that points in any direction and have any length we choose in two-dimensional space.

FIGURE 2.11   Linearly independent vectors

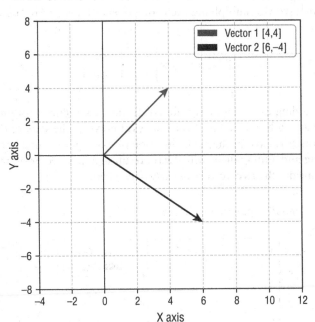

The Dot Product

A slightly more complicated approach to vector multiplication is known as the *dot product* (or scalar product). The dot product takes two vectors of identical dimensionality (i.e., they have the same number of components) and produces a scalar that is the sum of the products of each corresponding component. The dot product of the two vectors $\vec{v}$ and $\vec{w}$ is:

$$\vec{v} \cdot \vec{w} = \sum_{i=1}^{n} v_i w_i = v_1 w_1 + v_2 w_2 + \cdots + v_n w_n$$

The dot product plays a role when calculating the distance between vectors in n-dimensional space. This is known as the norm of their differences. Given two vectors $\vec{v}$ and $\vec{w}$, the norm of their differences is calculated as:

$$\|\vec{v} - \vec{w}\| = \sqrt{(\vec{v} - \vec{w}) \cdot (\vec{v} - \vec{w})}$$

which can be expressed in terms of their components as:

$$\|\vec{v} - \vec{w}\| = \sqrt{(v_1 - w_1)^2 + (v_2 - w_2)^2 + \cdots + (v_n - w_n)^2}$$

Common Distance Measures

Euclidean distance is the most common measure of distance in data science. It represents the straight-line distance between two points represented as vectors. For two vectors **A** and **B** in *n*-dimensional space, with coordinates $(a_1, a_2, \ldots, a_n)$ and $(b_1, b_2, \ldots, b_n)$, respectively, the Euclidean distance is defined as:

$$d_{Euclidean}(A, B) = ||A - B|| = \sqrt{\sum_{i=1}^{n}(a_i - b_i)^2}$$

You may have noticed that this is the same thing as the norm between two vectors. Euclidean distance is often used as a measure of similarity or dissimilarity in algorithms, such as k-means clustering and recommender systems (discussed in Chapter 8, "Unsupervised Machine Learning").

Manhattan distance, also known as the taxicab or L1 distance, is another common distance measure. It is the sum of the absolute differences between two vectors. For the same vectors **A** and **B** as above, the Manhattan distance is defined as:

$$d_{Manhattan}(A, B) = ||A - B||_1 = \sum_{i=1}^{n}|a_i - b_i|$$

$||A - B||_1$ is known as the L1 norm of the difference between vectors **A** and **B**. Manhattan distance is also used in clustering algorithms and in recommender systems.

Cosine distance and *cosine similarity* are measures based on the angle between two vectors, rather than their magnitudes or the distance between their endpoints. For two vectors **A** and **B**, the cosine similarity is given by the dot product of the vectors divided by the product of their magnitudes:

$$\text{cosine similarity}(A, B) = \frac{A \cdot B}{||A|| \, ||B||}$$

The cosine distance is defined as:

$$d_{Cosine}(A, B) = 1 - \text{cosine similarity}(A, B)$$

Cosine distance is particularly useful in text analysis and information retrieval, where the angle between vectors representing documents or words can indicate their semantic similarity, regardless of their length (magnitude).

Matrices

A *matrix* is a table of values arranged into columns and rows. Each value in the matrix is referred to as an element or entry and the size of the matrix provides a description of how many rows and columns it has. For example, an $m \times n$ matrix has m rows and n columns and can be represented as:

$$A_{m \times n} = \begin{bmatrix} a_{11} & a_{12} & \cdots & a_{1n} \\ a_{21} & a_{22} & \cdots & a_{2n} \\ \vdots & \vdots & \ddots & \vdots \\ a_{m1} & a_{m2} & \cdots & a_{mn} \end{bmatrix}$$

where a_{ij} represents the element in the i-th row and the j-th column. A matrix can be thought of as a collection of vectors, where each column of the matrix represents an individual vector.

A matrix where the number of rows, m, equals the number of columns, n, is known as a *square matrix*. Only square matrices have determinants, inverses, eigenvalues, and eigenvectors—concepts introduced later in this chapter.

The diagonal of a matrix comprises the elements within the matrix with identical subscripts ($a_{11}, a_{22}, a_{33}, \ldots$, etc.). If the only nonzero elements of a square matrix are on its diagonal, then the matrix is known as a *diagonal matrix*. If the values of a diagonal matrix are all equal to 1, then it is known as an *identity matrix* (I_n):

$$A = \begin{bmatrix} 1 & 0 & 0 \\ 0 & 1 & 0 \\ 0 & 0 & 1 \end{bmatrix} = I_n$$

Identity matrices play a crucial role in various matrix operations, such as finding the inverse of a matrix—one of the steps in solving a system of linear equations. The sum of the diagonal elements of an identity matrix is equal to the dimension of the matrix (n). We call this the *trace* of the matrix. For an $n \times n$ matrix, the trace is calculated as:

$$\text{tr}(A_{n \times n}) = \sum_{i=1}^{n} a_{ii} = a_{11} + a_{22} + \cdots + a_{nn}$$

Matrix Operations

The operations previously described for vectors extend to matrices as well. Specifically, if matrices A and B have the same dimensions, they can be summed on an element-by-element basis, as illustrated here:

$$A + B = \begin{bmatrix} a_{11} + b_{11} & a_{12} + b_{12} \\ a_{21} + b_{21} & a_{22} + b_{22} \end{bmatrix}$$

As we did with vectors, we can scale a matrix by multiplying its elements by a scalar:

$$cA = c \times A = \begin{bmatrix} c \times a_{11} & c \times a_{12} \\ c \times a_{21} & c \times a_{22} \end{bmatrix}$$

We can also apply a linear transformation to a vector, $\vec{v}$, by multiplying it with a matrix, A, to create a new vector, $\vec{v'}$:

$$\vec{v'} = A\vec{v} = \begin{bmatrix} a_{11} & a_{12} \\ a_{21} & a_{22} \end{bmatrix} \begin{bmatrix} v_1 \\ v_2 \end{bmatrix} = \begin{bmatrix} a_{11} \times v_1 + a_{12} \times v_2 \\ a_{21} \times v_1 + a_{22} \times v_2 \end{bmatrix}$$

Multiplying two matrices works a bit differently from the vector and matrix operations discussed earlier. To multiply two matrices, A and B, we multiply and add each row from A to each respective column of B, in an "over-and-down" pattern:

$$AB = \begin{bmatrix} a_{11} & a_{12} \\ a_{21} & a_{22} \end{bmatrix} \begin{bmatrix} b_{11} & b_{12} \\ b_{21} & b_{22} \end{bmatrix} = \begin{bmatrix} a_{11} \times b_{11} + a_{12} \times b_{21} & a_{11} \times b_{12} + a_{12} \times b_{22} \\ a_{21} \times b_{11} + a_{22} \times b_{21} & a_{21} \times b_{12} + a_{22} \times b_{22} \end{bmatrix}$$

It's important to note that to multiply two matrices, A and B, the number of columns in A must be equal to the number of rows in B. And if A is an $m \times n$ matrix and B is an $n \times p$ matrix, their product will be an $m \times p$ matrix.

Matrix Inversion

An *inverse matrix* is a matrix that undoes the transformation of another matrix. In other words, multiplying a matrix A by its inverse A^{-1} will return an identity matrix I_n. For example, let's say we have a matrix A:

$$A = \begin{bmatrix} 2 & 3 \\ 1 & 2 \end{bmatrix}$$

Using mathematical software, we can find its inverse as:

$$A^{-1} = \begin{bmatrix} 2 & -3 \\ -1 & 2 \end{bmatrix}$$

If we multiply both matrices, we get an identity matrix:

$$A \times A^{-1} = \begin{bmatrix} 2 & 3 \\ 1 & 2 \end{bmatrix} \begin{bmatrix} 2 & -3 \\ -1 & 2 \end{bmatrix} = \begin{bmatrix} 1 & 0 \\ 0 & 1 \end{bmatrix}$$

This property is fundamental in linear algebra and is used in solving systems of linear equations, among other applications. However, it's important to note that not every matrix has an inverse. A matrix can only be inverted if it has full *rank*, which implies that all the columns (or rows) of the matrix are linearly independent.

Solving a System of Linear Equations

Let's say we are provided with the following set of equations:

$$2x + 8y + 4z = 2$$

$$2x + 5y + z = 5$$

$$4x + 10y - z = 1$$

We can represent these equations in matrix form as $AX = B$, where A is the coefficient matrix, X is the vector of variables (the unknowns), and B is the vector of constants:

$$A = \begin{bmatrix} 2 & 8 & 4 \\ 2 & 5 & 1 \\ 4 & 10 & -1 \end{bmatrix}, X = \begin{bmatrix} x \\ y \\ x \end{bmatrix}, B = \begin{bmatrix} 2 \\ 5 \\ 1 \end{bmatrix}$$

Using mathematical software, we find A^{-1} to be:

$$A^{-1} = \begin{bmatrix} -5/6 & 8/3 & -2/3 \\ 1/3 & -1 & 1/3 \\ 0 & 2/3 & -1/3 \end{bmatrix}$$

The solution to the system can be found using the formula $X = A^{-1}B$, where A^{-1} is the inverse of the matrix A:

$$X = A^{-1}B = \begin{bmatrix} 2 & 8 & 4 \\ 2 & 5 & 1 \\ 4 & 10 & -1 \end{bmatrix}\begin{bmatrix} 2 \\ 5 \\ 1 \end{bmatrix} = \begin{bmatrix} 11 \\ -4 \\ 3 \end{bmatrix}$$

Therefore, the solution to the system of equations is $x = 11$, $y = -4$, and $z = 3$.

Matrix Transposition

Matrix transposition is the operation of flipping a matrix over its diagonal, which results in swapping the matrix's rows and columns. The transpose of a matrix A is denoted as A^T. Consider the following matrix:

$$A = \begin{bmatrix} 1 & 2 \\ 3 & 4 \\ 5 & 6 \end{bmatrix}$$

The transpose of the matrix will be:

$$A^T = \begin{bmatrix} 1 & 3 & 5 \\ 2 & 4 & 6 \end{bmatrix}$$

Matrix transposition is a fundamental operation in data science with various applications across different domains. In feature engineering, a key step in building predictive models, transposing a matrix can be instrumental in creating new features from existing ones. One common technique involves multiplying a matrix by its transpose to create interaction features, which are combinations of the original features. This can help capture complex relationships between variables in regression models.

In neural networks, which are the cornerstone of deep learning, the weights associated with layers of a network are typically represented as matrices. During the model training process, specifically in the backpropagation algorithm, transposing weight matrices to ensure the correct alignment of dimensions for mathematical operations is common.

Matrix Decomposition

Matrix decomposition, also known as *matrix factorization*, is the process of breaking up a matrix into its basic components. This is similar to how a number such as 12 can be factored into its components: $2 \times 2 \times 3$. There are several types of matrix decompositions. One of the most common is known as eigendecomposition.

Given a square matrix A, *eigendecomposition* involves finding its *eigenvectors* and *eigenvalues*. An eigenvector of A is a nonzero vector v such that when A is multiplied by v, the result is a scalar multiple of v. The scalar multiplier is known as the eigenvalue λ associated with the eigenvector v. Mathematically, this relationship is expressed as:

$$Av = \lambda v$$

Eigendecomposition has a wide variety of applications in data science. It is core to principal component analysis (PCA), a widely used technique for dimensionality reduction, where eigenvectors are used to represent the directions of maximum variance in the data, and eigenvalues indicate the magnitude of the variance along these directions (see Chapter 8). Eigendecomposition is also used in collaborative filtering, a recommender system, to decompose the user-item interaction matrix.

Summary

Differential and integral calculus are core concepts in machine learning. They are useful in the areas of optimization, neural networks, and performance estimation, to name a few. Derivatives measure rates of change, whereas integrals measure accumulation.

Probability distributions describe the likelihood of various outcomes within a dataset. A continuous probability distribution, used for variables with an infinite number of values, can be represented using a probability density function (PDF). A discrete probability distribution, used for countable outcomes, can be represented using a probability mass function (PMF).

The use of inferential statistics involves making predictions about a population based on a sample. It relies on the central limit theorem, which allows for normal distribution-based statistical inference techniques. Inferential statistics allow us to estimate population parameters based on a sample and to conduct hypothesis testing.

Linear algebra provides a framework for manipulating data represented as vectors and matrices. Key concepts include vectors (objects with magnitude and direction), vector operations (addition, scaling, and the dot product), and matrices (tables of values arranged in rows and columns). Matrix operations include addition, scaling, multiplication, inversion, and transposition. Matrix decomposition breaks down matrices into core components.

Exam Essentials

Explain how derivatives are used in machine learning.   Derivatives are crucial for optimization, particularly in gradient descent, where they guide parameter updates to minimize the cost function. They're also used in backpropagation for neural network training and in finding optimal parameters in models like linear regression by solving for where the derivative of the cost function is 0.

Know the differences between how Euclidean, Manhattan, and cosine distance measures are used.   Euclidean distance is used for clustering and geometric data analysis. Manhattan distance is applied in grid-like structures and high-dimensional data. Cosine distance is primarily for text analysis and information retrieval, focusing on the orientation of vectors rather than their magnitude.

Explain how a probability density function (PDF), a cumulative distribution function (CDF), and a probability mass function (PMF) are used.   A probability density function (PDF) calculates probabilities for continuous variables. A cumulative distribution function (CDF) determines the likelihood of a variable falling within a specific range. A probability mass function (PMF) quantifies the probabilities of discrete outcomes.

List some common statistical tests and what they're used for.   Common statistical tests include the t-test for comparing means between two groups, ANOVA for comparing means among more than two groups, the chi-squared test for comparing observed and expected frequencies in categorical data, Pearson's correlation coefficient for measuring linear relationships, and Spearman's rank correlation coefficient for assessing monotonic relationships.

Explain what a confidence interval is and why it is used.   A confidence interval is a range of values that is likely to contain the true value of an estimated population parameter, based on a sample statistic. They are used to quantify the uncertainty of an estimate.

Review Questions

1. Which of these best describes what a cumulative distribution function (CDF) is used for?

    A. Describing the probability that a random variable takes on a value greater than a threshold

    B. Calculating the mean of a probability distribution

    C. Describing the probability that a random variable takes on a value less than or equal to a threshold

    D. Representing the probability at any threshold

2. What does Spearman's rank correlation coefficient measure?

    A. The linear relationship between two continuous variables

    B. The monotonic relationship between two variables

    C. The difference between the means of two groups

    D. The association between two categorical variables

3. Thalia is using a mathematical equation to model house prices as a function of square footage. The model is represented by the function $f(x) = 2x + 3$, where x is the square footage. Based on her function, at what rate does the price of a house change with each unit increase in square footage?

    A. 2

    B. 3

    C. 5

    D. 6

4. Ali is studying the distribution of IQ scores in a large population. The IQ scores are assumed to have a symmetric distribution around the mean. Which probability distribution is most appropriate for modeling the IQ scores?

    A. Continuous uniform

    B. t

    C. Power law

    D. Gaussian

5. What does the rank of a matrix represent?

    A. The number of linearly independent rows or columns in the matrix

    B. The sum of the diagonal elements of the matrix

    C. The number of nonzero elements in the matrix

    D. The size of the largest square matrix that can be extracted from the matrix

6. You are provided with a 95% confidence interval for a population mean. What does the confidence level indicate?

   A. The probability that the sample mean is equal to the population mean

   B. The probability that the population mean lies within the interval

   C. The percentage of the sample that lies within the interval

   D. The range of values within which the population mean is expected to lie

7. Which of these is a valid use of integrals?

   A. To find the maximum value of a function

   B. To calculate the area under a curve

   C. To determine the rate of change of a function

   D. To calculate the slope of a function at any point

8. A small sample of data is collected from a normally distributed population, but the population standard deviation is unknown. Which continuous probability distribution is most suitable for estimating the mean of this sample?

   A. Uniform

   B. Pareto

   C. Student's t

   D. Normal

9. Nadine wants to determine if there is an association between the category of product purchased (A, B, or C) by her customers and their satisfaction level (–1, 0, or +1). Which of these statistical tests should she use?

   A. A one-sample t-test

   B. ANOVA

   C. A paired-samples t-test

   D. A chi-squared test of independence

10. What does it mean for two vectors to be linearly independent?

   A. One vector can be written as a linear combination of the other.

   B. The vectors have unlimited span and can create new vectors in any direction.

   C. The vectors exist on the same line and have the same direction.

   D. The dot product of the vectors is 0.

11. Althea is studying the relationship between calorie intake and weight gain in adults. She collects data on daily calorie intake and weight gain over a month for a sample of individuals. Which of these tests would best quantify the strength and direction of the linear relationship between calorie intake and weight gain?

   A. Pearson's correlation coefficient

   B. Spearman's rank correlation coefficient

   C. Chi-squared test of independence

   D. Two-sample t-test

12. Emeka is working on a project to optimize delivery routes for a logistics company. He needs to calculate the shortest path between various delivery points in a city grid, where movement is restricted to horizontal and vertical streets. Which distance measure should he use to calculate the shortest path between two points in the city grid?

    A. Euclidean distance

    B. Manhattan distance

    C. Cosine distance

    D. Dot product distance

13. According to the central limit theorem, what happens to the sampling distribution of the mean as the sample size increases?

    A. It becomes positively skewed.

    B. It becomes uniformly distributed.

    C. It becomes normally distributed.

    D. It becomes negatively skewed.

14. Yetunde is investigating whether there is a significant difference in the average time spent on a website between two different age groups. She collects data from a sample of users in each age group and calculates the average time spent on the website for each group. Which of these statistical tests should Yetunde use to test whether the difference in average time spent is statistically significant?

    A. A chi-squared goodness-of-fit test

    B. A two-sample t-test

    C. A paired-samples t-test

    D. A chi-squared test of independence

15. Which of these mathematical concepts is most useful in transforming skewed data to a more normal distribution?

    A. Derivatives

    B. Exponents

    C. Integrals

    D. Logarithms

16. In a game of chance, a fair six-sided die is rolled. The outcome of the roll is an integer between 1 and 6, with each outcome being equally likely. Which of these probability distributions best describes the outcome of the die roll?

    A. Discrete uniform

    B. Poisson

    C. Continuous uniform

    D. Normal

17. Nitesh is investigating the impact of three different diets (Diet A, Diet B, and Diet C) on weight loss. Participants are randomly assigned to one of the three groups, and the change in their weights are tracked over a 12-week period. To determine if there is a significant difference in average weight loss among the three groups, Nitesh should use:

    A. Pearson's correlation coefficient

    B. A chi-squared test of independence

    C. A paired-samples t-test

    D. ANOVA

18. Enzo is working on a recommendation system for a music streaming service. The system needs to recommend songs that are similar to the user's current playlist. To measure the similarity between songs, Enzo decides to calculate the angle between vectors representing each song's features. Which distance measure is he using?

    A. Euclidean distance

    B. Manhattan distance

    C. Cosine distance

    D. Radial distance

19. A neural network model is being trained using the backpropagation algorithm. During the training process, connection weights, which are represented as matrices, are updated. Which of the following operations is commonly used to ensure proper alignment of the dimensions of matrices?

    A. Matrix inversion

    B. Dot product

    C. Matrix multiplication

    D. Matrix transposition

20. Danielle is conducting a statistical analysis of a manufacturing process that is known to produce an average of five defective products per hour. She wants to model the probability distribution of the number of defective products produced in any given hour. Which of the following discrete probability distributions is most suitable for this purpose?

    A. Student's t

    B. Poisson

    C. Binomial

    D. Gaussian

Chapter 3

Data Collection and Storage

THE COMPTIA DATAX EXAM OBJECTIVES COVERED IN THIS CHAPTER INCLUDE:

✓ **Domain 4: Operations and Processes**

- 4.2 Explain the process of and purpose for obtaining different types of data.

- 4.3 Explain data ingestion and storage concepts.

In today's digitally driven landscape, data isn't just a byproduct of operations—it's a prized asset. Data acquisition is the first phase in the data science lifecycle. It involves acquiring accurate, timely, and relevant data to ensure that downstream operations, analyses, and insights are robust and reliable. Data acquisition isn't just about amassing vast amounts of information; it's about gathering the right data for a specific purpose. Every piece of data acquired should have intent behind it, serving as a lens through which we can better understand a phenomenon or make more informed decisions. In this chapter, you will learn about some of the most common sources of data, why and when we need them, how they are collected, and how best to store and manage them.

Common Data Sources

As data continues to drive innovation and transformation across industries, it becomes imperative for organizations to leverage diverse data sources to inform decision-making, improve operations, and innovate products. Data sources, based on their origin and use, can be broadly categorized into *generated data*, *synthetic data*, and *commercial or public data*. Each type offers unique opportunities and challenges. In this section, we explore some of these common sources of data in order to understand their nature and how they can be used to extract meaningful insights and achieve strategic goals.

As you prepare for the DataX exam, you should be able to explain the process of and purpose for obtaining different types of data. Make note of this as you read about the common data sources introduced in this section.

Generated Data

Generated data is data that is collected through surveys, administrative records, sensors, transactions, and experiments. In other words, generated data is data born out of actions. Every time a user logs into a website, a sensor registers a temperature change, or a customer makes a purchase, generated data is created. Its immediacy and relevance make it invaluable for data science projects.

Surveys

Surveys are a common source of generated data. They are an important way to collect data about people's opinions, attitudes, preferences, and behaviors. Surveys are often collected through structured questionnaires, interviews, or feedback forms and can be conducted in person, over the phone, or online. They can be used for a variety of data science projects, such as predicting customer behavior, understanding public opinion, and identifying trends.

Surveys are not conducted with every single person in the population. Instead, they are gathered from a subset of the population (known as a sample) with the expectation that the subset will be representative of the larger group. As we collect survey data, it's important to keep a few key considerations in mind. They include:

- **Sampling Design:** The survey's sample must be carefully designed to faithfully represent the population of interest, guaranteeing the validity of the conclusions drawn from the data.

- **Question (or Item) Design:** Crafting well-constructed survey questions is essential to obtain clear and unbiased responses that truly capture the perspectives of respondents.

- **Data Cleaning:** Addressing issues such as missing data, outliers, and response bias is necessary to enhance the quality of the collected data.

If these considerations are not properly addressed, survey data may lead to incomplete or errant conclusions, be influenced by personal biases, or yield results with very high variability. It's important to note that surveys can yield both numerical data (e.g., ratings) and textual data (e.g., open-ended responses). An example of a numerical survey question can be seen in Figure 3.1. Surveys can be subjected to a wide range of statistical analyses, from simple descriptive statistics to advanced modeling.

FIGURE 3.1   Example of a quantitative survey question

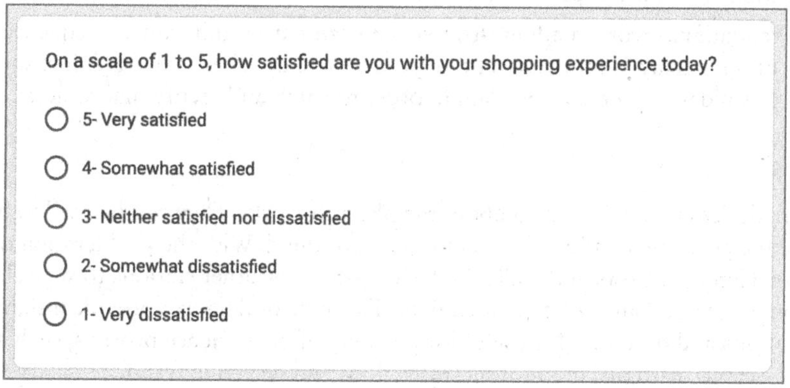

On a scale of 1 to 5, how satisfied are you with your shopping experience today?

○ 5- Very satisfied

○ 4- Somewhat satisfied

○ 3- Neither satisfied nor dissatisfied

○ 2- Somewhat dissatisfied

○ 1- Very dissatisfied

Administrative Records

Another common source of generated data are administrative records. Administrative records are data that is collected by governments and other organizations as part of their normal operations. This can include data found on birth certificates, death certificates, income tax returns, and school records. Administrative records can be used for a variety of data science projects, such as studying population trends, predicting crime rates, and evaluating government programs.

Administrative data has two main characteristics that make it suitable for data science. The first is recurrence. Administrative data is generated at regular intervals, making it highly suitable for longitudinal studies, where repeated observations are made over long periods of time. For example, recurrent administrative records such as weekly payroll data, monthly attendance records, or yearly tax filings can allow data scientists to analyze trends over time and understand how variables change and evolve with time.

The second characteristic of administrative data that makes it suitable for data science is its high granularity. Administrative data is often highly detailed, capturing specific information like timestamps, individual transactions, or user behaviors. This level of granularity enables data scientists to perform intricate analyses and gain insights into specific aspects of an organization's operations.

When working with administrative data, the following are some critical considerations to keep in mind:

- **Data Privacy:** Administrative data often contains sensitive information. It is imperative to implement robust data privacy measures to protect personal and confidential data, ensuring compliance with privacy regulations like GDPR (General Data Protection Regulation), CPRA (California Privacy Rights Act), or HIPAA (Health Insurance Portability and Accountability Act).

- **Data Integration:** To harness the full potential of administrative data, organizations may need to combine data from various sources to create comprehensive datasets. Data integration can be a complex process, but it is essential for holistic data analysis.

- **Data Validation:** Errors in administrative data can have significant consequences in terms of both analysis outcomes and organizational decision-making. Effort should be made to validate administrative data in order to catch and rectify inaccuracies.

Sensors

Sensors are devices that collect data about the physical world. They can be used to measure things like temperature, humidity, light, motion, and sound. With the proliferation of IoT (Internet of Things), sensors embedded in devices—from weather stations to wearable tech—have become a major source of generated data. This type of data can provide insights into real-time events and trends and is useful for a variety of data science projects, such as predicting weather patterns, monitoring traffic flow, and detecting fraud.

Working with sensor data comes with its unique set of challenges and considerations, some of which include:

- **Data Volume Management:** Sensors often generate large volumes of data, especially when collected at high frequencies. Managing and storing this data efficiently can be a significant challenge. It requires a scalable storage solution and a well-defined data archiving strategy.

- **Real-Time Processing:** Sensor data generated by critical system monitors or IoT devices often require real-time processing. Ensuring that data processing and analysis can keep up with the incoming stream of data is crucial.

- **Data Quality and Calibration:** Sensors can drift or become inaccurate over time. Regular calibration and quality checks are necessary to ensure the accuracy of the data. As a result of drift, outliers and errors in sensor data may need to be identified and addressed frequently.

- **Data Integration:** In many cases, sensor data needs to be integrated with other types of data to provide a comprehensive view of a system or an environment. Integrating sensor data with contextual information from other sources can be complex but is often essential.

- **Data Privacy and Security:** Sensor data can contain sensitive information, especially in applications like healthcare or security. Protecting this data from unauthorized access and ensuring compliance with data privacy regulations is critical.

 Real World Scenario

Flock Safety Cameras

Flock Safety cameras are a type of surveillance camera system designed primarily for use by communities and law enforcement agencies to enhance security and assist in crime prevention and investigation. They are notable for their ability to capture and process images of vehicles, including details such as license plates, make, model, and color, even at high speeds or in low-light conditions.

The data they capture is a prime example of the use of sensor data in the domain of urban safety and security. This data often has to be processed in real time to ensure a timely response to potential threats or incidents. The ability to integrate captured data with police databases facilitates the quick identification of persons or vehicles associated with criminal activity.

Due to the large volume of data generated by Flock cameras, the data is often stored for a limited duration to allow for sufficient time to review and act upon the information without unnecessarily prolonging the storage of personal information. This short-term data retention approach, along with ensuring that the data is encrypted, and access restricted to authorized personnel only, helps mitigate the risks related to privacy and security breaches.

The effectiveness of Flock cameras in accurately reading license plates relies heavily on their proper positioning and calibration. Regular review and maintenance are essential to ensure that these sensors operate optimally.

Transactions

Transactional data (another source of generated data) is data that is generated by business transactions. This can include data such as sales records, customer purchase history, and website traffic data. Transactional data offers insights into business health, customer preferences, and market dynamics.

Transactional data is characterized by its event-based nature and relational structure, making it particularly well suited for data science projects. These projects can range from predicting customer churn to recommending products and optimizing marketing campaigns. When dealing with transactional data, it's crucial to consider several key factors to ensure its reliability and utility:

- **Data Consistency:** One of the foremost considerations is maintaining data consistency. This involves ensuring that the transactional data is both accurate and uniform, thus providing a solid foundation for making sound financial and operational decisions.

- **Data Aggregation:** To unearth meaningful insights and discern relevant trends within the vast sea of transactional data, effective data aggregation techniques must be employed. This process involves summarizing the data across different timeframes or categories to extract actionable knowledge.

- **Data Security:** The protection of transactional data is paramount. Establishing robust data security measures, such as encryption, access controls, and regular security audits, is essential to safeguard against potential threats such as fraud and unauthorized access.

Experiments

Another source of generated data is experimental data. Experimental data is the product of carefully controlled experiments or studies, frequently conducted in scientific research or product development endeavors. Experiments serve as a means to test hypotheses and deepen our understanding of the world around us. In these experiments, researchers deliberately manipulate one or more variables to observe their impact on a desired outcome, thereby generating data that enables them to draw conclusions and make informed decisions. The use of experimental data is instrumental in establishing cause-and-effect relationships toward objectives such as developing new drugs, improving manufacturing processes, and understanding social phenomena.

Experimental data frequently involves the utilization of control groups. These control groups serve as essential reference points in the experimental process, enabling researchers to compare the outcomes of specific treatments or interventions against a baseline. By having control groups in place, researchers can discern and quantify the effects of the variables under investigation, enhancing the reliability of their findings.

Meticulous attention must be paid to the definition and measurement of variables in experimental data. Researchers adhere to standardized protocols, ensuring that variables are consistently and rigorously defined and measured. This commitment to standardized measures not only promotes uniformity in data collection but also bolsters the precision and accuracy of the data, ultimately contributing to the robustness of the research.

Some of the key principles that underpin the generation and analysis of experimental data include:

- **Randomization:** This involves the random assignment of subjects or samples to different treatment groups. This deliberate randomness serves to minimize bias and confounding variables, bolstering the validity of the conclusions drawn from the data.

- **Data Collection Protocols:** The rigorous application of well-defined data collection procedures is a hallmark of experimental data. Researchers meticulously follow established protocols to gather data systematically and consistently. This commitment to adhering to data collection protocols not only ensures replicability, allowing others to reproduce the experiment's results, but also guards against errors and inaccuracies, which are critical considerations in maintaining the integrity of the data.

- **Hypothesis Testing:** Hypothesis testing enables researchers to determine whether the observed outcomes align with the hypothesized relationships, shedding light on the validity and practical implications of the research findings.

How Is Generated Data Used in Data Science?

Here are some ways generated data is used in data science:

- **Predicting Customer Behavior:** Companies can use data from surveys, transactions, and customer support tickets to predict customer behavior, such as which customers are likely to churn and which customers are likely to buy a particular product.

- **Understanding Public Opinion:** Government agencies and political campaigns can use data from surveys and social media to understand public opinion on a variety of issues.

- **Identifying Trends:** Data scientists can use data from sensors, transactions, and social media to identify trends in consumer behavior, economic activity, and social media use.

- **Detecting Fraud:** Financial institutions and other organizations can use data from transactions and sensors to detect fraud, such as credit card fraud and insurance fraud.

- **Developing New Drugs:** Pharmaceutical companies can use data from experiments to develop new drugs and treatments.

- **Improving Manufacturing Processes:** Manufacturers can use data from sensors and experiments to improve their manufacturing processes and reduce waste.

- **Understanding Social Phenomena:** Social scientists can use data from surveys and experiments to understand social phenomena, such as the spread of misinformation or the causes of poverty.

Synthetic Data

In situations where generated data is either unavailable or insufficient, synthetic data is used instead. Synthetic data is artificially generated data designed to mimic real-world data. It can be used for a variety of purposes, including training machine learning models, testing software, and simulating real-world scenarios.

There are a number of ways to create synthetic data. One common approach is to use statistical models to generate data that matches the distribution of real-world data. Another approach is to use generative adversarial networks (GANs), a type of machine learning model that can be trained to generate realistic data.

There are several benefits to using synthetic data in data science. They include:

- **Cost:** Synthetic data is often less expensive to generate than collecting real-world data.

- **Control:** Synthetic data can be generated with specific characteristics in mind, which can be useful for training machine learning models or testing software.

- **Privacy:** Synthetic data enhances privacy since it can be created without any personally identifiable information (PPI) of real individuals or entities.

While synthetic data offers a number of benefits, it is important to also be aware of its limitations. Some of the limitations of synthetic data are:

- **Realism:** Synthetic data may struggle to capture certain characteristics in real-world data such as outlier behavior. This can impact its effectiveness for training machine learning models.

- **Bias:** Depending on the data generation process, synthetic data can be biased. It is important to carefully evaluate synthetic data to ensure that it is representative of the real-world data that it will be used to model.

- **Expertise:** Depending on the approach used, generating synthetic data can be computationally expensive and require significant domain expertise.

How Is Synthetic Data Used in Data Science?

Here are some ways synthetic data is used in data science:

- **Image Generation:** In computer vision and image analysis, synthetic images are often created using generative models such as generative adversarial networks (GANs). These images are generated to augment the training data available to machine learning models.

- **Autonomous Systems:** In fields like autonomous vehicles, robotics, and IoT, synthetic sensor data is used to train and test algorithms. For instance, lidar, radar, or camera data can be synthetically generated to simulate various real-world scenarios.

- **Natural Language Processing:** Synthetic text data is often used in natural language processing (NLP) tasks, including text classification, sentiment analysis, and chatbot training. Language models like GPT-4 can generate coherent text passages that mimic human-generated text.

- **Healthcare:** Synthetic healthcare data is crucial for developing and testing medical data analysis algorithms without exposing sensitive patient information. It can include synthetic patient records, medical images (such as in the following graphic), or diagnostic data.

- **Genomic Research:** In bioinformatics, synthetic genomic data is generated to create artificial DNA sequences for testing genetic analysis algorithms and understanding the properties of DNA.

- **Fraud Detection:** In financial and cybersecurity applications, synthetic data is used to simulate fraudulent activities to train fraud-detection systems.

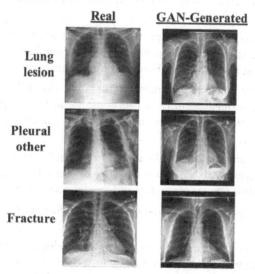

Source: Shobhita et al., (2021) / with permission of ACM (The Association for Computing Machinery)

Commercial or Public Data

Sometimes, when an organization's internal data isn't enough, it may need to purchase (commercial) or access (public) external data to complement or supplement its in-house data. Commercial or public data is data that is collected and sold by companies or provided by government agencies and other public institutions. Such data can range from demographic studies to industry trends and can be used for a variety of purposes, including training machine learning models, conducting research, marketing, and developing new products and services.

There are several ways to obtain commercial or public data. One approach is to purchase data from data brokers—intermediaries who collect data from a variety of sources and sell it to businesses and other organizations. Another approach is to download commercial or public data directly from the source. Many government agencies, public institutions, and private organizations provide data for free download or for sale on their websites. These include platforms like Kaggle (www.kaggle.com), University of California, Irvine Machine Learning Repository (http://archive.ics.uci.edu), and various commercial or governmental portals such as the Chicago Data Portal (http://data.cityofchicago.org).

Some of the benefits of using commercial or public data in data science include:

- **Rich and Diverse Information:** Commercial and public datasets typically cover a wide range of topics, industries, and geographic regions, providing a rich source of diverse information for analysis. This breadth of data allows data scientists to explore various research questions and applications.

- **Cost-Efficiency:** Public data sources are often freely accessible. Though they may come with a cost, commercial datasets can provide substantial return on investment due to the insights they offer.

- **Timeliness:** Many commercial data providers regularly update their datasets, ensuring that users have access to the most up-to-date information. Timely data is crucial for businesses operating in dynamic markets and for researchers analyzing current trends.

- **Support for Decision-Making:** Commercial and public data help organizations and individuals make informed data-driven decisions. For instance, market research data can guide business strategy, while economic indicators can enable policymakers to base decisions on empirical evidence.

- **Accessibility and Transparency:** Public data sources published by governments and organizations are typically open to a wide range of users. This democratizes access to information and promotes transparency and greater accountability.

Using commercial or public data for data science does also present some challenges, such as:

- **Data Access and Cost:** Commercial data, being a valuable asset for its providers, often comes at a significant cost. Access to high-quality, comprehensive datasets can be expensive, making it difficult for smaller organizations or individual researchers to utilize these resources.

- **Quality and Reliability:** Depending on the source, commercial and public datasets may vary in terms of data quality, accuracy, and reliability. Errors, inconsistencies, and missing values can be prevalent, requiring extensive data cleaning and preprocessing.

- **Data Privacy and Ethics:** Public datasets may contain sensitive information or PII. Handling this data without appropriate precautions can raise privacy and ethical concerns.

- **Usage Restrictions:** Commercial data may also have usage restrictions. Misusing this data can result in legal consequences.

- **Limited Control:** Data scientists have limited control over how commercial and public datasets are collected, formatted, and maintained. This lack of control can hinder the customization of data for specific research or business needs.

- **Data Availability and Coverage:** While commercial and public data sources offer valuable information, they may not always have the data needed for a particular analysis or research question. Gaps in data coverage can limit the scope of work.
- **Data Integration:** Combining data from different commercial or public sources can be challenging due to differences in data formats, schemas, and data definitions.

When using commercial or public data, it is important to be aware of the licensing and restrictions that apply to the use of the data (see Table 3.1). Some data may be free to use for any purpose, while other data may require a license or have restrictions on how it can be used or distributed. Understanding these licensing terms and implications is crucial. Violating license terms can lead to legal and ethical issues. This makes it essential for data scientists and organizations to adhere to the rules and guidelines set forth in data licenses. When in doubt, consult with legal experts to ensure compliance.

TABLE 3.1 Common licensing types

License	Description
Public domain	Public domain data is data that isn't protected by copyright or other intellectual property laws, or whose copyright has expired. No permission is needed to use, modify, or distribute this data. An example of a public domain license is the Creative Commons Zero (CC0) license. See `http://creativecommons.org/about/cclicenses` for more information on Creative Commons licenses.
Open license	An open license allows data to be freely used, modified, and shared by anyone for any purpose. The data can be used for both commercial and noncommercial projects. Some open licenses might require attribution (credit to the source). Others might require derivative works to be released under the same open license, often referred to as a "share-alike" clause. Examples of this type of license include the Creative Commons Attribution (CC BY) license and the Creative Commons Attribution-ShareAlike (CC BY-SA) license.
Noncommercial license	This license allows users to use, modify, and distribute the data but not for commercial purposes. Definitions of "commercial use" may vary, so users need to read the license terms carefully. This type of license is ideal for educational, research, or personal projects. An example of a noncommercial license is the Creative Commons Attribution-Noncommercial (CC BY-NC) license.
No-derivatives license	A no-derivatives license permits the original work to be redistributed, copied, and exhibited, but does not allow the work to be altered or used as the basis for creating new works. One of the most recognized no-derivatives licenses is the Creative Commons Attribution-NoDerivatives (CC BY-ND) license. This license allows others to redistribute the work, both commercially and noncommercially, as long as the content remains unchanged and is properly credited to the creator.

(continues)

TABLE 3.1   Common licensing types *(continued)*

License	Description
Proprietary or commercial license	Commercial licenses are licenses that allow users to use commercial data for commercial purposes. These licenses are generally provided by the owner or creator of the product or content in exchange for compensation, often monetary. The compensation can be a one-time fee, a recurring subscription, or based on usage metrics. The terms of commercial licenses can vary widely, so it is important to carefully review the license before using the data.

How Are Commercial and Public Data Used in Data Science?

Here are some ways commercial and public data are used in data science:

- **Benchmarking and Validation:** Well-known public datasets serve as benchmarks in the data science community. For instance, the MNIST dataset (handwritten digits) and CIFAR-10 (images in 10 classes) are often used to compare the performance of various image classification algorithms.

- **Academic Research:** Public datasets are widely used in academic research because they are freely accessible and can be shared across the community, ensuring reproducibility of results. In some cases, academic researchers might purchase commercial datasets if they provide unique insights not available in public datasets, especially for specialized research topics.

- **Learning:** Public datasets are invaluable for students, beginners, and even experienced data scientists looking to hone their skills. With platforms like Kaggle offering competitions based on public datasets, they provide practical experience in solving real-world problems.

- **Business Decision-Making:** Businesses frequently invest in commercial datasets to gain insights into areas outside their immediate purview. For example, market research firms offer datasets that can inform businesses about industry trends, competitive landscapes, and emerging market segments.

Data Ingestion

Data ingestion is the process of importing, processing, and storing data for later use. It's a crucial first step in the data pipeline, where data is collected from various sources and transferred to a place where it is easily accessible for analysis.

As you prepare for the DataX exam, you should be able to explain various concepts related to data ingestion such as the two main data ingestion methods, infrastructure requirements, and the data ingestion pipeline. Make note of these concepts as you read.

Data Ingestion Methods

The ingestion method we choose impacts how quickly the data we're working with becomes available for analytics and other tasks. Data ingestion can either be done in scheduled intervals (*batch data ingestion*) or in real time (*streaming data ingestion*). The choice of method is often determined by the specific operational requirements of the data science project and the nature of the data source.

Batch Data Ingestion

Batch data ingestion is a method where data is collected and processed in predefined chunks or batches, typically at scheduled intervals. Batch processing is a cost-effective approach, suitable for scenarios where immediate, real-time analysis is not a strict requirement, and where data can be aggregated or transformed before storage.

With batch data ingestion, data is continuously collected until a batch is formed or a predetermined time interval has elapsed, at which time the data is ingested as a whole. Batch processing frameworks such as Apache Hadoop or Spark are commonly used to ingest and process data in batch prior to being stored in a data warehouse, database, data lake, or other storage platform optimized for querying and reporting.

Streaming Data Ingestion

Streaming data ingestion is a dynamic approach that focuses on the real-time collection and processing of data as it flows into an organization's systems. It's like sipping from a constantly flowing stream of data, where information is processed and analyzed the moment it becomes available.

Streaming data sources can vary widely, from sensor data in IoT devices to social media posts to website clickstreams. Stream processing tools like Apache Kafka, Apache Flink, or Amazon Web Services Kinesis are useful for ingesting and buffering data in real time. Using these tools, streaming data can undergo real-time processing—filtering, enrichment, aggregation, and transformation—as it's being ingested. It can then trigger real-time alerts and actions or be stored in a persistent storage medium such as a database or data lake for future analysis. Streaming data ingestion is useful for applications that demand real-time insights and quick responses to events, such as fraud detection, system health monitoring, or real-time analysis of online user behavior.

Infrastructure Requirements

A robust infrastructure isn't just about having the capacity to store data. It's about ensuring data can be accessed, processed, and analyzed seamlessly. Adequately addressing *resource sizing* and leveraging specialized hardware are two ways to ensure this.

Resource Sizing

Resource sizing in data ingestion is the process of determining and allocating compute, storage, and network resources required to efficiently and effectively ingest and process data. This process is crucial to ensure that data ingestion pipelines can handle the volume, velocity, and variety of the data. Here's how resource sizing comes into play:

- **Compute Resources:** The type of central processing unit (CPU), number of CPU cores, or amount of memory allocated affects the throughput and speed of data ingestion and processing. Making sure that these resources are appropriately sized to handle processing load is critical. For example, with streaming data ingestion, resource sizing dictates whether real-time processing can occur with or without bottlenecks.

- **Storage Resources:** Choosing adequate and appropriate storage resources is also essential for data ingestion. These can include short-term storage for buffering incoming data, such as Kafka topic partitions, and long-term storage, such as data lakes or databases. The choice of storage resources must align with data volume and retention requirements.

- **Network Bandwidth:** High-speed network connections are crucial, especially in streaming data scenarios where data is ingested continuously. Sufficient bandwidth ensures that data can flow seamlessly from sources to processing systems without latency or congestion.

Specialized Hardware

Graphics processing unit (GPU) and tensor processing unit (TPU) are specialized hardware accelerators that can significantly enhance data processing capabilities, particularly for tasks involving machine learning and deep learning. They provide some key advantages during the data ingestion process:

- **Parallel Processing:** Both GPUs and TPUs are renowned for their parallel processing capabilities. They excel at handling multiple computational tasks simultaneously, which can be highly advantageous in data preprocessing, feature extraction, and real-time analytics. This parallelism can help maintain smooth data flow, especially in streaming data scenarios.

- **Resource Isolation:** GPUs and TPUs also offer the benefit of resource isolation. In situations where data ingestion coexists with compute-intensive tasks, these specialized accelerators can be employed to separate and prioritize workloads. This ensures that data ingestion pipelines do not compete for CPU resources, resulting in improved overall system performance.

Data Ingestion Pipeline

At the heart of data ingestion is the *extract, transform, load (ETL)* process, a fundamental and transformative phase in data management. ETL encompasses a series of operations that enable organizations to collect, cleanse, transform, and ultimately load data from various sources into a destination system, typically a data warehouse, data lake, or database. This process is pivotal in ensuring that data is structured, consistent, and ready for analysis. Let's delve into each component of the ETL process.

Extract

The first step involves extracting data from diverse sources, which can include databases, flat files, application programming interfaces (APIs), cloud services, and more. Data extraction is performed using specialized tools or scripts designed to access and retrieve data from these sources. The goal is to gather raw data without altering its original format.

Transform

Once data is extracted, it often requires cleansing and transformation to prepare it for analysis. This phase involves various operations, including data cleaning to remove errors or inconsistencies, data validation to ensure accuracy, and data enrichment to enhance its quality. Additionally, data is transformed to align with the destination schema and meet specific business requirements. Transformations can range from simple tasks like data type conversions to complex operations like aggregations or pivoting.

Load

After data is extracted and transformed, it is loaded into the destination system. This could be a data warehouse, data lake, or database, depending on the organization's architecture and needs. Loading involves populating tables, files, or data structures within the destination, making the data readily accessible for analytics, reporting, and other downstream processes.

The ETL process is not a one-time event; it is typically executed on a regular basis to keep the data up to date and synchronized with source systems. In the modern data ecosystem, manual handling is impractical. *Orchestration* and *automation* both play crucial roles in ETL to improve efficiency, reduce human error, and ensure consistency in data ingestion. ETL tools and frameworks, such as Apache NiFi, Apache Airflow, Talend, and Informatica, are commonly used to streamline and automate these processes.

Furthermore, ETL processes are evolving to adapt to modern data integration challenges. Organizations are increasingly adopting real-time ETL and *extract, load, transform (ELT)* approaches to handle streaming data and big data technologies. ELT, in particular, involves loading raw data into the destination first and then performing transformations within the target system using tools like Apache Hadoop or cloud-based services like Amazon Web Services (AWS) Glue.

Orchestration vs. Automation

In the context of the data ingestion pipeline, the terms *orchestration* and *automation* are sometimes used interchangeably. However, they refer to two different but related concepts.

Automation is the process of using software to perform tasks that would otherwise be done manually. This can include tasks such as extracting data from sources, transforming it into a desired format, and loading it into a target system. Automation can help to improve the efficiency and accuracy of the data ingestion process.

Orchestration is the process of coordinating and managing the execution of multiple automated tasks. It ensures that the tasks are executed in the correct order and with the correct dependencies. Orchestration can be done manually, but it is often automated using a data pipeline orchestration tool.

In summary, orchestration is about managing the execution of multiple automated tasks, whereas automation is about automating individual tasks.

Data Storage

Data storage is the culmination of the acquisition and ingestion processes. It is when data is organized, preserved, and made accessible for future use. Data storage isn't just about finding a space for data to reside; it's about ensuring accessibility, integrity, and longevity. The approach or platform we choose often depends on how we want to structure the data, the scale of the data, and the specific use cases or retrieval needs.

 As you prepare for the DataX exam, you should be able to explain various data storage concepts. Make note of these as you read about the different approaches to data storage.

Structured Storage

We use structured storage when we want to store data in a highly organized, tabular, or schema-driven format. Structured storage systems are ideal for data with well-defined attributes and a consistent structure. One of the most prominent examples of structured storage is a *relational database*. Relational databases, such as MySQL, PostgreSQL, Oracle, and SQL Server, use tables to organize data into rows and columns. For instance, in a customer database, each row represents a unique customer, and each column corresponds to specific attributes like name, address, and contact information. Structured storage is prevalent in various industries and is crucial for applications requiring data integrity and relational queries.

It's widely used in finance for managing financial transactions, in e-commerce for product catalogs, and in human resources for employee records. An example of a relational database structure for an e-commerce site can be seen in Figure 3.2.

FIGURE 3.2   Relational database schema

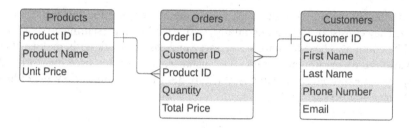

Another example of structured storage is a *data warehouse*. These specialized databases are designed for analytical queries and reporting. Data warehouses, like Amazon Redshift and Snowflake, store structured data efficiently, often employing star or snowflake schemas (as shown in Figure 3.3) to organize data for business intelligence and data analysis.

FIGURE 3.3   Star schema diagram

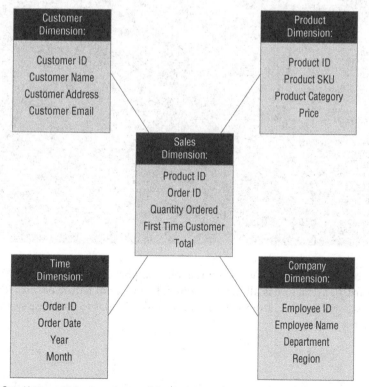

Source: StreamSets / https://streamsets.com/blog/schemas-data-warehouses-star-galaxy-snowflake /
Last accessed on February 26, 2024.

In situations where the complexity and overhead of a relational database or data warehouse is not necessary, opting for structured data storage in text-based flat files is a viable alternative. This approach is especially useful for smaller datasets or projects where the advanced features of a database management system (DBMS) are not required.

Comma-Separated Values (CSV)

CSV files are one of the simplest and most widely used text-based formats for storing structured data. They consist of rows and columns, with each line representing a record and fields separated by commas. These formats are versatile and easy to work with, making them suitable for various data manipulation tasks. For instance, CSV is often used for storing datasets, logs, or data exported from databases. Figure 3.4 shows a sample CSV file of historical winning lottery numbers.

FIGURE 3.4 Lottery data in the form of a CSV file

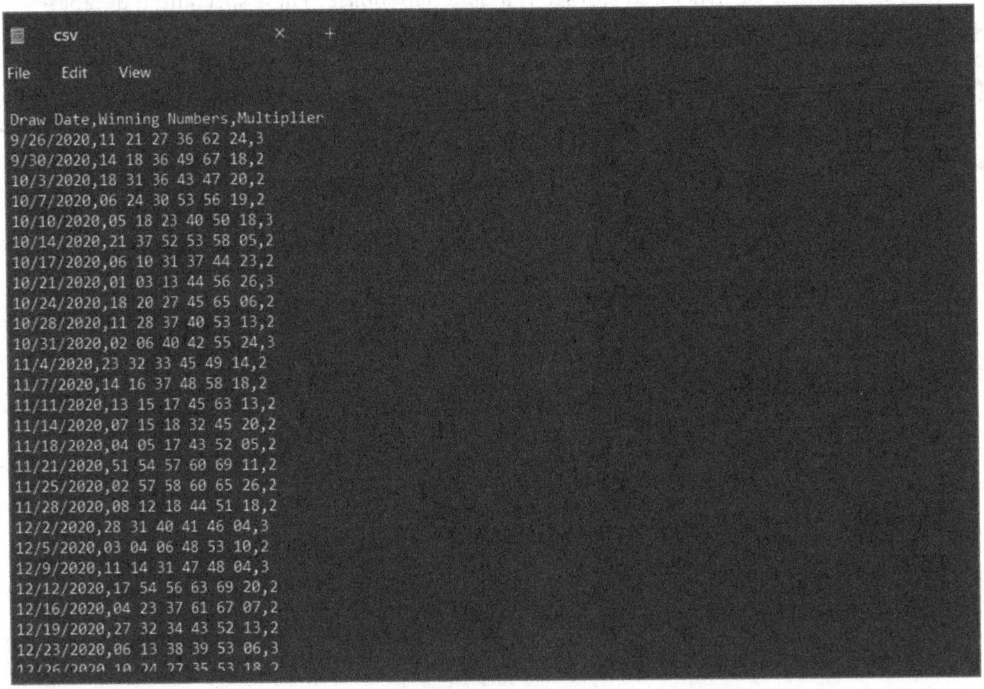

```
Draw Date,Winning Numbers,Multiplier
9/26/2020,11 21 27 36 62 24,3
9/30/2020,14 18 36 49 67 18,2
10/3/2020,18 31 36 43 47 20,2
10/7/2020,06 24 30 53 56 19,2
10/10/2020,05 18 23 40 50 18,3
10/14/2020,21 37 52 53 58 05,2
10/17/2020,06 10 31 37 44 23,2
10/21/2020,01 03 13 44 56 26,3
10/24/2020,18 20 27 45 65 06,2
10/28/2020,11 28 37 40 53 13,2
10/31/2020,02 06 40 42 55 24,3
11/4/2020,23 32 33 45 49 14,2
11/7/2020,14 16 37 48 58 18,2
11/11/2020,13 15 17 45 63 13,2
11/14/2020,07 15 18 32 45 20,2
11/18/2020,04 05 17 43 52 05,2
11/21/2020,51 54 57 60 69 11,2
11/25/2020,02 57 58 60 65 26,2
11/28/2020,08 12 18 44 51 18,2
12/2/2020,28 31 40 41 46 04,3
12/5/2020,03 04 06 48 53 10,2
12/9/2020,11 14 31 47 48 04,3
12/12/2020,17 54 56 63 69 20,2
12/16/2020,04 23 37 61 67 07,2
12/19/2020,27 32 34 43 52 13,2
12/23/2020,06 13 38 39 53 06,3
12/26/2020,10 24 27 35 53 18,2
```

For many data scientists, a CSV file is a reliable first port of call, particularly when a straightforward, flat structure is all that's required. Its universal nature ensures it's recognized by a vast array of tools, from Python libraries like Pandas to database systems and data visualization tools.

However, CSV's strength—its simplicity—can also be its Achilles' heel. Datasets that inherently contain commas or newline characters can disrupt the format, potentially causing data misalignment or loss during parsing. Another challenge with CSV files is the lack of a standardized way to handle text qualifiers or escape characters. While double quotes are commonly used, variations exist, making it imperative to be vigilant during data ingestion. Finally, CSV files are not the most storage-efficient for vast datasets and are not suitable for capturing complex hierarchical relationships.

Tab-Separated Values (TSV)

TSV files are very similar to CSV files with just one key difference—they use tabs instead of commas as separators (as shown in Figure 3.5). This nuance makes TSV a better choice when handling data containing natural textual content, which often includes commas. Yet, just like a CSV file, TSV isn't without its challenges. Data containing tab characters can also disrupt the structure of a TSV file, leading to parsing errors. Similar to CSV files, TSV files are also not great for extremely large datasets or for capturing data with intricate, nested structures.

FIGURE 3.5 Lottery data in the form of a TSV file

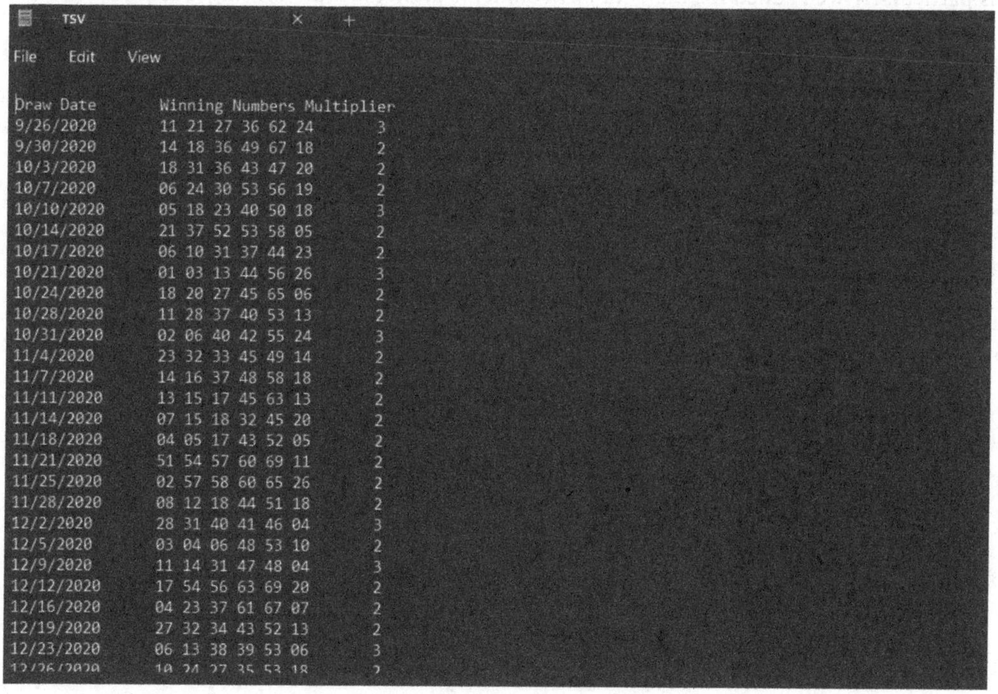

Spreadsheets

Spreadsheet applications, such as Microsoft Excel and Google Sheets, store data in structured tables, which make them suitable for organizing and analyzing structured data. While not a text-based format, spreadsheets are frequently used to manipulate structured data, making them a popular choice for tasks like data entry, data visualization, and reporting. They can also contain multiple sheets with formulas, charts, and graphs, making them useful for organizing and sharing data within organizations.

When it comes to data processing or model training, spreadsheets are not the most efficient format to work with. They can be bulkier and slower to read or write when compared to plain-text formats. Furthermore, parsing spreadsheet files may require specialized libraries, which do not come by default with some data ingestion tools.

While text-based flat files and spreadsheets are straightforward and widely compatible for storing structured data, binary file formats like Parquet and Hierarchical Data Format version 5 (HDF5) present advanced features, efficiency, and performance improvements, especially beneficial for handling large and complex datasets.

Parquet

Parquet is a columnar storage format that is highly efficient for analytics workloads. Parquet is particularly well suited for big data environments and data warehousing. Parquet files are optimized for performance and compression, making them ideal for tasks that require quick querying of large datasets. They are commonly used in Apache Spark, Hive, and other big data frameworks.

If you're not working within a Big Data framework, Parquet is overkill and might introduce unnecessary complexity. It doesn't do well with simple, lightweight analytics tools or applications that aren't designed to handle columnar data.

HDF5

HDF5 is a binary format used for storing and managing large volumes of scientific data, such as numerical simulations, sensor data, and scientific measurements. It allows for efficient storage of multidimensional arrays and supports complex data structures.

Its hierarchical structure means you can store datasets and metadata in a tree-like fashion in HDF5. This makes it particularly suited for complex projects where various datasets are interrelated. Moreover, HDF5 supports on-the-fly compression, allowing for efficient storage and I/O operations.

However, HDF5's specialized nature means it might not be the best choice for everyday, lightweight tasks. And while HDF5 shines in scenarios like neuroimaging or fluid dynamics simulations, it might be overkill for simpler, tabular datasets. An additional aspect to be mindful of is ensuring compatibility with tools and libraries. Not all data processing tools support HDF5 out of the box.

For projects that require complex queries, transactions, or relationships between datasets, structured storage is invaluable. The deterministic structure allows for efficient querying, joining, and aggregating operations.

Unstructured Storage

On the other end of the spectrum is unstructured storage. Unstructured storage systems accommodate data without a specific schema or predefined organization. They are versatile and capable of handling various data formats, making them ideal for diverse content types. A prime example of unstructured storage is the filesystem. Operating systems like Windows, Mac, and Linux use filesystems to store unstructured data such as documents, images, videos, audio files, and more. These files are typically organized into directories, but the content within the files may vary widely.

Additionally, *content repositories* are designed for unstructured content management. Content management systems (CMSs) and digital asset management (DAM) systems are examples of repositories that store web pages, multimedia files, documents, and other unstructured content. Such systems are vital for organizations managing extensive media libraries, website content, and document archives.

Cloud object storage services provided by platforms like Amazon S3, Google Cloud Storage, and Microsoft Azure Blob Storage offer scalable and cost-effective unstructured data storage. They are commonly used for backing up and archiving, storing media and log files, and serving static website assets.

The inherent challenge with unstructured data is its unpredictability. It is not as straightforward to query or analyze as structured data and often demands more storage space and specialized processing techniques to work with. However, when harnessed correctly, unstructured data can be a gold mine for data science. Fields like sentiment analysis, image recognition, and natural language processing (which will be discussed in later chapters) all depend heavily on unstructured data.

Semi-Structured Storage

Semi-structured storage bridges the gap between structured and unstructured storage, offering a degree of organization while maintaining flexibility. Semi-structured data is data that has a self-describing structure (usually with tags) and doesn't always follow a predefined form.

Semi-structured data formats include JSON (JavaScript Object Notation), XML (Extensible Markup Language), YAML (Yet Another Markup Language), and data in NoSQL (Not Only SQL) databases like MongoDB. These formats offer some organization using tags, labels, or hierarchical structures, but they lack the rigid schema of structured data. Attributes may vary between records, making semi-structured storage suitable for scenarios where data schemas may evolve over time or when dealing with data that doesn't fit the mold of traditional relational databases. Semi-structured storage is often used in web applications, APIs, and data exchange formats.

JavaScript Object Notation (JSON)

One of the most ubiquitous examples of semi-structured storage is JavaScript Object Notation (JSON). JSON is a lightweight, text-based format for storing data in a structured and hierarchical manner using key-value pairs, as seen in Figure 3.6. It is particularly popular for representing data in web applications and APIs due to its compatibility with JavaScript. JSON is commonly used to exchange data between systems and also has the advantage of being human-readable. It is well suited for storing complex data structures and nested objects. However, JSON's nested nature can become a burden when dealing with flat, tabular data structures. It's not as straightforward to query as a simple table, and it can be more memory-intensive to process than columnar storage formats.

FIGURE 3.6 Lottery data in the form of a JSON file

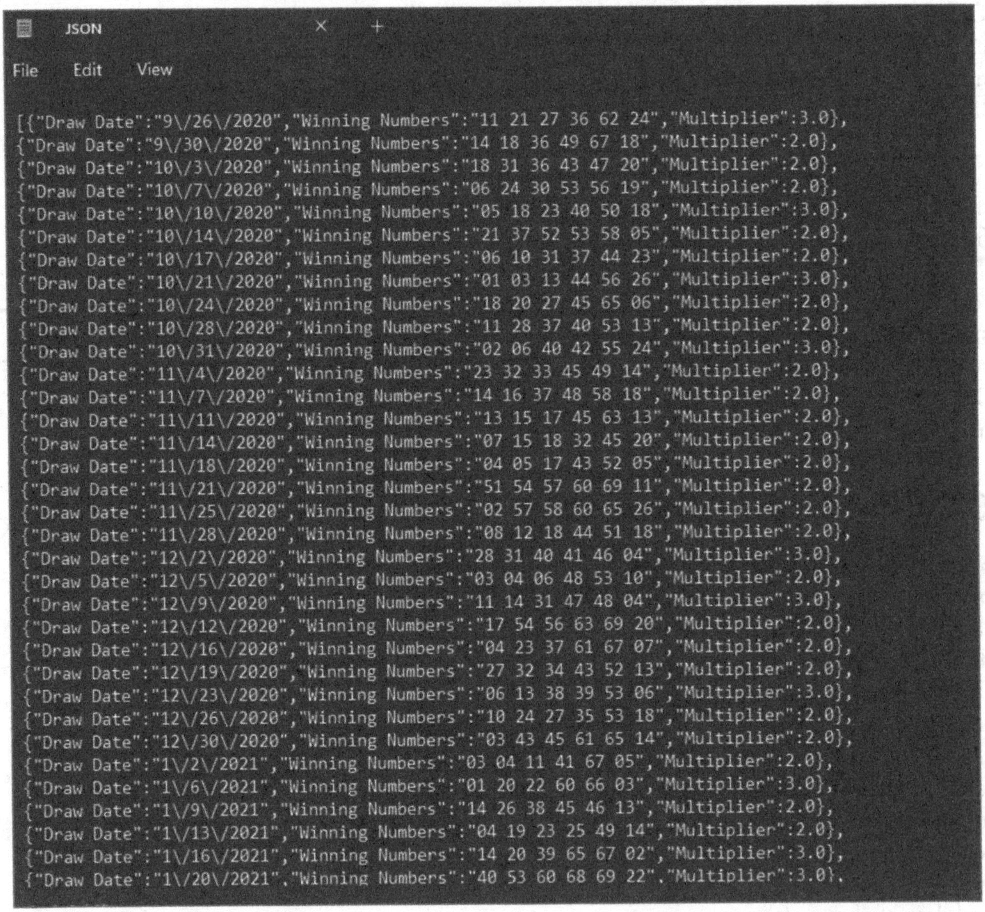


```
[{"Draw Date":"9\/26\/2020","Winning Numbers":"11 21 27 36 62 24","Multiplier":3.0},
{"Draw Date":"9\/30\/2020","Winning Numbers":"14 18 36 49 67 18","Multiplier":2.0},
{"Draw Date":"10\/3\/2020","Winning Numbers":"18 31 36 43 47 20","Multiplier":2.0},
{"Draw Date":"10\/7\/2020","Winning Numbers":"06 24 30 53 56 19","Multiplier":2.0},
{"Draw Date":"10\/10\/2020","Winning Numbers":"05 18 23 40 50 18","Multiplier":3.0},
{"Draw Date":"10\/14\/2020","Winning Numbers":"21 37 52 53 58 05","Multiplier":2.0},
{"Draw Date":"10\/17\/2020","Winning Numbers":"06 10 31 37 44 23","Multiplier":2.0},
{"Draw Date":"10\/21\/2020","Winning Numbers":"01 03 13 44 56 26","Multiplier":3.0},
{"Draw Date":"10\/24\/2020","Winning Numbers":"18 20 27 45 65 06","Multiplier":2.0},
{"Draw Date":"10\/28\/2020","Winning Numbers":"11 28 37 40 53 13","Multiplier":2.0},
{"Draw Date":"10\/31\/2020","Winning Numbers":"02 06 40 42 55 24","Multiplier":3.0},
{"Draw Date":"11\/4\/2020","Winning Numbers":"23 32 33 45 49 14","Multiplier":2.0},
{"Draw Date":"11\/7\/2020","Winning Numbers":"14 16 37 48 58 18","Multiplier":2.0},
{"Draw Date":"11\/11\/2020","Winning Numbers":"13 15 17 45 63 13","Multiplier":2.0},
{"Draw Date":"11\/14\/2020","Winning Numbers":"07 15 18 32 45 20","Multiplier":2.0},
{"Draw Date":"11\/18\/2020","Winning Numbers":"04 05 17 43 52 05","Multiplier":2.0},
{"Draw Date":"11\/21\/2020","Winning Numbers":"51 54 57 60 69 11","Multiplier":2.0},
{"Draw Date":"11\/25\/2020","Winning Numbers":"02 57 58 60 65 26","Multiplier":2.0},
{"Draw Date":"11\/28\/2020","Winning Numbers":"08 12 18 44 51 18","Multiplier":2.0},
{"Draw Date":"12\/2\/2020","Winning Numbers":"28 31 40 41 46 04","Multiplier":3.0},
{"Draw Date":"12\/5\/2020","Winning Numbers":"03 04 06 48 53 10","Multiplier":2.0},
{"Draw Date":"12\/9\/2020","Winning Numbers":"11 14 31 47 48 04","Multiplier":3.0},
{"Draw Date":"12\/12\/2020","Winning Numbers":"17 54 56 63 69 20","Multiplier":2.0},
{"Draw Date":"12\/16\/2020","Winning Numbers":"04 23 37 61 67 07","Multiplier":2.0},
{"Draw Date":"12\/19\/2020","Winning Numbers":"27 32 34 43 52 13","Multiplier":2.0},
{"Draw Date":"12\/23\/2020","Winning Numbers":"06 13 38 39 53 06","Multiplier":3.0},
{"Draw Date":"12\/26\/2020","Winning Numbers":"10 24 27 35 53 18","Multiplier":2.0},
{"Draw Date":"12\/30\/2020","Winning Numbers":"03 43 45 61 65 14","Multiplier":2.0},
{"Draw Date":"1\/2\/2021","Winning Numbers":"03 04 11 41 67 05","Multiplier":2.0},
{"Draw Date":"1\/6\/2021","Winning Numbers":"01 20 22 60 66 03","Multiplier":3.0},
{"Draw Date":"1\/9\/2021","Winning Numbers":"14 26 38 45 46 13","Multiplier":2.0},
{"Draw Date":"1\/13\/2021","Winning Numbers":"04 19 23 25 49 14","Multiplier":2.0},
{"Draw Date":"1\/16\/2021","Winning Numbers":"14 20 39 65 67 02","Multiplier":3.0},
{"Draw Date":"1\/20\/2021","Winning Numbers":"40 53 60 68 69 22","Multiplier":3.0},
```

Extensible Markup Language (XML)

Extensible Markup Language (XML) is another widely used semi-structured data format. XML files use tags to define data elements and their relationships, making them a great choice for applications—like web services, data interchange, and configuration files—where data needs to be self-describing and machine-readable.

In data science, XML can often be found in contexts such as web scraping or when working with certain types of configuration and metadata files. Its hierarchical structure, as depicted in Figure 3.7, is adept at capturing nested relationships in data, akin to JSON, but with a more verbose syntax. This verbosity can be a drawback. XML files can become large and unwieldy, making them less efficient for storage and parsing compared to formats like JSON. Furthermore, when working with tabular data structures, XML might introduce unnecessary complexity. It's essential to have a good XML parsing library at your disposal and be wary of potential bloat in data storage.

FIGURE 3.7   Lottery data in the form of an XML file

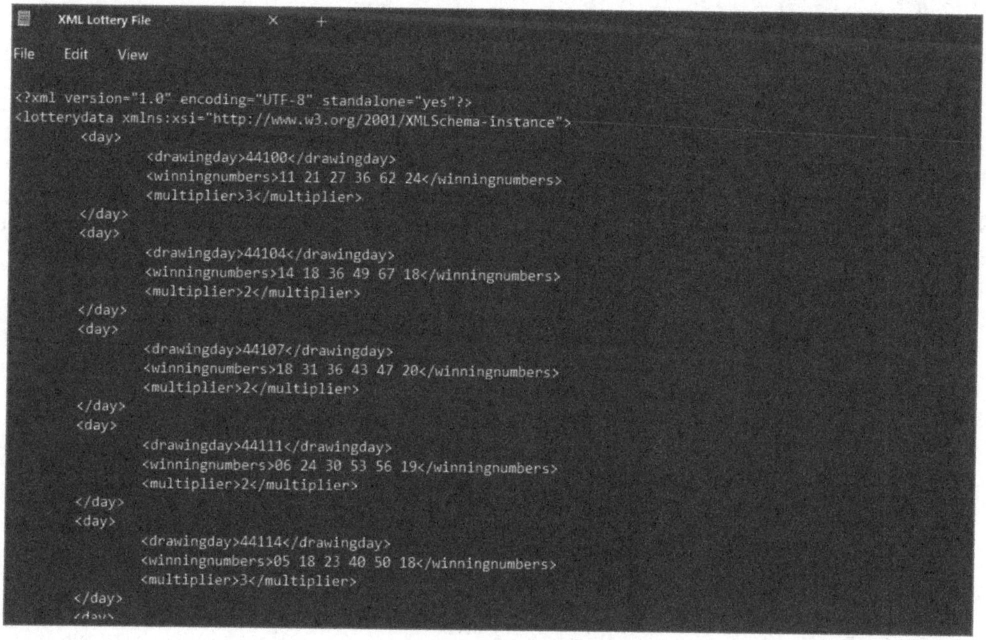

```xml
<?xml version="1.0" encoding="UTF-8" standalone="yes"?>
<lotterydata xmlns:xsi="http://www.w3.org/2001/XMLSchema-instance">
    <day>
        <drawingday>44100</drawingday>
        <winningnumbers>11 21 27 36 62 24</winningnumbers>
        <multiplier>3</multiplier>
    </day>
    <day>
        <drawingday>44104</drawingday>
        <winningnumbers>14 18 36 49 67 18</winningnumbers>
        <multiplier>2</multiplier>
    </day>
    <day>
        <drawingday>44107</drawingday>
        <winningnumbers>18 31 36 43 47 20</winningnumbers>
        <multiplier>2</multiplier>
    </day>
    <day>
        <drawingday>44111</drawingday>
        <winningnumbers>06 24 30 53 56 19</winningnumbers>
        <multiplier>2</multiplier>
    </day>
    <day>
        <drawingday>44114</drawingday>
        <winningnumbers>05 18 23 40 50 18</winningnumbers>
        <multiplier>3</multiplier>
    </day>
    <day>
```

In data science, semi-structured data finds its niche in areas like web scraping or when interacting with certain APIs. It offers a balanced blend of flexibility and organization, enabling data scientists to work with dynamic data sources without completely forgoing structure.

Data Lakes

Data lakes play a significant role in modern data management and analytics. They offer a unified, scalable, and cost-effective solution for storing and managing structured, unstructured, and semi-structured data. A data lake is particularly useful in scenarios where organizations need to store vast amounts of raw data in its native format for future use, including unstructured, semi-structured, and structured data. Unlike data warehouses or traditional relational databases that require data to be cleaned, structured, and processed before it can be stored, a data lake allows for the storage of data without the need for immediate transformation. It is essential to implement proper data governance practices, metadata management, and data cataloging within the data lake to maintain data quality and usability, regardless of the data type being stored or processed.

Compressed Formats

Sometimes, to reduce the size of data for storage efficiency, transmission, and management, data files are compressed using popular algorithms, resulting in formats like ZIP, GZ (gzip), and BZ2 (bzip2). Compressed files retain the characteristics of the original format while being significantly reduced in size. This makes data transfer faster, which is especially beneficial when downloading datasets from the internet or sharing them between systems.

Most modern data science tools and languages, like Python's Pandas, can directly read compressed files, providing seamless integration into data workflows. For a data scientist, the choice of a compression format depends on the type of data, the desired compression ratio, and compatibility with tools and platforms used in the data science workflow.

While compression significantly reduces file size, it introduces an additional step in the data access pipeline. Reading compressed data requires decompression, which, depending on the size and compression method, might introduce latency. For real-time applications or scenarios where speed is paramount, it's essential to weigh the benefits of reduced storage and transfer times against the potential cost of decompression delays.

Choosing the right data storage approach depends on factors such as the nature of the data, the tools and frameworks being used, and the specific data manipulation or analysis tasks at hand. Whether it's the simplicity of CSV and TSV, the versatility of spreadsheets and JSON, or the efficiency of Parquet, each format offers its unique advantages tailored to specific objectives and limitations. Being proficient in working with different data storage formats is an essential skill for data scientists in whatever industry or domain they find themselves in.

Managing the Data Lifecycle

Effective management of the data lifecycle is crucial for maintaining the reliability, availability, and optimal utility of data within an organization. The data lifecycle covers the diverse phases that data undergoes, from its inception and acquisition to its ultimate retirement and deletion. This path involves delineating the *data lineage*, formulating a strategy for refreshing data, and establishing an archiving plan. This holistic approach ensures that data remains an asset by providing consistent value and insight throughout its lifecycle within the organization.

Data Lineage

Data lineage refers to a detailed illustration or map, like Figure 3.8, that documents the journey of data from its source to its final destination within an organization. It traces the path and various transformations data undergoes, offering a comprehensive view of how data is processed and utilized across diverse systems and processes. This visual representation is vital for understanding and documenting the complexities of data movement and modifications within an organization's ecosystem.

The main components of data lineage include the source, transformations, data flows, and destination. The source refers to the origin or initial source of the data, which could be an external data provider, databases, or any of the data sources we discussed earlier in the chapter. Transformations encompass all the changes the data undergoes as it moves through various systems and workflows, including cleaning, normalization, and aggregation. Data flows represent the paths through which data travels as it gets transferred within and between systems, applications, or processes. The destination is the final endpoint where data is stored or utilized for analysis, reporting, or other data science tasks.

Understanding data lineage brings numerous benefits to organizations. It plays a crucial role in enhancing data quality by enabling organizations to trace data back to its source to identify and address issues. This understanding also ensures regulatory compliance by offering an auditable trail of data movement and modifications. Data lineage supports robust data governance by providing valuable insights into data dependencies and the potential impact of changes to data or processes. Furthermore, it enables efficient troubleshooting of data issues and supports informed, data-driven decision-making by offering clarity and transparency regarding the origins and transformations of organizational data.

Refresh Cycles

A *refresh cycle* is the regular and scheduled process of updating data to ensure that it remains current, accurate, and relevant. This can involve adding new data, updating existing data, or purging outdated or irrelevant data.

The importance of refresh cycles is multifaceted. First, refresh cycles guarantee relevance. In today's fast-paced business environment, decisions need to be made based on the latest

FIGURE 3.8 Example of a data lineage diagram

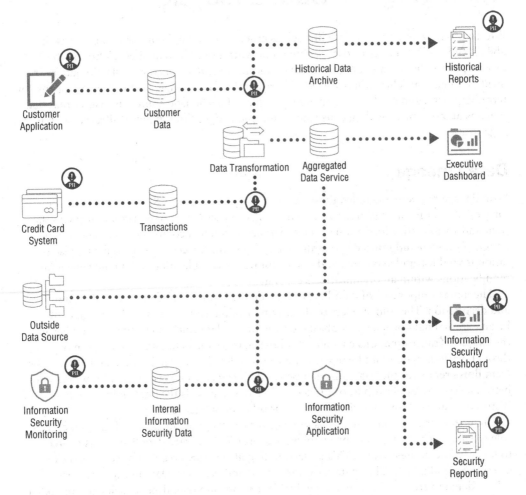

available information. Second, regular refresh cycles offer an opportunity to rectify inaccuracies or discrepancies in historical data that come to light as new data becomes available. Finally, refresh cycles provide an avenue to continuously refine and optimize algorithms or analytical models, by making sure that models are exposed to patterns within data as the data evolves over time.

Refresh cycles do come with some potential challenges. The most evident is resource intensity. Regularly updating vast swaths of data often requires significant computational resources. Additionally, frequent updates increase the risk of data integrity issues. Each update can introduce a potential point of failure, which increases the risk of data corruption.

Archiving

Archiving is the process of moving older data that may no longer be in active use (but needs to be retained for various reasons) to long-term storage. Archived storage is usually more cost-effective and less accessible compared to active storage.

The utility of archiving is manifold. From an operational standpoint, archiving enhances efficiency. As active datasets grow larger, having all data on hand can be both costly and operationally cumbersome. Archiving older data clears up primary storage, ensuring resources are optimized for immediate data needs. From a regulatory perspective, many industries are bound by stringent norms that necessitate data retention for specific periods. Archiving ensures compliance without clogging primary systems. Furthermore, in the quest for insights, having a historical trail of data can be invaluable. Archived data offers a panoramic view of long-term trends and patterns, serving as a rich reservoir for longitudinal analysis.

Archiving isn't without its challenges. One inherent challenge is the reduced accessibility of archived data. Retrieving archived data from storage sometimes takes hours to days depending on the storage platform or medium. Cost-effective media such as magnetic tapes are often used for archive storage. Over protracted periods, this physical medium of storage might degrade, increasing the risk of data loss. As technology evolves, certain data storage formats risk becoming outdated. Data archived in a storage format that is current today might become challenging to access or analyze in the future when the format becomes obsolete.

In the broad context of managing the lifecycle of data, using both refresh cycles and archiving is a balancing act. While refresh cycles ensure that data systems remain up to date and relevant, archiving ensures that as data matures and becomes less relevant, it's stored efficiently without being lost. Implementing robust strategies for both is critical for effective and efficient data lifecycle management.

Summary

Data acquisition, the initial phase in the data science lifecycle, is crucial in today's digital environment, emphasizing not just the collection of vast quantities of data, but more importantly, securing accurate, timely, and relevant information for robust, reliable analysis and insights.

Data acquisition sources vary widely and include surveys, administrative records, sensors, transactional data, and experimental data.

In cases lacking actual data, synthetic data, created artificially to mirror real-world data, becomes invaluable. Organizations sometimes turn to commercial and public data. However, understanding and adhering to licensing restrictions is pivotal to avoid legal complications.

Data ingestion can be executed in real time (streaming) or at scheduled intervals (batching). Central to data ingestion is the ETL process, which involves extracting data from varied sources, transforming it by cleaning and enriching it, and then loading it into a destination system.

Data storage can be broadly categorized into structured, unstructured, and semi-structured storage. Structured storage, exemplified by relational databases, data warehouses, and structured file formats, offers a consistent, schema-driven format optimal for data with well-defined attributes. Unstructured storage is suitable for diverse content like images or audio files. Between structured and unstructured storage lies semi-structured storage, such as JSON and XML, which strikes a balance, possessing some organization while maintaining flexibility.

Managing the lifecycle of data involves understanding data lineage, adhering to refresh cycles, and implementing effective archiving strategies. Data lineage tracks the journey of data from its origin to its endpoint. Refresh cycles refer to the regular updating of data to maintain its accuracy and relevance. Archiving involves transferring inactive data to long-term, cost-effective storage.

Exam Essentials

Explain the importance of data collection and storage in the data science lifecycle.   Effective data collection ensures that accurate, relevant, and diverse datasets are gathered, forming the basis for insightful, reliable analysis and prediction. Proper storage, on the other hand, guarantees data integrity, accessibility, and security, while also enabling efficient retrieval and processing.

Understand the differences between generated data, synthetic data, and commercial or public data.   Generated data comes from specific activities, like transactions or sensors; synthetic data is artificially created to mimic real data for testing or privacy; and commercial/public data is aggregated information released by organizations or governments for public or business use. Each type varies in source, purpose, and privacy considerations.

Identify which scenarios are best suited for generated data, synthetic data, and commercial or public data.   Generated data is best suited for real-time analysis, trend identification, and decision-making due to its immediacy and relevance. It's particularly beneficial in scenarios demanding high granularity and recurrence, such as longitudinal studies, detailed operational analyses, and real-time monitoring. Synthetic data is ideal when original data is scarce or confidential, or when creating training sets for machine learning models, especially in simulated environments or stress-testing scenarios. Commercial and public data is valuable when an organization's internal data is insufficient. It's used to supplement in-house data, providing additional insights for research, product development, or market analysis. Its usage often requires adherence to specific licensing agreements and restrictions.

Explain the difference between streaming and batch data ingestion.   Streaming data ingestion involves the continuous, real-time collection and processing of data, enabling immediate analysis and response to incoming information. This method is ideal for applications requiring instant insights or actions, such as fraud detection or real-time user behavior analysis. Conversely, batch data ingestion collects data in predefined segments or at scheduled intervals, processing it as a single unit. This approach is more cost-effective and suitable for scenarios without the need for immediate analysis, like for ingesting data into data warehouses or data lakes.

Describe the extract, transform, load process.   The ETL (extract, transform, load) process begins with the extraction of raw data from diverse sources like databases or cloud services. Next, the data undergoes transformation, where it is cleaned, validated, and enriched to meet specific business needs, ensuring it aligns with the destination's schema. The final step is loading the refined data into the target system for convenient access and analysis.

Identify which scenarios are best suited for structured, unstructured, or semi-structured storage.   Structured storage is ideal for organized, tabular data, commonly found in transactional systems. Unstructured storage, like filesystems and cloud object storage, is best suited for diverse data without a specific schema, such as documents and multimedia files. Semi-structured storage, which includes data stored in JSON and XML formats, caters to data that has an evolving structure or schema.

Describe the difference between a refresh cycle and archiving.   A refresh cycle is a scheduled update of data to maintain its accuracy, relevance, and currency. It is essential for informed decision-making, algorithm optimization, and data integrity. In contrast, archiving involves transferring data that's no longer actively used but needs to be retained to a more cost-effective, long-term storage platform. This process enhances operational efficiency by freeing up primary storage and ensuring compliance with data retention regulations.

Review Questions

1. Which of the following is *not* a common data source for data science?

   A. Generated data

   B. Synthetic data

   C. Commercial or public data

   D. Transformed data

2. Generated data can be created when a user _____.

   A. Writes a poem

   B. Creates realistic images using a GAN

   C. Logs into a website

   D. Reads a book

3. Your tech startup is looking to develop a system for real-time health monitoring. The goal is to detect abnormal heart rates and alert the user. What type of data source would be the most crucial for your system?

   A. Synthetic data generated by GANs

   B. Survey data about a user's behaviors

   C. Sensor data from wearable devices

   D. Transactional data from your e-commerce platform

4. Which of the following is *not* a key consideration when collecting survey data?

   A. Sampling design

   B. Question design

   C. Font size

   D. Data cleaning

5. A government agency is working on a project to track and predict economic trends. They have a trove of yearly tax filings and want to utilize this data. Which characteristic of administrative data makes it particularly suitable for their needs?

   A. Its low granularity

   B. Its ability to capture public opinions

   C. Its event-based nature

   D. Its recurrence at regular intervals

6. Transactional data is generated by _____.

   A. Business interactions

   B. Government regulations

   C. Administrative payroll forms

   D. Scientific experiments

7. You're working on a project to understand public sentiment toward a new policy initiative. You decide to gather opinions from a group of citizens. Which method would be the most appropriate to collect data?

   A. Conduct experiments in a laboratory.

   B. Use administrative records from the local government.

   C. Launch an online survey targeting a diverse group of respondents.

   D. Analyze transactional data from e-commerce platforms.

8. One of the main differences between administrative and transactional data is _____.

   A. Transactional data is event-based and tends to change more frequently.

   B. Administrative data is only about finances.

   C. Transactional data is generated by internal operations.

   D. Administrative data is always public.

9. Synthetic data is _____.

   A. Generated by sensors

   B. Generated by synthetic data brokers

   C. Artificially generated to mimic real-world data

   D. Generated from experimental research

10. Which of the following best describes data ingestion?

    A. The storage of data in databases

    B. The process by which data is acquired and transformed for use

    C. The real-time analysis of data

    D. The method by which data is encrypted for security purposes

11. What is the primary purpose of the transform step in the ETL process?

    A. To load data into the destination system

    B. To gather raw data without altering its original format

    C. To cleanse and modify data to prepare it for analysis

    D. To determine the computational and storage resources required for data ingestion

12. How do GPUs and TPUs benefit data ingestion processes?

    A. By ensuring that data is stored securely

    B. By enhancing parallel processing capabilities and offering resource isolation

    C. By prioritizing streaming over batching

    D. By ensuring the full use of network bandwidth

13. What distinguishes streaming data ingestion from batch data ingestion?

   A. Streaming involves processing data in real time, whereas batching involves processing data at scheduled intervals.

   B. Streaming is only used for social media posts, whereas batch is for IoT devices.

   C. Streaming uses Apache Hadoop, whereas batch uses Apache Kafka.

   D. Streaming data ingestion is more cost-effective than batch data ingestion.

14. Which of these is structured storage ideal for?

   A. Text documents, images, videos

   B. Customer information in a CRM

   C. Unpredictable data

   D. Data that doesn't conform to a fixed schema or structure

15. What characterizes unstructured storage?

   A. Organized in a tabular or schema-driven format

   B. Used for analytical queries and reporting

   C. Stores data that doesn't conform to a fixed schema or structure

   D. Stores data with well-defined attributes and a consistent structure

16. Which of these is a common example of semi-structured storage?

   A. Relational databases

   B. JSON

   C. Filesystems

   D. Data warehouses

17. What is a notable feature of the Parquet file format?

   A. It is particularly well suited for simple, lightweight analytics tools.

   B. It is particularly well suited for big data environments and data warehousing.

   C. It is a binary format used for storing and managing scientific data.

   D. It uses tags to define data elements and their relationships.

18. What does data lineage refer to?

   A. The process of storing old data

   B. The refresh of data on a regular schedule

   C. Tracking data as it moves through various stages of a data pipeline

   D. The trustworthiness of data

19. What is the primary purpose of refresh cycles?

   A. To store data in a cost-effective manner

   B. To ensure data remains current, accurate, and relevant

   C. To demonstrate compliance with data handling regulations

   D. To trace the journey of data for transparency purposes

20. Why is data archived?

   A. To rectify inaccuracies in the data

   B. To provide a common language for collaboration

   C. To store older data that may not be in active use but is still needed

   D. To track the journey of data from its origin to its endpoint

Chapter

4

Data Exploration and Analysis

THE COMPTIA DATAX EXAM OBJECTIVES COVERED IN THIS CHAPTER INCLUDE:

✓ **Domain 2: Modeling, Analysis, and Outcomes**

- 2.1 Given a scenario, use the appropriate exploratory data analysis (EDA) method or process.

- 2.2 Given a scenario, analyze common issues with data.

Data exploration and analysis is the second phase in the data science lifecycle. It empowers data scientists to unearth valuable insights, recognize underlying patterns, and comprehend the inherent characteristics of the data acquired during the data collection and storage phase introduced in the previous chapter. This chapter begins by introducing exploratory data analysis (EDA), variable types, and which EDA techniques are most appropriate depending on the type of variable we're working with and our analytic objective. The chapter concludes by addressing how to identify and deal with some of the most common data quality challenges often encountered during data analysis, such as data sparsity, nonlinearity, and missingness (or missing data).

Exploratory Data Analysis

Exploratory data analysis (EDA) is an iterative and interactive open-ended process to learn about data, understand its characteristics, and identify patterns or irregularities in the data that might not be immediately obvious. EDA is often performed before formal statistical techniques are applied or machine learning models are built. During the EDA process, data scientists use summary statistics and graphical representations to discover patterns, spot anomalies, test hypotheses, or check assumptions. It also helps data scientists determine if the statistical methods they are considering are appropriate for the data they're working with.

Exploratory data analysis can be performed using graphical and nongraphical methods. Graphical methods provide visual insights that are intuitive and easily interpreted, allowing you to see patterns, relationships, and outliers. Nongraphical methods offer a more quantitative analysis, giving precise measurements and statistics that describe the data. The combined use of both these techniques allows for a comprehensive and in-depth understanding of the dataset, laying the foundation for further analysis and modeling.

Later in this chapter, we will focus our attention on the graphical methods of EDA for univariate, bivariate, and multivariate statistical analysis. Before we do so, understanding the characteristics of the variables we're working with will help inform and guide the exploratory data analysis method we choose.

Quantitative Variables

Quantitative variables, also known as numerical variables, are variables that have a numerical value. They represent a measurable quantity and can be classified into two main types: discrete and continuous variables.

Discrete Variables

Discrete variables are a type of quantitative variable that can take on certain specific values only within a given range. They often represent countable items or events where the values are distinct and separate, meaning there are no intermediate values between two adjacent values. Examples of discrete variables include the number of employees in a company, the number of cars in a household, or the number of siblings one has.

Imagine conducting a survey in a residential area to find out the number of pets each household owns. The number of pets is a discrete variable because households can only have a whole number of pets (0, 1, 2, 3, . . .).

Continuous Variables

Continuous variables are quantitative variables that have an infinite number of values within a range. Unlike discrete variables, continuous variables can take on any value within a given range, including fractions and decimals. They are often used to represent measurements such as height, weight, temperature, and time, where the values can be expressed in decimals. Continuous variables are essential for various statistical analyses and mathematical modeling because they allow for a precise measurement and calculation.

Imagine conducting a scientific study to measure the height of a specific plant species in a garden. The height of the plants is a continuous variable because it can take on any value within a possible range. For example, the plant heights could be 13.5 inches, 13.55 inches, or 13.555 inches.

Qualitative Variables

Qualitative variables, also known as categorical variables, are variables that represent types or categories and cannot be measured on a numerical scale. They are used to label or categorize elements in a dataset into distinct groups based on certain attributes. Qualitative variables can be classified into three main types: nominal, ordinal, and binary variables.

Nominal Variables

Nominal variables are those that have no inherent order among their categories. Examples include colors (Red, Green, Blue), gender (Male, Female), or types of fruits (Apple, Banana, Orange). These variables are often handled in data analysis and machine learning models by using one-hot encoding (introduced in Chapter 5, "Data Processing and Preparation"). This technique converts each category into a binary vector, enabling the use of mathematical models without assuming any order.

Ordinal Variables

Ordinal variables have categories that follow a meaningful sequence, even though the intervals between these categories are not defined. Examples of ordinal variables include education level (High School, Bachelor's, Master's, PhD) or satisfaction rating (Poor, Average, Good, Excellent). Ordinal variables can be encoded by assigning ordered numbers or other techniques that maintain the order information.

Binary Variables

Binary variables, also known as dichotomous or Boolean variables, are a type of categorical variable that have only two possible values. These two values can represent outcomes such as yes/no, true/false, success/failure, and more.

 Real World Scenario

Analyzing Public Health Policy Survey Data

Imagine you are conducting a survey to understand the impact of a new public health policy in your community. You collect various types of data from each respondent, including their age, gender, whether or not they have received a vaccine, their income level, and their satisfaction with the new public health policy. The data you collect could look like the following table:

Respondent ID	Age	Gender	Vaccination Status	Income Level	Satisfaction
1	25	Female	Yes	Medium	Satisfied
2	42	Male	No	High	Unsatisfied
3	33	Other	Yes	Low	Neutral
4	29	Female	Yes	Medium	Satisfied
5	55	Male	No	High	Unsatisfied

In this table, Respondent ID is simply a numerical representation of a categorical attribute. We cannot perform numerical calculations against it. Age is a quantitative variable. You might calculate the average age or look at the age distribution among the respondents. Gender, Vaccination Status, Income Level, and Satisfaction are categorical variables. For Gender, a nominal variable, you might visualize the number of respondents in each category. For Vaccination Status, a binary variable, you might calculate the proportion of respondents who have been vaccinated. Income Level and Satisfaction are ordinal variables. You could look at the distribution of income levels and satisfaction levels. You could also analyze how income level relates to policy satisfaction.

By analyzing this data, you can gain insights into the community's vaccination rates, how income level might relate to vaccination status or policy satisfaction, and overall opinions on the new public health policy. Understanding and recognizing each type of variable allows us to use appropriate analysis techniques for each, ensuring more meaningful and valid results from our data analysis.

As you prepare for the DataX exam, you should be able to choose an appropriate exploratory data analysis method or process given a particular scenario. Make note of the scenarios used to highlight each data analysis method as you read through the sections on univariate, bivariate, and multivariate analysis.

Univariate Analysis

Univariate analysis is the simplest form of EDA, focusing solely on one variable at a time. This method of analysis aims to outline the data, discern patterns, and identify anomalies without exploring causes or relationships. It aids in understanding each variable's distribution, revealing details such as central tendency, spread, and shape.

Univariate analysis allows data scientists to delve into each variable by offering a clear understanding of each variable's characteristics and distribution, before advancing to more complex analysis methods such as bivariate and multivariate analysis. In this section, we look at some of the common tools and visualizations used in univariate exploratory data analysis, including frequency distributions, histograms, and box plots, among others.

Frequency Distribution

Frequency distributions play a pivotal role in univariate analysis, offering a structured view on how individual values are distributed within a dataset. They provide a comprehensive view of the data, showing the number of occurrences of each value or range of values. This technique is instrumental in revealing the patterns and trends inherent in the data, making it easier to extract meaningful insights.

Consider a teacher who wants to analyze student grades by creating a frequency distribution similar to Table 4.1. The teacher can easily observe the number of students falling into each grade category, providing a clear understanding of the class's overall performance. Similarly, businesses can use frequency distributions to identify the most popular products based on sales frequency, allowing them to tailor their marketing strategies or inventory accordingly.

TABLE 4.1   Frequency distribution of grades

Grade	Frequency
A	3
B	12
C	5
D	2
F	1

Frequency distributions can also be represented visually using histograms or bar charts. This makes them more accessible and interpretable. Visualizing frequency distributions also facilitates the identification of anomalies or outliers in data. An unusual data point would easily stand out, signaling a potential error or exceptional case that may require further investigation.

Histogram

A *histogram* is a graphical representation used in univariate analysis to illustrate the distribution of a dataset. The x-axis represents the bins or intervals into which the data is grouped, and the y-axis represents the frequency. Histograms are useful for understanding the shape, center, and spread of a data distribution, identifying any patterns, outliers, or anomalies in the data.

Consider a scenario where a teacher wants to analyze the distribution of scores from a recent math test to understand the performance of students, using a histogram that looks like Figure 4.1.

FIGURE 4.1   Histogram of student math test scores

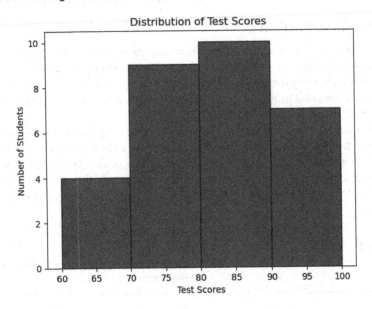

Analyzing the histogram, the teacher notices that the majority of students scored fairly high, with the highest concentration in the 80–89 range. The teacher could decide that most students performed well, and only a few might need additional assistance. The histogram could also reveal if the test was too easy or too difficult for the students, helping the teacher adjust accordingly for future tests.

In essence, a histogram is a powerful tool in univariate analysis, providing visual insight into the distribution and variability of a dataset, thereby assisting in making informed decisions based on the analysis of a single variable.

Box and Whisker Plot

A *box plot*, or *box-and-whisker plot*, is a graphical representation that provides a five-number summary of a dataset—the minimum, first quartile (Q1), median, third quartile (Q3), and maximum. It displays the *spread* and *skewness* in the data, and it is particularly useful for detecting outliers and understanding the distribution characteristics of a dataset. The "box" in the box plot represents the interquartile range (the middle 50 percent of the data), and the "whiskers" extend to the smallest and largest observations in the dataset.

Consider a scenario in which a company wants to analyze the monthly salaries of its employees to understand the distribution of pay within the organization. The HR department collects the salary data and constructs a box plot, as shown in Figure 4.2.

FIGURE 4.2   Box plot of employee salaries

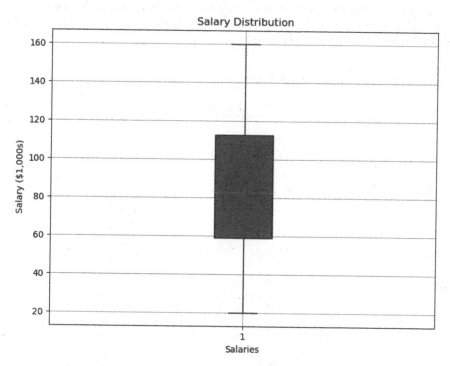

The box extends from Q1 ($60,000) to Q3 ($110,000), representing the interquartile range where the middle 50 percent of salaries lie. This means that 25 percent of employees earn less than $60,000, and another 25 percent earn more than $110,000. The line inside the box represents the median salary ($82,000).

The whiskers extend from the minimum salary ($20,000) to the maximum salary ($160,000). Any significant gap between the whiskers and the box may suggest the presence of outliers, or employees who earn significantly more or less than the rest.

Through this box plot, the company can better understand its salary distribution, identify any pay disparities, and make informed decisions about salary adjustments or restructuring. It gives a clear, concise visual summary of the data, enabling easy comparison and analysis for the company's HR department.

Density Plot

A *density plot*, also known as a *kernel density estimate (KDE)* plot, is a graphical representation used to estimate the probability density function of a continuous variable. It visualizes the distribution of a single variable by drawing a smoothed curve, where the y-axis represents the density and the x-axis represents the data values. Density plots are especially useful for identifying the shape of the data distribution, such as detecting multimodality or assessing skewness.

Imagine a scenario where we wish to analyze the age distribution of a population. Using a density plot like what we have in Figure 4.3, we can visualize the distribution of ages, helping to identify patterns such as peaks (indicating a high density of a certain age group), valleys (indicating a low density of a certain age group), or gaps.

FIGURE 4.3   Density plot of age distribution

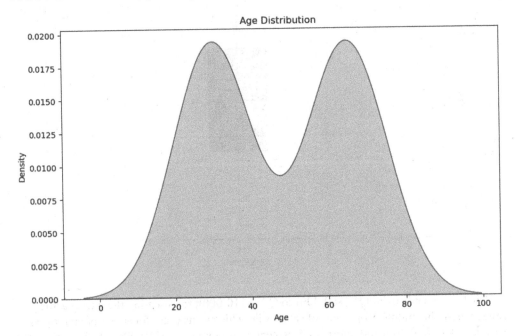

Quantile-Quantile (Q-Q) Plot

A *Q-Q plot*, or *quantile-quantile plot*, is a graphical tool used in univariate analysis to assess if a dataset follows a particular theoretical distribution. It compares the quantiles of the observed data to the quantiles of the chosen theoretical distribution. Each point on a Q-Q plot corresponds to a quantile in both datasets, with the x-coordinate representing the quantile from the theoretical distribution and the y-coordinate representing the quantile from the observed data. If the data follows the chosen distribution, the points on the Q-Q plot should approximately lie on a straight line.

Imagine analyzing a dataset of exam scores to determine if they follow a normal distribution. A Q-Q plot (Figure 4.4) can be used to plot the theoretical quantiles on the x-axis and the actual quantiles of the exam scores on the y-axis.

FIGURE 4.4   Quantile-quantile (Q-Q) plot of exam scores against a theoretical normal distribution

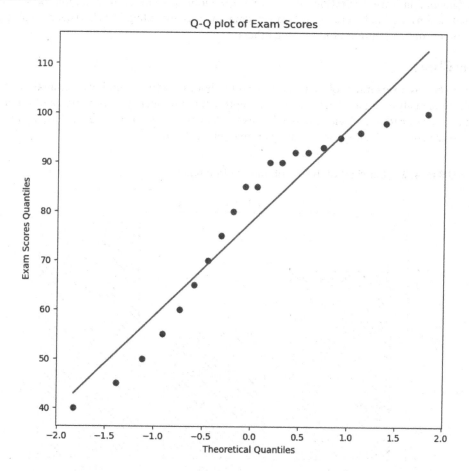

The results show that most of the points deviate slightly from the line, which means that the exam scores loosely follow a normal distribution curve. If the points lie approximately on the line, it suggests that the exam scores are normally distributed. And if the points deviate significantly from the line, it suggests a deviation from normality.

Bivariate Analysis

Unlike univariate analysis, which is focused on understanding the characteristics of individual variables, *bivariate analysis* aims to understand the interactions and associations between pairs of variables. It helps in understanding cause-and-effect relationships, if any, and aids in predicting outcomes and making better data-driven decisions.

Bivariate analysis is also very useful in identifying potential outliers, trends, patterns, and insights that can be beneficial for further analysis and modeling. This understanding is crucial for building predictive models, as understanding the relationships between variables is fundamental in feature selection. In this section, we look at some of the common tools and visualizations used in bivariate exploratory data analysis, including bar charts, scatterplots, line plots, and correlation plots, among others.

Bar Chart

A *bar chart* is a versatile tool that can be useful in both univariate and bivariate analysis. In univariate analysis, a bar chart can visually represent the frequency or proportion of different categories within a single variable. For example, you can use a bar chart to display the frequency count of fruit types within a variable (Figure 4.5).

FIGURE 4.5   Bar chart of the distribution of fruit types

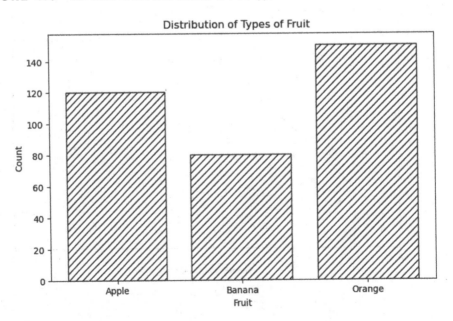

In bivariate analysis, a bar chart can be used to compare a categorical variable and a continuous variable, or two categorical variables. For example, a bar chart can display the average cost (a continuous variable) of different types of vehicles (a categorical variable), as shown in Figure 4.6. Similarly, a grouped or stacked bar chart can be used to display the frequency or proportion of two categorical variables, allowing for comparison of the distribution of one categorical variable across the levels of another categorical variable.

FIGURE 4.6   Bar chart of the average cost per vehicle type

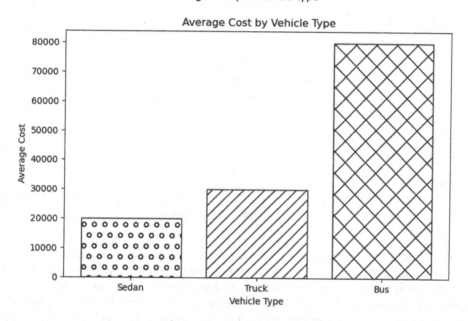

Scatterplot

A *scatterplot* is a graphical representation used in bivariate analysis to visualize the relationship between two quantitative variables. It plots one variable on the x-axis and the other on the y-axis, with each point on the plot representing an observation. The position of each point on the horizontal and vertical axes indicates values for an individual data point. Scatterplots are useful for observing relationships between variables, identifying trends, and spotting outliers or anomalies.

Consider a scenario where a researcher wants to analyze the relationship between the years of experience and the salaries of a group of workers. The researcher could create a scatterplot, as shown in Figure 4.7.

FIGURE 4.7 Scatterplot showing the relationship between salary and years of work experience

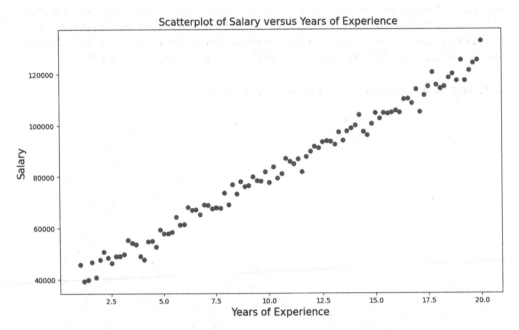

By examining the scatterplot, the researcher can visually assess the relationship between years of experience and salary. If the points cluster along a relatively straight line that ascends from left to right, this would suggest that salary tends to increase with years of work experience. Conversely, a descending line would suggest that salary decreases as years of experience increases. A random distribution of points would suggest no clear relationship or correlation between the two variables.

Line Plot

A *line plot* is a graph that displays data points on a two-dimensional plane and connects them with straight lines. It is commonly used to visualize the change in a variable over time, making it especially useful for time-series analysis, though it can be used for any two continuous variables.

Imagine a scenario where a company wants to assess its monthly revenue over a 12-month period. A line plot, like the one shown in Figure 4.8 that shows the relationship between time (months) and revenue, would be useful for this.

This visual representation allows the company to easily observe trends, patterns, and fluctuations in monthly revenue, enabling them to make more informed business decisions.

FIGURE 4.8   Line plot of monthly sales revenue over 12 months

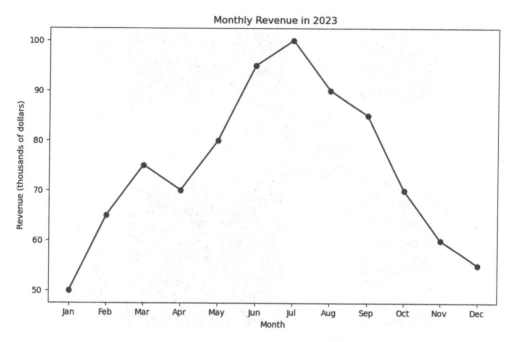

Correlation Plot

In bivariate analysis, a *correlation plot* allows us to quantify the strength and direction of the relationship between a pair of variables. However, it can also be useful in the context of multivariate analysis, where it can be used to simultaneously identify pairs of variables that are strongly correlated. This is important for feature selection, dimensionality reduction, and understanding the interplay between multiple variables.

In a correlation plot, variables are often displayed as rows and columns in a grid, and the cells of the grid are filled with correlation coefficients, ranging from –1 to 1. The *correlation coefficient* quantifies the degree of the linear relationship between two variables: A positive value near 1 indicates a strong positive correlation, meaning that as one variable increases, the other tends to increase as well; a negative value near –1 signifies a strong negative correlation, which means that as one variable increases, the other decreases; and a correlation coefficient near 0 indicates little to no linear relationship.

Consider a scenario where a real estate company wants to understand the relationship between various features of a house and its selling price to make informed pricing and investment decisions. The company has collected data on several variables, including the size of the house (in square feet), the number of bedrooms, the age of the house, and the selling price. It can use this data to create a correlation plot to visualize the pairwise correlation coefficients between the selling price and the other variables. Figure 4.9 shows a sample correlation plot based on the four features in the dataset.

FIGURE 4.9   Sample correlation plot

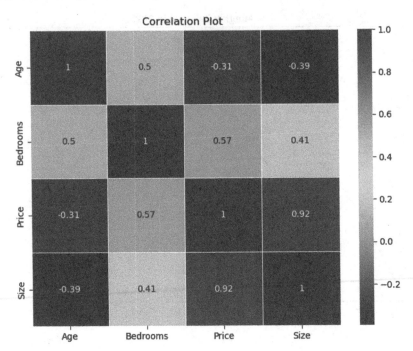

Here's how to read the visual:

- **Color Intensity:** The intensity of the color indicates the magnitude of the correlation: darker colors signify stronger correlations, and lighter colors indicate weaker correlations.

- **Correlation Values:** Inside each cell of the plot is a numeric value. This value is the correlation coefficient, which quantifies the degree of linear association between a pair of variables.

From the visual, we can quickly tell that there is a negative linear relationship between the age of a house and price (the boxes with a correlation coefficient of –0.31). This means that older houses tend to be cheaper. Conversely, the relationship between size and price is positive (the boxes with a correlation coefficient of 0.92). This means that the larger a house is, the more expensive it will be.

Correlation Plots vs. Heatmaps

It's important to note that while similar, correlation plots and *heatmaps* are not the same thing. A heatmap is a graphical representation of data where values in a matrix are represented as colors. It is a way to visualize data and the intensity of some metric. Heatmaps are used in various types of analysis besides just showing correlation. For instance, heatmaps can be used to represent the magnitude of web traffic over time, where darker colors might represent higher traffic and lighter colors represent lower traffic.

A correlation plot specifically visualizes the correlation coefficients between multiple variables. It is often realized as a heatmap, where darker colors represent strong correlations and lighter colors represent weak correlations. In other words, a correlation plot is a specific type of heatmap. So, while all correlation plots are heatmaps, not all heatmaps are correlation plots.

Violin Plot

A *violin plot* is a type of data visualization that combines aspects of a box plot and a kernel density plot. It provides a visualization of the distribution of the data, its probability density, and its cumulative distribution. The thicker part of a violin plot represents where the data is concentrated, and the thinner part represents where the data is sparse. Violin plots are useful for comparing the distribution of data across different categories or groups.

In bivariate analysis, a violin plot can effectively illustrate the relationship between a categorical variable and a continuous variable. For example, consider a study examining the correlation between the vehicle types (Sedan, SUV, Truck) and the ages of individuals who purchase them. The violin plot in Figure 4.10 illustrates this relationship.

FIGURE 4.10   Violin plot of the relationship between vehicle type and customer age

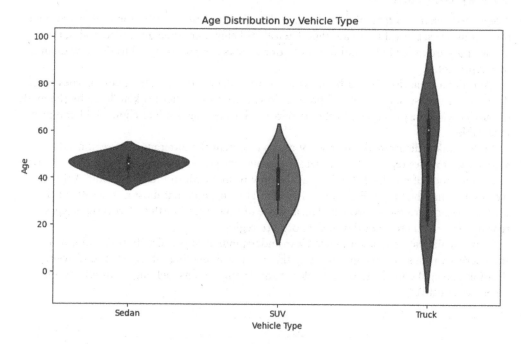

From the plot, we can tell that:

- Sedans are mostly bought by middle-aged individuals, as the widest part of the sedan violin is in the middle.
- SUVs have a more uniform distribution, which indicates a broad age group of buyers.
- Trucks are most popular among younger and older age groups, represented by the bimodal distribution of the violin at the lower and upper age ranges.

Multivariate Analysis

The objective of *multivariate analysis* is to understand the relationships and interactions between multiple variables and how they collectively impact outcomes. It can be used to derive insights, detect patterns, and unearth hidden relationships between variables in a dataset. Multivariate analysis often involves the use of visualization and analysis tools such as Sankey diagrams, cluster analysis, and principal component analysis (PCA) in order to form a more comprehensive understanding of the behavior of data.

In exploratory data analysis, multivariate analysis is a vital step that helps data scientists build more accurate and robust models by considering the interdependence of multiple variables and factors. It assists in making more informed decisions by providing a holistic view of the data and uncovering hidden patterns and relationships that might not be noticeable in univariate or bivariate analysis. In this section, we look at some of the common visualizations and techniques used in multivariate exploratory data analysis, including Sankey diagrams, cluster analysis, and principal component analysis.

Sankey Diagram

A *Sankey diagram* is a type of flow diagram that visualizes the distribution of flows or quantities from one set of values to another. The values being connected are called nodes, the connections are called links, and the width of the links are proportional to the flow quantity they represent.

Consider a scenario where a business wants to understand the distribution of sales across different regions, segmented by the product categories and further broken down by the mode of purchase (online or offline). In this scenario, a Sankey diagram like Figure 4.11 can prove invaluable.

In the Sankey diagram, the first set of nodes represent the different sales regions, the second set of nodes represent the different product categories, and the third set of nodes represent the mode of purchase. Looking at the flow from North to Electronics and Apparel, we observe that the link to Electronics is wider. This suggests that most of the sales in the northern region are for electronics. The absence of flow from North to Groceries suggests that there were no grocery sales in the northern region.

This visualization enables a quick, clear understanding of the distribution and flow of sales across various dimensions, assisting the business in making informed, data-driven decisions. It highlights the strongest sales channels and regions, helping focus efforts and resources effectively.

FIGURE 4.11   Sankey diagram of sales by region, category, and mode of purchase

Sales Distribution by Region, Category, and Mode of Purchase

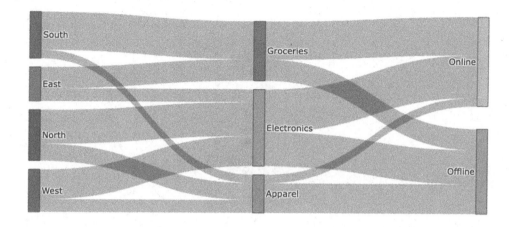

Cluster Analysis

Cluster analysis, or *clustering*, is a technique in multivariate analysis used to group similar data objects together based on certain attributes. It aims to maximize intracluster similarity (similarity between items in the same cluster) and minimize the intercluster similarity (similarity between items in different clusters). Cluster analysis is useful in multivariate exploratory data analysis to reveal hidden patterns and insights, which become apparent when similar data points are grouped together.

Imagine a scenario where a retail chain wants to understand how its products are being sold, based on factors like average income and population density of the customers in the city in which an item was sold. The retail chain can use cluster analysis to segment each product into groups (or clusters) based on units sold, average income, and population density, as shown in Figure 4.12.

The cluster visualization reveals that the retail chain's products can be segmented into three main clusters based on average income, population density, and units sold. It also reveals that items in cluster 3 (the square cluster) have higher sales volume and are typically sold in cities with higher-than-average population density but lower-than-average income. With this high-level insight, the retail chain can make more informed decisions about marketing and sales strategies, such as investing more resources in advertising and promotion in cities with higher population densities and average income to boost the sales of the items currently in cluster 1 (the circle cluster).

FIGURE 4.12 Cluster visualization of items segmented by average income, population density, and units sold

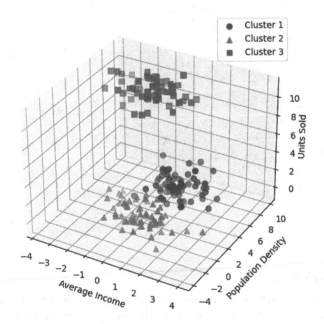

Principal Component Analysis

Principal component analysis (PCA) is a *dimensionality reduction* technique used in multivariate analysis. It works by identifying the "principal components" of the data, which are dimensions along which the variation in the data is maximized. These principal components can then be used to represent the data in a lower-dimensional space without losing significant information, making the data easier to explore and visualize. PCA is most useful when we want to understand the relationship between variables in a high-dimensional dataset.

Suppose a company wants to understand the relationship among multiple variables related to its products, like cost, weight, durability, and customer satisfaction ratings. A dataset with these variables will have multiple dimensions, making it challenging to analyze and visualize. By using PCA to reduce the dimensionality of the dataset, the data can be visualized in two dimensions, as shown in Figure 4.13.

By transforming the original variables into a new set of uncorrelated variables (principal components), PCA enables the visualization and analysis of high-dimensional datasets in two- or three-dimensional space. Analyzing the spread and clustering of the data points in Figure 4.13 provides insights into the underlying patterns and relationships in the dataset. For example, we can clearly see that the products are grouped into three distinct clusters. This indicates that products within each cluster are similar in terms of cost, weight, durability, and customer satisfaction. Insights such as this can inform marketing strategy, product development roadmaps, and other business decisions.

FIGURE 4.13   Sample visualization using principal component analysis (PCA)

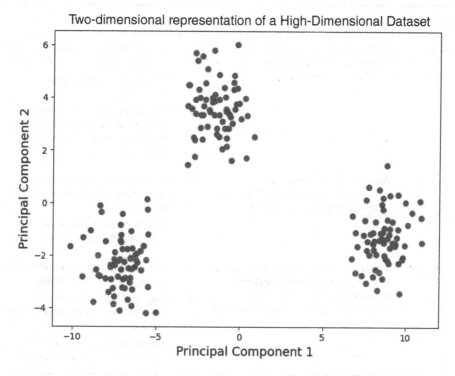

Two-dimensional representation of a High-Dimensional Dataset

    For a more detailed coverage of cluster analysis and principal component analysis, see Chapter 8, "Unsupervised Machine Learning."

Choosing an Exploratory Data Analysis Method

Exploratory data analysis is a crucial early step in the data science lifecycle that helps us better understand our data before applying more sophisticated modeling techniques. Univariate analysis looks at one variable. Bivariate analysis looks at two variables and their relationship to each other. Multivariate analysis looks at more than two variables, their relationship to each other, and their impact on an outcome variable. Understanding which analysis method to use and knowing when to use it helps data scientists navigate through the data in preparation for modeling. Table 4.2 provides a high-level summary of the approaches and the best situations in which to use them.

TABLE 4.2   Summary of exploratory data analysis methods

Analysis Type	Description	Scenarios and Use Cases
Univariate	Analyzes a single variable to understand its distribution, central tendency, and dispersion	• Understanding the distribution of a variable (e.g., customer age) • Identifying outliers and anomalies • Summarizing and describing the data with metrics like mean, median, mode, and standard deviation
Bivariate	Analyzes two variables to understand the relationships and associations between them	• Exploring the relationship between two variables (e.g., age and income) • Testing hypotheses about associations between variables
Multivariate	Analyzes more than two variables to understand the interactions between them and identify patterns and structures in the data	• Understanding the relationships among multiple variables • Segmenting or classifying observations based on multiple features • Reducing dimensionality and extracting important features

Common Data Quality Issues

Exploratory data analysis is not only useful for understanding data, it also is a vital step in ensuring the quality, integrity, and readiness of data for analysis and modeling. By effectively identifying and addressing data quality issues such as multicollinearity, seasonality, and missingness during the EDA process, data scientists set a solid foundation for subsequent phases of the data science lifecycle, ensuring more reliable, accurate, and insightful results.

There are several ways to categorize data quality issues. One approach is to categorize them based on the specific characteristics of the data that is affected. Using this approach, data quality issues can be categorized as structural issues, temporal issues, and completeness issues.

As you prepare for the DataX exam, you should be able to identify and suggest mitigating strategies for common data quality issues. Make note of the approaches highlighted in this section for identifying and handling data quality issues.

Structural Issues

Structural issues pertain to the inherent properties and relationships within the data. They can significantly impact the performance of data analyses and predictive models. Structural issues can include problems such as granularity misalignment, outliers, nonlinearity, and multicollinearity.

Granularity Misalignment

Granularity misalignment in data quality refers to the mismatch in the level of detail or specificity in data, where different datasets are represented at varying levels of detail, making it difficult to analyze or compare effectively. This issue is typically encountered in integrated datasets, where data from different sources or categories is combined.

Addressing the issue of granularity misalignment generally involves restructuring the data to ensure a uniform level of granularity. This usually involves aggregating more granular data, obtaining additional data to make aggregated data more granular, or removing unnecessary or excessive detail to ensure that a consistent level of granularity is achieved throughout the dataset. For example, consider a scenario where one attempts to combine and analyze sales data from two different sources. If one dataset provides detailed information about sales for each day, while the other provides a summary of sales for each month, we have a granularity misalignment issue. To resolve the issue, the daily sales data would need to be aggregated to monthly totals in order to align with the granularity of the monthly sales data.

Outliers

Outliers are values in data that significantly deviate from the rest. The presence of outliers can disproportionately affect statistical calculations and models, leading to unreliable results and conclusions. Exploratory data analysis tools such as box plots and scatterplots are useful in identifying outliers in data. Once identified, outliers need to be analyzed to determine whether they represent genuine values or errors.

To resolve outlier data, we must first decide whether to retain, transform, or remove them. In cases where outliers represent errors or anomalies that do not contribute valuable information to the analysis, they can be removed from the dataset. When outliers hold critical information, data transformation techniques like logarithmic transformation or binning can be applied to minimize their impact.

 See Chapter 5 for some of the other data transformation techniques that are commonly used to deal with outliers.

Nonlinearity

Nonlinearity arises when the relationship between the independent and dependent variables in a dataset cannot be adequately represented with a linear model. If not properly accounted for, this can lead to suboptimal or incorrect results because traditional linear models will fail to capture the underlying patterns in the data. To identify nonlinearity, visualization techniques such as scatterplots are useful. By plotting the data, we can visually inspect the relationships between pairs of variables. If the data points do not follow a straight line or plane, a nonlinear relationship might be present.

To accommodate or handle nonlinearity, we can use nonlinear approaches such as polynomial regression or decision trees (discussed in Chapter 9, "Supervised Machine Learning") when modeling our data. Where appropriate, we can also use a data transformation technique to linearize the relationships between variables, allowing the use of linear models for analysis and prediction.

Multicollinearity

Multicollinearity is a data quality issue encountered in regression analysis where two or more independent variables in a dataset are highly correlated. This high correlation means that these variables essentially contain similar information about the variance within the dataset, making it difficult to determine the individual influence of each predictor variable on the dependent variable. This situation can lead to unreliable and unstable estimates of regression coefficients, reducing the predictive performance of the model and making it harder to interpret the results.

Identifying multicollinearity involves examining the relationships between the independent variables. A correlation matrix, variance inflation factor (VIF), and condition index are common tools and metrics used to detect multicollinearity. A correlation matrix provides pairwise correlations between all variables, where a high correlation between two independent variables signals potential multicollinearity. A VIF value greater than 10 is often considered an indicator of multicollinearity. The condition index, computed on the independent variables, can also be used to assess multicollinearity, with values above 30 suggesting possible multicollinearity.

Resolving multicollinearity typically involves removing one of the highly correlated variables, combining variables, or applying dimensionality reduction techniques like PCA on the data. Another approach is to use regularization methods like ridge regression, which can mitigate the impact of multicollinearity by adding a penalty term to the regression.

Regularization methods and their use in regression modeling is discussed in more detail in Chapter 9.

Temporal Issues

Temporal issues are related to time-based aspects of the data. They are particularly relevant in time-series analysis and forecasting models. The temporal issues covered here include nonstationarity and seasonality.

Nonstationarity

Nonstationarity is a common data quality issue in time-series analysis where the statistical properties of a sequence of data points vary with time. This implies that the data does not have a stable or predictable behavior, and that the past observations may not be representative of the future ones. A nonstationary time series will have a time-dependent mean or variance (or both), which can add complexity and unpredictability to the analysis, making it difficult to model and forecast accurately.

Nonstationarity is a critical issue because many time-series modeling techniques, such as autoregressive integrated moving average (ARIMA), assume stationarity in the data. Nonstationarity can result from factors such as seasonality, cycles, shocks, and structural breaks, and can affect the validity, accuracy, and interpretation of trend analysis methods.

ARIMA and other temporal models will be covered in more detail in Chapter 6, "Modeling and Evaluation."

To identify nonstationarity, visual inspection of the data is the first step. Plotting the data will often reveal the presence of trends or seasonality, indicating nonstationarity. More formally, statistical tests such as the Augmented Dickey–Fuller (ADF) test can be used. This test compares the null hypothesis of nonstationarity against the alternative hypothesis of stationarity and provides a p-value that indicates the probability of rejecting the null hypothesis. Generally, a low p-value (less than 0.05) suggests that the data is stationary, whereas a high p-value (more than 0.05) suggests that the data is nonstationary.

Resolving nonstationarity typically involves transforming the data to make it stationary. A common approach is differencing, which involves subtracting the current value of the data from the previous value or a lagged value to remove the trend or seasonality component. Another approach is decomposition, where the time series is decomposed into trend, seasonal, and residual components.

To illustrate how to deal with nonstationarity, consider a time-series dataset of monthly sales revenue of an online store over several years, as shown in Figure 4.14. Visual inspection of the data shows an increasing trend, suggesting nonstationarity. Applying the ADF test could further confirm this.

To resolve the nonstationarity in the data, we can apply differencing to the data by subtracting the revenue of the previous month from the current month for each data point. The differenced data, now more likely to be stationary, is shown in Figure 4.15. We can also perform the ADF test on the differenced data to confirm stationarity. If confirmed, the stationary data can then be used for further analysis and modeling to create more accurate forecasts.

FIGURE 4.14   Sample nonstationary monthly sales revenue over a 60-month period

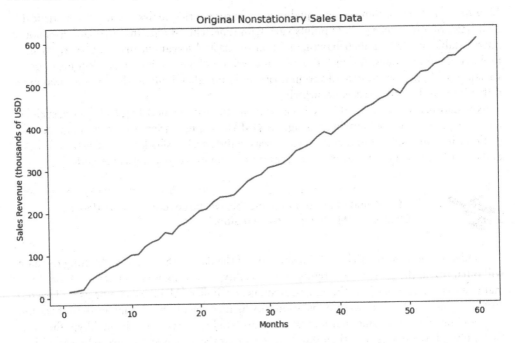

FIGURE 4.15   Sample stationary monthly sales revenue over a 60-month period after differencing

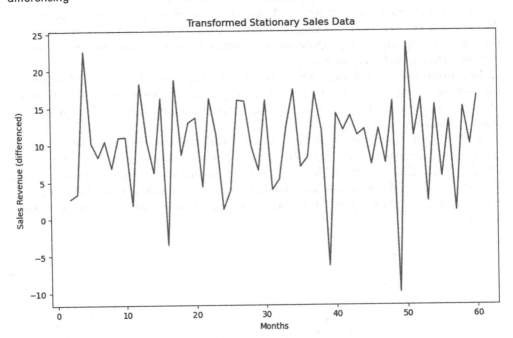

Seasonality

Seasonality is another common data quality issue often encountered in time-series analysis, where patterns in the data repeat at regular intervals, corresponding to specific seasons or times of the year. It is a type of nonstationarity. While seasonality is an expected and natural pattern in many datasets, it can confound time-series analyses and forecasts if not accounted for, making it seem like a dataset is experiencing unexpected growth or decline.

Identifying seasonality involves visual inspection of the data and conducting a seasonal decomposition of the time-series data. Visual inspection using line plots can reveal repeating patterns at specific intervals, and a seasonal decomposition can statistically confirm the presence of seasonality by isolating the seasonal component of the time-series data.

To resolve seasonality, we remove the seasonal component in the data by calculating the average seasonal effect and subtracting it from the original data. To illustrate how this works, consider Figure 4.16, which is a visualization of the monthly sales data of a clothing store over a 60-month period. We clearly see seasonality in the data based on visual inspection.

FIGURE 4.16   Sample seasonal monthly sales data over a 60-month period

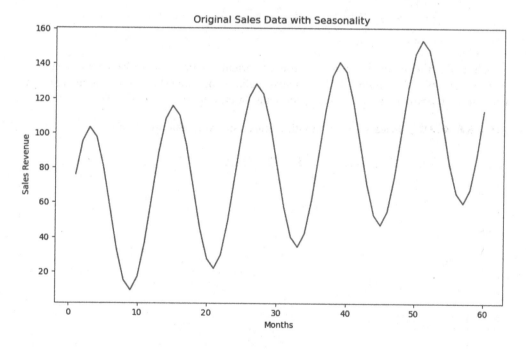

To analyze the underlying sales trends or make future sales predictions, the data would need to first be "deseasonalized" by subtracting the seasonal component from the original sales figures. A seasonal decomposition of the time-series data produces the trend, seasonal, and residual components, as shown in Figure 4.17.

FIGURE 4.17   Decomposed seasonal monthly sales data showing the trend, seasonal, and residual components

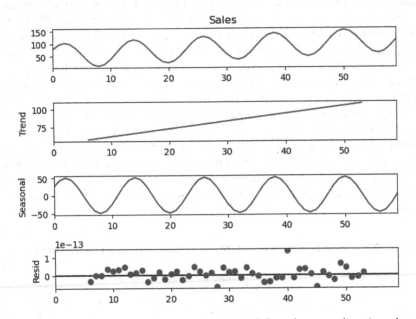

Subtracting the seasonal component from the original data deseasonalizes it and results in data that looks like Figure 4.18. The deseasonalized data now shows the underlying trend without the repeating seasonal pattern, allowing for clearer analysis and modeling of the data.

FIGURE 4.18   Deseasonalized monthly sales data over a 60-month period

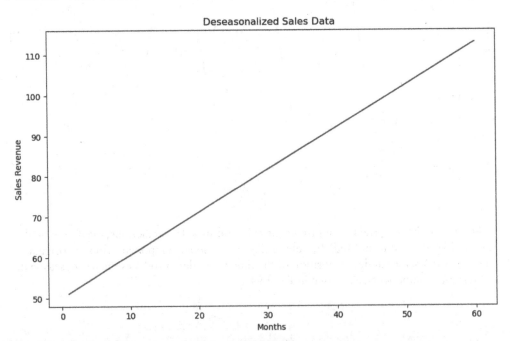

Completeness Issues

Completeness issues refer to the absence or insufficiency of data required for comprehensive analysis. These include the issues of insufficient features, sparse data, and missing data.

Insufficient Features

The data quality issue of insufficient features refers to the scenario where the available data does not contain enough features (variables) to adequately model and understand the problem at hand. This issue is particularly relevant in machine learning and predictive modeling, where the goal is to make predictions or inferences based on patterns in the data. Insufficient features can lead to underfitting, where a model is too simple to capture the underlying structure of the data, resulting in poor performance in both the training and test data.

Identifying that we have insufficient features in our data can be challenging. Generally, we can suspect that we have insufficient features in our data if, after adding complexity to a model, extensive tuning, and optimization, performance still does not increase. This could be an indication that the model is lacking sufficient information from the features to make accurate predictions.

Resolving the issue of insufficient features usually involves feature engineering, which is the process of creating new features or transforming existing ones to improve model performance, gathering additional data that contains more features, and using techniques such as feature extraction or dimensionality reduction to create more informative features from the existing data.

Sparse Data

Sparse data refers to a scenario where a dataset has insufficient useful information because the majority of the values in the dataset are missing or zero. Sparsity in data can be problematic for analytic models because the absence of sufficient information means that the model may fail to detect underlying patterns in the data, which can lead to bias, overfitting, underfitting, and poor performance.

Identifying sparsity in data typically involves quantifying the degree of sparsity in a dataset by calculating the proportion of missing or zero values. Visualizing the data is also a useful approach. An EDA tool such as a heatmap can enable us to quickly identify areas of sparsity in a dataset.

The resolution of sparse data depends on the specific context and dataset. One common approach is to use *imputation* methods to fill in missing or zero values with estimated values. Another approach is to model the data using algorithms specifically designed to handle sparse data, such as certain types of decision trees or ensemble methods. Alternatively, dimensionality reduction techniques can be used to compress the sparse dataset into a lower-dimensional space, reducing the impact of the sparse features.

Missing Data

Missing data refers to the absence of values in a dataset where they would be expected. It's a common data quality issue that can arise due to factors such as errors in data collection, incomplete survey data, data entry mistakes, issues with data integration, or simply the lack of certain information. Missing data can potentially introduce bias, reduce the power of statistical tests, and lead to invalid conclusions.

While sparse data and missing data are both data quality issues, they differ in their nature and implications. Sparse data implies that a variable itself has mostly missing values, while missing data refers to specific data points or observations with missing values for one or more variables.

Identifying missing data typically involves conducting a preliminary analysis of the dataset to determine the presence and extent of missing values. Visualization techniques like heatmaps or missing data plots can also be employed to visually represent the areas where data is missing. The specific steps we take to identify and resolve missing data is usually dependent on the nature of the missingness. Broadly, missing data can be classified into one of three categories:

Missing Completely at Random (MCAR)   This is when missing data occurs independent of any observed or unobserved variables. In other words, there are no systematic differences between observations with missing data and those without. Deleting missing data or basic imputation techniques can typically be used to handle data that is MCAR without adding bias to the data analysis process.

Missing at Random (MAR)   This occurs when missingness is systematically related to other observed variables in the dataset. Handling data that is MAR effectively requires sophisticated imputation methods, such as regression or model-based imputation, which considers the relationships between the missing data and other variables.

Missing Not at Random (MNAR)   In this scenario, missingness is systematically related to unobserved data or the expected value of the missing data itself. In other words, missingness is related to events or factors which are not captured by the data. Addressing data that is MNAR requires advanced techniques, such as sensitivity analysis, which involves making different assumptions about the cause of missingness and observing how these assumptions affect the results of data analysis.

See Chapter 5 for a more detailed discussion on how to resolve missing data using various imputation techniques.

To further illustrate the different categories of missing data, consider a scenario where income data is missing from a survey conducted on the relationship between income and health outcomes. If the income data is missing due to technical errors during data collection that randomly affects entries, then we say that the data is MCAR. However, if the income data is more likely to be missing for participants of a certain age (which is observed in the dataset), then it is MAR. Alternatively, if the income data is missing because participants with lower income are less likely to report it, then we can say that the data is MNAR.

Summary

Exploratory data analysis (EDA) is used to understand the main characteristics of a dataset by summarizing its main features, often visually. It allows data scientists to identify patterns and anomalies, test assumptions, and check for inconsistencies and model suitability without applying formal statistical tests. The type of EDA chosen is often dependent on the type of variable(s) being analyzed.

Quantitative variables are either discrete (with specific, countable values) or continuous (with an infinite range). Qualitative variables categorize data into nominal (no inherent order), ordinal (with a meaningful sequence), and binary (two possible values).

Univariate analysis is a fundamental step in exploratory data analysis, focusing on one variable at a time to outline data patterns and anomalies without examining relationships. It provides insights into a variable's distribution using tools like frequency distributions, histograms, and box plots.

Bivariate analysis explores relationships between pairs of variables, revealing cause-and-effect connections and aiding prediction and decision-making. It uncovers outliers, trends, and insights, essential for feature selection in predictive models. Tools such as bar charts compare categorical and continuous variables, scatterplots visualize relationships between two quantitative variables, line plots track variable changes over time, and correlation plots quantify and display relationships between variables.

Multivariate analysis explores the complex interactions between multiple variables to uncover insights and hidden patterns. It employs visualization and tools like Sankey diagrams for understanding flow distributions, cluster analysis for grouping similar data objects based on attributes, and principal component analysis (PCA) for dimensionality reduction.

Exploratory data analysis not only helps in understanding data but is also crucial for ensuring data quality and readiness for analysis and modeling. Data quality issues can be categorized as a structural issue, a temporal issue, or a completeness issue based on the characteristics of the affected data. Structural issues include granularity misalignment, outliers, nonlinearity, and multicollinearity. Temporal issues include nonstationarity and seasonality, and completeness issues include insufficient features, sparse data, and missing data.

Exam Essentials

Explain the importance of data exploration and analysis in the data science lifecycle. Data exploration and analysis play a pivotal role in the data science lifecycle by enabling data scientists to gain valuable insights, uncover hidden patterns, and grasp the intrinsic properties of the data collected during the data collection and storage phase. It serves as an essential bridge between data acquisition and data modeling.

Understand the difference between quantitative and qualitative variables. Quantitative or numerical variables are either discrete (with distinct values) or continuous (with infinite values within a range). Qualitative or categorical variables are nominal (with no inherent order), ordinal (with meaningful order), or binary (with only two outcomes).

Explain univariate analysis and the best times to use it.   Univariate analysis is a simple form of exploratory data analysis where only one variable (univariate) is considered, focusing on describing the characteristics of that single variable through measures such as the mean, median, mode, range, variance, maximum, minimum, quartiles, and standard deviation. It is particularly useful when summarizing large datasets, identifying trends or patterns in one dimension, or simply presenting simplified data insights without the influence of other variables.

Explain bivariate analysis and the best times to use it.   Bivariate analysis involves the statistical examination of two variables (bivariate) to determine the empirical relationship between them, often visualized through scatterplots, line graphs, or correlation matrices. It is most effective when the goal is to understand the interactions between two variables—for example, determining if a relationship is causal or coincidental, identifying trends, forecasting outcomes, or investigating hypotheses about underlying connections.

Explain multivariate analysis and the best times to use it.   Multivariate analysis examines more than two variables simultaneously to understand the relationships among them and their combined impact on outcomes. It is most useful when the goal is to understand interactions among multiple variables or to control for the influence of multiple variables on an outcome.

Describe how to identify common structural data quality issues.   Granularity misalignment can be detected by comparing the levels of detail across datasets. Outliers are identified using visual exploratory tools like box plots and scatterplots. Nonlinearity is identified through scatterplots or residual plots. Multicollinearity is detected using statistical measures like correlation matrices or VIF.

Describe how to identify common temporal data quality issues.   Identifying temporal data quality issues begins with visual inspection. For nonstationarity, plot the data to detect trends or seasonal effects, then use statistical tests like the Augmented Dickey–Fuller (ADF) test to formally assess stationarity. For seasonality, visually inspect for cyclical behaviors and perform seasonal decomposition to statistically verify seasonality.

Describe how to identify common completeness data quality issues.   Identifying completeness data quality issues requires different approaches. For the issue of insufficient features, we can suspect that this issue is at play when model performance doesn't improve in spite of extensive tuning. The issue of data sparsity is identified by quantifying the proportion of missing or zero values in the data. Missing data is detected through preliminary data analysis or visualization techniques such as heatmaps or missing data plots.

Review Questions

1. Discrete variables are _____.
   A. Variables that have an infinite number of values within a range
   B. Variables that represent countable items or events with distinct and separate values
   C. Variables that do not have an inherent order among their categories
   D. Variables that have an inherent order among their categories

2. Which of the following is *not* an example of a continuous variable?
   A. Weight
   B. Number of siblings
   C. Temperature
   D. Time

3. Which of these is a distinguishing feature of nominal variables?
   A. They have an inherent order among their categories.
   B. They can only take two possible values.
   C. They represent countable items.
   D. They have no inherent order among their categories.

4. In a box-and-whisker plot, what does the "box" primarily represent?
   A. The entire dataset
   B. The interquartile range
   C. The minimum and maximum
   D. The median

5. What is the main purpose of a Q-Q plot?
   A. To represent the distribution of a dataset
   B. To provide a five-number summary of a dataset
   C. To assess whether a dataset follows a particular theoretical distribution
   D. To show the frequency distribution of a dataset

6. Which of these is a valid use of a bar chart in bivariate analysis?
   A. To represent the frequency of a single categorical variable
   B. To visualize the relationship between two continuous variables
   C. To compare a categorical variable and a continuous variable
   D. To show the correlation coefficient between two variables

7. In a correlation plot, what does a positive value close to 1 signify?

    A. A strong negative correlation

    B. No correlation

    C. A strong positive correlation

    D. A weak positive correlation

8. What is the difference between correlation plots and heatmaps?

    A. Correlation plots visualize data, whereas heatmaps show correlations.

    B. All heatmaps are correlation plots, but not all correlation plots are heatmaps.

    C. Correlation plots are a specific type of heatmap.

    D. Heatmaps and correlation plots are the same thing.

9. What does a Sankey diagram visualize?

    A. The relationship between two variables

    B. The distribution of flows or quantities from one set of values to another

    C. The dimensionality reduction of data

    D. The similarity between data points in different clusters

10. What does cluster analysis aim to maximize?

    A. Intercluster similarity

    B. The number of clusters

    C. Intracluster similarity

    D. The number of variables in a dataset

11. What is principal component analysis (PCA) primarily used for?

    A. Grouping similar data objects

    B. Understanding flow distribution

    C. Reducing the dimensionality of a dataset

    D. Increasing the number of dimensions in a dataset

12. Which of these is a valid approach to address granularity misalignment?

    A. Removing outliers from the data

    B. Aggregation or obtaining additional data

    C. Checking for multicollinearity

    D. Applying regularization methods

13. When the relationship between the independent and dependent variables cannot be represented by a linear model; this is known as:

    A. Outliers

    B. Multicollinearity

    C. Granularity misalignment

    D. Nonlinearity

14. What is nonstationarity in time-series analysis?

   A. Repeating patterns at regular intervals in time

   B. Statistical properties of data that remain constant over time

   C. High correlation between two variables

   D. Statistical properties of data that vary with time

15. How is seasonality typically resolved in time-series data?

   A. By differencing the data

   B. By conducting the Augmented Dickey–Fuller (ADF) test

   C. By removing the seasonal component

   D. By adding more data points to the series

16. Which of the following best describes seasonality in time-series analysis?

   A. A trend in data that varies with time

   B. Patterns in data that repeat at regular intervals

   C. A consistent behavior in data over time

   D. A sudden change in the structure of time-series data

17. What does the issue of insufficient features in a dataset imply?

   A. The dataset has too much information.

   B. The use of insufficient features can lead to overfitting.

   C. The dataset lacks enough information to model the problem adequately.

   D. The dataset is too large and needs to be reduced.

18. Which of these is one way to identify sparsity in a dataset?

   A. Looking at the model's accuracy

   B. Calculating the proportion of missing or zero values

   C. Observing the variables with abundant information

   D. Checking the consistency of the data

19. What is missing completely at random (MCAR) data?

   A. Missingness that is related to events or factors not captured by the data

   B. Missingness that is systematically related to other observed variables in the dataset

   C. Missingness that occurs independent of any observed or unobserved variables

   D. Missingness that is always related to unobserved data

20. What distinguishes sparse data from missing data?

   A. Sparse data refers to the absence of values, whereas missing data implies that a variable mostly has missing values.

   B. Sparse data implies a variable mostly has missing values, whereas missing data refers to specific observations with missing values.

   C. Sparse data and missing data have no distinguishable differences.

   D. Sparse data refers to the missing of quantitative variables, whereas missing data refers to the missing of qualitative variables

Chapter

5

Data Processing and Preparation

THE COMPTIA DATAX EXAM OBJECTIVES COVERED IN THIS CHAPTER INCLUDE:

✓ **Domain 2: Modeling, Analysis, and Outcomes**

- 2.3 Given a scenario, apply data enrichment and augmentation techniques.

✓ **Domain 4: Operations and Processes**

- 4.4 Given a scenario, implement common data-wrangling techniques.

The third phase in the data science lifecycle is data processing and preparation. The primary objective of data processing and preparation is to transform raw data into a refined and structured form that allows for more advanced analytics and modeling. In the previous chapter, you learned how the data exploration and analysis process empowers data scientists to unearth valuable insights, recognize underlying patterns, and comprehend the inherent characteristics of the data they are working with. In this chapter, we begin with an exploration of various data transformation techniques such as encoding, standardization, and flattening, to name a few. Then we discuss various data enrichment and augmentation concepts such as ground truth labeling, feature engineering, and joins. Building on the concepts introduced in the previous chapter, we also examine techniques and strategies for handling data quality issues such as outliers, duplicate data, and missing data, among others. Finally, the chapter concludes with a discussion of how to handle the critical issue of class imbalance.

Data Transformation

Data transformation refers to the process of converting data from one format, structure, or representation into another to meet specific requirements or to make it more suitable for a particular task or analysis. It's a fundamental step in data processing and preparation. It encompasses a range of techniques such as encoding, scaling, normalizing and transforming values in data, transforming the structure of data and feature extraction. Effective data transformation is crucial in preparing data for analysis, as it helps improve the consistency and usability of data.

As you prepare for the DataX exam, you should be able to decide which data transformation technique(s) to use given a scenario and explain why. Make note of the different data transformation approaches introduced in this section and how they are used to prepare data for analysis.

Encoding

To make categorical data more interpretable or suitable for certain analytic models, we sometimes have to transform it from categorical form to numerical form. This is known as *encoding*. Two of the most common types of encoding are one-hot encoding and label encoding.

One-Hot Encoding

The main idea behind one-hot encoding is to convert each category of a categorical variable into a new binary column with a value of 0 or 1. For instance, let's say we have a dataset containing a column for vehicle colors with three distinct values: Red, Green, and Blue, as shown in Table 5.1.

TABLE 5.1 Categorical vehicle color values

ID	Colors
0	Red
1	Green
2	Blue
3	Red

Using one-hot encoding, this single column will be split into three separate columns, one for each color, as shown in Table 5.2.

TABLE 5.2 One-hot encoded vehicle color values

ID	Colors_Blue	Colors_Green	Colors_Red
0	0	0	1
1	0	1	0
2	1	0	0
3	0	0	1

If a row in the original dataset had the color Red, then in the transformed dataset, the Red column would have a value of 1, while the Green and Blue columns would have values of 0.

Label Encoding

Label encoding involves assigning a unique integer value to each category of a categorical variable. It's a simple and efficient way to represent categories. However, it is important to note that label encoding can introduce an artificial order that might not exist in the original data.

This could lead to misleading results with certain algorithms. As a result, label encoding is most suitable for ordinal data where an inherent order exists.

To illustrate how label encoding works and how it differs from one-hot encoding, consider a dataset (Table 5.3) with a column for shirt sizes: Small, Medium, and Large.

TABLE 5.3   Ordinal shirt size values

ID	Sizes
0	Small
1	Medium
2	Large
3	Small

Using label encoding, Small might be encoded as 0, Medium as 1, and Large as 2 (Table 5.4).

TABLE 5.4   Label encoded shirt size values

ID	Sizes
0	0
1	1
2	2
3	0

Both encoding techniques are fundamental for improving the interpretability of data and for preparing categorical data for more advanced analytic tasks such as machine learning. The choice between both encoding methods is dependent on the type of categorical data (nominal or ordinal) we are working with, and the specific requirements of the model being used. For example, one-hot encoding is preferred over label encoding when working with nominal variables without a natural order or when building a linear model (which does not handle categorical variables intrinsically).

Scaling and Normalization

Certain machine learning algorithms, especially those that rely on distance calculations, perform better and converge faster when features have consistent scales. The idea is simple: Ensure that numerical features have values in comparable scales to prevent one feature from disproportionately influencing the model due to the scale of its values. For example, in a machine learning model, a feature with values that range in scale from 2,000 to 100,000 will diminish the influence of a feature with values that range in scale from 1 to 10. To make the scale of different features more compatible or consistent, we *scale* or *normalize* the features in our data during data preparation by reshaping the distribution and range of the data. Two of the most prevalent techniques for scaling and normalizing features are min-max normalization and standardization.

Min-Max Normalization

Min-max normalization is a technique used to transform the values of a feature so that they fall within a given range, typically between 0 and 1. The idea is to rescale the feature's values so that they are bounded within this defined range. The formula for min-max normalization is:

$$value_{normalized} = \frac{value_{original} - min}{max - min}$$

where $value_{original}$ is each original value for a feature, *min* is the smallest value in the feature, and *max* is the largest value in the feature.

For example, consider a dataset like Table 5.5 of age values ranging from 20 to 60.

TABLE 5.5   Original age values

ID	Age
0	20
1	40
2	60
3	30
4	50

Using min-max normalization, we can normalize the age values to fall within a range of 0 and 1, as shown in Table 5.6. A value of 20 becomes 0, an age of 60 becomes 1, and an age of 40 (the midpoint) becomes 0.5.

TABLE 5.6   Age values min-max normalized

ID	Age	Normalized_Age
0	20	0.000000
1	40	0.500000
2	60	1.000000
3	30	0.250000
4	50	0.750000

Standardization

Standardization, often referred to as Z-score normalization, is a scaling technique that transforms features to have a mean of 0 and a standard deviation of 1. Unlike min-max normalization, which scales features to a specific range, *standardization* adjusts features based on their distribution's mean and standard deviation. This method is particularly useful for algorithms that assume that input data is normally distributed or algorithms that are sensitive to variance. The formula for standardization is:

$$value_{standardized} = \frac{value_{original} - \mu}{\sigma}$$

where $value_{original}$ is each original value for a feature, μ is the average value in the feature, and σ is the feature's standard deviation.

Consider Table 5.7, which holds test scores ranging from 50 to 100 with a mean score of 75 and a standard deviation of 18.7.

TABLE 5.7   Original test scores

ID	Scores
0	50
1	60
2	70
3	80
4	90
5	100

Table 5.8 shows the same text scores standardized. The standardized values represent how many standard deviations each original score is from the mean. A score of 70 has now become –0.267, as it's slightly below the average. A score of 80 has now become 0.267, indicating that it's slightly above the average (or 0.267 standard deviations above the mean).

TABLE 5.8   Test scores standardized (Z-score)

ID	Scores	Standardized_Scores
0	50	–1.336306
1	60	–0.801784
2	70	–0.267261
3	80	0.267261
4	90	0.801784
5	100	1.336306

Transformation Functions

Not all datasets readily conform to the assumptions or requirements of specific algorithms or the statistical tests that we intend to perform. Data might exhibit skewness in its distribution, non-constant variance, or nonlinearity, all of which could potentially reduce the efficacy of our analysis. Transformation functions allow us to reshape data to meet certain conditions, so as to enhance model performance, improve interpretability, and satisfy statistical assumptions. Two commonly used transformation techniques are *log transformation* and *Box-Cox transformation*.

Log Transformation

Log transformation is a mathematical operation that applies the logarithm to each data point in a dataset. It is especially useful for handling data that exhibits an exponential growth trend, data that is skewed, or data spanning several orders of magnitude. Log transformations can compress the range of data. They can also convert an exponential growth trend into a linear one. This is known as *linearization*. Log transformations can also be used to stabilize variances across the levels of an independent variable.

The Importance of Linearization

There are several reasons why it's important to linearize data before modeling, especially when fitting the data to a linear model:

- **Model Assumptions:** Many statistical models, especially linear regression models, assume that the relationships between variables are linear. However, if the data is inherently nonlinear, using a model that assumes linearity will produce inaccurate and unreliable predictions.

- **Homoscedasticity:** Another critical assumption for linear models is homoscedasticity, which means that the variance of errors is consistent across all levels of the independent variables. Nonlinear data often leads to heteroscedasticity, where variances differ at different values of the independent variable(s).

- **Interpretability:** Linear relationships are generally easier to interpret than nonlinear ones. The coefficients of linear models can be directly interpreted in terms of the association between predictors and the response variable. This makes it easier to communicate findings to non-experts.

- **Performance:** Many optimization algorithms used in modeling, such as gradient descent, converge faster and more reliably when the relationships between variables are linear.

- **Reduced Complexity:** Linearizing data allows us to model our data using linear models. Linear models are usually simpler and often less prone to overfitting compared to nonlinear models, which tend to be more complex.

Before deciding whether to linearize data, it's crucial to understand the nature of the data, the problem at hand, and the chosen modeling technique. In some cases, nonlinear models like decision trees, random forests, or neural networks might be more appropriate than a linear model. In that case, it would not be necessary to linearize the data.

To illustrate how log transformation is used, consider a dataset that represents the population growth for a species of mice over a period of time. If the population growth is exponential, the data might look something like Table 5.9.

TABLE 5.9 Exponential population growth data for mice

ID	Population
0	10
1	100
2	1000
3	10000
4	100000
5	1000000

Building an analytic model using this data as it currently is would pose a challenge for a linear model. However, if we applied log transformation to the data, the values would become more evenly spread out and would exhibit a linear trend, as shown in Table 5.10. This log transformed version of the original data will be more amenable to linear modeling.

TABLE 5.10 Log transformed population growth data

ID	Population	Log_Population
0	10	2.302585
1	100	4.605170
2	1000	6.907755
3	10000	9.210340
4	100000	11.512925
5	1000000	13.815511

It's important to note that log transformation assumes all data points are positive. It cannot be applied directly to negative values. If negative values do exist, they can first be made positive by adding a constant, and then applying a log transformation. We must also be mindful of the fact that building a linear model based on log transformed data impacts the way we interpret the results of our model. We explore this concept in more detail in Chapter 9, "Supervised Machine Learning."

Box-Cox Transformation

The *Box-Cox transformation* is part of a family of power transformations that aim to stabilize the variance in values of a feature and to transform the values so they closely resemble a normal distribution. Box-Cox transformations are often applied to response variables prior to building a statistical model to improve the predictive power of the model. The formula for the Box-Cox transformation is:

$$y(\lambda) = \begin{cases} \dfrac{y^{\lambda} - 1}{\lambda}, & \text{if } \lambda \neq 0 \\ \ln(y), & \text{if } \lambda = 0 \end{cases}$$

where y is the response variable (or dependent variable) and λ is what is known as the transformation parameter. The value of λ affects the shape of the transformed distribution. As a result, our objective when using Box-Cox transformation is to choose the λ value that provides the best approximation of a normal distribution. It's important to note that, similar to log transformation, the Box-Cox transformation only works with positive values.

To illustrate the impact of the Box-Cox transformation on a response variable, imagine that the distribution of the values of your response variable are right skewed, similar to what is shown on the left side in Figure 5.1. Applying the Box-Cox transformation to the variable, we can reduce the skewness and make the distribution of the values more symmetric, similar to what can be seen on the right side in Figure 5.1. Doing this will improve the performance of a statistical model built using the data.

FIGURE 5.1   Sample skewed distribution before (left) and after (right) being transformed with Box-Cox transformation

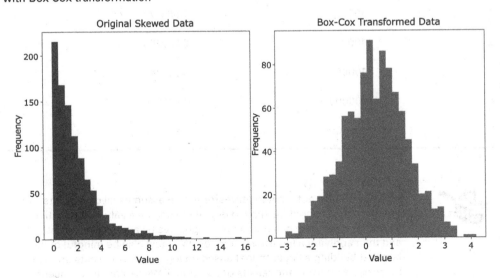

Structural Transformation

Instead of changing the value of the data we use for modeling to meet certain requirements, we can restructure how the data is represented instead. Some of the common techniques used to reshape the structure of data are *binning*, *pivoting*, and *flattening*.

Binning

Binning, which is often referred to as discretization, is the process of representing continuous data as distinct categories or intervals, known as bins. It serves multiple purposes: It can enhance data visualization, mitigate the effects of minor observation errors, or transform continuous data into a categorical form suitable for certain analytical methods. Bins are typically created by defining specific ranges within the data and then classifying each data point into a bin based on where it falls within the ranges.

For instance, consider the age values in Table 5.11. Based on these values, we can define three age ranges with categorical labels such as Minor (for ages 0 to 18), Adult (for ages 19 to 60), and Senior (for ages 61 and above).

TABLE 5.11   Sample age data

ID	Age
0	15
1	22
2	29
3	34
4	42
5	55
6	67
7	72

The original age values can then be represented by each one of the new age categories, as shown in Table 5.12.

TABLE 5.12   Binned sample age data

ID	Age	Age_Group
0	15	Minor
1	22	Adult
2	29	Adult
3	34	Adult
4	42	Adult
5	55	Adult
6	67	Senior
7	72	Senior

Binning can be particularly helpful in understanding the distribution of data, recognizing patterns in data, or preparing data for machine learning models that require categorical input features.

Pivoting

Pivoting is a data reshaping technique used to transform long-format data into wide-format data (or vice versa). By rearranging data this way, relationships and trends become more visible, facilitating easy comparison and enhanced visualization. Pivoting often involves converting the unique values of one or more columns of the original data to row indices, the unique values of another column to column labels, and the values from yet another column to cell values.

To illustrate how pivoting works, consider sales data of products A and B over two months, as shown in Table 5.13.

TABLE 5.13   Monthly sales data by product

ID	Month	Product	Sales
0	Jan	A	100
1	Jan	B	150
2	Feb	A	110
3	Feb	B	160

Pivoting the sales data by Month and Product would transform the data into a format like Table 5.14.

TABLE 5.14   Sales data pivoted by month and product

	Product	
Month	**A**	**B**
Feb	110	160
Jan	100	150

In this new format, we can much more easily compare the sales for products A and B across months.

Flattening

Flattening refers to the process of transforming hierarchical or multilevel structured data into a flat, tabular format. Data is often stored in nested structures using formats like XML and JSON, which inherently support multilevel data. While this nested format is excellent for representing complex relationships or maintaining data integrity, it can be cumbersome for analysis and querying, or when interacting with tools that expect flat, tabular input. Flattening seeks to resolve this by collapsing these nested layers into a single level, making the data more accessible and straightforward. For instance, consider this XML snippet:

```
<record>
    <name>Fred Nwanganga</name>
    <address>
        <street>Main Street</street>
        <city>South Bend</city>
        <state>Indiana</state>
    </address>
</record>
```

Flattening this data would result in a table like Table 5.15.

TABLE 5.15   Flattened XML address data

ID	name	address.street	address.city	address.state
0	Fred Nwanganga	Main Street	South Bend	Indiana

Feature Extraction

Feature extraction is an integral data transformation technique that enables us to transform high-dimensional data into a lower-dimensional form while retaining the most important information in the original data. It makes it easier to process, visualize, and analyze data using fewer variables, and without a significant loss of information. Techniques like principal component analysis (PCA), linear discriminant analysis (LDA), and independent component analysis (ICA) are among the most widely used.

PCA transforms a set of correlated variables into a set of orthogonal (uncorrelated) ones, known as principal components. These principal components are ranked by the amount of variance they capture from the original data, allowing for dimensionality reduction by limiting our focus to the most significant principal components. LDA identifies features that maximize variance between classes, and ICA decomposes signals into independent non-Gaussian (non-normally distributed) signals.

Consider an e-commerce company that wants to understand the behavior of their customers to create targeted marketing strategies. They have a dataset containing several features like age, annual income, spending score, number of purchases, average purchase amount, total purchase amount, website visits, time spent on website, and more for each customer. However, the marketing team needs to simplify the customer data into more manageable groups without losing significant information about the customer behaviors and patterns. Using a feature extraction technique, the marketing team can reduce the dimensionality of the customer data, which would allow them to leverage cluster analysis to segment each customer or to use other machine learning models to derive valuable insights into customer behavior.

For a more detailed coverage of cluster analysis and principal component analysis (PCA), see Chapter 8, "Unsupervised Machine Learning."

Data Enrichment and Augmentation

Data enrichment and augmentation refers to a set of techniques designed to enhance the quality and depth of datasets, making them more valuable and insightful for analytics and machine learning. It involves *ground truth labeling*, *feature engineering*, and several techniques for merging and combining data from disparate sources to create a richer and more comprehensive view of information.

As you prepare for the DataX exam, make note of how each of the data enrichment and augmentation techniques introduced in this section work. Know when to use them and when not to.

Ground Truth Labeling

Ground truth labeling is the process of providing an authoritative and accurate annotation or label for data. In supervised machine learning, having accurate ground truth labels is critical, as the quality of labeled data directly impacts a model's ability to learn patterns. Ground truth labeling usually involves human annotators who meticulously tag, or label, data based on expertise, observation, or defined criteria. For instance, to build an image recognition model that can differentiate between images of cats and dogs, the model would need to be exposed to a lot of previously labeled images of cats and dogs—the training data. To create such training data, human annotators would have to gather, review, and annotate as many images of cats and dogs as possible, ensuring that each image is accurately labeled.

Feature Engineering

Feature engineering is the process of creating new features from existing data. It requires domain expertise, to understand which features might be relevant, and creativity, to devise new features. Consider a sample housing dataset like what we have in Table 5.16. It includes features like the number of bedrooms, total square footage, and proximity of the house to the city center (in miles).

TABLE 5.16   Sample housing data

bedrooms	square_footage	proximity
3	1,500	1.6
4	2,000	0.3
2	900	0.8
5	5,000	0.4

Based on the data, we could create (feature engineer) a new binary feature called close_to_city that indicates whether or not a house is close to the city center based on a threshold, say within 0.5 miles (see Table 5.17).

TABLE 5.17   Sample housing data with engineered variable

bedrooms	square_footage	proximity	close_to_city
3	1,500	1.6	0
4	2,000	0.3	1
2	900	0.8	0
5	5,000	0.4	1

Geocoding

In an age when location data plays a pivotal role in a myriad of applications—from logistics to real estate—*geocoding* serves as a bridge between descriptive location information and spatial location data. Geocoding is the feature engineering technique of converting addresses or place names into geographical coordinates, typically latitude and longitude. It allows for the spatial representation and analysis of location-based data. Conversely, *reverse geocoding* is the process of converting geographic coordinates into human-readable addresses or place names.

Consider a business that wants to visualize its customer distribution on a map based on a list of customer addresses. Through geocoding, these addresses can be converted into latitude and longitude pairs, which can then be plotted on a map. For example, using geocoding, we can convert the address of the University of Notre Dame, "Holy Cross Dr, Notre Dame, IN 46556," into its respective geographical coordinates:

Latitude: 41.701345, Longitude: −86.243352

In this format, the address can then be represented spatially on a map or used in subsequent spatial analyses.

Merging and Combining Data

Merging and combining data from various sources is a powerful and often used data enrichment and augmentation technique. By integrating relevant data from different sources, it's possible to construct a multidimensional view of a subject, revealing patterns and relationships that might not be apparent from a single source. Integrating data this way, however, requires careful consideration of data consistency, alignment, and the resolution of potential conflicts.

Set operations such as a *union* or *intersection* are often used as a simple way to merge and combine data. Sometimes, a more powerful operation, such as a *join*, is used to combine two or more sources of data based on the expected or observed relationships between columns in the data.

Union

A *union* is an operation that combines two or more datasets (or tables) vertically, meaning one on top of the other. The primary condition for executing a union is that the datasets being combined must have the same number of columns and corresponding columns must have compatible data types. The result of a union operation is a new dataset that includes all rows from each of the constituent datasets, typically with duplicates removed. Consider the two datasets in Figure 5.2, one containing the names of students in a statistics course (Table A), and the other, students in a coding course (Table B). If we wish to create a single list containing names of all students from both courses, we can use a union operation to combine both datasets into one.

FIGURE 5.2   Union of Table A and Table B

Table A

ID	Name	Major	Year
1	Melissa	Economics	Freshman
2	Richard	History	Senior
3	Melinda	Nursing	Freshman
4	Alex	Engineering	Junior
5	Andrew	Physics	Sophomore

Table B

ID	Name	Major	Year
1	Fred	Art	Junior
2	Melissa	Economics	Freshman
3	Abigail	Biology	Freshman
4	Andrew	Physics	Sophomore
5	Melinda	Nursing	Freshman

Table A **UNION** Table B

ID	Name	Major	Year
1	Melissa	Economics	Freshman
2	Richard	History	Senior
3	Melinda	Nursing	Freshman
4	Alex	Engineering	Junior
5	Fred	Art	Junior
6	Abigail	Biology	Freshman
7	Andrew	Physics	Sophomore

Intersection

An *intersection* is an operation that identifies common elements or rows shared between two or more datasets (or tables) and yields a new dataset containing only the rows that are present in all of the input datasets. Imagine two datasets in Figure 5.3, one containing the names of students who participate in sports (Table A) and another containing the students who are part of the debate team (Table B). If we wish to find students who are both athletes and part of the debate team, then we use an intersection operation on the two datasets to return a single list of the students in question.

FIGURE 5.3   Intersection of Table A and Table B

Table A

ID	Name	Major	Year
1	Melissa	Economics	Freshman
2	Richard	History	Senior
3	Melinda	Nursing	Freshman
4	Alex	Engineering	Junior
5	Andrew	Physics	Sophomore

Table B

ID	Name	Major	Year
1	Fred	Art	Junior
2	Melissa	Economics	Freshman
3	Abigail	Biology	Freshman
4	Andrew	Physics	Sophomore
5	Melinda	Nursing	Freshman

Table A **INTERSECT** Table B

ID	Name	Major	Year
1	Melissa	Economics	Freshman
3	Melinda	Nursing	Freshman

Match Rates

In the context of combining and merging data, *match rate* refers to the percentage of records in one dataset that have a corresponding match in another dataset. Match rates can be a critical metric, especially when integrating or deduplicating datasets. High match rates indicate effective alignment of records across datasets, whereas low match rates may suggest inconsistencies, gaps in data, or inefficient matching criteria. For example, when comparing a company's internal customer database to a purchased mailing list, the match rate might reveal the percentage of the mailing list contacts already present in the internal database. A 70 percent match rate would mean that 70 percent of the contacts in the mailing list are already known to the company.

Joins

A join operation refers to the process of combining rows from two or more tables based on related columns known as *keys*. Keys serve as links or bridges, aligning records from distinct sources to create a coherent, unified dataset. For instance, when joining a table of customers with a table of customer orders, a CustomerID column from both tables could serve as a key, linking each order to a specific customer based on the value of the column. Join operations are fundamental in relational databases, enabling data retrieval from multiple tables as if they were a single data source. There are several types of join operations, each yielding different results based on how non-matching rows are treated. They include:

Inner Join   An inner join returns rows when there is at least one match in both tables. If a row in one table doesn't have a corresponding match in the other table, it is excluded from the results. Consider a company that wants to retrieve employee data along with department details, but only for employees assigned to a department. The HR system has two tables, as shown in Figure 5.4: an Employees table (Table A) and a Departments table (Table B). An inner join will combine data from both tables using the ID column as the key. The result will include only those employees who have a corresponding department, as shown.

FIGURE 5.4   Inner join between Table A and Table B

Table A

ID	Name
0001	John
0003	Chrissy
0005	Luna
0007	Miles

Table B

ID	Department
0004	Operations
0005	Marketing
0006	IT
0007	Sales

Table A **INNER JOIN** Table B

ID	Name	Department
0005	Luna	Marketing
0007	Miles	Sales

Left (or Left Outer) Join　Given two tables, A and B, a left join returns all rows from the left table (A) and only the matched rows from the right table (B). If the keys do not match for a particular row, the result will be a null in the column representing the right table. Consider a school that wants to list all students along with their grades, even students who have not yet received a grade. The gradebook system has two tables, as shown in Figure 5.5: a Students table (Table A) and a Grades table (Table B). A left join will list *all students*, with all available grades displayed in the Grades table.

FIGURE 5.5　Left join between Table A and Table B

Table A

ID	Name
A01	Zac
B02	Kevin
C03	Sable
D04	Michelle

Table B

ID	Grade
B02	B+
D04	A-
G06	A
I08	A-

Table A **LEFT JOIN** Table B

ID	Name	Grade
A01	Zac	-
B02	Kevin	B+
C03	Sable	-
D04	Michelle	A-

Right (or Right Outer) Join　This is the opposite of the left join. Given two tables, A and B, a right join returns all rows from the right table (B) and only the matched rows from the left table (A). If the keys do not match for a particular row, the result will be a null in the column representing the left table. Consider a business that wants to list all orders along with customer data, even if some orders are from previous customers who are no longer stored in the order management system. The system has two tables, as shown in Figure 5.6: a Customers table (Table A) and an Orders table (Table B). A right join will list *all orders*, along with customer data where available.

FIGURE 5.6　Right join between Table A and Table B

Table A

ID	Name
090	Melissa
105	Hailan
246	Caroline
358	Filip

Table B

ID	Amount
246	$10,000
300	$22,000
358	$13,000
451	$11,000

Table A **RIGHT JOIN** Table B

ID	Name	Amount
246	Caroline	$10,000
300	-	$22,000
358	Filip	$13,000
451	-	$11,000

Full (or Outer) Join　Given two tables, A and B, a full join returns rows when there is a match in either the left or the right table. It essentially combines the results of both left and right joins. Say a health system wants to analyze all records of doctors and patient appointments, even if some doctors haven't seen patients yet or some patients haven't yet been assigned a doctor. The appointment management system has two tables, as shown in Figure 5.7: a Patients table (Table A) and a Doctors table (Table B). A full outer join shows all doctors and all appointments, including doctors without patient appointments and patients without assigned doctors.

FIGURE 5.7 Full join between Table A and Table B

Table A

ID	Patient
A	Melinda
B	Alexander
C	Abigail
D	Andrew

Table B

ID	Doctor
C	Freud
D	Jackson
E	Pepper
F	Phil

Table A **FULL JOIN** Table B

ID	Patient	Doctor
A	Melinda	-
B	Alexander	-
C	Abigail	Freud
D	Andrew	Jackson
E	-	Pepper
F	-	Phil

Anti-Join   An anti-join can be thought of as the opposite of the inner join. Given tables A and B, an anti-join returns rows from Table A where no matches exist in Table B. It's essentially a way to find unmatched rows. Consider a scenario where a cleaning company wants to identify employees who have not completed any tasks. The task management system has two tables, as shown in Figure 5.8: an Employees table (Table A) and a Tasks table (Table B). An anti-join lists all employees who don't have a corresponding task in the Tasks table.

FIGURE 5.8 Anti-join between Table A and Table B

Table A

ID	Name
1	Chase
2	Luka
3	Alex
4	Ian

Table B

ID	Task
1	Sweep
4	Mop

Table A **ANTI-JOIN** Table B

ID	Name
2	Luka
3	Alex

Cross Join   A cross join returns the Cartesian product of the two tables, which means it combines each row of the first table with each row of the second table. Consider a retailer who wants to create a promotional matrix where every product in one line is paired with every product in a second line for a sale. As shown in Figure 5.9, a cross join between the products from the first line (Table A) and the products from the second line (Table B) returns a combination of products from both lines.

FIGURE 5.9   Cross join between Table A and Table B

Table A

ID	Product
A	Pens
B	Pencils
C	Notebooks
D	Bookbags

Table B

ID	Product
E	Laptops
F	Headphones
G	Tablets
H	Chargers

Table A **CROSS JOIN** Table B

Product A	Product B
Pens	Laptops
Pens	Headphones
Pens	Tablets
Pens	Chargers
Pencils	Laptops
Pencils	Headphones
Pencils	Tablets
Pencils	Chargers
Notebooks	Laptops
Notebooks	Headphones
Notebooks	Tablets
Notebooks	Chargers
Bookbags	Laptops
Bookbags	Headphones
Bookbags	Tablets
Bookbags	Chargers

Fuzzy Joins

In some scenarios, records between two datasets might not match perfectly due to various factors such as typos, abbreviations, or slight variations in naming conventions. A *fuzzy join*, unlike a regular join, which requires exact matches, allows for approximate or "fuzzy" matching of records. It employs algorithms and techniques to find potential matches between datasets based on the likelihood or degree of similarity, rather than exact equality. For instance, consider two rows with the names "Jonathan Doe" and "Jon Doe." A standard join would treat these as distinct, but a fuzzy join might recognize them as a probable match based on their similarity.

Data Cleaning

Data cleaning, often referred to as data cleansing or data scrubbing, is the process of identifying and correcting (or removing) errors and inconsistencies in data. It is undertaken to improve the quality, reliability, and accuracy of data for subsequent analysis and modeling. Without thorough data cleaning, any subsequent data analysis or modeling could lead to flawed conclusions based on misleading results.

As you prepare for the DataX exam, you should be able to apply an appropriate data cleaning technique when presented with a scenario that requires it. Make note of the common data quality issues presented in this section and the recommended data-wrangling techniques to resolve them.

Identifying Data Errors

Data errors refer to inaccuracies or discrepancies in data that can be misleading or distort analytical results. They can occur because of human error, sensor malfunction, software bugs, or data transfer issues, among other things. Data errors can generally be classified into one of two major groups—*idiosyncratic errors* and *systematic errors*.

Idiosyncratic Errors   Idiosyncratic errors occur randomly, are unpredictable, and do not follow a specific pattern. They can arise from isolated incidents or unforeseeable circumstances. For instance, if an individual mistakenly enters an incorrect value while filling out a form or if a sensor momentarily glitches due to a transient issue, the data error that occurs would be classified as idiosyncratic.

Systematic Errors   Systematic errors are consistent and follow a specific pattern. They often occur due to a persistent issue or bias in the data collection process. These errors affect data uniformly and can lead to consistently misleading results if not addressed. Consider a scale that is consistently off by 5 pounds due to calibration issues. If this scale was used to collect the weight of multiple people for analysis, it would introduce a systematic error into the dataset.

Recognizing the distinction between idiosyncratic and systematic errors is important prior to data cleansing. While the impact of idiosyncratic errors might diminish as a dataset grows larger, systematic errors consistently skew data in one direction and need to be identified and rectified to ensure accurate analysis.

Handling Inconsistent Data

Some of the most pervasive forms of data inconsistency include disparate units of measure, inconsistent date/time formats, variances in textual representation, and inconsistency in categorization. These data inconsistencies usually stem from human error, issues with data integration, regional differences, or variance in data collection protocols.

Disparate Units of Measure

When datasets incorporate measurements in different units, it's imperative to convert or standardize them to a consistent unit to ensure compatibility and accuracy. For instance, if you're analyzing a dataset with temperatures recorded in both Celsius and Fahrenheit, direct comparisons or aggregations would be misleading without unit standardization. Before analysis you would need to convert all values to either Celsius or Fahrenheit.

Inconsistent Data/Time Formats

Date and time formats can vary widely based on regional settings, software defaults, or personal preferences. For reliable data analysis, it's essential that all date/time data adhere to a consistent format. This standardization can involve ensuring that all date entries follow a consistent format such as YYYY-MM-DD, that time zones are aligned, or that all times are represented in a 24-hour format. Consider a dataset in which one entry records the date in the format as 02/01/2024 and another as January 2, 2024. While both represent the same day, their differing formats can cause issues when sorting, filtering, or aggregating. Before analysis, we would need to standardize all date values to the same format, such as 2024-01-02.

Textual Inconsistencies

Textual inconsistencies occur in data when similar or identical entities have multiple representations. Common examples include spelling errors, differences in capitalization, the use of special characters, or variations in abbreviation. For example, a company name like McDonald's might appear in a dataset as Mcdonalds, Mc Donald's, or even MacDonald's. Such variations, while seemingly trivial, can obstruct data analysis, leading to skewed aggregations or misleading insights. Addressing these inconsistencies requires the use of techniques such as string normalization (e.g., converting all text to lowercase), string matching, or more sophisticated approaches like Levenshtein distance calculations, which measure the "distance" between two strings. Textual inconsistencies can also be prevented by limiting variability in data entry with the use of drop-down menus in place of free text, where appropriate.

Levenshtein Distance

The Levenshtein distance, also known as the "edit distance," is a measure of the similarity between two strings. It is defined as the minimum number of single-character edits (insertions, deletions, or substitutions) required to change one string into the other. For example, the Levenshtein distance between **kitten** and **sitting** is 3:

1. kitten → sitten (replace k with s)
2. sitten → sittin (replace e with i)
3. sittin → sitting (insert g at the end)

The Levenshtein distance between flaw and lawn is 2:

1. flaw → law (delete f)
2. law → lawn (insert n at the end)

The Levenshtein distance between apple and apple (the same string) is 0 since no changes are needed.

The Levenshtein distance has a wide range of applications in fields such as computational biology, natural language processing, and spell checking, to name a few.

Categorical Inconsistencies

Categorical inconsistency in data often arises from variations in naming convention or representation for identical categories within a dataset. Such inconsistencies can stem from a variety of factors, including human error during data entry, merging data from diverse sources, or simply the absence of standardized data entry protocols.

Consider a column that holds customer contact method preferences. In an ideal scenario, the column should have a distinct set of expected values such as Email, Phone, and Mail. However, upon close inspection, we may find entries such as Cell Phone, Home Phone, Work Email, Daytime Number, and so forth. To handle these inconsistencies, we would need to first define a standard set of categories. Then, we'd map the varied entries to these standard categories. This might involve manual curation, especially when domain expertise is required, making use of joins or even clustering techniques to group similar categories together.

Addressing Duplicate Data

Duplicate data refers to repeated entries within a dataset that don't add new information, but rather inflate record counts and distort analytical outcomes. There are several common causes of duplicate data. They include but are not limited to merging data from multiple sources, human error during data entry, and software glitches. Regardless of the origin, it's essential to identify and manage duplicate data to maintain data integrity.

To illustrate how to effectively address duplicate data, consider a dataset of registered users for an online platform. Suppose Jane Doe registers twice using the same email but with different usernames—once as JaneD and later as JDoe. At face value, these two entries may seem like two distinct users, but further examination would reveal that they share the same email, indicating a probable duplication.

To effectively handle the duplicate data in this scenario and others like it, a structured approach is recommended:

1. The first step is to determine which column or set of columns should uniquely define a record. In our example, the email address might serve as a unique identifier. However, oftentimes a combination of fields might be necessary to uniquely identify a record, such as First Name, Last Name, and Date of Birth.

2. With the unique identifier(s) determined, the next step is to search for duplicate entries and flag duplicate rows based on the selected columns.

3. Once duplicates are identified, decide on an action. If the duplicate data doesn't offer any new information, it might be best to simply remove it. However, duplicates might contain bits of unique data. For example, JaneD might have a phone number listed but no address, while JDoe might have an address. In such a scenario, merging the two records into one comprehensive entry would be the ideal approach.

4. Once resolved, to avoid future incidences of duplicate data, implement checks and constraints during data entry and as part of the data integration process when merging data from different sources.

Resolving Missing Data

Missing data refers to the absence of values in a dataset where they would be expected. There are a myriad of reasons for missingness, from individuals choosing not to answer specific survey questions to sensor malfunctioning during data collection. Regardless of the cause, missing data can compromise the reliability and validity of analytic models and can lead to potentially misleading conclusions.

There are several approaches to resolve missing data, two of which are listed here:

- **Deletion:** One of the simplest methods to handle missing data is to remove records with missing values. While this approach is quick and reduces data complexity, it might not be ideal if the dataset is small, or if it results in a significant loss of data.

- **Flagging:** Another simple approach is to create an additional column to flag records with missing values. This is useful in scenarios where the fact that data is missing is informative in itself.

In most scenarios, the better approach is usually one of several *imputation* methods. Imputation is the process of replacing missing, incomplete, or erroneous values within a dataset with substituted values. The method of imputation chosen often depends on the nature of the data and the reason for the missingness:

- **Mean/Median/Mode Imputation:** For numerical data, we can replace missing values with the mean or median (to reduce the impact of outliers) of the observed values. For categorical data, we replace missing values with the mode (or most frequent category) instead.

- **Interpolation and Extrapolation:** For ordered data, like time-series data, interpolation and extrapolation methods can be used to estimate the missing value based on its neighbors. Interpolation estimates the missing value using available data points in the same vicinity, whereas extrapolation ventures outside the known data range.

- **Model-Based Imputation:** This approach involves training a machine learning model like linear regression, k-nearest neighbors, decision trees, or even deep neural networks on the portion of the data without missing values to predict and impute the missing values.

- **Stochastic Imputation:** This is an extension of the model-based approach. Instead of imputing a missing value directly, randomness is added to the prediction to introduce variability in the imputation, making the imputation process less deterministic.

- **Multiple Imputation by Chained Equations (MICE):** Instead of predicting a single value as a substitute for missing data, MICE uses a model-based approach to create different plausible imputed datasets. These datasets can then be used for analysis separately, after which results are pooled.

- **Hot-Deck Imputation:** This method involves randomly choosing a value from an observed data point to replace the missing value. The selected observed value typically comes from a similar record in the dataset.

In all imputation methods, it's crucial to understand the potential biases introduced and the assumptions made about the missing data. For example, mean imputation could artificially decrease the variance or standard deviation of a feature with a lot of missing values. After imputation, it's important to evaluate the data to make sure the imputed values align well with the observed data. It's also important to maintain awareness of the impact of imputation on the subsequent analyses and the conclusions drawn from the data.

Dealing with Outliers

Outliers are data points that deviate significantly from the typical pattern observed in the rest of the data. The presence of outliers can be a result of genuine variations in data, or they can be erroneous data points. Whether outliers are informative or detrimental to data analysis depends on the context and the nature of the analysis.

There are several ways to detect outliers in data. Plots such as box plots, scatter plots, or histograms can visually highlight outliers in data. A statistical method such as a Z-score can also be used to identify outlier data. Z-scores quantify how far away a data point is from the mean. A common threshold for outliers is a Z-score above 3 or below –3. Similarly, the interquartile range (IQR) for a dataset can be used to define outliers. A typical rule of thumb is to treat values higher than the third quartile plus 1.5 × IQR range as outliers and values below the first quartile minus 1.5 × IQR range as outliers.

Once detected, outliers must be evaluated to determine the cause. Whether outlier data is due to data entry or measurement error or whether the outlier data is a genuine extreme value determines how we deal with it using one or more of the following approaches:

- **Removal:** In some cases, outright removal of outliers is the best approach. This is especially so if they are caused by errors in data entry or collection. However, caution should be exercised, as this is a destructive approach that reduces the size of the data and can potentially remove valuable insights.

- **Transformation:** Using a data transformation technique such as log transformation can minimize the impact of outliers by pulling in extreme values, making the data more uniform or normally distributed.

- **Separate Treatment:** In some scenarios, we can gain additional insights from our data by treating outliers separately. For instance, in a sales dataset, exceptionally high sales values might be the result of seasonal sales or promotional offers. Such outlier data can provide unique insights and may need to be analyzed separately rather than being removed or transformed.

- **Winsorization:** One of the most systematic methods to handle outliers is *winsorization*. Instead of removing outliers, which reduces the data size and might discard valuable information, winsorization modifies these extreme values, making them less extreme. The process involves setting boundaries, such as the 5th and 95th percentiles. Data points below the 5th percentile are replaced with the value at the 5th percentile, and data points above the 95th percentile are replaced with the value at the 95th percentile. The beauty of winsorization lies in its ability to retain the structure and size of a dataset while curtailing the undue influence of extreme values.

- **Robust Statistical Methods:** Another approach to dealing with outliers is to use robust statistical methods or models that are resistant to outliers, such as decision trees, robust regression models, and ensemble methods. This approach is useful when it's difficult to determine whether an outlier represents a genuine observation or an error.

When handling outliers, the overarching goal is to ensure the integrity and reliability of the subsequent analysis. The chosen treatment method should align with the nature of the data, the cause of the outlier, and the objective of the analysis. It's also essential to be transparent about any changes made to the original data due to outliers, especially when presenting findings or drawing conclusions.

Handling Class Imbalance

Supervised machine learning algorithms learn to predict an outcome based on previously labeled historical data known as training data. The more training examples an algorithm gets, the better it does at learning the patterns in the data that lead to a particular outcome. In some scenarios the predicted outcome rarely occurs, which means that examples of the outcome are infrequent in the training data. This results in what is known as *class imbalance*.

For instance, consider that we intend to build a model that can flag financial transactions as either fraudulent or legitimate based on certain patterns in the data. Historically, the number of financial transactions that can be considered fraudulent is significantly smaller than the number of legitimate transactions. This imbalance would also be reflected in any training data sourced from historical transactions.

There are two primary challenges with class imbalance. The first has to do with the effectiveness of the learning process. Because there are fewer examples of the minority class (the outcome that occurs the least) in the training data, it is more challenging for a model to effectively learn the patterns that differentiate them from those associated with the majority class (the outcome that occurs more frequently).

The second challenge with class imbalance has to do with the reliability of performance metrics. Let's assume that 99 percent of all financial transactions are legitimate (the majority class). If a model simply predicted the majority class for all future transactions, it would achieve an accuracy of 99 percent. Despite being very "accurate," such a model would be of little practical use, as it would fail to capture the minority, yet crucial, class. This is known as the *accuracy paradox*. The predictive accuracy of the model would simply reflect the underlying class distribution of the data.

There are several approaches to handling class imbalance:

Collect more data.   To minimize the imbalance in the distribution between the majority and minority classes, we can attempt to collect more examples of the minority class.

Change the performance metric.   Since we know that predictive accuracy can be misleading when working with imbalanced data, we can use other measures of performance when evaluating a model trained against imbalanced data. Metrics like precision, recall, and the area under the receiver operating characteristic (ROC) curve provide a more holistic view of a model's performance. These metrics are covered in Chapter 6, "Modeling and Evaluation."

Choose a robust algorithm.   Certain machine learning algorithms are particularly sensitive to class imbalance, while others are not. When training a model on imbalanced data, we should consider algorithms such as decision trees and random forest, which are better at handling class imbalance. Some algorithms also allow us to set class weights, which can be used to encourage a model to minimize the misclassification of the minority class.

Resample the data.   We can also deal with class imbalance by attempting to balance the distribution of outcomes in the data. This is typically done by *undersampling* the majority class or *oversampling* the minority class.

Undersampling

Undersampling involves reducing the number of examples in the majority class so that it more closely aligns with the number of examples in the minority class. It's a simple and valuable technique for large datasets, where reducing the number of examples in the data does not result in substantial loss of information. With the simplicity of undersampling comes the risk of discarding valuable data, which could introduce bias and skew the results of the model.

There are several approaches to undersampling. One of them is *random undersampling*. As the name suggests, random undersampling involves randomly discarding examples from the majority class. A more nuanced approach is *cluster-based undersampling*. This approach uses clustering to group similar instances, ensuring that only redundant data points within each cluster are discarded. Another approach is to use what are known as *Tomek links*, which is a nearest neighbors approach, to identify and remove certain majority class examples.

Oversampling

Oversampling involves increasing the number of instances in the minority class by replicating them or by generating synthetic examples. It's a particularly useful approach in scenarios where the training data is limited. Unlike undersampling, oversampling has the advantage that all the original data is retained. However, by replicating examples of the minority class, oversampling does introduce the risk of overfitting (see Chapter 6).

Random oversampling is the simplest oversampling approach. It involves randomly duplicating copies of examples from the minority class. A more sophisticated approach is *SMOTE (synthetic minority oversampling technique)*. SMOTE involves the creation of synthetic examples based on the differences between existing data points and their neighbors. A variant of SMOTE is *ADASYN (adaptive synthetic sampling)*. ADASYN is an adaptive approach that generates more synthetic instances in regions where a model is expected to perform poorly, resulting in more focused improvement of a model's performance on difficult regions of the data. Care must be taken when using synthetic sampling techniques because they can lead to overfitting if the synthetic examples generated are too numerous or not diverse enough.

Summary

Data transformation improves the consistency and usability of data by converting it from one form to another. It includes various methods like encoding, scaling, normalizing, value transformation, structural changes, and feature extraction.

Data enrichment and augmentation involves techniques that enhance the quality of data such as ground truth labeling, feature engineering, and merging and combining data from different sources.

Merging and combining data involves integrating multiple data sources to form a comprehensive view, revealing otherwise hidden patterns and relationships. Simple set operations like unions and intersections vertically combine datasets or identify shared rows, respectively, while join operations combine rows from multiple tables based on key columns.

Data cleaning is a crucial step in ensuring the integrity of data analysis. It involves the detection, alteration, or deletion of faulty, inconsistent, or anomalous data points.

Handling inconsistent data involves addressing disparities in units of measure, standardizing date/time formats, rectifying textual inconsistencies, and resolving categorical variances.

Duplicate data inflates records and skews analytics. Upon detection, duplicates can be either removed or merged, depending on whether they hold unique information. Proactively implementing data entry checks and constraints during data collection and integration can minimize future occurrences of duplicate data.

Handling missing data is essential for reliable analytics. It includes simple techniques like deletion or flagging and advanced imputation methods such as using average values, applying machine learning models, generating multiple plausible datasets, or randomly selecting similar observed values.

Addressing outliers involves strategies based on their cause: removal for errors in data collection, transformation to normalize data, separate treatment for potentially insightful data, winsorization to adjust extreme values while maintaining data structure, or robust statistical methods for ambiguous cases.

Class imbalance in supervised machine learning poses challenges due to unequal representation of outcomes in training data, affecting both the learning process and the reliability of performance metrics. Class imbalance is addressed through strategies like collecting more data, using more suitable performance metrics, choosing robust algorithms, and resampling data via undersampling or oversampling.

Exam Essentials

Explain the importance of data processing and preparation in the data science lifecycle. Data processing and preparation is a foundational stage in the data science lifecycle that directly impacts the quality of insights derived. It involves transforming raw, messy data into structured, clean, enriched, and balanced data. Without proper data processing and preparation, even the most advanced algorithms and models would struggle to produce accurate, reliable, and meaningful results.

Understand how encoding, scaling, normalization, transformation functions, and structural transformation are used for data transformation. Encoding converts categorical data into numerical form, with techniques like one-hot encoding and label encoding. Scaling and normalization adjust the scales of numerical features for consistency, using methods like min-max normalization and standardization. Transformation functions like log transformation and Box-Cox transformation reshape data to meet algorithm assumptions or improve model performance, addressing issues like skewness or nonlinearity. Structural transformation techniques like binning, pivoting, and flattening are used to make data more suitable for specific analytical or visualization purposes.

Explain when to use a union, intersection, or join operation. Union, intersection, and join operations serve distinct purposes in data manipulation: Union combines datasets with the same structure into one, useful for aggregating similar data from different sources; intersection identifies common records between datasets, ideal for finding exact similarities across different groups; and joins merge datasets based on a key, crucial for retrieving interconnected data from separate tables in a database. The choice among them hinges on the layout of your data and your analytical goals—whether to aggregate, find commonalities, or explore relationships within your data.

Understand the difference between idiosyncratic and systemic errors. Idiosyncratic errors are random and unpredictable, with no fixed pattern, often arising from isolated mishaps or unforeseen glitches. Systematic errors, however, are uniform and recur consistently, usually due to an inherent bias or flaw in the data-gathering process. The key distinction lies in the nature of their occurrence: although idiosyncratic errors are sporadic and diminish in larger datasets, systematic errors present a consistent deviation, posing a continuous threat to data integrity unless specifically identified and corrected.

Explain how to handle inconsistent data, duplicate data, missing data, and outlier data. Resolving inconsistencies requires standardizing formats and measurements; duplicate entries must be identified and either merged or purged; missing data calls for methods ranging from deletion to sophisticated imputation techniques, depending on the context and data type; and outliers necessitate careful scrutiny, with responses varying from removal to statistical adjustments, all depending on whether they represent true data points or anomalies. Each approach demands a nuanced understanding of the nature of the data and the intended analysis.

Understand what class imbalance is and how to handle it.   Class imbalance in supervised machine learning arises when there's a disparity between class examples in training data, affecting model performance and metric reliability. Addressing this involves gathering more data for the minority class, adopting metrics like precision and recall instead of mere accuracy, utilizing algorithms less sensitive to imbalance, and resampling data through methods like undersampling (reducing majority class instances) and oversampling (increasing minority class instances or generating synthetic ones). Properly implementing these strategies can enhance model effectiveness on imbalanced datasets.

Review Questions

1. What is the primary purpose of data transformation?
   A. To convert data into a specific format or structure
   B. To combine different sources of data
   C. To improve the quality of data
   D. To reduce the complexity of data

2. What potential issue could arise from using label encoding on categorical data?
   A. Introduction of an artificial order
   B. Conversion of categories to binary format
   C. Duplication of categories
   D. Loss of data during transformation

3. In the context of machine learning, why is scaling and normalization of features important?
   A. It increases data volume.
   B. It enhances the interpretation and visualization of data.
   C. It prevents a single feature from disproportionately influencing a model.
   D. It compresses data storage.

4. What is a significant limitation of the Box-Cox transformation?
   A. It can only be applied to negative values.
   B. It linearizes only noncontinuous data.
   C. It can only be applied to positive values.
   D. It is not suitable for machine learning algorithms.

5. As a data scientist for a real estate company, you're analyzing property data. How could you use feature engineering to enhance this dataset for a more insightful analysis?
   A. By removing redundant property listings
   B. By gathering data from additional real estate agencies
   C. By generating a new feature, like "total square footage above ground" from existing data
   D. By flattening JSON data scraped from competitor real estate

6. Your logistics company relies heavily on location data. How could geocoding be utilized to enhance your operational efficiency?
   A. By importing geographical coordinates from public data sources
   B. By importing address data from postal route data
   C. By consolidating multiple datasets into a single database
   D. By converting warehouse addresses into geographical coordinates

7. In the process of data reconciliation, you notice some vendor records in one database that don't have corresponding entries in another. You suspect that there are more. Which type of join would help you identify the remaining unmatched records?

   A. A left join

   B. An inner join

   C. An anti-join

   D. A cross join

8. What does log transformation specifically help with in data preparation?

   A. Addressing skewness and stabilizing variances

   B. Removing outliers in data

   C. Assigning integer values to categories

   D. Creating a visual representation of data

9. Your dataset has several missing values. What's a potential risk of simply deleting records with these missing values?

   A. Deleting data is a time-consuming process.

   B. Losing valuable insights or significant data is possible.

   C. It will make the dataset more difficult to visualize.

   D. No risk. It's always the recommended approach.

10. Which of these techniques is primarily used for reducing the dimensionality of data?

   A. Feature engineering

   B. Pivoting

   C. Feature extraction

   D. Flattening

11. A dataset contains distance measures in both miles and kilometers. What should be done before this data is analyzed?

   A. Remove the records with the distance measured in miles.

   B. Convert all records to a single unit of measurement.

   C. Analyze the data separately in miles and then by kilometers.

   D. Remove the records with the distance measured in kilometers.

12. A company collects data on how users find their website. They expect options like Search Engine, Social Media, Email, and Referral. However, when analyzing the data, they come across entries such as Google, Facebook, Newsletter, and Friend. What is this an example of?

   A. Systematic error

   B. Categorical inconsistency

   C. Duplicate data

   D. Textual inconsistency

13. What is a potential downside of undersampling for handling class imbalance?

   A. It leads to overfitting by creating synthetic examples.

   B. It makes the model computationally expensive.

   C. It increases the number of examples in the minority class.

   D. It can discard potentially important information from the majority class.

14. For an imbalanced dataset, why can accuracy be considered a misleading metric?

   A. It always underestimates model performance.

   B. It may simply reflect the class distribution.

   C. It overcomplicates the evaluation process.

   D. It is computationally too demanding to calculate.

15. During the data cleaning process, you identify that a sensor malfunctioned, leading to systematic errors in your dataset. What is the potential impact of these errors if not corrected?

   A. They will cancel each other out over time.

   B. They will likely lead to random inaccuracies in analysis.

   C. They could consistently skew data.

   D. They have no impact on the analysis.

16. What is the purpose of binning in data transformation?

   A. It flattens data into XML format.

   B. It increases the variance among data features.

   C. It categorizes continuous data.

   D. It standardizes the mean and variance of data.

17. When analyzing a dataset, you notice that some outliers could be genuine extreme values while others are errors. Which of these approaches is most appropriate to handle these outliers?

   A. Remove the outliers from the data.

   B. Ignore the outliers during analysis.

   C. Apply log transformation to minimize the impact of all outliers.

   D. Apply winsorization to adjust extreme values.

18. Your school administration has separate lists for students who have registered for music and art classes. Which of these conditions must be met to combine these lists into one comprehensive list using a union operation?

   A. Both lists must originate from the same source.

   B. Both lists must have the same number of columns with compatible data types.

   C. Both lists must have the same number of rows with compatible data types.

   D. Both lists must have the same number of columns and originate from the same source.

19. Why is class imbalance in training data a problem for supervised machine learning algorithms?

   A. It makes learning patterns that differentiate the minority class from the majority class difficult.

   B. It increases the computational time that it takes the algorithm to learn the difference between the minority and majority classes.

   C. It forces the model to overfit to the minority class.

   D. It automatically makes the model less accurate.

20. Which of these is a benefit of linearizing data before modeling?

   A. It simplifies data augmentation.

   B. It enhances interpretability.

   C. It increases the data processing speed.

   D. It reduces the need for data cleaning.

Chapter

6

Modeling and Evaluation

THE COMPTIA DATAX EXAM OBJECTIVES COVERED IN THIS CHAPTER INCLUDE:

✓ **Domain 1: Mathematics and Statistics**

- 1.1 Given a scenario, apply the appropriate statistical method or concept.

- 1.4 Compare and contrast various types of temporal models.

✓ **Domain 3: Machine Learning**

- 3.1 Given a scenario, apply foundational machine learning concepts.

Following data processing and preparation is the fourth phase in the data science lifecycle—modeling and evaluation. This stage focuses on constructing and evaluating predictive models that can accurately reflect the trends and patterns discovered during the data exploration and preparation phases. In this chapter, we delve into the different types of predictive models, which include regressors, classifiers, and temporal models. We'll explore the essential aspects of model design, such as understanding what a loss function is, the crucial balance between bias and variance errors, and the intricacies of hyperparameter tuning. We'll also discuss how to systematically evaluate the performance of regression and classification models, the challenges in evaluating models, and strategies to effectively interpret the performance evaluation results.

Types of Models

A *model* is a mathematical representation or computational algorithm that is used to infer relationships, recognize trends, or predict future outcomes based on historical data. There are various types of models in data science. The type of model we build is dependent on the nature of the data, the problem to be solved, and/or the desired outcome. Regressors, classifiers, and temporal models are three common types of what are known as predictive models.

As you prepare for the DataX exam, you should be able to compare and contrast various types of predictive models. Make note of the differences and similarities between the models introduced in this section and when to use them.

Regressors

Regressors are analytic models specifically constructed for tackling *regression* problems. Regression problems are problems where the primary objective is to predict a continuous target variable based on the input features. The input variables are commonly referred to as *independent variables* or *predictors*, while the output variable is often referred to as the *dependent variable* or *response*.

One of the most elementary and extensively used regression techniques is *linear regression*. Linear regression presumes that a linear relationship exists in the data between the independent variables and the dependent variable. In cases where the relationship between the independent and dependent variables is intricate or hierarchical, tree-based methods such as *decision trees* and *random forests* ensembles are usually more effective.

Regression models are used in a wide variety of domains. In finance, they can be used to forecast stock prices; in real estate, they can help estimate housing prices; within healthcare, they can predict disease outbreaks; and in sports, they are used to forecast player performance and ticket sales.

See Chapter 9, "Supervised Machine Learning," for a more detailed introduction to linear regression, decision trees, random forests, and other supervised machine learning models.

Classifiers

Classifiers are analytic models designed to identify the class to which a new observation belongs based on a set of input variables. Essentially, classifiers predict a categorical dependent variable using a set of independent variables. This is known as *classification*. Classifiers can be categorized as either binary or multiclass depending on the number of unique values in the dependent variable.

Binary classifiers allow us to categorize data into one of two distinct classes. This is the simplest approach to classification and includes examples such as determining whether a tumor is malignant or benign, labeling an email as either spam or non-spam, or deciding if a bank transaction is fraudulent or legitimate.

On the other hand, *multiclass classifiers* help us with scenarios where there are three or more potential categories into which a data point can be classified. Examples of multiclass classification include identifying handwritten letters based on an image or assigning predefined topic labels to a set of news articles based on the text.

Temporal Models

Temporal models, often referred to as sequence models, are a class of analytical models used for predicting future values or understanding patterns within data that is sequential or time ordered. These types of models are distinct from typical regression or classification models because they specifically account for the dynamic component of time, where the order of data points is crucial for accurate analysis and prediction.

Time-Series Analysis

Time-series models are temporal models that are focused on forecasting the future values of a series based on the patterns identified in the historical data. These models are useful in any domain where quantitative data is collected sequentially over time, such as financial markets, epidemiology, and weather forecasting. Some of the most used time-series techniques are:

- *Autoregressive (AR) Models*: These are statistical models that are based on the concept that the current value in a time series can be explained by a linear combination of its previous values. Autoregressive models assume that historical data is stationary, which means that the mean and variance is constant over time. They are useful in predicting nonseasonal trends such as trends in the financial market, economic indicators, or (non-seasonal) environmental patterns.

- *Moving Average (MA) Models*: Unlike autoregressive models that leverage past observations to make future predictions, MA models predict future data based on past forecast errors. The idea is that random errors are propagated to future values and can be used to improve predictions. An MA model assumes that any value in a time series is generally related to a weighted sum of past errors.

- *Autoregressive Integrated Moving Average (ARIMA) Models*: ARIMA models combine elements of both AR and MA models and can handle nonstationary data (where means and variances fluctuate over time) by differencing. ARIMA models *are* particularly powerful because by differencing and combining the features of both autoregressive and moving average models, they can capture a wide range of behaviors in data.

Survival Analysis

Survival analysis models are temporal models that deal with predicting the time until an event of interest or a certain endpoint occurs. There are two primary approaches to survival analysis: parametric and nonparametric. Each approach has its advantages and disadvantages, and the choice between them depends on various factors such as the availability of data, the presence of censoring, and the specific objectives of the analysis.

Parametric Survival Analysis

Parametric survival analysis involves specifying a particular statistical distribution that survival times are assumed to follow. Common distributions used in parametric survival analysis include the exponential, Weibull, log-normal, and gamma distributions. The choice of distribution shapes the survival function, which is used to estimate various quantities of interest in the analysis, such as the median survival time.

Parametric survival analysis is beneficial in that it provides an efficient and precise estimate of survival times when the underlying assumptions are appropriate. It also allows for extrapolation beyond the observed data range, which can be useful for predicting survival probabilities at times beyond the last observed event time. Additionally, parametric survival analysis models can accommodate complex, time-dependent covariates and scenarios.

The major drawback to parametric survival analysis is that the entire analysis hinges on the assumption that the data follows a specified distribution. If this assumption is incorrect, then the model can provide biased estimates, which can lead to incorrect conclusions.

Nonparametric Survival Analysis

Nonparametric survival analysis makes very few assumptions about the form of the survival distribution. Instead, a survival function is estimated directly from the observed data. Because they don't make assumptions about the data, nonparametric survival analysis methods are more versatile and broadly applicable. However, they are limited in their ability to make predictions beyond the range of the observed data (i.e., no extrapolation). They also often require large sample sizes to make reliable predictions.

In practice, the choice between parametric and nonparametric survival analysis involves a trade-off between model assumptions and flexibility. Researchers might use nonparametric methods for an initial analysis to understand the data without making strong assumptions. If there's reason to believe that survival times follow a specific distribution, or if there's a need to predict survival beyond the range of the data, parametric methods might be preferred. Often, a combination of approaches is used in comprehensive survival analysis.

The Challenge of Censoring in Survival Analysis

A unique challenge in survival analysis is censoring, which is when the exact time of an event is unknown for certain individuals in the study. As illustrated here, there are several ways in which censoring can manifest:

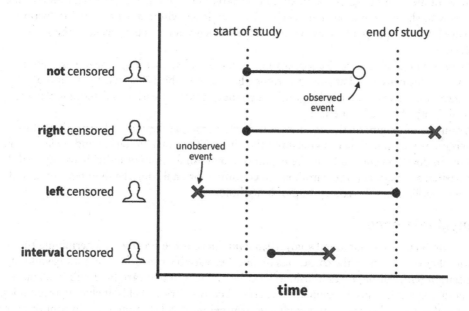

- **Right censoring** occurs when the study ends before the event occurs for an individual. For example, a study on patient survival might end before some patients experience a relapse of the disease. Essentially, we know the event didn't occur up to a certain time but don't know when (or if) it will occur afterward.

> - **Left censoring** arises when the event starts before the observation window, making the exact starting point elusive. For instance, if cancer recurrence is detected at a three-month check but might have begun earlier, the exact time is left censored because we do not know exactly when it recurred.
>
> - **Interval censoring** is when event times fall between two observation points. For example, if a patient is disease-free at three months but passes away before the six-month checkup, the exact time of recurrence is unknown and is thus interval censored.
>
> In all these cases, censoring introduces uncertainties that survival analysis techniques must account for to provide reliable predictions and insights.

Longitudinal Studies

A *longitudinal study* is a research approach that involves conducting repeated observations of the same subjects over a period. The period could span several years to several decades. Longitudinal studies are used to analyze the dynamics of change and continuity across the life span of a subject or subjects being studied. Unlike cross-sectional studies, which analyze a population at a single point in time, longitudinal studies offer valuable insights by tracking the development and progression of specific variables in *cohorts*. A cohort is a group of individuals who share a common characteristic or experience within a defined period (people who are born in a particular year, people who experience a particular event at the same time, etc.).

By observing the same subjects over time, longitudinal studies help researchers better understand the causes and effects of various phenomena. This is because the temporal sequence of events is clearer in longitudinal studies, making it easier to determine whether a cause did in fact precede an effect.

Examples of longitudinal studies include tracking the development of a group of children born at the same time to understand the effects of various biological and social factors on human development, studying the health outcomes of a group of individuals exposed to a particular treatment or environmental condition, or analyzing the long-term effects of economic policies on the same group of households.

Causal Inference

When conducting a longitudinal study, *causal inference* is the process of determining the impact that one variable (the cause) has on another variable (the effect). It goes beyond mere association (correlation) by establishing whether changes in one variable result in changes to another variable. This determination is crucial across various fields, including economics, epidemiology, social sciences, and medicine, as it helps in understanding the impact of different factors, policies, treatments, or interventions.

Several methodologies and analytical techniques are employed in the pursuit of causal inference. They include:

- **Counterfactuals:** These are hypothetical scenarios used to imagine what would have happened to a group of individuals under an alternative set of circumstances—for example, evaluating what would have happened to patients if they had not received a particular treatment.

- **Randomized Controlled Trials (RCTs):** This is an approach in which subjects or participants in a study are randomly assigned to one of two groups. One group is known as the treatment group and the other is known as the control group. Subjects in the treatment group receive an intervention or treatment, while subjects in the control group do not. Randomly splitting participants in this way ensures that both observed and unobserved confounding variables are evenly distributed between the groups, which helps provide a more reliable basis for inferring causality from the treatment to the outcome.

- **Difference-in-Differences (DiD):** This is another statistical technique commonly used to evaluate the effect of a treatment, policy change, or intervention. It's often employed when randomization is not possible. DiD estimates causal effects by comparing the differences before and after the treatment, on both the control and the treatment groups. It assumes that in the absence of the treatment, the difference between the two groups would have remained constant over time. This is known as the "parallel trends assumption."

- **A/B Testing:** Also known as split testing or treatment effect testing, A/B testing is a randomized experiment with two variants, A and B, which are the control and treatment in the context of causal inference. It's widely used in industries like marketing, software development, and healthcare to compare two versions of a product or element (like a web page) to determine which performs better in terms of a specific outcome metric. A/B testing directly facilitates causal inference by controlling all other variables and randomly assigning participants to each group, ensuring any difference in outcome is attributable to the treatment.

- **Causal Diagrams:** These are visual tools used in causal inference to help researchers conceptualize and communicate assumptions about the causal structure among variables. One of the most common is the *directed acyclic graph (DAG)*, which illustrates the directed relationships (arrows) between variables (nodes). They are crucial for determining the variables to control when estimating causal effects, thus guiding the modeling strategy. For example, the DAG in Figure 6.1 helps us understand the multiple factors that could influence lung cancer. Looking at one set of connections, we see that genetics might increase the propensity to smoke and also directly affect the likelihood of developing lung cancer.

FIGURE 6.1   Directed acyclic graph showing the relationships between smoking, lung cancer, and other factors

DAG for Smoking, Lung Cancer, and Other Factors

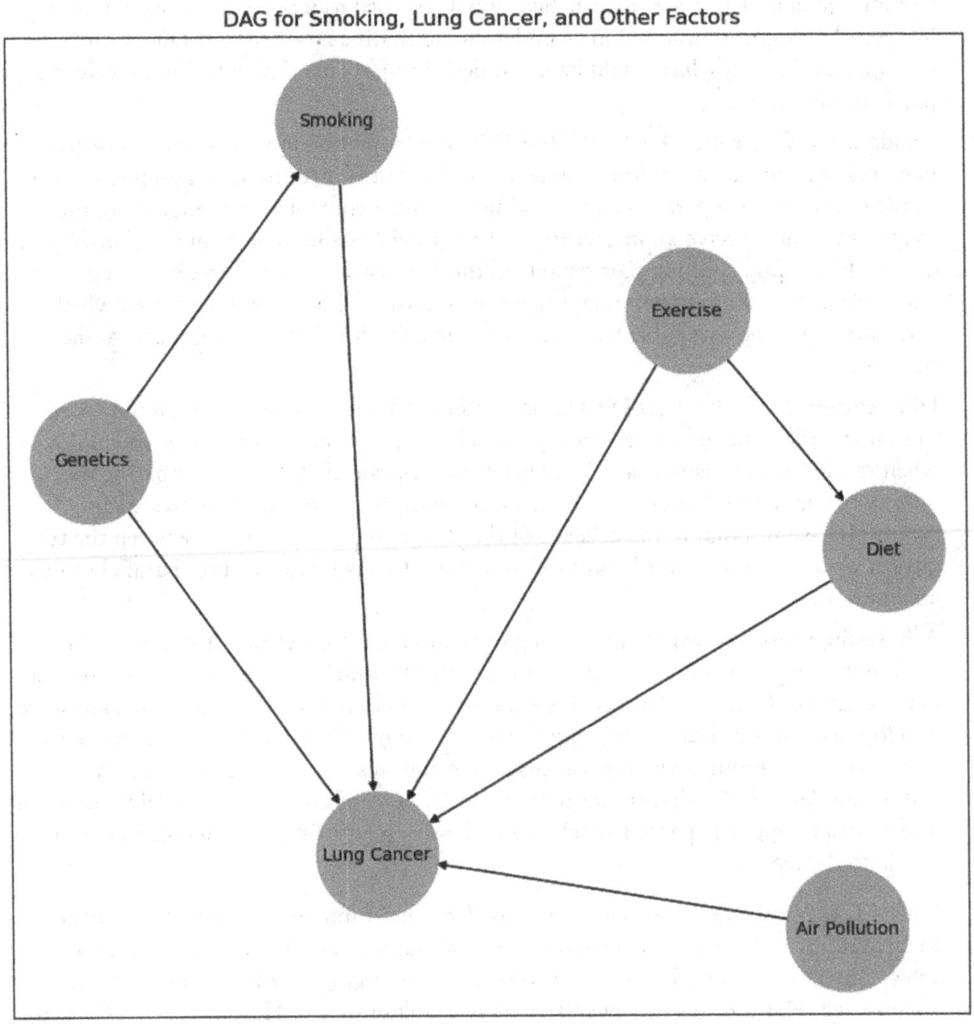

Real World Scenario

Beware of Confounders

A confounding factor, often simply termed a *confounder,* is a third variable in a study that can falsely distort or mask the relationship between the independent variable (or predictor) and the dependent variable (or outcome). This can lead to erroneous conclusions about the association between the predictor and the outcome.

Consider a study investigating the relationship between coffee consumption (predictor) and productivity (outcome). The initial data analysis might suggest that individuals who drink more coffee tend to have lower productivity levels. This could lead to the preliminary conclusion that coffee consumption directly reduces productivity.

However, let's consider the role of sleep quality (confounder) in this relationship. Sleep quality could influence both coffee consumption and productivity. Individuals who have poor sleep quality might drink more coffee to counteract their tiredness, and poor sleep could independently decrease productivity due to fatigue. Conversely, individuals with better sleep quality are both more productive and less inclined to consume large amounts of coffee, as they are already well rested.

Once sleep quality is controlled in the study, it becomes apparent that coffee consumption is less significant in predicting productivity than initially thought. The true relationship between coffee consumption and productivity was masked by the confounding variable of sleep quality.

Model Design Concepts

As we build data science models, it is important to note some of the common design concepts that are fundamental to creating effective models. These concepts help ensure that models are accurate, reliable, and relevant to the problem being addressed. Some of these concepts include the holdout method, the bias-variance trade-off, feature selection, cross-validation, bootstrapping, and hyperparameter tuning.

As you prepare for the DataX exam, you should be able to apply foundational machine learning concepts to a given scenario. Make note of the model design concepts introduced in this section and when best to use them.

The Holdout Method

The *holdout method* is a foundational concept in machine learning model design, primarily used to train and evaluate the performance of a model. When employing the holdout method, the available dataset is divided into two distinct subsets: the training set and the test set.

The training set is utilized to train the machine learning model, allowing it to learn and adapt to patterns, relationships, and structures within the data. Meanwhile, the test set is reserved and remains untouched during the training process. Once the model has been trained, it is then evaluated on the test set. Since the test data was not used during training, it acts as new, unseen data, providing an unbiased evaluation of the model's ability to generalize.

One of the key characteristics of the holdout method is its simplicity and straightforwardness, offering a clear demarcation between the training dataset and the dataset used for testing. However, care must be taken to ensure that both subsets are representative of the overall data distribution in order to be confident that the model adequately learns the patterns in the data. A common way to ensure this is by using a stratified random sampling approach to split the training and test data (except in the case of time-series data). In some cases, practitioners may further split the data into three parts, adding a validation set to fine-tune model parameters or hyperparameters before the final evaluation on the test set.

Data Leakage

Data leakage is a problem that occurs in machine learning when data is inadvertently shared between the training and test datasets. Data leakage often leads to overly optimistic performance estimates for a model. There are several forms and sources of data leakage:

- **Leakage Through Data Preprocessing:** This can happen during data normalization or standardization if the parameters used in scaling (like mean or standard deviation) are derived from the entire dataset and not just the training data. As a result, data indirectly leaks from the test set into the training set.

- **Leakage Due to Inappropriate Data Splitting:** This occurs when the split between training and test datasets is done improperly. For instance, if chronological data is split randomly and not chronologically, a model may inadvertently be trained on future data and tested on past data.

- **Leakage from Target Variables:** When a predictor variable inadvertently contains data that should only be available in the target, the model may perform exceptionally well but fail to generalize to new, unseen data.

The Bias-Variance Trade-off

The bias-variance trade-off is a central concept in model design that has to do with the balance between a model's ability to fit the data closely (low bias error) and its ability to generalize well to new, unseen data (low variance error).

Bias errors are errors that occur due to overly simplistic assumptions in model design or in the chosen learning algorithm. It can cause a model to miss relevant relationships between features and the target outputs, leading to high error rates on the training data as well as the test data. This is known as *underfitting*. An example of bias error is the error that is introduced when we try to fit a linear model to inherently nonlinear data.

Variance errors are errors due to too much complexity in a learning algorithm. They can cause a model to capture too much of the random noise in the training data, which leads to great performance on the training data but poor performance on the test data or previously unseen data. This is known as *overfitting*. *Variance minimization* is crucial for building robust machine learning models. The goal of variance minimization is to ensure that a model's predictions are consistent across different datasets, improving its ability to generalize from the training data to unseen data.

Ideally, the goal in model design is to find a good balance between bias and variance that allows us to minimize the total error of a model. This sweet spot is where the model performs well on both training and previously unseen data. Techniques like regularization, ensemble methods, cross-validation, bootstrapping, feature selection, and dimensionality reduction can help us find the right balance between bias and variance.

See Chapter 9 for more detailed coverage of regularization and ensemble methods such as bagging and boosting.

Feature Selection

Feature selection is the process of selecting a subset of the most relevant features (or predictors) for use in constructing a predictive model. The goal is to choose the most relevant features that provide the best predictive performance while discarding those that don't contribute significantly or might even degrade the performance of a model.

Feature selection reduces the number of irrelevant or redundant features in a dataset, which decreases the potential for a model to overfit, hence improving a model's ability to generalize against unseen data. Reducing the number of features used to train a model also speeds up the training process, improves the interpretability of the model, and reduces the amount of storage needed by the model, which can be significant in big data scenarios.

Some of the techniques used in feature selection are:

- **Filter methods:** These work by first applying a statistical measure to each feature to individually determine its relevance and importance to the target variable. Features are then ranked based on their importance scores, and a decision is made to keep or remove features based on whether their score meets or exceeds a threshold or ranking. Common statistical measures used in filter methods include the Pearson correlation coefficient (for continuous predictors and a continuous target), the chi-squared test (for categorical predictors and a categorical target), and analysis of variance, or ANOVA (for continuous predictors and a categorical target).

- **Wrapper Methods:** Also known as stepwise methods, wrapper methods involve evaluating subsets of variables to determine which combination of variables results in the best model performance. Examples are forward selection (iteratively adding features to improve performance), backward elimination (iteratively removing features that have the least impact), and recursive feature elimination (recursively removing features and identifying which remaining features contribute the most to the model's performance).

- **Embedded Methods:** These integrate the feature selection process into the model training process. Examples of embedded feature selection methods include L1 regularization, which is used in linear regression, or feature importance scores, which are generated by tree-based algorithms such as a decision tree.

The Law of Parsimony (Occam's Razor)

Occam's Razor, or the *Law of Parsimony*, is a philosophical principle that suggests that when presented with competing hypotheses, one should select the solution with the fewest assumptions or the simplest one. In essence, it posits that simplicity is preferable to complexity, and that unnecessary complexity should be avoided, if possible.

In the context of model design, Occam's Razor suggests that, given two models that perform similarly well on the training data, the simpler model—the one with fewer features or less complexity—is more likely to perform better on new data. This principle is helpful when dealing with the trade-off between bias and variance. However, it's important to note that Occam's Razor is a guideline rather than an irrefutable principle. Simplicity should not come at the expense of performance. In some cases, a more complex model may be necessary to adequately capture the intricacies of the data. The key is to find the right balance between simplicity and performance.

Cross-Validation

Cross-validation is a resampling technique that involves partitioning the data we intend to use to train a model into subsets, training the model on one subset (training data) and evaluating its performance on the remaining subset (validation data). Note that the validation data is not the same as the test data held out prior to cross-validation; the validation data is only used to estimate the future performance of a model against unseen data.

In the most common approach to cross-validation, known as k-fold cross-validation, the data is divided into k different subsets (or folds). For example, in the case of 5-fold cross-validation (i.e., k is set to 5), the data is divided into five subsets. The model is first trained on four of the folds and validated on the remaining fold. This process is repeated five times, with each of the five subsets used exactly once as the validation data. After the five iterations, the performance across all five iterations is averaged to obtain a single performance estimate for the model.

The process of systematically training and testing a model on different subsets provides a more robust estimation of a model's performance and helps to minimize the impact of errors due to bias and variance.

Bootstrapping

Bootstrapping is another resampling technique that is also helpful in minimizing bias and variance. It involves creating a subset of the data by randomly sampling the data with replacement. The model is trained on the random sample and then evaluated on the remaining data. This process is repeated many times, resulting in a distribution of model performance scores. Similar to cross-validation, by repeatedly sampling from the dataset and reevaluating the model, bootstrapping provides a more comprehensive estimation of the stability and performance of a model on different data samples.

Hyperparameter Tuning

Hyperparameter tuning is a key concept in machine learning that refers to the process of selecting a set of optimal hyperparameters for a learning algorithm. A hyperparameter is a parameter or setting whose value is used to control the learning process. Some examples of hyperparameters include the depth of a decision tree, the number of hidden layers in a neural network, or the k in k-nearest neighbors. By systematically tuning these hyperparameters, we can find a configuration that significantly improves the performance and computational efficiency of a model. Hyperparameter tuning also minimizes variance by producing a model that generalizes well to unseen data. Two of the most common methods for hyperparameter tuning are:

- **Grid Search:** This involves performing an exhaustive search through a manually specified subset of the hyperparameter space (usually a grid of hyperparameter values). A model is built for every hyperparameter combination, and the best one is selected.

- **Random Search:** This method involves randomly selecting combinations of hyperparameters from a given range. It's less exhaustive but is more efficient than grid search, especially when only a few hyperparameters have a significant impact.

Loss Functions

The primary objective of a model during the training phase is to learn to make predictions that are as close as possible to the expected results in the training data. Models accomplish this by minimizing what is known as a loss function. A *loss function*, also known as a cost function or an objective function, quantifies the disparity between the predicted values of a model and the observed values in the training data. If a model's predictions deviate from the actual results, loss functions penalize the model for its errors.

Loss functions are often used in conjunction with an optimization algorithm, such as gradient descent, which attempts to minimize loss gradually through each iteration of a training cycle. They do this by recursively making gradual changes to model parameters that slightly reduce the difference between the predicted and observed values during each cycle. This process is repeated until the model achieves the lowest possible (or what it considers sufficiently low) loss. See Chapter 12, "Specialized Applications of Data Science," for a more detailed discussion of optimization algorithms.

Model Evaluation

Model evaluation is the process of assessing the performance of a predictive model to determine how well it generalizes to unseen data. It involves using various metrics and techniques to measure the accuracy, reliability, and effectiveness of the model in making predictions or decisions. Depending on the type of model (i.e. classification or regression), there is a wide range of metrics we can employ to evaluate the performance of a predictive model.

As you prepare for the DataX exam, make note of the model performance metrics introduced in this section and how they differ from each other. Know which are used by regression models and which are used by classification models.

Regressor Performance Metrics

The effectiveness of regressors is typically evaluated by specific performance metrics that measure the difference between the model's prediction and the observed data. Commonly used metrics include R-squared, adjusted R-squared, root mean squared error (RMSE), F-statistic, Akaike information criterion (AIC), and Bayesian information criterion (BIC).

R-squared

R-squared, also known as the coefficient of determination, is a statistical measure that represents the proportion of the variance of a dependent variable that's explained by an independent variable or variables in a regression model. It is a commonly used metric to evaluate the goodness of fit of a regression model.

R-squared values range from 0 to 1. An R-squared value of 0 indicates that a model explains none of the variability of the response data around its mean. An R-squared value of 1 indicates that the model explains all the variability of the response data around its mean. It's important to note that a high R-squared value doesn't always indicate a good model. A model might have a high R-squared value and yet be ill-suited for prediction because it may have overfit to the training data. Conversely, a low R-squared value doesn't necessarily signify a bad model, particularly if the data is noisy and if the model's objective is to make accurate predictions rather than explain the relationship between features.

Adjusted R-squared

Because R-squared increases as more variables are included in a model (regardless of whether the new variables are significant predictors of the outcome), the *adjusted R-squared* is often used alongside R-squared. It essentially is an "adjusted" version of the R-squared statistic based on the number of independent variables in the model. The adjusted R-squared of a model only increases if a newly added predictor improves the model by more than expected by chance. The adjusted R-squared will also decrease if a newly added predictor improves the model by less than expected by chance.

Root Mean Squared Error (RMSE)

RMSE, or *root mean squared error*, is a reliable and straightforward way to evaluate the quality of a regression model and compare it to other models. It measures how well a model predicts the outcome of a dependent variable based on a set of independent variables. RMSE is calculated by taking the square root of the average of the squared differences between the predicted values and actual (or observed) values of the response variable.

RMSE shares the same unit of measure as the dependent variable, which makes them easy to interpret. Lower RMSE values indicate better fit, while higher RMSE values indicate poorer fit. When using RMSE to evaluate model performance, it's important to note that because differences are squared before they are averaged, RMSE gives a relatively high weight to large errors. This makes RMSE rather sensitive to outliers.

F-Statistic

In the context of regression, the *F-statistic* is used to test the overall significance of a model. It is a way to see if the variance explained by the entire model is significantly greater than the variance unexplained. The F-statistic can be used to compare statistical models that have been fitted to a dataset, to identify which model best fits the population from which the data was sampled. A high F-statistic value in a linear regression model indicates that the presence of independent variables improves the performance of the model compared to a model that only includes the intercept. Alternatively, a low F-statistic implies that the independent variables do not provide a significantly better fit than the intercept-only model and that the additional complexity of including the variables may not be justified.

When using the F-statistic as a measure of performance for a regression model, it's important to note that a large F-statistic only indicates that the model explains a good deal of variability in the dependent variable. It does not indicate which variables in your model are important predictors, nor does it say anything about the size of the effect the independent variables are having on the dependent variable. That's why it's important not just to rely on the F-statistic, but also to look at other statistics, like adjusted R-squared, and the individual t-statistic p-values for each predictor to get a comprehensive understanding of your model.

Akaike Information Criterion (AIC)

Akaike information criterion (AIC) is a metric used for model selection, where several statistical models of different complexities have been fitted to the same dataset and are ranked against each other based on how well they fit the data. Because AIC estimates the quality of each model relative to each of the other models, the absolute value of AIC is not as important as the relative values of AIC between different models in the set of candidate models. When you're choosing between candidate models, consider the model with the lowest AIC score the best.

Bayesian Information Criterion (BIC)

Also known as the Schwarz information criterion, *Bayesian information criterion (BIC)* is closely related to the AIC. However, it imposes a heavier penalty for models with more parameters, making it more stringent about the trade-off between the complexity of a model and the goodness of fit to the data. Like AIC, BIC doesn't provide an absolute measure of a model's performance. Instead, it offers a way to compare different models on the same dataset. The model with the lowest BIC value is considered the best among a set of models.

While both AIC and BIC help in model selection, the choice between them depends on the specific context and goals of your analysis. BIC's preference for simpler models can be particularly valuable when there's a risk of overfitting or when the model's interpretability is crucial.

Classifier Performance Metrics

Evaluating the performance of a classification model requires assessing how well the model performs on previously unseen data. To do this, a variety of metrics can be used; each offers a different perspective on the strengths and weaknesses of the model. This section introduces some of the most widely used classifier performance metrics, such as accuracy, precision, recall, sensitivity, specificity, and a few others.

Confusion Matrix

A *confusion matrix* is a table or matrix that describes the performance of a classification model by tabulating how many observations the model correctly or incorrectly predicted by class value. Figure 6.2 shows a sample confusion matrix for a binary classification problem. It consists of four cells, which give us different perspectives on the performance of the model on the test data. If we assume that the model the confusion matrix is based on was trained to predict whether an email is a solicitation (spam) or legitimate (ham), we can interpret the cells as follows (clockwise starting from the top left cell):

- **True Positives (TP):** 135 emails were correctly labeled as spam.
- **False Negatives (FN):** 80 spam emails were incorrectly labeled as ham. These are known as *Type II errors* or missed detections.
- **True Negatives (TN):** 203 emails were correctly labeled as ham.
- **False Positives (FP):** 2 ham emails were incorrectly labeled as spam. These are referred to as *Type I errors* or false alarms.

FIGURE 6.2   A sample confusion matrix showing actual versus predicted values

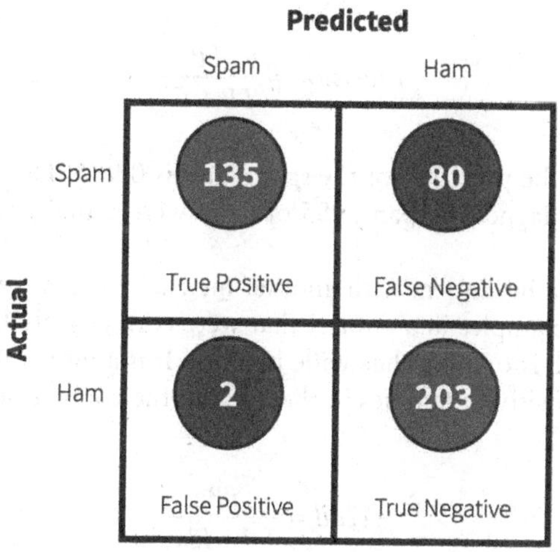

Accuracy

Accuracy, or *predictive accuracy*, is the simplest and most straightforward classifier performance metric. It represents the number of observations that a model predicted correctly as a ratio of the total number of observations in the data. In the context of a confusion matrix, accuracy is calculated as:

$$Accuracy = \frac{TP + TN}{TP + TN + FP + FN}$$

Using the values from the confusion matrix in Figure 6.2, the accuracy of the spam filter is calculated as follows:

$$Accuracy = \frac{135 + 203}{135 + 203 + 2 + 80} = 0.8$$

This result means that the model will correctly label 80 percent of incoming emails as either spam or ham.

Though useful, accuracy can be a deceptive measure of model performance, particularly when the data suffers from class imbalance. For this reason, accuracy is often used in conjunction with other metrics like precision, recall, F1 score, sensitivity, and specificity, which provide more detailed insight into the performance of a classification model.

Precision and Recall

Precision, which is also known as the positive predictive value, is the proportion of positive predictions made by a model that are indeed truly positive. A model with high precision is one that is trustworthy. In the context of a confusion matrix, precision is calculated as follows:

$$precision = \frac{TP}{TP + FP}$$

Based on Figure 6.2, the precision of the spam filter is 0.985. This means that for every 1,000 emails the model flagged as spam, 985 of them were actually spam, while 15 of them were ham.

Precision is often used in tandem with another metric known as recall. *Recall* is the proportion of positive examples in a dataset that were correctly predicted by a model. A model with high recall is one that has wide breadth. It is a model that correctly identifies a large number of the positive examples in the data. In the context of a confusion matrix, recall is calculated as:

$$recall = \frac{TP}{TP + FN}$$

Based on Figure 6.2, the recall of the spam filter is 0.628. We interpret this to mean that out of every 1,000 actual spam emails, the model correctly identified and flagged 628 of them as spam, while 372 spam emails went undetected and landed in a user's inbox.

F1 Score

In many real-world contexts, there's a trade-off between precision and recall, where improving one may reduce the other. The *F1 score* is often used as a single metric that combines both precision and recall. It is the harmonic mean of precision and recall, taking both false positives and false negatives into account. F1 score is calculated as:

$$F1\ score = \frac{2 \times precision \times recall}{precision + recall}$$

The F1 score ranges from 0 to 1, where 1 represents perfect balance between precision and recall, and 0 represents the worst balance between both metrics. One of the limitations of the F1 score is that it gives equal weight to precision and recall. In some cases, one might be more important than the other, so it's essential to consider the context in which you're using this metric.

Matthews Correlation Coefficient (MCC)

For binary classification problems, the *Matthews correlation coefficient (MCC)* provides a balanced measure of model performance even when the classes are of very different sizes. This makes it a better metric than accuracy for datasets that suffer from class imbalance. In the context of a confusion matrix, MCC is calculated as follows:

$$MCC = \frac{TP \times TN - FP \times FN}{\sqrt{(TP + FP) \times (TP + FN) \times (TN + FP) \times (TN + FN)}}$$

As is evident in this formula, the main advantage of the Matthews correlation coefficient over other metrics like accuracy, precision, and recall is that it considers all four quadrants of the confusion matrix. MCC values range from −1 to +1, with +1 representing a perfect prediction, 0 an average random prediction, and −1 an inverse prediction.

Sensitivity and Specificity

Another pair of performance measures used in tandem are sensitivity and specificity. *Sensitivity*, also known as the true positive rate, is synonymous with recall and represents the ability of a model to correctly identify the positive cases in a dataset.

Specificity, also known as the true negative rate, is the proportion of actual negative examples that a model correctly identifies. A model with high specificity is one that correctly labels most of the examples in the negative class. In the context of the confusion matrix, the specificity of a model is calculated as follows:

$$specificity = \frac{TN}{TN + FP}$$

The values for both sensitivity and specificity range from 0 to 1, with higher values representing better performance. Based on Figure 6.2, the specificity of the spam filter is 0.99. This means that for every 1,000 ham emails, the model correctly identified and flagged 999 of them, while incorrectly flagging 1 as spam.

Each of the classifier performance measures introduced here provides different insights into the strength and weakness of a model. As a result, they should be used collectively to get a comprehensive understanding of the performance of a model.

Real World Scenario

Choosing the Appropriate Performance Metric

You are a machine learning engineer at SecureTech, a top software security company. The company is known for its state-of-the-art malware detection system. After the latest software update, you reevaluated the performance of your system on a test dataset of 478 files (100 unsafe and 378 safe). The confusion matrix in the following graphic describes the results from that test.

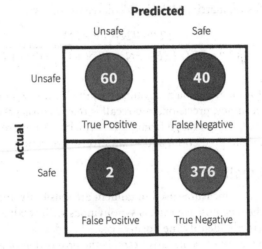

Based on the confusion matrix, we know the following:

- The accuracy of the model is 0.912. This means that out of 1,000 files, the model is expected to accurately flag 912 of them as safe or unsafe.

- The precision of the model is 0.968. This means that of the 62 files that the model predicted to be unsafe, 96.8 percent of them were actually unsafe.

- The recall (or sensitivity) of the model is 0.6. This means that of the 100 files that were unsafe, the model accurately flagged 60 percent of them. Conversely, this means that the model failed to correctly flag 40 malware files.

- The specificity of the model is 0.995. This means that of the 378 files that were safe, the model accurately flagged 99.5 percent of them and incorrectly quarantined 0.5 percent of them as malware.

These metrics provide different perspectives on the performance of the model, each important in its own way. However, considering that the primary objective of the software is to ensure that no malware goes undetected, the most impactful metric is recall (or sensitivity). While false positives can be a minor inconvenience, a single undetected malware (false negative) can compromise an entire system or network. A 40 percent false negative rate is unacceptable. SecureTech should retrain their model, incorporating the latest malware signatures and leveraging advanced detection techniques to push the recall closer toward 100 percent before releasing this version of the product.

Receiver Operating Characteristic (ROC) Curve

When classifiers make predictions, they usually do so by estimating the probability that an individual instance belongs to a particular class. Based on the estimated probability and a cutoff threshold, the model assigns a label to the instance. For most classification algorithms, the default two-class cutoff threshold is 0.5. To illustrate how this works, consider a spam filter model. If the model estimates that the probability that a particular email is spam as 0.6, then the email is labeled as spam. However, if the estimated probability was 0.3, then the email would be labeled as ham. As you can imagine, adjusting the cutoff threshold will have an impact on whether emails are ultimately labeled as spam or ham. Consequently, it will also have an impact on the true positive (sensitivity) and true negative (specificity) rates of a classifier.

By adjusting the cutoff threshold of a classifier from 0 to 1, we can calculate and visualize the true positive rate (sensitivity) and false positive rate (1-specificity) of the classifier at various cutoff values. This visualization is known as the *receiver operating characteristic (ROC) curve*. The ROC curve for a classifier shows the tradeoff that exists between the sensitivity and specificity of a model—as one goes up, the other goes down.

The shape of an ROC curve also provides insight into a classifier's ability to discriminate between the positive and negative classes in the data. Figure 6.3 shows the ROC curves for three different classifiers. The classifier represented by the diagonal dotted line is a classifier with no predictive value. This classifier performs no better than chance. The classifier represented by the dotted line closest to the y-axis is an ideal classifier. This classifier correctly identifies all of the positive examples and all of the negative examples. In practice, the ROC curve for most classifiers will fall somewhere between the two extremes, as represented by the solid line. The closer a classifier's ROC curve is to the top left corner of the chart, the better it is. Conversely, the closer a classifier's ROC curve is to the diagonal dotted line, the worse it is.

FIGURE 6.3 The ROC curve for a sample classifier, a perfect classifier, and a classifier with no predictive value

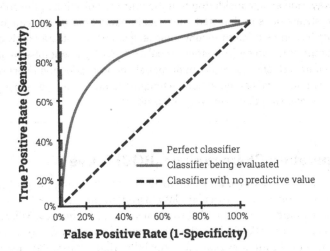

Area Under the Curve (AUC)

The ROC curve can be condensed into a single metric called the *area under the curve (AUC)*. Simply put, the AUC quantifies the entire region beneath the ROC curve. AUC values vary between 0.5 (indicating a classifier lacking predictive ability) and 1.0 (representing a flawless classifier). Generally, the higher the AUC of a classifier, the better it is. The AUC of a classifier can be interpreted as the probability that a classifier ranks a randomly chosen positive instance above a randomly chosen negative instance.

Summary

Regressors are models for predicting continuous outcomes, like housing prices or disease trends. Linear regression models assume that a direct linear relationship exists between predictors and the outcome, whereas tree-based models don't make assumptions about the data and can handle complex relationships.

Classifiers are models used to assign observations to categories, based on input features. They are referred to as binary when categorizing observations into two classes or multiclass when there are three or more classes.

Temporal models predict outcomes by accounting for the sequential nature of certain data. Time-series models forecast future values from historical patterns. Survival analysis predicts time to an event. Longitudinal studies track subjects over time, offering insights into cause and effect, and are central to causal inference, which uses methodologies such as randomized controlled trials, difference-in-differences, and A/B testing.

In model design, we use the holdout method to split data into training and testing sets to evaluate model generalization. Minimizing a loss function during training reduces prediction errors. The bias-variance trade-off balances model simplicity with generalization, while cross-validation and bootstrapping improve performance estimation. Hyperparameter tuning optimizes model settings for better performance. Feature selection removes irrelevant inputs to enhance model generalization and efficiency, using statistical, iterative, or integrated techniques.

Regressor performance is evaluated using metrics like R-squared and adjusted R-squared for quality of fit, RMSE for predictive accuracy, and F-statistic for model significance. AIC and BIC aid in model selection, penalizing complexity to prevent overfitting and ensuring interpretability.

Classifier performance is assessed by metrics like accuracy, precision, recall, F1 score, MCC, sensitivity, specificity, ROC curve, and AUC. These metrics offer insights into a model's ability to effectively discriminate between classes.

Exam Essentials

Understand the difference between regressors and classifiers. The key difference lies in the nature of the output. Regressors are designed to predict continuous values, such as stock prices, whereas classifiers are used to assign categorical class labels to observations, like distinguishing between spam and non-spam emails.

Explain the differences between time-series analysis, survival analysis, and a longitudinal study. The main differences are that time-series analysis is used to predict future values from historical data patterns, survival analysis is used to estimate the time until an event, and longitudinal studies allow us to observe the same subjects over time.

Understand how cross-validation, bootstrapping, hyperparameter tuning, and feature selection minimize variance. Cross-validation and bootstrapping both reduce variance by evaluating model performance across different data subsets. Hyperparameter tuning reduces variance by optimizing model settings to generalize well. Feature selection prevents overfitting by retaining only relevant predictors. Together, these techniques enhance a model's predictive performance and generalizability to new, unseen data.

Explain the difference between R-squared and adjusted R-squared. In a linear regression model, R-squared is the proportion of variance in the dependent variable explained by the independent variables. Adjusted R-squared modifies R-squared to account for the number of independent variables in the model. It increases only if the addition of a new variable enhances the model significantly.

Explain the difference between Akaike information criterion (AIC) and Bayesian information criterion (BIC). The Akaike information criterion (AIC) and Bayesian information criterion (BIC) are both used for model selection. BIC, while similar to AIC, adds a stronger penalty for models with more parameters. BIC favors simpler models and is better when overfitting is a concern or model interpretability is important.

Know the difference between precision and recall.   Precision is the proportion of true positives among all positive predictions made by the model, whereas recall is the proportion of actual positives correctly identified by the model. Both metrics are crucial for understanding a model's performance on the positive class.

Know the difference between sensitivity and specificity.   Sensitivity, which is synonymous with recall, measures a model's ability to correctly identify positive cases, while specificity measures how well a model identifies the negatives cases. Together, they offer a balanced view of a model's ability to classify both positive and negative cases accurately.

Describe how to use the receiver operating characteristic (ROC) curve to evaluate model performance.   When choosing between models using the ROC curve, you should typically choose the model whose ROC curve is closest to the top left corner of the plot. This represents the highest true positive rate (sensitivity) with the lowest false positive rate (1-specificity). Also, the model with the largest area under the ROC curve (AUC) is often considered the best, as it indicates the model that has a better overall performance across all classification thresholds.

Review Questions

1. A health app company wants to use an uploaded image to predict whether a mole is benign or malignant. Which type of model is best suited for this task?

    A. A multiclass classifier

    B. A binary classifier

    C. A temporal model

    D. A regressor

2. What does R-squared represent in a regression model?

    A. The number of variables in the model

    B. The proportion of variance for a dependent variable explained by an independent variable or variables

    C. The quality of each model, relative to each of the other models

    D. The proportion of negative predictions made by a model that are truly negative

3. An online shopping platform wants to understand if changing the color of their Add To Cart button will lead to more purchases. They show half of their visitors the old version and the other half a new version with a different color. What technique are they using to determine the impact of the button color?

    A. Longitudinal study

    B. Difference-in-differences (DiD)

    C. A/B testing

    D. Time-series analysis

4. A bank has developed multiple models to detect fraudulent transactions. One model has a BIC value significantly lower than the others. Why might this model be preferred?

    A. It is the most complex model with the highest number of parameters.

    B. It balances model complexity and fits the data better than the other models.

    C. It has the highest RMSE, indicating a better fit to the data.

    D. It guarantees that fraudulent transactions will be detected with 100 percent accuracy.

5. A researcher is comparing multiple statistical models to select the best one for forecasting weather patterns. She decides to use AIC as her criterion for model selection. If Model A has an AIC of 300 and Model B has an AIC of 280, which model should she choose?

    A. Model A

    B. Model B

    C. AIC values are irrelevant when comparing models.

    D. She needs the BIC values as well to make this determination.

6. Sandy developed a machine learning model to forecast sales. The RMSE of the model on the test data is very high. What does this tell Sandy about her model?

   A. The model fits the data perfectly.

   B. The model is likely overfitting and may not generalize well.

   C. The model is likely underfitting and does not capture the data trends well.

   D. The model has a perfect balance between bias and variance.

7. Which of the following metrics is synonymous with recall?

   A. Precision

   B. Sensitivity

   C. Specificity

   D. Accuracy

8. According to the Law of Parsimony, when two models perform similarly well on the training data, which one is more likely to perform better on new data?

   A. The one with more features

   B. The more complex model

   C. The simpler model

   D. The one with more hyperparameters

9. James is building a regression model to predict consumer spending. He notices that the R-squared value for his model increases with each additional variable he includes in the model. To ensure that the new variables meaningfully contribute to the model's predictive power, which additional metric should he also consider?

   A. Adjusted R-squared

   B. RMSE

   C. F-statistic

   D. AIC

10. You are a data scientist working at a real estate company. Your boss asks you to predict the future selling price of houses based on various features like the number of bedrooms, square footage, and location. Which type of analytic model would you most likely use?

    A. A classifier

    B. A temporal model

    C. A regressor

    D. A time series model

11. Sam is researching the growth patterns of a certain plant species. He observes the same set of plants over multiple years to understand the factors affecting their growth rate. What research approach is Sam using?

    A. Time-series analysis

    B. Longitudinal study

    C. Randomized controlled trials

    D. A/B testing

12. A data scientist has developed a regression model to predict housing prices and is now analyzing the model's performance. The R-squared value comes out to be 0.95. Which of these statements is true regarding the model?

    A. The model explains 5 percent of the variability of the housing prices around its mean.

    B. The model predicts the correct result 95 percent of the time.

    C. The model explains 95 percent of the variability of the housing prices around its mean.

    D. The model's predictions are within 5 percent of the expected value.

13. Which of the following scenarios best illustrates data leakage due to inappropriate data splitting?

    A. Using current data to train a model to predict past events

    B. Splitting the data randomly without considering categories

    C. Splitting the data based on user IDs

    D. Splitting data into training and test sets only

14. An educational tech company is developing an AI-based essay grading tool. They want the tool to rate student essays as Very Good, Good, Average, or Below Average. Which kind of model is best suited for this?

    A. A binary classifier

    B. A regressor

    C. A multiclass classifier

    D. A temporal model

15. What does the receiver operating characteristic (ROC) curve visually represent?

    A. The trade-off between a model's precision and recall

    B. The absolute performance of a model

    C. The trade-off between a model's true positive rate and false positive rate

    D. The trade-off between a model's sensitivity and specificity

16. While testing the performance of a new AI-assisted cancer diagnostic system, the data science team found the precision to be very high. This means that when the system predicts that a tumor is malignant, it is usually correct. However, the team also wants to make sure that the model is correctly identifying as many malignant tumors as possible. Which additional metric should the team evaluate to address this concern?

    A. AUC

    B. Sensitivity

    C. Specificity

    D. F-statistic

17. How is the Matthews correlation coefficient (MCC) different from accuracy, precision, and recall?

    A. It is only suitable for multiclass problems.

    B. It doesn't consider false positives or false negatives.

    C. It considers all four quadrants of the confusion matrix.

    D. It is exclusively used in tandem with other metrics.

18. When evaluating the performance of two models (A and B), you find that the AUC for Model A is 0.9, while that of Model B is 0.6. Based on these results, which of these statements is correct?

    A. Model B has a higher true positive rate than Model A at all cutoff thresholds.

    B. Model A has a higher true negative rate than Model B at all cutoff thresholds.

    C. Model A is better than Model B at distinguishing between positive and negative classes.

    D. Both models perform worse than random guessing.

19. A weather forecasting agency collects temperature data every hour and wants to predict temperatures for the next week based on patterns in the collected data. Which type of model would be best suited for this?

    A. A binary classifier

    B. A regressor

    C. A time-series model

    D. A multiclass classifier

20. A fraud detection model has an accuracy of 0.95. However, the dataset contains 95 percent legitimate transactions and 5 percent fraudulent transactions. What potential issue should be considered before deploying this model?

    A. The model might have high precision but low recall.

    B. The class imbalance in the data is likely skewing the accuracy.

    C. The model might have high recall but low precision.

    D. The model's AUC is likely too high.

Chapter 7

Model Validation and Deployment

THE COMPTIA DATAX EXAM OBJECTIVES COVERED IN THIS CHAPTER INCLUDE:

✓ **Domain 2: Modeling, Analysis, and Outcomes**

- 2.4 Given a scenario, conduct a model design iteration process.

- 2.5 Given a scenario, analyze results of experiments and testing to justify final model recommendations and selection.

- 2.6 Given a scenario, translate results and communicate via appropriate methods and mediums.

✓ **Domain 4: Operations and Processes**

- 4.6 Explain the importance of DevOps and MLOps principles in data science.

- 4.7 Compare and contrast various deployment environments.

Model validation is a critical stage in the data science lifecycle, focusing on evaluating a model's performance to ensure it aligns with design specifications, requirements, and standards. In this chapter, the importance of assessing a model's performance against key metrics and real-world constraints like time, resources, and costs is emphasized. We also explore how models must align with business needs, the role of benchmarking, and the significance of effective communication of model results. Later in the chapter, various model deployment strategies are described and the integration of DevOps practices in machine learning through machine learning operations (MLOps) is discussed.

Model Validation

Model validation in the data science lifecycle is a critical phase where the performance and effectiveness of a model are rigorously evaluated to ensure it meets design specifications, satisfies requirements, and is standards compliant, prior to deployment.

As you prepare for the DataX exam, you should know what role design specifications, performance evaluation, and requirements validation play in model design and selection. Make note of those concepts in context as they are introduced.

Performance Metrics

When validating the performance of a model, key statistical metrics (covered in Chapter 6, "Modeling and Evaluation") such as accuracy, R-squared, precision, recall, and RMSE are useful for assessing a model's effectiveness in learning the underlying patterns in the data. For regression models, diagnostic plots such as a residual versus fitted value plot are useful in assessing a model's goodness-of-fit to the training data. For classification problems, a visualization such as the receiver operating characteristics (ROC) curve can provide insight into how the model will perform in different scenarios.

Inference Performance

Another crucial aspect of model validation is evaluating a model's inference performance over time to ensure that it stays stable and reliable. This continuous assessment is crucial for detecting and mitigating *data drift* and *concept drift*, both of which can potentially diminish the accuracy of a model over time.

Regularly evaluating a model's inference performance over time helps assess the model's robustness against data variations and anomalies by identifying when the model needs updates or retraining in response to new trends and patterns in the data. This is especially important in dynamic production environments where data changes quickly. For example, for a stock price prediction model, its ability to adapt to market changes over time is a crucial aspect of its suitability.

Data Drift vs. Concept Drift

Data drift refers to changes in the statistical properties of the input data over time. This can happen due to various factors such as changes in the environment, user behavior, or data collection processes. Data drift can lead to a decrease in model performance because the model was trained on a dataset with different characteristics than the current data.

Concept drift, on the other hand, refers to a change in the underlying relationship between the input data and the target variable. In other words, the concept that the model is trying to predict has changed. This can happen due to changes in external factors, market dynamics, or other influences that affect the way inputs are related to outputs.

Data drift and concept drift are related but distinct phenomena. Both impact the performance of a model over time. Both can be addressed by retraining the model with more recent data.

Design Constraints

Model validation goes beyond just measuring the statistical performance of a model against a given dataset. It also involves assessing how well a model meets the time, resource, and cost constraints specified during the modeling and design stage of the data science lifecycle.

Time Constraints

Time constraints dictate a project's timeline and influence the complexity of algorithms used. During model validation, we must confirm that a model can be trained and deployed within the allocated time frame. This is critical in projects with tight deadlines, where the speed of model development and validation is as important as the model's accuracy. For example, in a scenario where a model must be deployed within three months, the use of simple algorithms or prebuilt frameworks would be preferred over a custom purpose-built solution with higher predictive performance.

Resource Constraints

Resource constraints refer to the amount of data and computing resources (processing, storage, and networking) available to a model during the training stage as well as when the model is deployed. A limited training dataset may restrict a model's complexity and potentially its predictive power. Similarly, models designed for deployment in environments with limited computational resources must be validated to ensure that they can run efficiently under those constraints. The model's resource requirements cannot exceed the processing power, memory, and storage available on the intended hardware. This is particularly important for models intended for real-time applications or edge devices, where hardware capabilities can be a limiting factor.

Cost Constraints

Cost constraints also play a significant role in model validation. The costs associated with the training, validation, deployment, and ongoing operation of a model must be weighed against the expected benefits of the model. In essence, model validation can act as a reality check, confirming that the model not only performs well statistically but it is also operationally and financially viable.

Business Requirements Alignment

Another critical aspect of model validation is verifying that a model aligns with actual business requirements. This involves distinguishing between essential business needs and additional wants or preferences. For example, a model that can accurately predict customer behavior is a need if it directly affects the company's ability to increase sales or enhance customer satisfaction. On the other hand, the ability of the model to provide interpretable insights, while beneficial for understanding the "why" behind the predictions, could be classified as a want. Business "needs" are the non-negotiables that a model must fulfill to be considered successful, whereas business "wants" are enhancements that provide value but are not critical for success.

Requirements validation prior to modeling can help with the delineation between business needs and wants. Requirements validation is the process of confirming that the documented requirements align with stakeholder expectations. The process involves checking that every requirement is articulated clearly, completely, correctly, and consistently. It also involves making sure that requirements can be tested and that they do not conflict with each other. By validating requirements up front, teams can avoid costly and time-consuming revisions later in the project lifecycle.

Benchmarking

Benchmarking plays a pivotal role in model validation. It provides a means to objectively evaluate a model's performance and its practical utility in comparison to existing standards or methods. Benchmarking for model validation involves two key comparative analyses—benchmarking against a baseline and benchmarking against conventional processes.

Benchmarking Against a Baseline

Benchmarking against a baseline involves comparing a new model's performance with a predefined standard. This standard could be an existing model, a simpler algorithm, or established industry metrics or requirements. The objective is to determine whether the value added by a new model justifies the potential increase in complexity that comes with it. For instance, if a more complex model only marginally improves upon the performance of a simpler existing model, it might not be worth the additional resources and complexity that it brings.

Benchmarking Against Conventional Processes

Benchmarking against conventional processes evaluates a model's performance in comparison to non–machine learning methods or existing business practices. It's a crucial step for assessing the real-world impact of a model—the practical benefits of adopting a machine learning solution over traditional methods. This type of benchmarking is not just about technical performance metrics but also about demonstrating tangible improvements in operational efficiency, decision making, or other business outcomes. Successfully showing a clear advantage over conventional processes can be instrumental in convincing stakeholders and decision makers of the value of implementing a new model.

 Real World Scenario

Developing a Product Recommendation Model

You are a data scientist leading a team tasked with developing a recommender system for a retail company. The goal is to launch the system just in time for the holiday season, which is four months away. The company has existing customer data, including browsing history, purchase records, and user feedback. The budget for the project is moderate, and the model needs to be deployable on the company's current server infrastructure.

Phase 1: Model Design and Development

Requirements Validation: Before diving into model development, you engage with stakeholders to validate business requirements. You distinguish between essential needs and additional wants. It's determined that the primary need is to increase sales during the holiday season by providing personalized product recommendations to customers. A want is for the model to also provide interpretable insights for nontechnical stakeholders.

Design Constraints: Given the moderate budget and existing infrastructure, the team decides that the model should be optimized for efficient resource usage to ensure cost-effectiveness. With a tight four-month deadline, you decide to prioritize speed and simplicity in model development. Collaborative filtering is chosen as the initial core algorithm due to its effectiveness and relatively quick implementation.

Phase 2: Model Validation

Performance Evaluation: Key statistical measures like accuracy, precision, and recall are used to evaluate the model's ability to provide accurate recommendations. You also monitor training time and resource usage.

Business Requirements Alignment: The model is evaluated to make sure that it fulfills the primary business need of increasing sales through personalized recommendations. While interpretable insights are a "want," they are considered secondary to the core goal of boosting revenue during the holiday season.

Benchmarking: You compare the collaborative filtering model's performance against a simpler baseline model to justify the additional complexity of the approach. You also benchmark the model against the company's existing recommendation methods, which involve manual curation of holiday product lists. Your goal is to show how the new model can significantly improve operational efficiency and sales.

Phase 3: Model Selection

Based on the results of model validation, it becomes apparent that the collaborative filtering model performs better than the baseline and existing processes. The model can also be trained and deployed within the four-month deadline while staying within the budget. Continuous monitoring of the model's inference performance over time shows it can adapt to changing customer preferences without frequent retraining, ensuring its stability and reliability. The rigorous validation process helps justify the selection of the collaborative filtering model as the final choice and provides confidence in its ability to boost sales during the holiday season.

Communicating Results

Effectively communicating the results of a model is just as critical as the analysis itself. To successfully convey complex results in a clear and impactful manner, we must know how to select appropriate data, utilize varied visualization techniques, and tailor our communication to diverse audiences. We must also maintain ethical standards and design for accessibility. Additionally, comprehensive documentation of the entire process ensures the longevity and credibility of the analysis. Adhering to these standards ensures that model insights are not only shared but also understood and valued by all stakeholders.

Data

Choosing the right data to include in reports is foundational to effective communication. It involves a careful selection process where data that directly supports the core message of the report is prioritized. This selection must be precise, focusing on data that offers clear insights and avoids overwhelming the audience with unnecessary details.

Additionally, considering the level of data aggregation is crucial. Granular data can provide in-depth insights but may be too complex for some audiences, whereas aggregate data can offer a clearer, broader view of a concept but might miss subtle nuances. Striking the right balance based on the objective and the audience is key.

Visuals

Visualizations are a crucial tool in communicating model insights and the results of data analysis. Effective communication often requires a mix of different types of visualizations and reports, each tailored to highlight specific aspects of the data and the insights derived from the model. A few of the common types of visualizations and reports that are used to communicate model results are discussed next.

Confusion Matrix

Confusion matrices are pivotal in classification models. They display the number of correct and incorrect predictions, categorized by each class. A confusion matrix helps in identifying the overall accuracy of a model but also provides insights into the types of errors it makes, such as the percentage of false positives and false negatives. By breaking down the performance of a classification model into categories, stakeholders can assess a model's performance in real-world scenarios, where different types of errors might have varying consequences.

Receiver Operating Characteristics (ROC) Curve

ROC curves are essential for understanding the performance of classification models, especially binary classification models. The ROC curve plots the true positive rate against the false positive rate at various threshold settings, providing a comprehensive view of a model's performance across different scenarios.

Precision-Recall Curve

Precision-recall curves are particularly important in the context of imbalanced datasets, which are quite common in real-world scenarios. They highlight the trade-off between precision (the accuracy of positive predictions) and recall (the ability of a model to find all positive instances). For applications where the cost of false negatives is high, such as fraud detection or medical diagnosis, precision-recall curves offer a more relevant evaluation of model performance than traditional accuracy metrics or a confusion matrix.

See Chapter 6 for more detail on the confusion matrix, precision, recall, and the receiver operating characteristics (ROC) curve.

Decision Tree Visualization

Visual representations of decision trees (as shown in Figure 7.1) demystify the decision-making process of a tree-based model. They show how different features and their values lead to specific predictions. This transparency is vital for validating the model's logic, especially in sectors like finance or healthcare, where explainability is just as important as accuracy.

FIGURE 7.1   Sample decision tree showing the decision logic for a predictive model

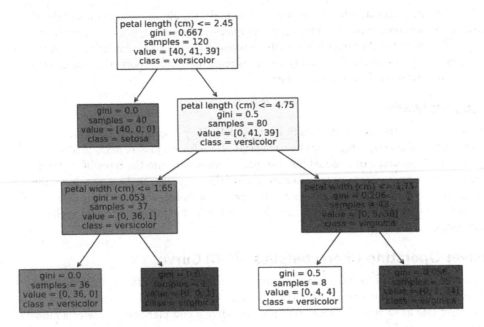

Feature Importance Chart

Feature importance charts are invaluable in understanding what drives a model's decisions. In tree-based models like decision trees, random forests, or gradient-boosting machines, feature importance charts rank the independent variables (or predictors) based on their influence on the model's predictions. Ranking features this way not only enhances the interpretability of a model, but it also helps in identifying which variables are most significant, guiding future data collection and feature engineering efforts. For example, in the feature importance chart shown in Figure 7.2, you can see that petal length is the most predictive feature in the model, while sepal width is the least predictive.

FIGURE 7.2   Sample feature importance chart for a predictive model

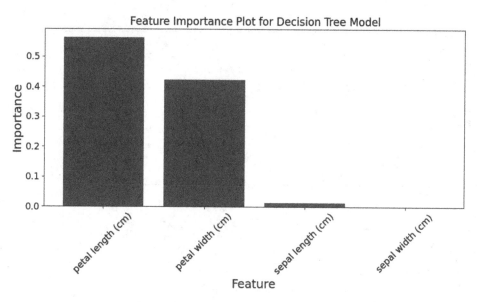

Residual Plot

A residual versus fitted values plot, also known as a residual plot, is a common diagnostic tool used to assess the goodness of fit of a regression model. By displaying the difference between observed and predicted values, residual plots help in identifying any systematic errors in the model. If the residuals are randomly scattered around the horizontal axis (as shown in Figure 7.3), it suggests that the model is appropriately capturing the data patterns. Conversely, any clear pattern in the residuals indicates issues like nonlinearity or heteroscedasticity (which is where variances differ at different data points). Figure 7.4 shows a clear and systematic pattern in the residuals as you move along the predicted (fitted) values. In other words, the variance of residuals depends on the fitted value.

Time-Series Decomposition Plot

A time-series decomposition plot breaks down a time-series dataset into its trend, seasonal, and residual components. This decomposition makes it easier to understand complex time dependencies in the data. For instance, identifying and adjusting for seasonal trends is crucial in making accurate forecasts. By visualizing these components separately, stakeholders can better understand the underlying patterns and anomalies in the data, leading to more informed decision making.

FIGURE 7.3   Sample residual vs. fitted values plot showing linearity

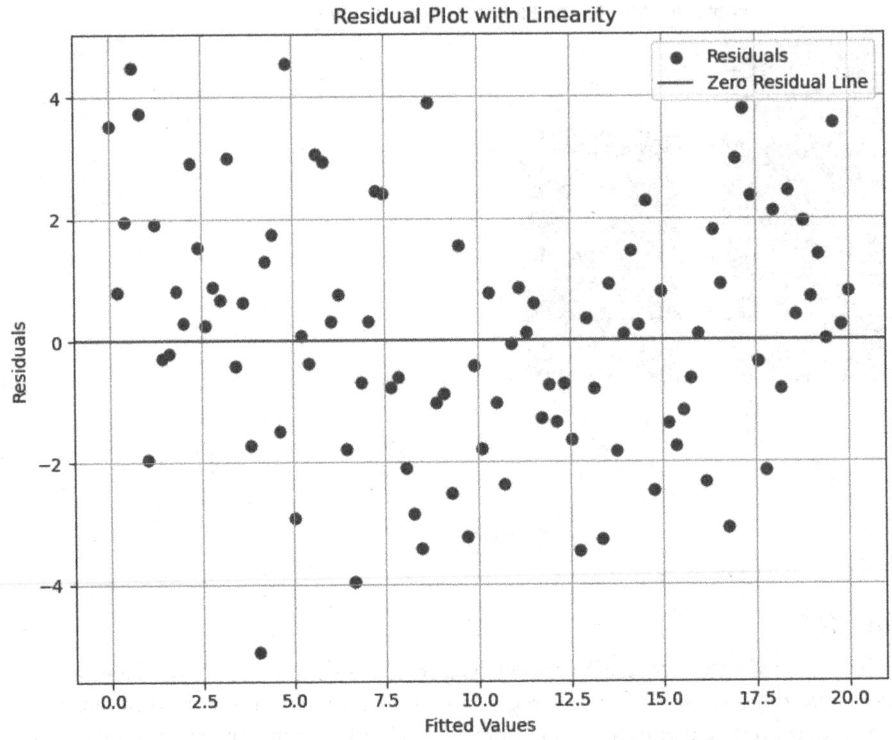

Interactive Dashboard

Interactive dashboards, similar to the one in Figure 7.5, provide a user-friendly platform to explore and interact with data and model results. They allow users to filter, drill down, and manipulate the data to discover patterns and insights by observing how model results change. The interactive nature of dashboards makes them especially useful for nontechnical stakeholders who are interested in a bit more in-depth exploration of a model and model results.

Stakeholders

Communicating effectively with diverse stakeholders requires tailoring our message to the background and information needs of the target audience. Business executives, such as CEOs, CFOs, and COOs, generally prefer high-level insights with strategic implications, presented clearly and succinctly. They focus on the overall impact of the insights on the company's direction, financial health, and operational efficiency.

FIGURE 7.4   Sample residual vs. fitted values plot showing heteroscedasticity

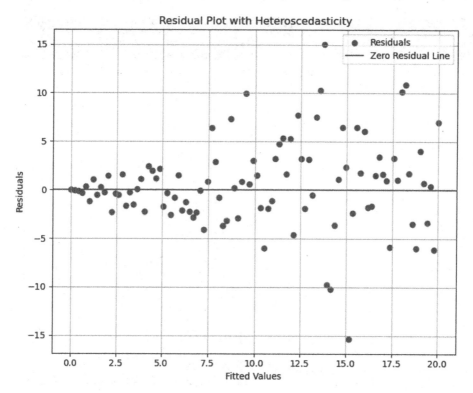

In contrast, business domain stakeholders, like marketing managers, sales managers, and human resources managers, value detailed insights specific to their areas of expertise. They seek information that can directly inform their strategies, such as customer behavior insights for the marketing team, sales opportunities for the sales team, and employee satisfaction information for the HR team.

Peers and professional stakeholders, including fellow data scientists, IT professionals, and project managers, often have a technical background and appreciate a deeper dive into the methodology, data analysis, and statistical nuances. They are interested in the technical details of the models, the infrastructure and security aspects of data management, and the impact of data analysis on project management. Adapting the communication style and depth of information to suit these different audiences is crucial for effectively conveying model insights and ensuring that each stakeholder group receives the information they need in a format that is accessible and actionable for them.

FIGURE 7.5   Sample interactive dashboard

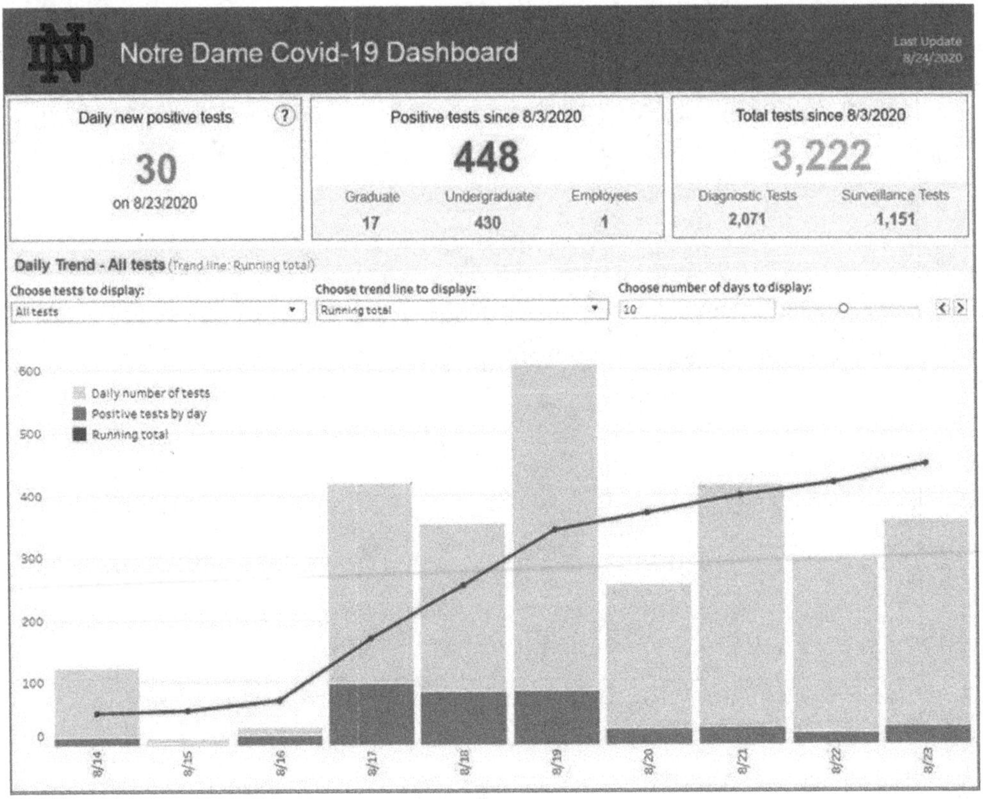

Source: University of Notre Dame / https://www.wndu.com/2020/08/24/notre-dame-reports-30-new-cases-of-covid-19 / Last accessed March 14, 2024.

Ethics

Accurate and ethical reporting is non-negotiable. This involves presenting data in a way that is truthful and not misleading, avoiding tactics like manipulative graph scales or cherry-picking data. Additionally, adherence to government regulatory standards, especially when handling sensitive or personal data, is paramount. This commitment to ethical reporting upholds the integrity of the data science field and ensures the credibility of the analysis.

Accessibility

Designing charts and reports with accessibility in mind is critical for ensuring that insights derived from data are accessible to a wide and inclusive audience. This involves making thoughtful choices in font style and size to ensure readability for all users, including those with visual impairments. Color schemes should be chosen with consideration for color-blind viewers, avoiding combinations that are difficult to distinguish for those with color vision deficiencies. Providing *content tagging* and descriptive text is essential for those using assistive technologies, such as screen readers, to understand graphical information.

Moreover, accessibility in data visualization and reporting is not just a matter of inclusivity but also a legal requirement in many contexts. Governments around the world have enacted regulations to ensure digital accessibility. For example, in the United States, the Americans with Disabilities Act (ADA) and Section 508 of the Rehabilitation Act require that electronic and information technology, including digital reports and charts, be accessible to people with disabilities. Similarly, the European Union's Web Accessibility Directive mandates that public sector websites and mobile apps be accessible to everyone.

Failure to comply with these regulations can result in legal consequences, including fines and lawsuits. Beyond legal compliance, accessible design demonstrates a commitment to social responsibility and can enhance an organization's reputation. Therefore, it is important for organizations to adhere to accessibility guidelines and standards, such as the Web Content Accessibility Guidelines (WCAG), when creating charts and reports. This not only ensures legal compliance but also promotes inclusivity and ensures that insights are available to all stakeholders, regardless of their abilities.

Documentation

The importance of thorough documentation cannot be overstated. *Code documentation* plays a pivotal role in ensuring that the analytical or modeling processes are transparent, reproducible, and maintainable. This involves thoroughly commenting the code to explain the logic behind each step, the choice of certain parameters, and the structure of the algorithms used. It's not just about what the code is doing, but also why certain decisions were made, which is essential for future reference or for other team members who may work on the project.

The *data dictionary* is a detailed description of each data element within your dataset. This includes the name of each field, its data type (e.g., integer, string, date), a description of what it represents, and any relevant metadata such as its source, the range of values it can take, and how it relates to other data elements. This dictionary is invaluable for anyone who needs to understand the data's structure and meaning, including data scientists, analysts, and decision makers.

Metadata goes beyond the data dictionary by providing context about the data. It includes information about the data's origins, how and when it was collected, any transformations it has undergone, and the quality and reliability of the data. Metadata can also include information about the models developed, such as the version of the model, the training and testing data used, and the performance metrics. This information is essential for evaluating the robustness and applicability of the models.

Finally, *change descriptions* are critical for maintaining the integrity of the data and models over time. This involves documenting any updates, modifications, or corrections made to the data, the code, or the models. Change descriptions ensure that there is a clear record of how and why the project has evolved, which is essential for troubleshooting, auditing, and improving models and analyses over time.

Real World Scenario

Effective Communication of Data Science Results

BuyIrish, a retail company, has recently implemented a data science model aimed at optimizing its inventory management by predicting product demand using various factors such as seasonality, market trends, and historical sales data. The data science team wants to communicate the impact of this new model to distinct groups of stakeholders: the executive team, inventory managers, and the data science team, each requiring a unique level of detail and focus.

The team begins by selecting critical data points that illustrate the model's impact. Key metrics include the reduction in overstock percentages, increase in sales due to improved stock availability, and the enhancement in forecast accuracy compared to previous methods. Comparative data showcasing inventory levels before and after the model's implementation is also prepared.

For the executive team, a high-level dashboard is designed, featuring pie charts depicting cost savings, line graphs showing sales improvements over time, and bullet points highlighting forecast accuracy improvements. This presentation is succinct, emphasizing strategic impacts like cost reduction and sales enhancement.

For inventory managers, a detailed report is created, focusing on operational insights. This includes bar charts comparing stock levels of key products pre- and post-model implementation, heat maps displaying demand patterns across regions, and scatter plots correlating marketing initiatives with demand surges. This report shows managers how the model impacts their day-to-day inventory decisions.

For the data science team and other data scientists at the company, an in-depth technical report is compiled, which includes complex model diagnostic plots, comprehensive performance metrics, error analyses, and data quality assessments. This report is intended to help the audience understand the model's performance in depth and identify potential areas for future improvement.

In all communications, ethical standards are upheld with a commitment to truthful, nondeceptive reporting. The design choices ensure accessibility, with attention to color and font selection and the inclusion of alternative text for visual elements, catering to those with visual impairments. Comprehensive documentation accompanies each report: an executive summary for top management, annotated details for managers, and extensive technical documentation for the technical team. This ensures that all stakeholders not only receive information in a format tailored to their needs but also have access to resources for a deeper understanding and reference.

Model Deployment

Model deployment is the process of releasing a new machine learning model or the integration of a trained machine learning model into an existing production environment. Effective model deployment requires careful consideration of the constraints and expectations inherent in the production environment. There are several deployment environments and strategies that you can choose based on the specific requirements and constraints of your project. Understanding these various environments helps organizations make informed decisions to effectively support their data science initiatives.

As you prepare for the DataX exam, you should be able to compare and contrast various deployment environments. Understanding the strengths and weaknesses of each deployment approach is crucial, as it will enable you to make an informed decision when choosing the most suitable deployment strategy for different scenarios.

Containerization

Containerization is a method of packaging an application along with its dependencies and configurations in a *container*, which is an isolated, lightweight environment. Containers are resource-efficient because they share the host system's operating system. This allows them to be spun up or down quickly in response to demand. Containers are especially useful in data science for deploying solutions consistently across various environments and platforms. Containerization ensures that a data science solution runs the same way on a developer's laptop as it does in a production environment, regardless of any differences in the configurations of both environments. Data scientists can also benefit from containerization by dividing complex applications into microservices, such as using separate containers for data preprocessing, model training, and inference services. This modularity makes it easier to update, manage, and scale each service independently.

Container orchestration is the automated provisioning, deployment, scaling, and management of containers. It plays a pivotal role in deploying and managing containerized data science applications, particularly in large and complex environments. Key functions of container orchestration include load balancing, service discovery, automatic scaling based on demand, and resource allocation. It also allows for seamless rolling updates and rollbacks, and the ability to maintain high availability and implement zero-downtime deployments. This facilitates the MLOps principles of CI/CD (continuous integration/continuous delivery) by enabling teams to rapidly iterate and deploy new versions of data science models and applications with confidence and minimal manual intervention. Tools like Kubernetes, Docker Swarm, and Apache Mesos are commonly used for container orchestration.

Virtualization

Virtualization is another technology that facilitates robust model deployment. It involves creating one or more virtual machines (VMs) on top of a single physical machine. This is accomplished through the use of software called a hypervisor, which abstracts the hardware resources of a physical machine and allocates them to virtual machines. Each virtual machine operates independently and can run its own operating system and applications, as if it were a separate physical machine.

In deploying data science solutions, virtualization offers several advantages. It allows for the efficient utilization of physical resources. Multiple data science environments, each with potentially different configurations, dependencies, and operating systems, can coexist on the same physical server without interference. This means resources can be allocated more efficiently, reducing hardware costs and simplifying infrastructure management.

Virtualization also enhances the flexibility and scalability of data science operations. VMs can be easily created, copied, moved, and resized, which is particularly beneficial during the experimental and development stages of a data science project. This allows data science teams to quickly set up and dismantle different environments for testing various models or algorithms.

Virtualization enables the reproducibility of data science experiments. Since each VM can encapsulate the entire environment needed for a particular experiment (data, model, operating system, additional software, configurations, etc.), it ensures that experiments can be reproduced reliably by simply spinning up another copy of the VM.

Virtualization also supports better isolation and security. Each VM is isolated from others, which reduces the risk that issues in one environment will affect others. Additionally, if a VM encounters a problem or is compromised, it can be shut down or rolled back to a previous state without impacting the physical host or other VMs.

Containerization vs. Virtualization

Virtualization involves the creation of virtual machines (VMs) on physical hardware using a hypervisor, where each VM houses not only the application but also an entire operating system. This approach is particularly suitable for scenarios requiring different operating systems or highly isolated environments on the same physical server.

Containerization, in contrast, encapsulates an application along with its dependencies into a container, which runs on the host's operating system kernel. This method is favored for its lightweight nature and the consistent environment it provides across various development, testing, and production stages. Containers are more resource-efficient compared to VMs, as they share the host system's kernel and do not require a separate operating system.

Cluster Deployment

Cluster deployment refers to the use of a group of interconnected computers, or nodes, working together as a single system to provide higher availability, reliability, and scalability. This approach is particularly useful for deploying data science solutions that require extensive computational resources or that need to handle large volumes of data.

In a cluster, tasks are distributed among the nodes, allowing for parallel processing and faster computation. This is especially beneficial for complex data processing tasks, deep learning model training, and large-scale data analysis. Clusters can be set up in dedicated on-premises servers or in cloud environments, depending on an organization's infrastructure and resource needs.

One of the key advantages of cluster deployment is its ability to handle big data workloads efficiently. Technologies such as Hadoop and Spark are often used in cluster environments to process and analyze large datasets distributed across multiple nodes. These frameworks provide the necessary tools for data partitioning, parallel processing, and fault tolerance, making them well suited for data-intensive tasks.

Cluster deployment also improves scalability by allowing nodes to be added or removed from the cluster in response to resource demand. Improved scalability ensures that data science applications can effectively handle growth in data volume and/or increased computational complexity without an appreciable impact on performance.

Finally, clusters provide high availability and failover capabilities. If one node fails, workloads can be automatically redistributed to other nodes in a cluster. This minimizes downtime and ensures continuity in operations. This is a critical benefit for data science applications where downtime can have significant consequences.

Cloud Deployment

The cloud has become a popular choice for deploying data science solutions due to its flexibility, scalability, and cost-effectiveness. In cloud environments, data scientists can access a wide range of computing resources and tools on demand, without the need for significant up-front investment in physical infrastructure. Being able to dynamically scale resources up or down based on workload is particularly beneficial for processing large datasets or handling variable computational loads typical in many machine learning tasks.

Another benefit of cloud deployment is the ease of access to specialized machine learning and analytics services. Most major cloud providers offer a suite of tools and platforms specifically designed for data science and machine learning, such as Google Cloud AI, Amazon SageMaker, and Azure Machine Learning. These platforms provide prebuilt algorithms, data processing workflows, and easy integration with other cloud services, which simplify the development and deployment of complex models.

Cloud environments also support a wide range of deployment models, from serverless architectures, which abstract the underlying infrastructure further, to containerized deployments, which offer greater control and flexibility. This versatility allows data science teams to choose the deployment strategy that best fits their specific requirements and constraints.

Deploying data science solutions to the cloud offers significant advantage in terms of collaboration and data accessibility. It allows team members to access the same central repository of resources and to collaborate more effectively regardless of their geographical locations. Cloud providers usually offer sophisticated access control mechanisms that allow administrators to define who can access specific resources. This ensures that sensitive information is only accessible to authorized personnel while still promoting collaboration among team members.

On-Premises Deployment

The cloud is an ideal deployment option for most data science solutions. However, in industries or for solutions with strict data privacy regulations such as healthcare, finance, and government projects, on-premises deployment may be preferred. Having full control over the data science environment, including the computing resources, data storage, and network infrastructure, means that organizations can enforce security protocols, compliance standards, and data management policies that govern access to sensitive data.

On-premises deployment also offers data scientists the flexibility to customize hardware and software to meet specific project needs or requirements. For example, servers can be customized for high-performance computing tasks, such as training complex machine learning models or processing very large datasets in parallel. This flexibility can lead to improved performance for resource-intensive data science applications.

However, on-premises deployment also requires significant investment in physical infrastructure—servers, storage, and networking equipment. It also involves ongoing maintenance costs and the need for a skilled IT team to manage and support the infrastructure. Additionally, scaling services on premises can be a challenge due to hard limitations in hardware capacity and physical space.

Hybrid Deployment

Hybrid deployment is a strategy that integrates both the cloud and on-premises deployment models in order to leverage the benefits of both. It enables organizations to keep sensitive data on premises, where they have direct control over security and compliance, while leveraging the cloud's scalability and flexibility for other aspects of their operations.

However, the major challenge with hybrid deployment lies in ensuring seamless integration and secure data exchange between the cloud and on-premises environments. This requires robust networking, consistent data management policies, and strong security measures to prevent data breaches and maintain data integrity. Organizations must also manage the complexity of operating across different platforms, which can involve compatibility issues, varying performance characteristics, and the need for specialized skills.

Edge Deployment

Edge deployment in data science refers to the practice of deploying machine learning models and data processing tasks closer to the source of the data (the "edge" of the network). This approach is used in scenarios where real-time data processing is crucial, such as in IoT

(Internet of Things) devices, mobile applications, and remote sensor networks. The primary advantage of edge deployment is the reduction in latency, as data doesn't have to be sent to a central server or the cloud for processing; instead, it gets processed directly on the edge device, leading to faster response times.

Another significant benefit of edge deployment is the reduction in network bandwidth and cost. By processing all or most of the data locally, edge deployment means that the amount of data that needs to be transferred over the network is minimized. This is particularly beneficial in cases where network connectivity is limited or expensive. It also helps in scenarios where continuous connectivity to a central server cannot be guaranteed.

Edge deployment also enhances privacy and security, as sensitive data can be processed locally without being transmitted over the network. This is particularly useful for applications that deal with personally identifiable or confidential information.

Deploying data science solutions at the edge does come with some challenges. Edge devices often have limited computational resources and storage capacity compared to traditional data centers or cloud environments. Additionally, managing and updating models across a large number of distributed edge devices can be a complex endeavor.

Machine Learning Operations (MLOps)

Machine learning operations (MLOps) is an interdisciplinary field that borrows from the principles of DevOps to improve the end-to-end lifecycle of machine learning applications. *DevOps* is a set of practices and cultural philosophies that aim to unify software development (Dev) and IT operations (Ops), with the goal of shortening the software development lifecycle and delivering high-quality software continuously and efficiently. Similarly, the goal of MLOps is to bridge the gap between the experimental phase of developing machine learning models and their operational deployment and maintenance in production environments.

At a high level, the MLOps process is structured into three main iterative and interconnected phases:

- **Design:** In the design phase, the focus is to understand the business and the data in order to craft an ML solution tailored to the user's needs. The activities in this phase involve defining and prioritizing machine learning use cases, evaluating available data for model training, and detailing both functional and nonfunctional requirements. These activities help guide the architectural design, the serving strategy, and the development of a test suite for the eventual model.

- **Experimentation and Development:** This is the phase where the feasibility of an end-to-end solution is tested through proof-of-concept models. It includes selecting and refining algorithms, data engineering, and model engineering, activities that are all aimed at creating a stable and high-quality model ready for production.

- **Operations:** The operations phase is about deploying the model into a production environment. It incorporates DevOps best practices such as testing, versioning, continuous delivery, and monitoring.

Explaining the importance of DevOps and MLOps principles in data science is a DataX exam objective. Make note of the principles of automation, versioning, testing, and monitoring introduced in this section and the important role they play in the MLOps pipeline.

Automation

A central component of MLOps is automation. MLOps requires that all or most of the machine learning pipeline or workflow be automated. This includes stages such as data preprocessing, model training, evaluation, deployment, and monitoring. By automating these steps, MLOps aims to increase the efficiency, speed, and repeatability of machine learning workflows.

The degree to which the stages in the workflow are automated reflects the maturity of the MLOps process. The ideal is a seamless ML workflow, where all steps—from data handling to model training and deployment—are automated without the need for manual intervention. The evolution toward a mature MLOps process can be characterized by three levels of automation:

- **Manual Process (Level 0):** This foundational level is typical of early ML implementations. At this maturity level, all tasks are performed manually and mostly in sequence (as shown in Figure 7.6). This includes data preparation, model training, and testing.

FIGURE 7.6   Sample ML pipeline illustrating Level 0 MLOps maturity

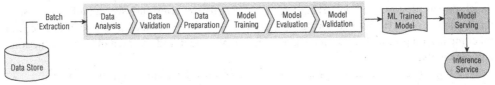

Source: Medium / https://medium.com/encora-technology-practices/introducing-mlops-9d5d2d35de04 / Last accessed March 18, 2024.

- **Automated ML Pipeline (Level 1):** This intermediate level includes an automated process of using new data to retrain models in production (as shown in Figure 7.7). Continuous training is possible in this stage, with new data automatically triggering retraining processes.

- **CI/CD Pipeline Automation (Level 2):** At the most advanced MLOps maturity level, the entire ML workflow, from data acquisition to model deployment, is automated using CI/CD systems. Continuous integration systems ensure that components are built, tested, and packaged when new code is committed to a source code repository, whereas continuous delivery systems ensure that new pipeline implementations are continuously delivered to the production environment. This process is illustrated in Figure 7.8.

FIGURE 7.7 Sample ML pipeline illustrating Level 1 MLOps maturity

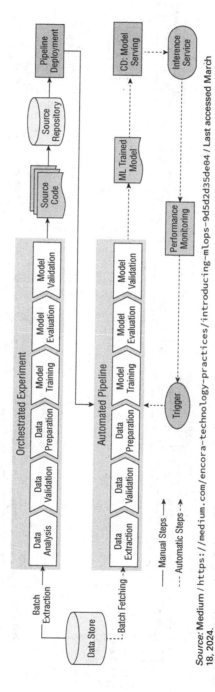

Source: Medium / https://medium.com/encora-technology-practices/introducing-mlops-9d5d2d35de04 / Last accessed March 18, 2024.

FIGURE 7.8 Sample ML pipeline illustrating Level 2 MLOps maturity

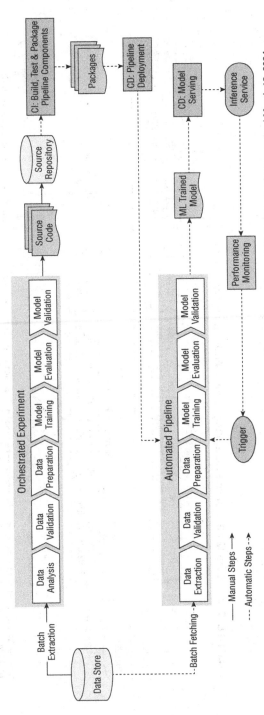

Source: Medium / https://medium.com/encora-technology-practices/introducing-mlops-9d5d2d35de04 / Last accessed March 18, 2024.

Versioning

Another core component of MLOps is robust version control. This extends beyond traditional code versioning to include versioning of the datasets used for training, the models themselves, and the MLOps pipeline.

Versioning offers numerous benefits that enhance the machine learning lifecycle:

- It ensures reproducibility, allowing teams to replicate results and fully understand the implications of each iterative change.

- In collaborative environments, versioning enables team members to work concurrently on different aspects of a project without conflict. This is particularly important for experiment tracking, where maintaining different versions of experiments allows for effective comparison and refinement of models.

- By providing a detailed history of data, models, and code changes, versioning facilitates auditability and compliance. This is critical in fields with stringent data governance standards.

Data Versioning

Data versioning involves keeping track of different versions of datasets used for training and evaluating machine learning models. By versioning data, teams can ensure reproducibility in experiments, track changes in data over time, and understand how these changes impact model performance. Common data versioning tools include DVC (Data Version Control), Pachyderm, Delta Lake, and Git LFS (Large File Storage).

Code Versioning

Code versioning refers to maintaining different versions of the codebase that does data pre-processing, model training, model evaluation, and model deployment in a machine learning pipeline. Code versioning facilitates MLOps pipelines by enabling teams to track changes, and to revert to earlier versions of the codebase if a new change causes issues. Common code versioning tools include Git, SVN (Subversion), and Mercurial.

Model Versioning

Each iteration of a machine learning model, including changes to its architecture, hyper-parameters, or deployment environment, can also be versioned. This practice allows teams to roll back to previous models when necessary and to understand the evolution of model performance over time. Common model versioning tools include MLflow and DVC.

Pipeline Versioning

The entire MLOps pipeline can be versioned as well. This involves keeping track of each aspect of the pipeline, from data ingestion to model deployment. Similar to data, code, and model versioning, pipeline versioning is essential for rolling back changes. However, it allows for an entire workflow to be rolled back, not just individual models or datasets. Common pipeline versioning tools in MLOps include Kubeflow Pipelines for managing machine learning workflows on Kubernetes, Apache Airflow for orchestrating complex data pipelines, and Pachyderm for version-controlled data pipelines.

Testing

Testing and validation are just as important in MLOps as they are in traditional software development. They involve not only ensuring that code is free of bugs but also that a model performs well on the intended tasks, generalizes well to new data, and adheres to ethical guidelines. Some of the testing and validation approaches used in MLOps are:

- **Offline Validation:** Offline validation involves testing a model against historical data. This is important for initial testing and for situations where live testing is impractical or risky. Offline validation typically includes techniques like cross-validation and the use of holdout datasets. In MLOps, this is often automated as part of the continuous integration pipeline, ensuring that every model iteration is rigorously tested before it is considered for deployment.

- **Online Validation:** Once a model is deployed, online validation comes into play. It involves evaluating a model's performance in the real world by monitoring how it performs with live data in production. Online validation is critical in MLOps for assessing the actual effectiveness of a model and for catching issues like concept drift, where a model's performance degrades over time due to unforeseen changes in the statistical properties of the target variable that the model is trying to predict.

- **Model A/B Testing:** This involves running two or more models simultaneously on similar data and comparing their performances. A/B testing is a powerful method for evaluating the effectiveness of new models or model changes in a controlled manner.

Monitoring

In an MLOps pipeline, continuous monitoring is essential once models are deployed into a production environment. It ensures that models perform as expected over time and that issues such as concept drift or model decay are identified and addressed promptly. Figure 7.9 illustrates how monitoring is used to remediate model decay over time. In the example, the F1 score is used as a key performance metric to evaluate a model's performance over time. If the model's performance declines (or decays) below a certain threshold as measured by the F1-score, an automated retraining process is triggered. The goal of this is to restore the model's performance back to acceptable levels.

FIGURE 7.9   Model decay monitoring as part of an MLOps pipeline

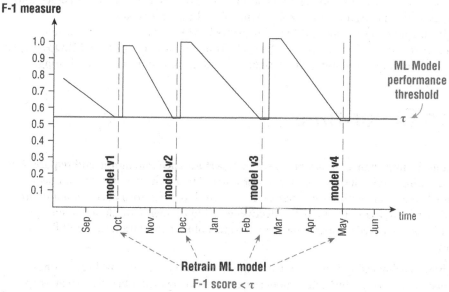

Source: Medium / https://medium.com/encora-technology-practices/introducing-mlops-9d5d2d35de04 / Last accessed March 18, 2024.

Summary

Model validation involves ensuring that a model meets design specifications and requirements before deployment. Key statistical metrics like accuracy, precision, recall, and RMSE are used to assess a model's effectiveness.

Validation also encompasses constraints specified during the design stage, like time, resource, and cost constraints. Time constraints influence algorithm complexity and the need for timely deployment. Resource constraints dictate the model's complexity and efficiency, especially for applications with limited computational resources. Cost constraints weigh the cost of building and maintaining a model against expected benefits.

Benchmarking is used to validate the choice of a model by measuring its performance against a standard baseline, to verify that it delivers substantial enhancements. Benchmarking is also used to evaluate a model against traditional methods to determine if it provides practical advantages.

Effective communication of model results involves the selection of relevant data, appropriate visualization techniques, and adapting the message to the needs of the audience. It is also crucial to uphold ethical practices, ensure accessible design for all users, and provide thorough documentation to support the communication of model findings.

Common deployment strategies include containerization for consistent deployment across environments, virtualization for resource efficiency, cluster deployment for scalability, cloud deployment for flexibility and scalability, on-premises deployment for increased control over data privacy and security, hybrid deployment for leveraging the benefits of both cloud and on-premises deployments, and edge deployment for real-time processing.

Machine learning operations (MLOps) integrates DevOps principles into machine learning. It covers the entire data science lifecycle from design to operations. MLOps emphasizes automation, robust version control, rigorous testing, and continuous monitoring.

Exam Essentials

Understand the importance of design constraints, performance evaluation, and requirements validation during model design.   Design constraints evaluate the viability of a model by assessing whether it fits within time, resource, and cost limits. Performance evaluation uses statistical metrics to assess the model's effectiveness. Requirements validation aligns the model with business needs, confirming it meets stakeholder expectations and fulfills core objectives.

Explain how benchmarking is used to justify model selection.   Benchmarking justifies model selection by comparing a new model's performance against a baseline, such as an existing model or industry standard, to determine if it offers significant improvements. It also compares the model to conventional processes to assess if it provides tangible benefits, like improved operational efficiency or decision making, which are critical for stakeholder acceptance.

Know the key concepts to consider when communicating model results.   When you're communicating model results, key concepts to consider include selecting relevant data that supports the core message, using appropriate visualizations to elucidate the model's insights, tailoring the communication to the audience's level of expertise, ensuring ethical reporting standards, designing for accessibility, and providing comprehensive documentation for transparency and credibility.

Know the differences between cloud, on-premises, hybrid, and edge deployment.   Cloud deployment involves using Internet-hosted server resources. On-premises deployment is where services are deployed within an organization's local infrastructure. Hybrid deployment combines cloud and on-premises deployment strategies. Edge deployment places resources closer to the source of data to minimize latency.

Explain the importance of MLOps principles in data science.   MLOps principles are critical in data science because they provide a framework for consistent, efficient, and scalable machine learning workflows, bridging the gap between experimental development and operational deployment. MLOps fosters automation, rigorous testing, version control, and monitoring, which are all essential for the long-term success and governance of data science projects.

Review Questions

1. A healthcare organization wants to deploy a data science solution that requires frequent updates and modular management of different services like data preprocessing and inference. Which deployment approach is best suited for their use case?

    A. Edge deployment

    B. Virtualization

    C. Containerization

    D. Cluster deployment

2. A data science team is tasked with communicating the results of a complex model to a group of peers and professional stakeholders with technical backgrounds. What type of documentation would be most appreciated by this audience for understanding the methodology and statistical nuances of the model?

    A. Metadata

    B. Data dictionary

    C. Code documentation

    D. Change descriptions

3. For a model that predicts housing prices, which of the following visualizations would be most appropriate to assess if the model captures the data patterns correctly without systematic errors?

    A. Time-series decomposition plot

    B. Decision tree visualization

    C. Residual plot

    D. Feature importance chart

4. A team is validating a model designed for use in mobile devices by focusing on ensuring that the model runs efficiently on limited hardware. Which of the following model validation concepts is the team primarily concerned with?

    A. Inference performance

    B. Cost constraints

    C. Business requirements

    D. Resource constraints

5. Why is benchmarking against a baseline important in model validation?

    A. To determine if the increased complexity of a new model is justified

    B. To determine if a model meets business requirements

    C. To determine if a model performs better than existing business processes

    D. To determine if an existing model is due for replacement

6. An e-commerce company needs to dynamically scale its machine learning resources based on varying workloads, especially during high-traffic events like holiday sales events. Which deployment option is most suitable?

   A. On-premises deployment

   B. Hybrid deployment

   C. Edge deployment

   D. Cluster deployment

7. A healthcare company has developed a model to predict patient outcomes. The cost of false negatives is high. Which of these visualization options is best suited to communicate the model results?

   A. An ROC curve

   B. A precision-recall curve

   C. A confusion matrix

   D. A feature importance chart

8. A retail business is deploying a new model to predict inventory stock levels. They decide to compare the model's performance against their current spreadsheet-based stock estimation process. What model validation activity are they doing?

   A. Benchmarking against a baseline

   B. Benchmarking against conventional processes

   C. Business requirements alignment

   D. Performance evaluation

9. A data science team has developed a model for predicting real estate prices. They notice that the variance of residuals depends on the fitted values. What does this indicate about their model?

   A. The model has high accuracy.

   B. The data might be nonlinear.

   C. The model's predictions are reliable.

   D. The model fits the data well.

10. A new model for loan approval has been developed. During validation, its performance is compared to an existing simpler model. This process is an example of:

   A. Benchmarking against a baseline

   B. Business requirements alignment

   C. Performance evaluation

   D. Benchmarking against conventional processes

11. A team is deploying a stock price prediction model. What aspect of model validation should be a primary focus?

    A. The model's accuracy

    B. The model's ability to adapt over time

    C. The time it takes to train the model

    D. The cost of training the model

12. A company's data science project involves multiple team members. Why is code versioning important in this context?

    A. To track individual contributions

    B. To restrict changes in the codebase

    C. To ensure all team members work at the same time

    D. To enable concurrent work without conflicts

13. A financial institution plans to deploy a machine learning model in a highly regulated industry. They are concerned about data privacy and security. Which deployment method should they prioritize?

    A. Cloud deployment

    B. On-premises deployment

    C. Hybrid deployment

    D. Edge deployment

14. In MLOps, which of these is the purpose of post-deployment monitoring?

    A. To determine when to switch to a different model

    B. To ensure that the model continues to perform well

    C. To track the model's cost-effectiveness

    D. To monitor how well the model is received

15. A company is deploying a real-time analytics model. Which deployment approach should they use if fast data processing is the main priority?

    A. Cloud deployment

    B. On-premises deployment

    C. Hybrid deployment

    D. Edge deployment

16. How is a residual plot used in model validation for regression models?

    A. To compare different models

    B. To assess a model's goodness of fit

    C. To visualize a model's accuracy

    D. To visualize a model's decision process

17. Which of these is an advantage of containerization?
    A. Increased privacy
    B. Improved model accuracy
    C. Consistent deployment
    D. Reduced need for monitoring

18. What is the primary goal of model validation in the data science lifecycle?
    A. To ensure the model meets performance expectations
    B. To ensure the model meets design specifications and satisfies requirements
    C. To ensure the model meets the needs of customers
    D. To ensure that the model is ready for deployment

19. A tech company wants to compare the performance of two different recommendation algorithms. They decide to run both algorithms simultaneously on their platform. What is this approach called?
    A. Model A/B testing
    B. Precision-recall analysis
    C. Residual analysis
    D. Online validation

20. A financial institution is deploying a fraud detection model. They need to ensure the model's decisions can be easily understood and explained. Which type of visualization is most appropriate?
    A. Decision tree visualization
    B. ROC curve
    C. Feature importance chart
    D. Interactive dashboard

Chapter

8

Unsupervised Machine Learning

THE COMPTIA DATAX EXAM OBJECTIVES COVERED IN THIS CHAPTER INCLUDE:

✓ **Domain 3: Machine Learning**

- 3.1 Given a scenario, apply foundational machine learning concepts.

- 3.5 Explain concepts related to unsupervised machine learning.

Unsupervised machine learning is an approach to machine learning that focuses on identifying patterns and relationships in unlabeled data. In this chapter, we explore several unsupervised machine learning approaches, such as the use of association rules to identify products frequently bought together and cluster analysis for customer segmentation and image processing. We also look at how certain unsupervised machine learning algorithms, such as principal component analysis (PCA), can be used for dimensionality reduction. The chapter concludes with an exploration of recommender systems and how they are used to predict user preferences and tailor recommendations.

Association Rules

Association rules are a set of if-then statements used in data science to describe the co-occurrence of items within a transaction set. Association rules are used in a wide variety of domains but are most often used for *market basket analysis*, which is the analysis of customer purchasing behavior.

In market basket analysis, the data or set of transactions being analyzed is referred to as market basket data. Table 8.1 is an example of a simple market basket dataset. Each row in the market basket data consists of a distinct set of items that were purchased together. These items are collectively known as a *transaction*. For example, transaction A consists of fruit, bread, and cereal, while transaction B consists of fruit, milk, cereal, and eggs. The amount or quantity of items purchased is not important. All we care about is that a particular item was purchased.

TABLE 8.1 Sample market basket data

Transaction	Items bought
A	Fruit, bread, cereal
B	Fruit, milk, cereal, eggs
C	Bread, milk, cereal, cheese
D	Fruit, bread, milk, cereal
E	Fruit, bread, milk, cheese

Within market basket data, any distinct set of one or more items within a transaction set is known as an *itemset*. Using an association rule, we can describe the relationship between two itemsets, as shown in Figure 8.1. This rule states that customers who bought bread and cereal also purchased milk. It suggests that a strong relationship may exist between the sales of bread, cereal, and milk. The itemset on the left side of the rule (before the arrow) is the condition that needs to be met. It is known as the *antecedent* of the rule, whereas the itemset on the right side of the rule (after the arrow) is the expected result of meeting the condition. It is known as the *consequent* of the rule. Note that the left and right itemsets that make up an association rule are disjoint. This means that they are distinct and have no items in common.

FIGURE 8.1 Sample association rule

For the most part, association rules can be classified into three major categories:

- **Trivial Rules:** Most association rules are trivial. These are rules that provide insight that is already well known by those familiar with the domain. For example, a rule that shows that customers who buy pencils often also buy erasers does not really provide meaningful new insight.

- **Inexplicable Rules:** These are rules that defy rational explanation, need more research to understand, or do not suggest a clear course of action. For example, a rule that suggests that customers who buy shirts are more likely to also buy backpacks does not provide clear insight and requires a little bit more research to understand why.

- **Actionable Rules:** These are rules that provide clear and useful insights that can be acted upon. They sometimes are rules that initially seemed inexplicable but then turn out to be actionable after some research. For example, we may discover that the rule that suggests that customers who buy shirts are more likely to also buy backpacks is strongest during the back-to-school shopping season. This provides some context to categorize this rule as actionable.

Association rules do not imply causality; they simply highlight the co-occurrence of events or items within a dataset. Understanding causality requires domain knowledge and further research into how items or events interact with each other over time, using an advanced analytic method such as a randomized control trial, which was introduced in Chapter 6, "Modeling and Evaluation."

Identifying Strong Rules

It often takes skill and patience to identify truly actionable rules. To determine which rules are potentially actionable, we need to first identify which rules are significant or interesting and limit our focus to those alone.

Support

One measure of the significance of a rule is how often the rule occurs. The frequency of a rule is measured using a metric called *support*. Also known as *coverage*, the support of a rule is the fraction of transactions that contain the rule. To illustrate how to calculate and interpret support, let's reconsider the market basket dataset from Table 8.1. The support of the rule {bread, cereal}→{milk} is:

$$Support_{\{bread,\ cereal\}\rightarrow\{milk\}} = \frac{Transactions\ with\ bread,\ cereal,\ and\ milk}{Total\ number\ of\ transactions} = 0.4$$

There are five transactions in the dataset, and two of them include bread, cereal, and milk, the itemsets contained in both the antecedent and the consequent. A support value of 0.4 means that 40 percent of all transactions in the dataset include bread, cereal, and milk. The support metric is useful in identifying strong rules because rules with low support are rules that don't occur a lot. They may occur simply by chance and are typically not actionable. By setting a minimum support threshold, we can improve our chances of finding actionable rules by limiting our focus to just those itemsets that occur a lot. These itemsets are known as *frequent itemsets*.

There are several approaches to generate frequent itemsets. Two of the most common are the Apriori algorithm and the FP-Growth algorithm. The particulars of both approaches are beyond the scope of this text and the DataX exam. For additional information, see https://en.wikipedia.org/wiki/Association_rule_learning.

Confidence

Another metric often used to quantify the strength of an association rule is *confidence*. The confidence of a rule is the predictive power or accuracy of the rule. It ranges in value from 0 to 1. The confidence of a rule is calculated by dividing the support of the rule by the support of the antecedent of the rule. For example, based on the market basket data in Table 8.1, the confidence of the rule {bread, cereal}→{milk} is:

$$Confidence_{\{bread,\ cereal\}\rightarrow\{milk\}} = \frac{Support_{\{bread,\ cereal\}\rightarrow\{milk\}}}{Support_{\{bread,\ cereal\}}} = \frac{0.4}{0.6} = 0.67$$

The support of the rule is 0.4 and the support of the antecedent, {bread, cereal}, is 0.6. A confidence value of 0.67 can be interpreted to mean that, of all the transactions where both bread and cereal were purchased, 67 percent of them also included the purchase of milk.

Lift

A third metric that is often used to quantify the strength of an association rule is *lift*. The lift of a rule tells us how much more the antecedent and consequent occur together in contrast to how often they occur independently. In other words, lift is the strength of association. Lift values range from 0 to infinity, where a value of 1 indicates independence between the antecedent and the consequent. Lift values less than 1 indicate a reduced likelihood of the antecedent and precedent occurring together, whereas values above 1 indicate an increased likelihood.

The lift of a rule is computed by dividing the confidence of the rule by the support of the consequent of the rule. For example, based on the market basket data in Table 8.1, the lift of the rule {bread, cereal}→{milk} is:

$$Lift_{\{bread, cereal\} \to \{milk\}} = \frac{Confidence_{\{bread, cereal\} \to \{milk\}}}{Support_{\{milk\}}} = \frac{0.67}{0.8} = 0.84$$

The confidence of the rule is 0.67, while 0.8 is the support of the consequent, {milk}. We can interpret the lift value of 0.84 to mean that customers who bought bread and cereal are 16 percent less likely to also buy milk compared to all customers who bought milk. Because the lift value was less than 1, we subtracted it from 1 to get the reduction in likelihood (0.16 or 16 percent). If the lift value were more than 1, we would interpret it as a multiplier of likelihood. For example, if our lift value were 2.4, this would mean that customers who bought bread and cereal are 2.4 times more likely to also buy milk.

Clustering

Clustering or *cluster analysis* is an unsupervised machine learning approach that is used to categorize or segment data into subgroups (*clusters*) based on similarity. There are two primary goals of clustering. The first is to ensure that the items within a particular cluster are as similar as possible (high intraclass similarity). The second goal is to make sure that items within one cluster are as different as possible from items in other clusters (low interclass similarity).

Clustering is used in a wide variety of domains. It is sometimes used in the domain of network security to detect anomalous behavior in computer networks. Clustering can also be used to automatically group or categorize documents based on similarity. In retail, clustering is often used to segment customers for marketing purposes. Clustering can also be used for image segmentation and compression.

There are several approaches to clustering, each with its own strengths and weaknesses. The type of clustering one chooses to use is often dependent on the characteristics of the data and the type of clusters needed. In general, clustering approaches can be categorized as either centroid-based, connectivity-based, or density-based.

As you prepare for the DataX exam, you should be able to explain concepts related to unsupervised machine learning. Make note of how each of the clustering approaches introduced in this section work. Also make note of when it is best to use each one.

Centroid-Based Clustering

Centroid-based clustering is a clustering approach that partitions items into distinct groups based on how close each item is to a *centroid*. A centroid is a central data point or vector that represents a typical value in each group. *k-means clustering* is the most widely used centroid-based clustering algorithm.

k-means clustering, often referred to as Lloyd's algorithm, consists of three basic steps. The first step is to randomly select k centroids (cluster centers), where k is a user-defined number representing the number of clusters desired. The second step involves assigning each item in the dataset to the cluster center nearest to it. "Nearest" is typically determined based on a distance measure such as *Euclidean (straight line) distance*. After each item has been assigned to a cluster center, the centroids are recalculated in the third step. This usually means that each centroid is moved to the mean (average) location of all the items assigned to its cluster. Steps 2 and 3 are repeated iteratively. With each iteration, the centroids move, and items might be reassigned to different clusters. The algorithm eventually terminates when the centroids no longer change significantly, items remain in the same clusters, or a maximum number of iterations is reached. The output is a set of k centroids and convex-shaped clusters like the ones shown in Figure 8.2.

The k-means clustering algorithm is efficient and easy to use. However, it does have some limitations. First, k-means is sensitive to outliers. Outliers can significantly impact the calculation of cluster centers, potentially leading to less accurate clustering. Another limitation is that k-means is nondeterministic. This means that the results can vary based on the initial choice of centroids. As a result, k-means is often run multiple times with different initializations and the best result is chosen. Third, k-means works best when the clusters are spherical and of similar size. It usually does not work as well with clusters of different shapes and densities. A fourth limitation is that k-means is sensitive to the scale of data. Features with larger scales (larger range of values) can dominate distance calculations such as Euclidean distance, so it's important to normalize or standardize the data before applying k-means. Finally, the number of clusters (k) needs to be specified in advance. Finding the right number of clusters can be challenging and often involves some trial and error.

FIGURE 8.2   k-means clustering result showing five clusters

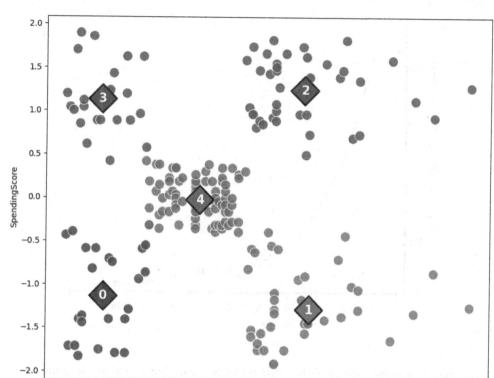

There are several approaches to choosing the "ideal" number of clusters in k-means clustering. One approach is to use a priori or domain knowledge. With this approach, we use our prior knowledge of the expected number of clusters to inform our choice of k. This could be based on existing business requirements or other known constraints. A more standard approach to choosing a value for k is to use one or more statistical approaches such as *the elbow method* or *the average silhouette method*.

The Elbow Method

The *Within Cluster Sum of Squares (WCSS)* metric quantifies the degree of similarity between items in a cluster. Specifically, it is the sum of the distances between the items in a cluster and the cluster centroid. As the value of k increases, the closer the items within each cluster become to the cluster centroid and the smaller the WCSS is. If we were to compute and plot the total WCSS for clusters created based on increasing values of k, we would get a convex curve with a negative slope much like the one in Figure 8.3.

FIGURE 8.3 The WCSS for clusters with *k* values from 1 to 10

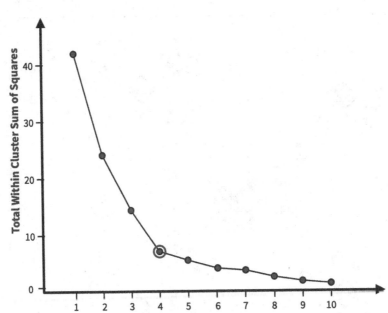

At some point in the curve, a visible bend typically occurs that represents the point at which increasing the value for *k* no longer yields a significant reduction in WCSS. This point is known as the elbow, and the *k* value at this point is usually expected to be the ideal number of clusters for the dataset.

The Average Silhouette Method

The *silhouette score* of an item within a cluster is a measure of how similar the item is to other items within the same cluster and how different it is from items in neighboring clusters. Similarity here is measured by Euclidean distance. The higher the silhouette value of an item, the more likely that it is in the right cluster (and vice versa). If most items in a cluster have a high silhouette value, then the average will also be high for a given *k*. If we were to compute and plot the average silhouette score for clusters created based on increasing values of *k*, we would get a plot much like the one in Figure 8.4. The *k* value corresponding to the highest average silhouette is expected to be the ideal number of clusters for the data.

FIGURE 8.4 The average silhouette score for clusters with *k* values from 1 to 10.

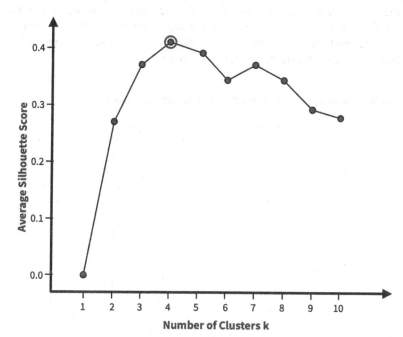

Connectivity-Based Clustering

Connectivity-based clustering or *hierarchical clustering* is an approach to clustering that creates a tree or hierarchy of clusters. It is a clustering approach well suited for working with hierarchical data, such as taxonomies. It is used in a wide variety of domains and tasks, such as gene and protein sequence analysis, information retrieval, and customer segmentation. The hierarchical clustering algorithm can take one of two approaches when creating the hierarchy of clusters:

- **The Agglomerative Approach:** This is a bottom-up approach, which starts by treating each data point as a single cluster. Then, the two closest clusters are merged into a single cluster. Next, the two next closest clusters are merged to form a larger cluster. This process is repeated iteratively to form progressively larger clusters until all data points are connected into a single cluster.

- **The Divisive Approach:** This is a top-down approach, which starts with all data points in a single cluster. In the next step, the cluster is divided into smaller clusters. This division process is repeated recursively in subsequent steps, leading to smaller and smaller clusters at each level. The process continues until each data point is in its own cluster or until a stopping criterion (such as a desired number of clusters) is reached.

The output of hierarchical clustering is often represented with a diagram known as a *dendrogram* (Figure 8.5). A dendrogram describes which clusters are connected at what distance, starting from the individual data points at the bottom all the way to the one single large cluster at the top. The height in the dendrogram at which two clusters are merged represents the distance between the two clusters in the data space.

FIGURE 8.5   Dendrogram showing result of hierarchical clustering

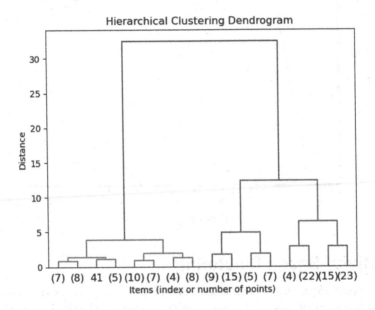

Unlike k-means clustering, where we need to first specify the number of clusters (*k*), there is no need to predefine the number of clusters with hierarchical clustering. The recommended choice of the "ideal" number of clusters for a dataset can be made by observing the dendrogram. It corresponds with the number of vertical lines in the dendrogram cut by a horizontal line that traverses the maximum vertical distance between the merger of two clusters.

In Figure 8.6, the maximum vertical distance between the merger of two clusters is between the dashed horizontal lines. The number of vertical lines cut by these two lines is two. This is the recommended choice for the "ideal" number of clusters.

FIGURE 8.6   Dendrogram showing the maximum vertical distance between the merger of two clusters

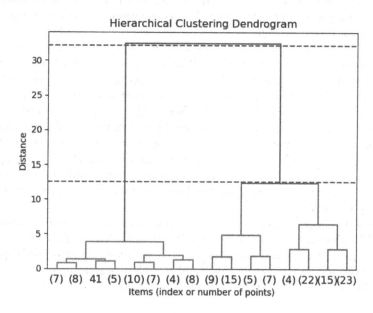

Hierarchical clustering, while useful in many contexts, does have several disadvantages. First, it can be more computationally intensive than other clustering methods, especially for large datasets, as it requires calculating the distances between all pairs of data points. Like k-means clustering, hierarchical clustering can be sensitive to noise and outliers because the presence of outliers can distort the distances between clusters, which leads to mis-groupings. Third, even with the use of a dendrogram, it can sometimes be difficult to determine the "ideal" number of clusters. The choice of where to cut the dendrogram to define clusters can be somewhat subjective and may not be clear-cut in practice. Another limitation is that there are several ways to calculate the distance between clusters. This can lead to different results, and there isn't always a clear reason to prefer one approach over another without domain-specific knowledge. Finally, hierarchical clustering may not perform well with certain types of data, such as high-dimensional data or datasets with complex shapes and varying densities.

Density-Based Clustering

Density-based clustering is an approach to clustering that creates clusters based on the density of data points within a region. Unlike k-means clustering and hierarchical clustering, which are based on distance metrics, density-based clustering focuses on separating regions of high data density from regions of low data density. The most well-known density-based clustering algorithm is *DBSCAN (density-based spatial clustering of applications with noise).*

The DBSCAN algorithm requires two parameters from a user. The first is the radius of a circle to be created around each data point. Items that fall within this circle are considered to be within the "neighborhood" of the data point. The second parameter is the minimum number of points that must fall within a neighborhood for a data point to be considered a *core point*.

To create clusters, the DBSCAN algorithm starts by randomly selecting a starting data point. If the starting point is a core point (as determined by the user-defined parameters), then the data points within its neighborhood are considered to be part of the same cluster as the starting point. The neighborhoods of each of the newly added points are then examined. If they are core points, then the points within their neighborhoods are also added to the cluster. This process is repeated until no additional points can be added to the cluster. Then another randomly selected point is chosen as the starting point for a new cluster. The process of determining whether a data point is a core point and adding items from its neighborhood to the same cluster is repeated until no more data points are available to be assigned to clusters. Any remaining data points are considered noise and are not included as part of a cluster. Basically, they are outliers.

Unlike k-means clustering, density-based clustering can discover clusters of arbitrary shapes (see Figure 8.7). This makes it suitable for complex datasets where clusters are not spherical, such as in geospatial applications, astronomy, and image analysis. With density-based clustering, we also do not have to predefine the number of clusters as we do for k-means clustering. The algorithm determines the "ideal" number of clusters based on the data.

FIGURE 8.7   Density-based clustering with DBSCAN

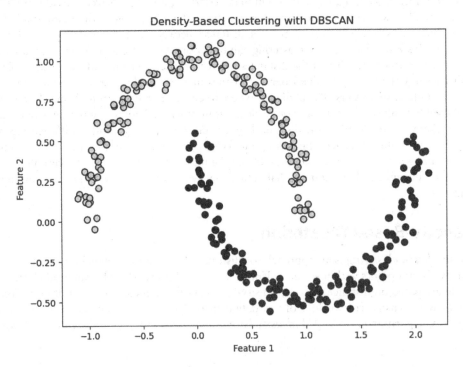

There are some inherent challenges with density-based clustering. The first is that choosing the "ideal" radius for a neighborhood and the minimum number of points for each neighborhood may require domain knowledge or some experimentation. Second, although density-based clustering performs better than hierarchical clustering on large datasets, its performance can degrade as the size and dimensionality of the dataset grows.

 Real World Scenario

Categorizing Customer Inquiries

TeleGlobe, a leading telecommunications company, is faced with the challenge of effectively streamlining customer support inquiries. They collect information about each inquiry, which includes the nature of the inquiry, demographic information about the customer, service type, and resolution time. Their objective is to categorize these inquiries into distinct groups to improve response time and quality of support.

Exploratory data analysis (EDA) on the inquiry dataset revealed that customers often have inquiries that span multiple categories. For example, a single inquiry might relate to both billing issues and technical support. EDA also revealed evidence of a nested structure to the inquiries. For example, some of the inquiries categorized as "Internet Connectivity" or "Device Troubleshooting" could both belong to a parent category called "Technical Issues."

The multidimensional and layered nature of TeleGlobe's customer support data makes *hierarchical clustering* an ideal choice. Its ability to uncover nested patterns and relationships without the need for a predefined number of clusters allows the company to gain a comprehensive understanding of its customer inquiries.

Dimensionality Reduction

Dimensionality reduction is the process of reducing the number of dimensions (or features) in a dataset while retaining as much of its information as possible. There are several reasons to reduce the dimensionality of a dataset, such as to improve the performance of a model, to reduce the computational complexity of the machine learning process, to minimize overfitting, to make it easier to visualize and interpret data, or to avoid *the curse of dimensionality*.

The curse of dimensionality refers to various phenomena that occur when working with high-dimensional data, which do not occur with lower-dimensional data. In machine learning, the curse of dimensionality is observed when the performance of a model trained on a fixed set of training samples first increases as the number of features increases, but eventually begins to degrade past a certain number of features (see Figure 8.8).

FIGURE 8.8   The curse of dimensionality

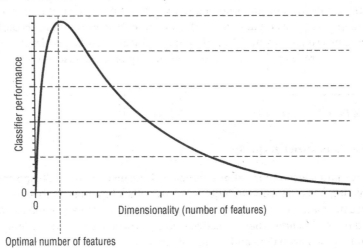

Optimal number of features

Source: Medium / https://towardsdatascience.com/dimensionality-reduction-for-machine-learning-80a46c2ebb7e / Last accessed March 19, 2024.

Several techniques are used in dimensionality reduction and they generally can be classified as either a *feature selection* technique or a *feature extraction* technique. Feature selection techniques focus on selecting a subset of the most significant features from the original data. We explored these techniques in Chapter 6. In this chapter, we will focus only on the techniques used for feature extraction.

Feature Extraction

Feature extraction (also known as *feature projection*) is the process of combining or transforming features into a new feature space of lower dimensionality. Unlike feature selection, feature extraction creates new features with different values from the original data. The goal is to capture as much of the significant information as possible from the original data using a new set of features. Some of the most commonly used feature extraction techniques are principal component analysis (PCA), singular value decomposition (SVD), t-distributed stochastic neighbor embedding (t-SNE), and uniform manifold approximation and projection (UMAP).

Principal Component Analysis

Principal component analysis (PCA) is a linear dimensionality reduction technique that transforms a set of correlated features into a smaller set of uncorrelated features (*principal components*), while retaining as much of the variation in the original data as possible.

There are several steps to the PCA algorithm. The first is to standardize the data so that each feature has a mean of 0 and a standard deviation of 1. Then a covariance matrix is computed. This matrix helps the algorithm understand how different features in the data are related to each other. Next, based on the covariance matrix, PCA computes a set of *eigenvectors* and corresponding *eigenvalues*. Eigenvectors are the principal components, and they represent the original data projected in a direction of increasing variance, whereas the eigenvalues represent the magnitude of variance in each direction. The eigenvectors are then sorted by their eigenvalues in descending order, which essentially ranks eigenvectors by how much information they hold about the data (or by importance). The idea is to pick the top few principal components that capture most of the important variations in the data. Finally, the original data is transformed or projected onto the principal components. If two components explain an adequate amount of variation, it has the advantage of being visualized with a scatter plot that may help with interpretability.

Singular Value Decomposition

Singular value decomposition (SVD) is a matrix factorization technique often used for dimensionality reduction. It reduces the dimensionality of a dataset by decomposing the data (as a matrix) into three matrices that allow the original data to be represented in reduced form.

Assuming the original data is represented as a data matrix A, SVD starts by factorizing this data matrix into three matrices:

- A matrix, U, that represents the relationship between the rows of A

- A diagonal matrix, Σ, with singular values sorted in descending order that represent the strength of each feature in A

- A matrix, V, that represents the relationship between the columns of matrix A

To reduce the dimensionality of matrix A, we can select the first k largest singular values in Σ and their corresponding vectors in U and V. We can call these new matrices U_k, Σ_k, and V_k. To obtain a new matrix, A_k, which is the reduced-dimensionality approximation of our original matrix A, we multiply U_k, Σ_k, and V_k. This new matrix has fewer features but still retains the most valuable information from the original data.

t-distributed Stochastic Neighbor Embedding

t-distributed stochastic neighbor embedding (t-SNE) is a nonlinear dimensionality reduction technique that is particularly well suited for the visualization of high-dimensional datasets. It is considered a nonlinear dimensionality reduction technique because the algorithm allows us to separate data that cannot be separated by a straight line.

The t-SNE algorithm begins by calculating the probability that pairs of data points in the high-dimensional space are related, effectively determining which points are "neighbors." It then maps the data to a lower-dimensional space, initially placing points randomly. Through an iterative process of attraction and repulsion—pulling neighbors closer and pushing non-neighbors further apart—it rearranges the points to maintain their high-dimensional relationships. The final output of t-SNE is a two- or three-dimensional map that visually represents the structure of the data, which may reveal patterns and relationships that were not apparent in higher-dimensional space.

Uniform Manifold Approximation and Projection

A relatively recent technique, *uniform manifold approximation and projection (UMAP)* is similar to t-SNE but is faster and scales better to larger datasets. It starts by exploring the data to understand its manifold structure—the way data points are grouped together in high-dimensional space. UMAP builds a network of these points, connecting each to its nearest neighbors. Unlike t-SNE, UMAP aims to preserve both the local and the global structure of the data using an optimization process, ensuring that points that are close in the high-dimensional space remain close in the lower-dimensional projection, while distant clusters remain far apart. The outcome is a simplified representation of the original dataset that brings out hidden patterns and structures in a form that is more accessible and easier to analyze visually.

It's important to note that the choice of which feature extraction technique to use depends on the goals of your data analysis, and the nature and size of your dataset. It also depends on the kind of insights you're looking to obtain. PCA and SVD are linear methods and are best for datasets where features exhibit a linear relationship. They are computationally efficient and widely used for preprocessing in machine learning pipelines. t-SNE and UMAP, on the other hand, are nonlinear techniques that are better suited for complex datasets with nonlinear relationships. They are primarily used for data visualization. While t-SNE is excellent for creating intuitive visualizations, it's not suitable for all types of quantitative analysis. UMAP, on the other hand, has more consistent and reproducible results, provides a good balance between preserving global and local structures, and is suitable for large datasets.

Recommender Systems

Recommender systems are information-filtering algorithms designed to predict or suggest items (such as movies, books, music, news, products) that are likely to be of interest to a user. They are particularly useful in helping users navigate the overwhelming number of available items a service may offer. There are several types of recommender systems, each using a different approach. Generally, recommender systems use a collaborative filtering approach, a content-based filtering approach, or a hybrid filtering approach.

As you prepare for the DataX exam, you should be able to apply foundational machine learning concepts to a problem. Make note of the core differences between the recommender systems introduced in this section and the best times to use them.

Collaborative Filtering

Collaborative filtering is a recommender system that uses a similarity-based approach to make recommendations between users and items. In other words, it assumes that if users A and B share similar interests, then they will also like similar items. The similarity between users and items is often calculated using measures such as cosine similarity, Pearson correlation, dot product, or Euclidean distance. Collaborative filtering makes use of a *user-item interactions matrix*, which stores past interactions between users and items, to produce new recommendations (see Figure 8.9). There are two common approaches to collaborative filtering: memory-based filtering and model-based filtering.

FIGURE 8.9   Illustration of a user-item interactions matrix

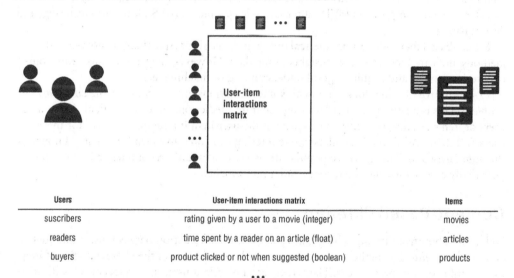

Users	User-item interactions matrix	Items
suscribers	rating given by a user to a movie (integer)	movies
readers	time spent by a reader on an article (float)	articles
buyers	product clicked or not when suggested (boolean)	products

• • •

Source: Medium / https://towardsdatascience.com/introduction-to-recommender-systems-6c66cf15ada / Last accessed March 19, 2024.

Memory-Based Collaborative Filtering

Also known as neighborhood-based collaborative filtering, memory-based collaborative filtering uses the entire user-item interactions matrix to generate predictions. The main idea is to find similar users or similar items to a target in the user-item interactions matrix, and then to use this information to predict what the target user will like. This is done in one of two ways:

- **User-User:** This approach attempts to find other users with a similar "interactions profile" as the target user and recommends items those users like to the target user. For example, if user A and user B tend to like similar items, then user B (the target user) will get recommendations for items that user A likes but that user B has not interacted with yet.

- **Item-Item:** This approach attempts to find other items with a similar "interactions profile" as the item liked by a target user and suggests those items to the user. For example, if users who liked item A also tend to like item B, then item B might be recommended to someone who liked item A.

Memory-based collaborative filtering methods are simple to implement and understand. However, they tend to suffer from scalability and sparsity issues as the number of users and items grows.

Model-Based Collaborative Filtering

In contrast to memory-based methods, model-based collaborative filtering involves building predictive models to estimate user preferences. These models are trained on the user-item interactions matrix using various machine learning and statistical techniques, such as singular value decomposition (SVD), alternating least squares (ALS), k-means clustering, and deep learning.

Model-based methods can handle scalability and sparsity better than memory-based methods and can uncover deeper insights in the data. However, they are usually more complex to implement and require a good understanding of machine learning.

Collaborative filtering does come with some limitations, one of which is the *cold start problem.* This is a situation where making accurate predictions becomes difficult for new users or items because very little data exists in the user-item interactions matrix for these users and items. Additionally, collaborative filtering can sometimes lead to what is known as the *popularity bias.* This is where popular items are consistently recommended more often, potentially overshadowing the recommendation of niche items.

Content-Based Filtering

Unlike collaborative filtering which relies solely on the interaction between users and items, *content-based filtering* methods make recommendations based on the characteristics of items and a profile of user preferences. They treat recommendations as a user-specific classification problem and learn to make recommendations based on *metadata* about a specific user and items. Content-based filtering is particularly useful in scenarios where a user's past behavior is limited or not available (the cold start problem). An example of a content-based filtering approach is a movie recommendation system that learns to recommend movies of certain genres, with certain actors or similar plot lines based on a user's profile and past activity.

Hybrid Filtering

In practice, most modern recommender systems use a combination of content-based and collaborative filtering approaches to leverage the strengths of both to provide more robust and diverse recommendations. There are various strategies for integrating content-based and collaborative filtering methods. Both approaches can be used independently and then merged. Both approaches can be used in sequence, and the results of collaborative filtering can be subsequently enhanced with content-based features, or vice versa. Another approach is to build a hybrid model that seamlessly blends both methodologies.

Summary

Association rules are used in data science to identify patterns in transaction data. These if-then statements are evaluated for strength and relevance using metrics like support, confidence, and lift, which help to distinguish between trivial, inexplicable, and actionable insights in customer purchasing behavior.

Clustering is an unsupervised machine learning technique that groups similar items into clusters based on similarity. It includes centroid-based clustering (like k-means), connectivity-based clustering (like hierarchical clustering), and density-based clustering (like DBSCAN). Each clustering approach has its unique advantages and limitations and is chosen based on the characteristics of the data and the clustering objectives.

Dimensionality reduction involves decreasing the number of features in a dataset, while maintaining as much information as possible. It helps to avoid the curse of dimensionality, improve model performance, and enhance visualization. Feature extraction is a dimensionality technique and includes approaches such as principal component analysis (PCA), singular value decomposition (SVD), t-distributed stochastic neighbor embedding (t-SNE), and uniform manifold approximation and projection (UMAP).

Recommender systems are algorithms that suggest items to users based on their interests. One approach is collaborative filtering, which is based on user-item interaction similarities. Another is content-based filtering, which focuses on item characteristics and user preferences. A third approach is hybrid filtering, which combines both collaborative filtering and content-based filtering to make robust recommendations.

Exam Essentials

Explain how support, confidence, and lift are used to evaluate the strength of an association rule.   Respectively, support, confidence, and lift evaluate association rules by measuring rule frequency, predictive strength, and the likelihood of items being purchased together versus separately. High support and confidence, along with a lift greater than 1, indicate a strong, non-random association between items.

Understand the difference between centroid-based, connectivity-based, and density-based clustering.   Centroid-based clustering, such as k-means, groups data points around a central point or centroid within the cluster. Connectivity-based clustering, like hierarchical clustering, creates a tree of clusters based on the proximity of data points. Density-based clustering, exemplified by DBSCAN, forms clusters in regions of high density, separated by areas of low density, and can detect clusters of arbitrary shapes.

Know the difference between feature selection and feature extraction. Feature selection involves choosing a subset of the most significant features from the original data, whereas feature extraction creates new features by transforming or combining the original features into a lower-dimensional space.

Understand when it's best to use linear and nonlinear dimensionality reduction techniques. Linear dimensionality reduction is suitable for datasets with linear correlations among features, where preserving global structure is important. Techniques like PCA and SVD are effective for this. Nonlinear dimensionality reduction is ideal for complex datasets where data forms manifolds or clusters not separable by a linear boundary. Techniques like t-SNE or UMAP are best for these.

Explain the difference between collaborative filtering and content-based filtering. Collaborative filtering makes recommendations by identifying patterns in user interactions, assuming users with similar behaviors have similar preferences. Content-based filtering, on the other hand, recommends items using the characteristics of the items themselves and a user's previous choices.

Review Questions

1. A new music streaming service has a vast library but limited user data. To recommend songs to its users, it should primarily use:

   A. Collaborative filtering

   B. Content-based filtering

   C. Hybrid filtering

   D. Predictive filtering

2. To reduce the dimensionality of her data, Oneshi applies a linear technique that transforms correlated features into uncorrelated ones. She is most likely using:

   A. t-SNE

   B. PCA

   C. UMAP

   D. SVD

3. A grocery store manager analyzes customer purchases and finds that customers who buy pasta often also buy tomato sauce. This observation is an example of:

   A. A trivial rule

   B. An inexplicable rule

   C. An actionable rule

   D. An infrequent rule

4. To choose the "ideal" number of clusters, Sharif plots the total Within Cluster Sum of Squares (WCSS) against various k values and looks for the point of inflection. Which of these approaches is he using?

   A. The Apriori method

   B. The elbow method

   C. The average silhouette method

   D. The centroid method

5. Scott enjoys books by Author X. A recommender system suggests more books by the same author. Which approach is this recommendation system most likely using?

   A. Collaborative filtering

   B. Content-based filtering

   C. Hybrid filtering

   D. Cluster filtering

6. A biologist wants to visualize complex high-dimensional genetic data in two dimensions. To achieve this while still maintaining the integrity of high-dimensional relationships, she should use:

   A. SVD

   B. PCA

   C. t-SNE

   D. UMAP

7. During market basket analysis, Fil determines that the rule {videogames}→{snacks} has a support of 0.3. This means:

   A. 30 percent of all transactions include both video games and snacks.

   B. 30 percent of transactions with video games also include snacks.

   C. The confidence of the rule is 0.3.

   D. The lift of the rule is 0.3.

8. A movie recommendation system uses a high-dimensional dataset of user preferences. Which of the following techniques could reduce the computational complexity of the system?

   A. Connectivity-based clustering

   B. Feature extraction

   C. Association rule mining

   D. Collaborative filtering

9. During market basket analysis, Alyssa determines that the rule {coffee}→{sugar} has a support of 0.25 and a confidence of 0.5. The total number of transactions is 400. How many transactions include both coffee and sugar?

   A. 50

   B. 100

   C. 200

   D. 300

10. An e-commerce platform uses a machine learning model to predict which products a user might like based on their past shopping behavior. This approach is:

   A. Memory-based collaborative filtering

   B. Association rule mining

   C. Content-based filtering

   D. Model-based collaborative filtering

11. When clustering her data, Melissa notices that the presence of outliers is affecting the centers of her clusters. Which of these clustering approaches is she most likely using?

   A. Density-based clustering

   B. Connectivity-based clustering

   C. Centroid-based clustering

   D. Hierarchical clustering

12. A movie recommender system recommends movies watched by others with viewing habits similar to yours. Which of these approaches is the system using?

   A. Content-based filtering

   B. Predictive filtering

   C. Collaborative filtering

   D. Cluster-based filtering

13. A cybersecurity team uses an unsupervised machine learning approach to detect anomalous behavior in their network. Which of these approaches are they likely using?

   A. Association rule mining

   B. Regression analysis

   C. Recommender systems

   D. Cluster analysis

14. During market basket analysis, Ricky determines that the rule {diapers}→{baby wipes} has a high confidence value of 0.9. This means:

   A. The rule occurs frequently.

   B. Most transactions that include diapers also include baby wipes.

   C. Most transactions include diapers and baby wipes.

   D. Most transactions that include baby wipes also include diapers.

15. Xiaojing frequently watches romantic comedies. A movie recommender system uses this information to suggest other romantic comedies to her. Which of these approaches is the system using?

   A. User-user collaborative filtering

   B. Item-item collaborative filtering

   C. Content-based filtering

   D. Hybrid filtering

16. A biologist uses a clustering method to group similar gene sequences. The method starts with each sequence as a separate cluster and merges them iteratively. This method is known as:

   A. k-means clustering

   B. Agglomerative hierarchical clustering

   C. Divisive hierarchical clustering

   D. DBSCAN

17. If the association rule {flour}→{yeast} has a lift value less than 1, it means that:

   A. Customers who buy flour are less likely to buy yeast.

   B. Flour and yeast are often bought together.

   C. Customers who buy yeast are less likely to buy flour.

   D. Flour and yeast are rarely bought together.

18. In a book recommendation app, the database of which books users have read and rated is known as:

    A. User profiles and preferences

    B. User market basket data

    C. User-item interactions matrix

    D. Item profiles and preferences

19. A popular social media platform continuously suggests trending posts, while ignoring less popular but relevant content. This issue is known as the:

    A. Popularity bias

    B. Cold start problem

    C. Scalability bias

    D. Complexity problem

20. A supermarket finds that the lift of the rule {beer}→{chips} is greater than 1. This suggests that:

    A. Customers who buy beer are less likely to buy chips.

    B. Customers who buy beer are more likely to buy chips.

    C. Beer and chips are bought independently.

    D. The rule is trivial.

Chapter

9

Supervised Machine Learning

THE COMPTIA DATAX EXAM OBJECTIVES COVERED IN THIS CHAPTER INCLUDE:

✓ **Domain 3: Machine Learning**

- 3.1 Given a scenario, apply foundational machine learning concepts.

- 3.2 Given a scenario, apply appropriate statistical supervised machine learning concepts.

- 3.3 Given a scenario, apply tree-based supervised machine learning concepts.

Supervised machine learning is an approach to machine learning where the goal is to learn from previously labeled training data to predict future outcomes. In this chapter, we explore several supervised machine learning techniques, starting with linear regression, an approach used to model the relationship between one or more predictors and a continuous dependent variable. Next, logistic regression and discriminant analysis will be introduced, both of which are useful for classification problems. Then we explore probabilistic learning using the naive Bayes model, and the use of decision trees to build machine learning models that are transparent and easy to interpret. The chapter concludes with an exploration of bagging, boosting, and stacking ensemble methods.

Linear Regression

As you prepare for the DataX exam, you should be able to apply appropriate statistical supervised machine learning concepts when presented with a scenario. As various supervised machine learning algorithms are introduced in this chapter, make note of how they work and consequently when best to use them.

Regression problems are supervised machine learning problems where the primary objective is to predict a continuous or numerical output variable based on a set of input variables. One of the simplest and most widely used regression techniques is *linear regression*. Linear regression makes the assumption that the relationship between the predictors (independent variables) and the response (dependent variable) is linear. It models this relationship using an equation in the following format:

$$Y \approx \beta_0 + \beta_1 X_1 + \beta_2 X_2 + \dots \beta_p X_p + \varepsilon \qquad (9.1)$$

There are four main components to Equation 9.1:

- A single response variable (Y), which represents the value or values that we intend to predict

- One or more predictor variables $(X_1, X_2, \dots, X_p)$

- Coefficients $(\beta_1, \beta_2, \dots, \beta_p)$, which describe the relationships between the predictors and the response variable, as well as an intercept (β_0)

- A random error (ε), which is also known as the *residual sum of squares* or *sum of squared errors*

When modeling data with the linear regression algorithm, we provide it with a training dataset that includes several examples of the predictor (or input) variables and corresponding response (output) values. The algorithm then uses an approach known as the *ordinary least squares (OLS)* method to estimate the best set of coefficients $(\beta_0, \beta_1, \beta_2, ..., \beta_p)$ that minimize the random error (ε).

The ordinary least squares method makes several key assumptions about the data. If these assumptions are violated, the results may be inefficient, biased, or misleading. The assumptions are:

- **Linearity:** The relationship between the independent variables and the dependent variable is assumed to be linear. This means the effect of a one-unit change in any independent variable on the dependent variable is constant. This assumption can be validated using a scatterplot or a residual plot. To remedy a violation of this assumption, we can transform our variables or use a nonlinear model instead.

- **Independence:** Observations are assumed to be independent of each other. This assumption ensures that the error term of one observation is not influenced by another and is especially vital in time-series data, where autocorrelation can occur. The Durbin–Watson test is often used as a test for this assumption. Using a model that accounts for correlation or using clustered standard errors are common ways to remedy a violation of this assumption.

- **Homoscedasticity:** The variance of the error terms is assumed to be constant across all levels of the independent variables. Heteroscedasticity (which is where variances differ at different data points) can be detected using residual plots. To resolve a violation of this assumption, we can transform the dependent variable or use the *weighted least squares (WLS)* method.

- **Normality:** The errors or residuals are assumed to be normally distributed. This is especially important when the sample size is small. Normality can be assessed with Q–Q plots (quantile–quantile plots) or a statistical test such as the Shapiro–Wilk test. To remedy a violation of this assumption, we can use a larger sample size for the training data, where the *central limit theorem* helps mitigate the impact of non-normality.

- **Little to No Multicollinearity:** Multicollinearity refers to the situation where two or more independent variables are highly correlated with each other. High multicollinearity, which can be detected based on the variance inflation factor (VIF) metric, makes it difficult to figure out the impact of individual predictors on the response. To resolve issues with multicollinearity, we can reduce the dimensionality of our data using a method like principal component analysis (see Chapter 8, "Unsupervised Machine Learning") or use a regularization technique.

The Weighted Least Squares Method

Weighted least squares (WLS) is an adaptation of ordinary least squares (OLS), designed to handle scenarios where different observations have different variances—a situation known as heteroscedasticity. In OLS, the objective is to minimize the sum of the squared differences $\Sigma(y_i - \hat{y}_i)^2$ (also known as residual sum of squares) between the observed values y_i in the data and the values predicted by the linear model $\hat{y}_i$.

WLS addresses the issues of heteroscedasticity by assigning different weights to different data points based on variance. Typically, weights are chosen as the inverse of the variance of the errors or residuals associated with each observation. This means that points with lower variance are given more weight (and vice versa). The WLS method then minimizes the sum of the squared product of these weights w_i and the residuals $\Sigma w_i(y_i - \hat{y}_i)^2$ to get the best set of coefficients for the model.

Regularization

A common challenge in supervised machine learning is the bias-variance trade-off (see Chapter 6, "Modeling and Evaluation"), which refers to the trade-off between a model's ability to fit the training data closely while also being able to generalize well to new, unseen data. To help linear regression models generalize well, we use a statistical modeling technique known as *regularization*.

To understand how regularization works, let's review how the OLS method estimates the coefficients of a linear regression model. The primary goal of OLS is to find the best-fitting line through a set of data points (see Figure 9.1).

FIGURE 9.1   Linear regression line of "best fit"

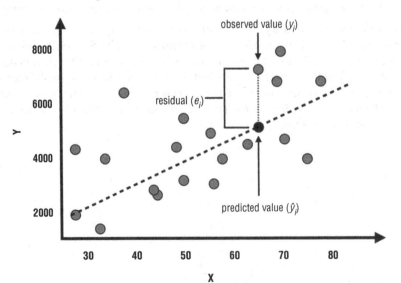

This "best fit" is defined as the line that minimizes the sum of the squared differences (or *residuals*) between the observed values and the values predicted by the linear model. Mathematically, this involves minimizing the value of the following residual sum of squares (RSS) loss function for a dataset with n observations and p predictors:

$$RSS = \sum_{i=1}^{n} \left(y_i - \beta_0 - \sum_{j=1}^{p} \beta_j x_{ij} \right)^2 \tag{9.2}$$

In Equation 9.2, y_i is the response value of the i-th out of n observations in the training data, β_0 is the intercept of the linear regression line, β_j is the coefficient of the j-th out of p predictors in the training data, and x_{ij} is the value of the j-th predictor of the i-th observation in the training data.

To enable a linear regression model to generalize well, we can regularize it by adding a penalty term to the loss function to discourage it from fitting the data too closely. Three of the most commonly used regularization approaches are L1 regularization, L2 regularization, and ElasticNet.

L1 Regularization

L1 regularization is also known as *least absolute shrinkage and selection operator (LASSO) regression*. It involves modifying the RSS loss function to include a penalty:

$$LASSO = RSS + \lambda \sum_{j=1}^{p} |\beta_j| \tag{9.3}$$

In Equation 9.3, (λ) is a tuning parameter that controls how much to penalize the absolute value of the coefficients (β_j). It takes on values between 0 and ∞. The larger the value of λ, the smaller the coefficients (β_j) become. In other words, increasing λ has the effect of simplifying the linear regression model by reducing the impact of the predictors. In fact, with LASSO regularization, as we increase the value of λ, some of the coefficients will eventually become 0, which effectively removes them from the model. Therefore, LASSO regularization is useful for feature selection.

L2 Regularization

L2 regularization is also known as *ridge regression*. Similar to LASSO regression, this regularization approach involves adding a penalty to the RSS loss function. However, the penalty this time is applied to the square of the coefficients (β_j):

$$Ridge = RSS + \lambda \sum_{j=1}^{p} \beta_j^2 \tag{9.4}$$

Like LASSO, the tuning parameter λ takes on values between 0 and ∞. The larger the value of λ, the smaller the coefficients (β_j) become. However, unlike LASSO, the coefficients approach 0 but never become 0.

ElasticNet

ElasticNet is a combination of both L1 and L2 regularization. It balances the feature selection of LASSO regression with the coefficient shrinkage of ridge regression and performs much better than both approaches, separately, when predictors are highly correlated or when the number of predictors is greater than the number of observations. The ElasticNet loss function is specified as:

$$ElasticNet = RSS + \lambda \left(\alpha \sum_{j=1}^{p} |\beta_j| + \frac{1-\alpha}{2} \sum_{j=1}^{p} \beta_j^2 \right) \tag{9.5}$$

Here, β_j are the coefficients, λ is the regularization parameter that controls the overall strength of the penalty, and α is a parameter that balances between L1 and L2 regularization.

As you can see, the parameters λ and α (for ElasticNet only) control the impact of bias and variance when regularizing a linear regression model. As the value of λ rises, it reduces the value of coefficients and thus reduces the variance of a model (hence avoiding overfitting). However, after a certain λ value, the model will start losing important information about the predictors, giving rise to bias in the model and thus underfitting. Therefore, it is important that we be careful when selecting the values of λ and α. This is usually done using cross-validation and hyperparameter tuning.

The choice between L1, L2, or ElasticNet regularization should be made based on the characteristics of the data and the importance of feature selection versus model stability in your analysis. If feature selection is the priority, then L1 regularization (LASSO) is useful, as it shrinks less important features to 0. If the goal is simply to build a more stable and robust model, then use L2 regularization (ridge) to shrink coefficients without eliminating features. ElasticNet is best when there are multiple correlated features, because it offers a balance between feature elimination and shrinkage.

Logistic Regression

Classification problems are supervised machine learning problems where the primary objective is to identify the class to which a new observation belongs. Essentially, the primary objective is to predict a categorical or discrete output variable based on a set of input variables. Depending on the number of possible outcomes, classification problems can be categorized as either binary (having only two possible outcomes) or multiclass (having more than two outcomes). *Logistic regression* is one of the most widely used binary classification techniques. It is similar to linear regression in that it is a linear model, but it differs in its goal and the way it achieves that goal.

In linear regression, the aim is to predict a continuous response variable (y) based on a set of predictor variables ($X_1, X_2, ..., X_p$). The model assumes a linear relationship between the predictors and the response (which can take on any value). On the other hand, instead of predicting the response directly, logistic regression uses a sigmoid function to model the probability that a given input (X) belongs to a particular category as shown in Figure 9.2. This probability, denoted as $p(X)$, is bounded between 0 and 1.

FIGURE 9.2   Curve of the logistic (sigmoid) function

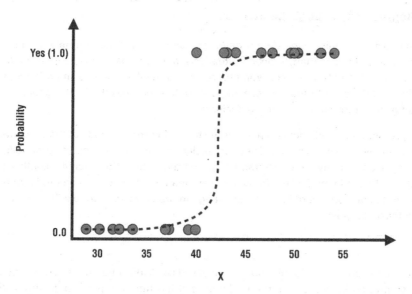

In order to use similar techniques as linear regression, and to improve interpretability and computational stability, the logistic regression algorithm expresses the relationship between the predictors and the response in terms of log-odds (or logit). In other words, it calculates the log-odds of $p(X)$ as a linear combination of the predictors:

$$log\left(\frac{p(X)}{1-p(X)}\right) = \beta_0 + \beta_1 X_1 + \beta_2 X_2 + ... \beta_p X_p \qquad (9.6)$$

To estimate the best set of coefficients ($\beta_0, \beta_1, \beta_2, ..., \beta_p$) that fit the training data, the logistic regression algorithm often uses a process known as *maximum likelihood estimation (MLE)* instead of the OLS method used by linear regression. To interpret the output or prediction of the logit function (Equation 9.6), they must be converted from log-odds to odds, and then to probability.

Suppose that a model predicts the log-odds of an observation as 0.5. To convert this to odds, we exponentiate:

$$Odds = e^{0.5} \approx 1.65$$

Then we can convert the odds to probability as follows:

$$Probability = \frac{1.65}{1+1.65} \approx 0.62$$

This means that the probability of the observation belonging to the target category is 62 percent.

Probit Regression vs. Logit Regression

Similar to logistic (or logit) regression, *probit regression* is another commonly used binary classification technique. In many practical situations, both approaches yield very similar results. However, the probit model is sometimes preferred when there is an underlying assumption that the error terms are normally distributed, whereas the logit model is preferred for the interpretability of its coefficients.

In logit regression, the coefficients represent the change in the log-odds of the outcome per unit change in the predictor variable. They can easily be converted to odds or probability, which are easy and intuitive to understand. In probit regression, however, the coefficients represent the change in the Z-score (how many standard deviations an element is from the mean) of the outcome variable per unit change in the predictor variable. This is a more abstract concept to grasp.

Logistic regression is a valuable tool for binary classification tasks, especially when interpretability and simplicity are important. However, it has limitations when dealing with more complex data structures, multiple categories, or nonlinear relationships. When the number of predictors is large relative to the number of observations, logistic regression models can be prone to overfitting. As is the case with linear regression, regularization techniques are useful in logistic regression to mitigate this issue.

Discriminant Analysis

Discriminant analysis is a classification technique used to determine which variables best distinguish between two or more naturally occurring groups. It does so by projecting the data onto a lower dimensional space based on two criteria, which it considers simultaneously. The first criterion is to maximize the distance between means, and the second is to minimize the variation (or scatter) within each category. Mathematically, discriminant analysis estimates the separation between two categories, j and k, as:

$$\frac{\left(\mu_j - \mu_k\right)^2}{\sigma_j^2 + \sigma_k^2} \qquad (9.7)$$

In Equation 9.7, μ_j and μ_k are the mean of the values that belong to categories j and k, respectively. Similarly, σ_j^2 and σ_j^2 represent the variation in values within categories j and k, respectively. The numerator in Equation 9.7 represents the distance between means, while the denominator represents the variation within each category. Ideally, the objective is to get a numerator that is as large as possible and a denominator that is as small as possible.

By maximizing the ratio between the numerator and denominator, discriminant analysis is able to construct a discriminant function for each class, which computes a score for each observation (the discriminant score). Classification is then done by assigning an observation to the class for which it has the highest discriminant score.

Discriminant analysis is useful for classification as well as for dimensionality reduction. In practice, it's often useful in preparing datasets for other classification methods by reducing dimensionality while preserving as much class discriminatory information as possible. Depending on the nature of the data, one of two approaches can be used for discriminant analysis: linear discriminant analysis or quadratic discriminant analysis.

Linear Discriminant Analysis

Linear discriminant analysis (LDA) operates under two key assumptions: first, the predictor variables in each class follow a Gaussian (normal) distribution, and second, all classes share the same covariance matrix, leading to linear decision boundaries between classes. It aims to find a linear combination of features that separate two or more classes within the data. The resulting combination can be used as a linear classifier or for dimensionality reduction before further classification.

Linear discriminant analysis and logistic regression are very similar in that they are versatile yet simple linear classification techniques. They often produce similar results. However, when the key assumptions of LDA hold true, it can outperform a logistic regression model. Also, unlike logistic regression, which is best suited for binary classification problems, discriminant analysis in general is preferred for multiclass problems.

 The covariance matrix of a dataset captures how much each of the variables (or features) in the dataset vary together. For a given class, the covariance matrix indicates how the features are correlated with each other. For instance, a high positive value in the covariance matrix for two features indicates that they tend to increase together (and vice versa).

Assuming that the covariance matrix is the same for every class in the dataset means that though different classes might have different means, the way their features vary and correlate with each other is the same across all classes.

Quadratic Discriminant Analysis

Quadratic discriminant analysis (QDA) is an extension of linear discriminant analysis (LDA). It also operates under the assumption that the predictor variables in each class follow a Gaussian (normal) distribution. However, unlike LDA, which assumes equal covariance matrices across different classes, QDA allows each class to have its own covariance matrix. This key difference allows QDA to have quadratic decision boundaries, which means they can take on elliptical, hyperbolic, or parabolic shapes.

Figure 9.3 illustrates the difference between the decision boundaries created using LDA (left plot) and QDA (right plot) on the same dataset. Compared to LDA, QDA is more flexible and capable of capturing complex relationships between classes. However, this flexibility comes at the cost of needing more data to avoid overfitting. The performance of QDA can suffer if there aren't enough observations to accurately estimate the covariance matrices for each class.

FIGURE 9.3 Decision boundaries created using LDA (left) and QDA (right) on the same data

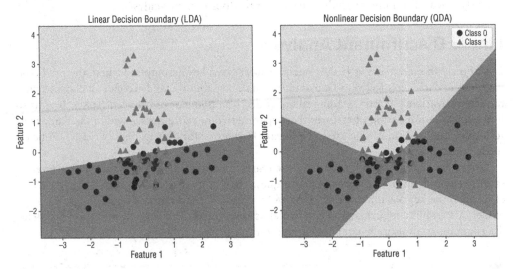

Naive Bayes

The *naive Bayes* algorithm is named after 18th-century clergyman and mathematician Thomas Bayes, who developed a class of mathematical principles known as *Bayesian methods*. Generally speaking, these methods allow for the updating of the probability estimate for a hypothesis as more evidence or information becomes available. The algorithm relies on one of those principles, known as the *Bayes theorem*, which describes the relationship between dependent events A and B as follows:

$$P(A|B) = \frac{P(B|A) \times P(A)}{P(B)} \tag{9.8}$$

In Equation 9.8, $P(A|B)$ is the conditional probability of event A occurring, given that event B has already occurred. It is known as the *posterior probability*. $P(B|A)$ is known as the *likelihood*. It is the probability of B given that event A already occurred. $P(A)$ is known as the *prior probability*. It describes the probability of event A by itself. $P(B)$ represents the probability of event B alone. It is known as the *marginal likelihood*.

To use the Bayes theorem for classification, we would need to compute the conditional probability that an observation belongs to each class given the values of the predictors. This calculation is terribly inefficient and becomes intractable as the number of predictors grows. To overcome this limitation, the naive Bayes algorithm makes the simplifying assumption of *class conditional independence* between predictors, which means that events are assumed to be independent as long as they are conditioned on the same class value.

With class conditional independence, given a dataset with n predictors $(x_1, x_2, \cdots, x_n)$ and m distinct class values $(C_1, C_2, \cdots, C_m)$, the conditional probability that an observation belongs to class C_k is denoted as follows:

$$P(C_k|x_1, x_2, \cdots, x_n) = \frac{P(C_k)P(x_1|C_k)P(x_2|C_k)\cdots P(x_n|C_k)}{P(x_1, x_2, \cdots, x_n)} \tag{9.9}$$

To make a prediction, the naive Bayes algorithm calculates the probability of an observation belonging to each class using Equation 9.9. The class with the highest probability is chosen as the output.

Due to the class conditional independence assumption, the naive Bayes algorithm is computationally efficient, making it fast for both training and prediction. It performs well with high-dimensional data and is less prone to overfitting than models such as decision trees (which are discussed next). It handles missing data well by ignoring it during calculations, and its probabilistic nature offers insights into the certainty of predictions.

However, the algorithm does have some limitations. The most significant is that the foundational assumption of class conditional independence often does not hold true for real-world data, which can lead to suboptimal performance. Additionally, some forms of the naive Bayes algorithm struggle with continuous data and can produce biased probability estimates. The algorithm can also face issues like the "zero frequency problem," where it assigns a zero probability to unseen features during training.

Decision Trees

As you prepare for the DataX exam, you should be able to apply tree-based supervised machine learning concepts when presented with a scenario. As you read through the text, make careful note of the main differences between the ensemble approaches in terms of their architectures.

Decision trees are a popular supervised machine learning technique used for both classification and regression tasks. They are particularly favored for their interpretability and simplicity. Unlike some other machine learning models that act as "black boxes," decision trees provide a clear and understandable representation of the decision-making process.

A decision tree uses a tree-like structure, which is essentially an inverted tree, to model the relationship between independent variables (also known as predictors or features) and the dependent variable (the target outcome). This structure is composed of nodes and branches, with each node representing a decision point based on a certain feature, and each branch representing the outcome of that decision. Figure 9.4 illustrates the structure of a basic decision tree.

FIGURE 9.4   Sample decision tree

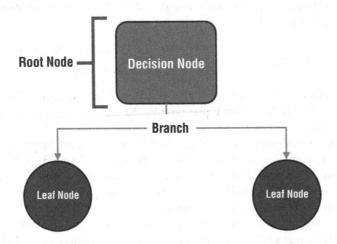

There are two main types of nodes in a decision tree:

- *Decision Nodes*: These are the internal nodes of the tree, where a test or decision is made based on the value of a particular feature. Each decision node corresponds to a feature that is used to split the data into two or more subsets. The decision at each node leads to further branches and nodes, representing the different outcomes of the decision. The topmost decision node is known as the *root node*.

- *Leaf Nodes*: Also known as *terminal nodes*, these are the nodes at the end of the tree where no further splitting occurs. Each leaf node represents a final decision or prediction, which could be a class label in a classification tree or a continuous value in a regression tree.

Decision trees are built using a process known as *recursive partitioning*—a process that involves repeatedly splitting the data into subsets in a recursive manner. The structure of the eventual tree that is built through this process tells a story about the underlying data.

The recursive portioning process begins with the entire dataset, considered the root of the tree. At each step, the algorithm selects the best split based on a specific criterion, such as maximizing *information gain* or minimizing an impurity measure such as *Gini impurity* or *entropy*. The splitting criterion determines which feature and threshold value to use when splitting the data, with the goal of creating subsets that are as homogeneous (i.e., contain similar labels) as possible with respect to the target variable.

Once the best split is determined at the current node, the dataset is divided into two or more subsets. This creates new nodes in the tree; each subset forms a child node of the current node. The algorithm then recursively applies the same splitting procedure to each child node.

The recursion continues until a stopping criterion is met. This could be when the nodes have a certain minimum number of samples, when all the samples at a node belong to the same class (in classification tasks), when the tree has grown to a certain size, or when further splitting no longer improves the homogeneity of the subsets.

The final result of recursive partitioning is a tree with decision nodes and leaf nodes that represent a set of rules. For instance, the decision tree in Figure 9.5 illustrates a tree trained on historical bank loan data. The logic of the tree can easily be interpreted as a set of rules that predict whether a future borrower will default on a bank loan. Following the nodes and branches of the tree, we can infer that "IF a customer borrows $40,000 or less (first left branch) AND earns less than $20,000 a year (second right branch) THEN the customer will most likely default on their loan."

FIGURE 9.5   Sample decision tree

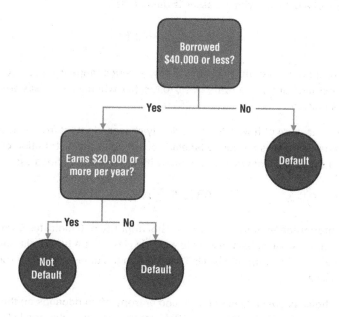

There are several benefits to using decision trees in supervised machine learning. The ease with which decision trees can be translated into simple and understandable IF-THEN-ELSE rules makes them attractive for decision-making processes where transparency is important and where the decision logic needs to be shared with nontechnical stakeholders. Decision trees can capture nonlinear relationships well, they can handle both numerical and categorical data, and they do not require much data preprocessing, such as feature engineering or scaling.

Decision trees, however, are prone to overfitting. To mitigate this, decision trees are often pruned by setting a maximum depth for the tree, requiring a minimum number of samples to split a node, or removing branches that add little predictive power. Decision trees can be very sensitive to small changes in the data, which end up changing the entire structure of the tree. This is often addressed by using an ensemble method. Finally, decision trees can be biased toward the dominant class, which means they may perform poorly if the class distribution is imbalanced.

Entropy vs. Gini Impurity Index

Entropy and Gini impurity are two commonly used measures in decision trees for determining the quality of a split. Both are used in the context of classification trees to quantify the "purity" or homogeneity of a subset of data. While they serve a similar purpose, they have different mathematical formulations and characteristics.

Entropy is a measure of the disorder or unpredictability in the data. It is derived from information theory and quantifies the amount of information (or uncertainty) present in the data. The entropy of a data set with J classes is defined as:

$$Entropy = -\sum_{i=1}^{J} p_i \times \log_2(p_i)$$

where p_i is the proportion of items in class i. Entropy values range from 0, when all data points within a partition are of the same class, to $\log_2(J)$, when all J classes are equally represented in a partition.

Gini impurity is a measure of how often a randomly chosen element from a dataset would be incorrectly labeled if it was randomly labeled according to the distribution of labels in the subset. For a set with J classes, the Gini impurity of the set is defined as:

$$Gini = 1 - \sum_{i=1}^{J} p_i^2$$

where p_i is the proportion of items in class i. A Gini impurity of 0 indicates perfect purity, meaning all elements in the subset belong to a single class. For a binary classification tree, the maximum value of Gini impurity is 0.5. That is when the data is perfectly split 50-50 between the two classes.

In practice, the choice between Gini impurity and entropy often depends on the specific problem and computational considerations. Gini impurity is computationally faster as it doesn't involve logarithmic functions. However, the difference in tree quality between the two methods is generally small.

Ensemble Methods

Ensemble methods are a class of supervised machine learning algorithms that enhance the accuracy and robustness of predictive models by combining the predictions of multiple individual models (known as base models). These methods are particularly effective in classification and regression tasks, where the goal is to make accurate predictions based on input data. The basic idea behind ensembles is that by leveraging the strengths of several base models, we can minimize their individual weaknesses to improve the overall predictive performance and stability of the collective. There are generally three approaches to building an ensemble: bagging, boosting, or stacking.

Bagging

One of the most common approaches to building an ensemble is known as *bagging,* which stands for *bootstrap aggregating.* The name comes from the fact that bagging ensembles use a bootstrap sampling approach for the allocation function (a set of rules that generate the data assigned to each model in the ensemble). Bagging ensembles are typically made up of homogenous learners trained independently and in parallel.

One of the most popular bagging ensemble methods is the *random forests* or *decision tree forests* ensemble technique. It gets its name from the fact that the ensemble consists of a large number of decision tree learners (which are collectively called a *forest*) and that its allocation function combines both bootstrap sampling and random feature selection to generate the data assigned to each learner in the ensemble. By limiting each member of the ensemble to a random subset of the full feature set, random forests are able to deal effectively with high-dimensional data.

The strength of bagging lies in its ability to reduce variance and overfitting, making the model more generalizable to unseen data. This is because while an individual model might have high variance and overfit the data, the predictions made by all models in the ensemble are combined into a single prediction. This aggregation process tends to cancel out extreme deviations, leading to a more stable model.

Boosting

Similar to bagging, *boosting* ensembles are built based on a homogenous set of base models. However, boosting differs from bagging in that, instead of independently training the base models in parallel, the base models in the boosting ensemble are trained in sequence. Within the sequence, each successive model attempts to improve upon the performance of the preceding model by learning from the mistakes of its predecessor. Each successive model boosts the performance of the ensemble.

Common boosting ensembles include *adaptive boosting (AdaBoost)* and *extreme gradient boosting (XGBoost),* which emphasize incremental improvement by weighting the training instances differently, typically giving more weight to the instances that were misclassified by previous models in the sequence. AdaBoost, for instance, adjusts the weights of the training data for each subsequent model, prioritizing the instances that were hardest to classify in the previous round. This effectively focuses the learning on the most difficult cases. XGBoost takes this idea further by using gradient descent to minimize errors in a more refined manner.

While boosting generally results in more accurate models than bagging, it can also be more prone to overfitting if not carefully managed. To counteract this, boosting algorithms often include parameters that control the complexity of the models and the rate at which they learn. These parameters need to be carefully tuned to balance the trade-off between bias and variance.

Stacking

Stacking is a nuanced ensemble technique that involves training multiple diverse (heterogenous) models and then using another model, known as the meta-learner, to integrate their predictions. In stacking, the base models are trained on the full dataset and their outputs are used as input features for the meta-learner, which then makes the final prediction. This method leverages the unique strengths of each individual model, potentially leading to better performance than any single model.

 Real World Scenario

Classifying Patient Conditions

A hospital seeks to develop a machine learning model to classify patients into different risk categories for a specific chronic disease based on medical history, test results, and demographic data. The categories are "Low Risk," "Moderate Risk," and "High Risk." The data is very wide (high-dimensional) and includes features such as age, gender, blood pressure, cholesterol level, and various categorical lifestyle factors. After the initial exploratory data analysis, the hospital comes to the following conclusions based on the benefits and limitations of each of the supervised machine learning techniques that could be used to build the model:

- **Linear Regression:** Inappropriate due to the categorical nature of the outcome.

- **Logistic Regression:** Suitable for binary classification, but less ideal for multiclass problems (such as this one).

- **Discriminant Analysis (LDA and QDA):** Would have been strong candidates as they handle multiclass problems well; however, it appears that the predictors are not normally distributed.

- **Naive Bayes:** Efficient with high-dimensional data, but its independence assumption might not hold in medical data, where symptoms often correlate.

- **Decision Trees:** Offers clear interpretability, which is crucial in medical settings. However, it could overfit and might not capture the complexity of the relationships in the high-dimensional data well.

- **Random Forests (Bagging):** Overcomes the limitation of overfitting and does well with high-dimensional data.

- **Extreme Gradient Boosting (Boosting):** Can improve predictive accuracy but requires very careful tuning to avoid overfitting.

- **Stacking:** Offers a comprehensive approach by leveraging the strengths of multiple models but is complex to implement and interpret.

Given the multiclass nature of the outcome and the high-dimensional nature of the data, the hospital leans toward random forests as the best approach, given its robustness and ability to handle complex data.

Summary

Linear regression is a supervised machine learning technique used to predict a continuous outcome. It assumes a linear relationship between the input variables and the response variable. Linear regression utilizes the method ordinary least squares (OLS) to minimize prediction errors. To improve their ability to generalize, linear regression models can be regularized using LASSO, ridge, or ElasticNet regularization.

Logistic regression is a supervised machine learning technique for binary classification. It predicts the probability of class membership by modeling the log-odds of an outcome as a linear combination of the predictors.

Discriminant analysis is useful for dimensionality reduction as well as multiclass classification. There are two approaches to discriminant analysis: linear discriminant analysis (LDA), which creates linear boundaries, and quadratic discriminant analysis (QDA), which can create nonlinear boundaries.

Naive Bayes, based on the Bayes theorem, is useful for both classification and regression. It works under the assumption of class conditional independence, which enables it to be computationally efficient, but often doesn't reflect the complexity of real-world data.

Decision trees, also used for both classification and regression, are valued for their interpretability and straightforward structure. They operate by recursively partitioning data into homogeneous subsets, using criteria like information gain or Gini impurity.

Ensembles are a supervised machine learning approach that improves performance by combining multiple weak models to form a stronger unit. Ensemble methods include bagging, boosting, and stacking.

Exam Essentials

Explain the difference between LASSO, ridge, and ElasticNet regularization.   LASSO uses L1 regularization, which adds a penalty equal to the absolute value of the magnitude of coefficients, leading to feature selection. Ridge regression employs L2 regularization, adding a penalty equal to the square of the magnitude of coefficients, causing them to shrink but not zero out. ElasticNet combines both L1 and L2 regularization, balancing feature selection and coefficient shrinkage, and is effective when predictors are correlated.

Understand the similarities between logistic regression, linear discriminant analysis, and quadratic discriminant analysis.   Logistic regression, linear discriminant analysis (LDA), and quadratic discriminant analysis (QDA) are all used for classification. Logistic regression and LDA are particularly similar in their use of linear decision boundaries, although logistic regression is primarily used for binary classification, whereas LDA extends to multiclass problems. QDA, an extension of LDA, also focuses on classification but allows for more complex, nonlinear decision boundaries.

Know the key benefits and limitations of naive Bayes.   Naive Bayes, known for its simplicity and efficiency, excels in handling high-dimensional data and is less prone to overfitting. Its probabilistic nature provides clear insights into prediction certainty, and it copes well with missing data. However, its key limitation is the assumption of class conditional independence among predictors, which is often unrealistic in real-world data.

Know the key benefits and limitations of decision trees.   Decision trees are favored for their interpretability and simplicity. They are capable of capturing nonlinear relationships and handling both numerical and categorical data with minimal preprocessing. They translate well into understandable rules, aiding transparent decision making. However, they are prone to overfitting, which can be mitigated through pruning. They're sensitive to small data changes and can perform poorly on imbalanced datasets.

Explain the difference between bagging, boosting, and stacking ensembles.   Bagging involves training multiple homogenous models independently, which reduces variance. Boosting involves sequentially training homogenous models, where each model learns from the errors of the previous one. It improves accuracy but also increases the risk of overfitting. Stacking trains multiple heterogenous models and then combines their predictions using a meta-learner.

Review Questions

1. Which of the following is an assumption of linear regression?

   A. The relationship between variables is quadratic.

   B. The variance of the error terms is assumed to be variable.

   C. The relationship between independent and dependent variables is linear.

   D. The error terms follow a uniform distribution.

2. Henry chooses linear discriminant analysis (LDA) over logistic regression for a classification problem because his dataset meets certain assumptions. Which of these is a key assumption that favors the use of LDA?

   A. Observations in each class have different covariance matrices.

   B. The predictor variables follow a Gaussian distribution.

   C. The relationship between the predictors and the class is nonlinear.

   D. The dataset has more features than observations.

3. Irene is using a decision tree to predict customer churn. She wants to ensure that the tree does not become too complex and lose generalizability. Which criterion might she use to stop the tree from growing too large?

   A. Maximizing the variance inflation factor (VIF)

   B. Setting a maximum depth for the tree

   C. Increasing the number of leaf nodes

   D. Applying the ordinary least squares method

4. Jack is working on a machine learning problem and decides to use a random forests model. He explains that his choice is driven by the model's ability to handle a specific issue associated with decision trees. What is this issue?

   A. Bias

   B. Variance

   C. Overfitting

   D. Underfitting

5. What method does linear regression typically use to estimate coefficients?

   A. Maximum likelihood estimation

   B. Gradient descent

   C. Ordinary least squares

   D. Bayesian inference

6. Olivia is concerned about the "zero frequency problem" in her naive Bayes classification model. Which of these causes this problem?

    A. Overfitting in the model

    B. The presence of continuous variables

    C. Unseen features in the test dataset

    D. High correlation between features

7. Which of these issues does the weighted least squares (WLS) method address in linear regression?

    A. Multicollinearity

    B. Heteroscedasticity

    C. Nonlinearity

    D. Model complexity

8. Karen is using a linear regression model for her research. During her analysis, she suspects that the error terms in her model might be correlated, which could violate an important assumption. Which of these tests should Karen use to check this assumption?

    A. Shapiro–Wilk test

    B. Durbin–Watson test

    C. Pearson correlation test

    D. Chi-square test

9. Which regularization technique is primarily known for feature selection?

    A. L1 regularization

    B. Ridge regularization

    C. L2 regularization

    D. Gradient descent

10. Emily is using a decision tree for a classification problem. She is concerned about overfitting and decides to limit the depth of the tree. What is she doing?

    A. Pruning

    B. Bootstrapping

    C. Regularization

    D. Cross-validation

11. Mia is building a logistic regression model and wants to ensure that her model does not overfit. Which of these techniques should she use?

    A. Increase the number of predictors.

    B. Apply a regularization technique.

    C. Reduce the sample size.

    D. Use a nonlinear transformation.

12. Alice plans to use linear regression to predict housing prices. Using historical data, she plots the relationship between the size of each house and the selling price. The plot shows a linear correlation between house size and selling price. Which linear regression assumption is being validated in this scenario?

   A. Autocorrelation

   B. Linearity

   C. Independence

   D. Normality

13. Linda is using a naive Bayes classifier for spam detection. She wants to improve the model's ability to handle continuous data. Which of these techniques can Linda use to better incorporate continuous data into her model?

   A. Discretize the continuous variables.

   B. Apply a regularization technique.

   C. Increase the size of the training set.

   D. Use an ensemble method.

14. David is using logistic regression for a binary classification problem. He wants to convert the log-odds output to odds. Which of these steps should he perform?

   A. Apply a linear transformation to the output.

   B. Exponentiate the output.

   C. Normalize the output.

   D. Calculate the residual sum of squares of the output.

15. Liam is working on a regression problem but realizes that his data violates the linearity assumption of linear regression. Which of these is a suitable next step?

   A. Switch to a logistic regression model.

   B. Remove the nonlinear predictors.

   C. Use a nonlinear model.

   D. Increase the sample size.

16. While building a text classification model using the naive Bayes algorithm, Julia notices that her model is having a hard time with certain words that exist in the test data but not in the training data. What problem is her model dealing with?

   A. Overfitting

   B. Underfitting

   C. Zero frequency

   D. Class imbalance

17. Bob is evaluating his linear regression model and notices that the variance of residuals is increasing with one of the predictors. To address this, which of the following should he use?

    A. Ordinary least squares

    B. Weighted least squares

    C. L1 regularization

    D. L2 regularization

18. Hannah is comparing LDA and QDA for her multiclass classification problem. She decides to use LDA because of a specific characteristic of her dataset. What could be a reason for choosing LDA over QDA in her scenario?

    A. Her dataset has a very large number of features.

    B. Each class in her dataset has a significantly different covariance matrix.

    C. Her dataset includes highly correlated features.

    D. She has a relatively small sample size for each class.

19. Kevin is trying to determine whether his dataset is well suited for LDA. He knows that LDA assumes that the predictors follow a Gaussian distribution. How can Kevin validate this assumption for his dataset?

    A. By performing a Durbin–Watson test

    B. By creating a scatter plot of each predictor

    C. By creating a box plot of each predictor

    D. By performing the Shapiro–Wilk test

20. Frank is using a linear regression model and notices that his residuals are not evenly distributed across all levels of the independent variables. This indicates a potential violation of which assumption?

    A. Independence

    B. Normality

    C. Homoscedasticity

    D. Linearity

Chapter 10

Neural Networks and Deep Learning

THE COMPTIA DATAX EXAM OBJECTIVES COVERED IN THIS CHAPTER INCLUDE:

✓ **Domain 3: Machine Learning**

- 3.1 Given a scenario, apply foundational machine learning concepts.

- 3.4 Explain concepts related to deep learning.

Deep neural networks represent an advanced facet of machine learning, focusing on constructing and training multilayered architectures capable of handling highly complex tasks. This chapter begins with an exploration of artificial neural networks, with a focus on network topology, activation functions, and the training algorithm. The discussion then extends to techniques for improving model generalization, such as dropout and batch normalization. Finally, we survey the landscape of deep learning, deep learning frameworks, and common deep learning architectures, such as convolutional neural networks, recurrent neural networks, long short-term memory networks, transformers, generative adversarial networks, and autoencoders. Each of these is tailored to specific types of data and learning tasks.

Artificial Neural Networks

Artificial neural networks solve learning problems by modeling the relationship between a set of input signals and an output signal, similar to the way biological neurons work. As a set of inputs is received by each node in the network, each input is weighted by importance. These weighted signals are then summed and passed through an activation function, which determines what value is forwarded by the node.

Figure 10.1 shows the basic architecture of a neural network, with signals flowing from the input nodes to the output nodes. This type of neural network is known as a *perceptron*. It is the most basic type of network. Neural networks come in different forms and differ in terms of:

- Network topology, which describes the number of neurons and/or layers in the model

- Activation function, which transforms a neuron's combined input signals into a single output signal

- Training algorithm, which specifies how connection weights and biases are set

FIGURE 10.1   Simple artificial neural network showing the flow of input and output signals

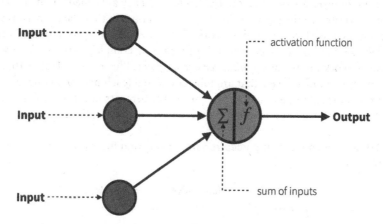

 As you prepare for the DataX exam, you should be able to explain foundational concepts related to neural networks and deep learning. Make note of the key terms introduced in this chapter and how they relate to deep learning. Endeavor to understand what each term means.

Network Topology

Neurons, which are also referred to as *nodes*, are the fundamental building blocks of an artificial neural network. The structure of interconnected nodes (or topology) within a neural network influences the way it learns. It determines the complexity of tasks that can be learned by the network. The larger and more complex the network is, the more capable it is of identifying subtle patterns in data. However, not only is the power of a network a function of the network size, but it also has to do with the way nodes are arranged. Nodes in a neural network are arranged in groups called layers. There are three main types of layers in neural networks: the input layer, the hidden layer(s), and the output layer.

Input Layer

The *input layer* is the first layer in the network. Each node in the input layer corresponds to one of the features in the input data. For instance, in a network that processes images, each input node might represent the intensity of a pixel from the input image. The role of the nodes in the input layer is to receive the input signals and pass them on to the next layer without any change.

Hidden Layer

Following the input layer are one or more *hidden layers*. They are called "hidden" because they are not directly exposed to the input or the output. The nodes in these layers perform the bulk of the computational work of a neural network. The more hidden layers and the more nodes per layer a network has, the more capable it is of capturing complex patterns. A very common type of neural network known as a *multilayer perceptron* is illustrated in Figure 10.2. It includes one or more hidden layers that are fully connected (each neuron in one layer connects to every neuron in the subsequent layer). The multilayer perceptron is foundational in the field of neural networks and has been used extensively in various applications.

FIGURE 10.2   The multilayer perceptron (MLP) showing the input, hidden and output layers

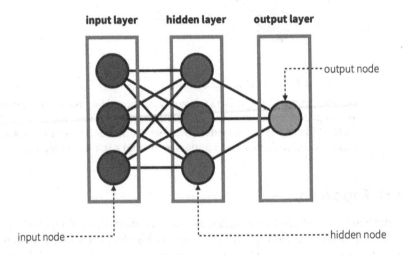

Output Layer

The final layer of nodes in a neural network is the *output layer*. It outputs the results of the computation that occurs within the network. The configuration of the output layer varies depending on the learning task. For example, if the learning goal is to classify whether an image is that of a dog, a cat, or something else, then the output layer might have three nodes—a node for each class. The output of each node would represent the probability that the image is either a dog, a cat, or something else.

Activation Function

An *activation function* is a component within a neural network that transforms a neuron's combined input signals into a single output signal. Activation functions serve two primary roles. First, they help to normalize the output of each node, typically to a range between

0 and 1, or –1 and 1, depending on the function. This is important because it keeps the output of each node within a manageable scale, which prevents the network from becoming unstable. Second, and more important, activation functions introduce nonlinearity into a neural network, which allows it to learn how to model complex patterns, such as image recognition, speech recognition, and natural language processing (NLP). Without activation functions, all neural networks, regardless of how many layers they have, would behave just like a perceptron, capable only of handling linear problems.

Several types of activation function are used within an artificial neural network, each with its unique characteristics and applications. The choice of activation function can significantly impact the performance of a neural network and largely depends on the specific requirements of the task at hand—the complexity of the problem, the architecture of the network (type of node or layer), and/or the nature of the input and output data expected.

Threshold Activation Function

Also known as the *unit-step activation function*, the *threshold activation function* (illustrated in Figure 10.3) is a simple, binary activation function that activates a node (outputs a 1) only if the weighted sum of its inputs is greater than or equal to a predefined threshold. If the weighted sum is less than the threshold, the node does not activate and outputs a 0. This binary output nature makes it suitable for tasks that require a clear dichotomy, such as basic binary classification problems. However, in the context of modern neural networks, the threshold activation function has significant limitations, such as a sensitivity to noise and a limitation to only linearly separable problems.

FIGURE 10.3   The threshold activation function

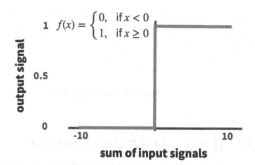

$$f(x) = \begin{cases} 0, & \text{if } x < 0 \\ 1, & \text{if } x \geq 0 \end{cases}$$

Sigmoid Activation Function

The *sigmoid activation function* (shown in Figure 10.4) is an activation function often used for binary response problems. Instead of an output of 0 or 1, the output of the sigmoid activation function can be any real number between 0 and 1. This makes it particularly suitable for models where the output is interpreted as a probability.

FIGURE 10.4   The sigmoid activation function

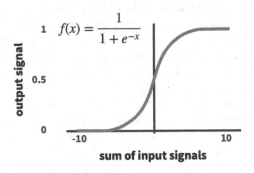

Hyperbolic Tangent (tanh) Activation Function

The *hyperbolic tangent activation function* (illustrated in Figure 10.5) differs from the sigmoid activation function in that it is 0-centered. The output of the hyperbolic tangent activation function falls between –1 and 1. The advantage of having outputs centered around 0 is that it often leads to faster convergence during training.

FIGURE 10.5   The hyperbolic tangent (tanh) activation function

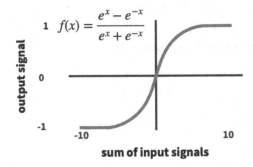

Rectified Linear Unit (ReLU) Activation Function

The *rectified linear unit activation function* (shown in Figure 10.6) is the most commonly used activation function. It transforms the sum of inputs by setting all negative values to 0 and leaving positive values unchanged. It is computationally efficient and has played a significant role in the success of deep neural networks. One of the major advantages of the rectified linear unit activation function is that it mitigates the impact of the *vanishing gradient problem*, which both the sigmoid and hyperbolic tangent activation functions suffer from. The vanishing gradient problem is discussed in more detail later in the chapter.

FIGURE 10.6   The rectified linear unit (ReLU) activation function

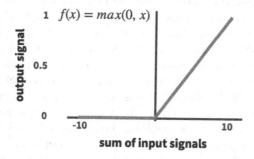

Softmax Activation Function

The *softmax activation function* is typically used in the output layer of a neural network to perform multiclass classification, as it converts logits to probabilities by normalizing the outputs. Normalization here means that the function assigns decimal probabilities to each class in a way that the total sums up to 1. The class with the highest probability is output as the model's prediction. We can think of the softmax activation function as a generalization of the sigmoid activation function to multiple dimensions.

Training Algorithm

Connections in an artificial neural network are the pathways through which neurons in different layers communicate with each other. Every connection carries a *weight*, a numerical value that signifies the strength and direction (positive or negative) of the influence one neuron has on another.

Each node in the network also has a parameter known as the *bias*. The bias of a node provides each neuron with an adjustable value that is added to the weighted sum of its inputs. The role of the bias is to shift the output of the activation function to the left or right. Without a bias, a neuron, regardless of its weights, might not be able to represent certain functions or patterns in the data.

During the training process, a neural network learns the patterns in the training data by adjusting the connection weights and biases across the entire network. One of the most common techniques for doing this is an algorithm known as *backpropagation*. The backpropagation process involves an iterative approach to adjusting connection weights and biases through cycles known as *epochs*. The algorithm runs through several epochs until some stopping criterion is met. Each epoch consists of two phases: a forward phase, which involves the activation of neurons in sequence from input to output, and a backward phase, in which the output from the forward phase is compared to the target value from the training data and the error propagated backward in the network to adjust connection weights and biases.

Because the network contains no a priori knowledge about the training data, the starting weights for the forward phase are typically set at random or using a specific initialization technique.

A loss function is also selected based on the specific task (e.g., mean squared error for a regression problem or cross-entropy for classification). The loss function quantifies the difference between the network's predictions and the actual target values in the training data.

The objective in the backward phase is to understand how each weight and bias contributes to the error and how they should be adjusted to minimize this error. An optimization algorithm (also known as an *optimizer*) is employed to adjust the weights and biases in a way that minimizes the loss function. Commonly used algorithms include *stochastic gradient descent (SGD)*, SGD with momentum, mini-batch gradient descent, adaptive gradient descent, *adaptive moment estimation (Adam)*, and *root mean square propagation (RMSprop)*. The extent to which the weights and biases are adjusted during the backward phase is governed by a hyperparameter known as the *learning rate*. Choosing the right learning rate is a delicate balance: too small, and the network may take too long to converge; too large, and the network may miss the optimal solution altogether. Often, techniques like learning rate schedules (discussed in a moment) or adaptive learning rate optimizers (like Adam) are used to mitigate these issues and achieve more effective training.

Throughout the learning process, various techniques like *dropout, batch normalization, early stopping*, and *learning rate schedulers* may be employed to improve training efficiency and prevent overfitting. The goal is to create a neural network that not only performs well on the training data but also generalizes well to new, unseen data.

Dropout

Dropout is a regularization technique used to prevent overfitting in neural networks. The basic idea is that during training, dropout randomly "drops out" or removes several outputs between nodes in one layer and a subsequent layer. This forces the network to learn more robust features and to generalize better to unseen data. The percentage of dropout between layers is a hyperparameter that is set before the training process.

Batch Normalization

Batch normalization is a technique used in neural networks to stabilize and accelerate the training process. It involves normalizing the inputs to a layer of a neural network on a per-feature basis. For each batch during training, the algorithm normalizes the inputs by subtracting the batch mean from each input and dividing by the batch standard deviation. A *batch* in this context refers to a subset of the training data used in one iteration of the training process. Batch normalization ensures that the range of activations remains consistent across different layers and training batches. The size of the batch, known as the *batch size*, is a hyperparameter that can significantly impact the training dynamics and performance of a neural network.

Early Stopping

Early stopping is another regularization technique used to prevent overfitting in neural networks. During training, a network's performance is continuously evaluated on a separate dataset known as the validation set. If the performance on the validation set starts to degrade in contrast to the training set (i.e., the model starts to overfit), the training process is stopped early. This helps in ensuring that the model doesn't learn the noise in the training data.

Learning Rate Schedulers

Learning rate schedulers are used to adjust the learning rate during training, which can lead to better convergence. The adjustment can be made according to a predefined schedule or in response to the current state of the training process, such as reducing the learning rate as the model's performance plateaus on the validation set.

The Vanishing and Exploding Gradient Problems

The *vanishing gradient problem* and the *exploding gradient problem* are two significant challenges encountered during the training of neural networks, especially when using gradient-based learning methods and backpropagation. Both problems are related to the way gradients are computed and propagated through the network, but they manifest in opposite ways.

To understand these problems, it's important to first explain what a gradient is in this context. In neural networks, a gradient is a vector of partial derivatives (see Chapter 2, "Mathematics and Statistical Methods") that represents the direction and rate of change of the loss function with respect to the network's weights. During training, gradients are used to update the weights in the opposite direction of the gradient to minimize the loss function. This process is known as *gradient descent*.

The vanishing gradient problem occurs when the gradients of the network's loss with respect to the weights become increasingly small as the backpropagation algorithm progresses through the layers. This happens especially in networks with many layers. The primary cause is the multiplication of gradients through the deep network layers during backpropagation. If these gradients are small (less than 1), multiplying them repeatedly leads to exponentially smaller gradients. As a result of the vanishing gradient, the weights in the early layers of the network (closer to the input) receive very small updates or none at all. This makes the training process extremely slow and inefficient.

The exploding gradient problem is the opposite of the vanishing gradient problem. It occurs when the gradients during training become excessively large. It typically happens in networks with a lot of hidden layers or large recurrent connections, where gradients can accumulate and grow exponentially during backpropagation, leading to very large updates to the network's weights. Large gradients can cause the learning process to become unstable, often leading to model divergence and the inability to converge to a solution.

Deep Neural Networks

The topology of interconnected neurons within a neural network influences the way it learns. Previously, we were introduced to the perceptron—a single-layer network that is only capable of learning simple patterns. As signals come into the input nodes, the perceptron passes them on to the output node exactly as received. To handle more sophisticated learning tasks, most practical neural networks are *multilayer networks* with one or more hidden layers that process incoming signals from the input layer before they are passed on to the output layer. These additional layers enable the network to perform more complex, higher-level feature extraction compared to traditional, shallower neural networks. The higher the number of hidden layers a network has, the "deeper" it is said to be. An artificial neural network with two or more hidden layers is referred to as a *deep neural network (DNN)* and the practice of training such a network is known as *deep learning*.

Deep neural networks have garnered significant attention due to their remarkable ability to perform a wide range of complex tasks. One of the primary benefits of deep neural networks is their ability to process and learn from enormous volumes of data, making them exceptionally well suited for applications like image and speech recognition, NLP, and autonomous systems. The layered structure of deep neural networks enables them to learn features and patterns at various levels of abstraction, allowing for intricate and nuanced understanding. This feature-learning capability eliminates the need for manual feature extraction, one of the most time-consuming aspects of traditional machine learning. Another advantage is the adaptability and versatility of deep learning models. With the same foundational architecture, deep neural networks can be adapted to solve a myriad of tasks, often outperforming more traditional algorithms. A benefit of deep neural networks that is receiving a lot of attention recently is their ability to leverage *transfer learning*. This is the ability of deep learning models to apply knowledge gained in one domain to tasks and problems in a different but related domain. Transfer learning is particularly useful for problems where data is scarce or expensive to acquire.

There are some challenges inherent with deep learning as well. One of the major challenges is that deep neural networks require massive amounts of labeled data to achieve their full potential. Collecting and labeling data can be costly and time-consuming. Due to this limitation, approaches such as *zero-shot learning*, *one-shot learning*, or *few-shot learning* are sometimes used when training a deep neural network. Another challenge is the issue of interpretability and explainability. Neural networks are "black box" models due to their complexity and the mechanics of how they work. This lack of transparency can be a significant hurdle in fields where explainability is crucial, like in healthcare and criminal justice. Training deep neural networks can be computationally intensive and time-consuming, requiring powerful and expensive hardware, such as graphics processing units (GPUs) or tensor processing units (TPUs). Finally, deep learning models are prone to overfitting. This is especially true when they are trained on datasets that are not sufficiently diverse or large enough. This means they might perform well on the training data but poorly on unseen data.

One-Shot, Zero-Shot, and Few-Shot Learning

Traditionally deep neural networks require large amounts of data to learn effectively. *One-shot learning* aims to overcome this by using techniques that allow a model to generalize from a minimal amount of data. It is particularly relevant in a field like facial recognition, where a system may only have one image of a person but still needs to be able to accurately identify them. A technique such as the use of Siamese networks, which focus on learning similarities and differences between pairs of examples, is often used for one-shot learning.

Zero-shot learning takes this concept a step further by attempting to classify data that belongs to classes not seen during training. This is achieved by linking the known and unknown classes through the use of auxiliary information like class attributes or semantic relationships. For example, a model trained on various animals might learn to recognize an unseen animal by relating it to learned attributes such as "has wings" or "can swim."

Few-shot learning is a middle ground between traditional machine learning and one-shot learning. It involves training neural networks to make accurate predictions with a very small dataset, typically ranging from a couple to a few dozen examples per class. Few-shot learning is particularly challenging because the model must avoid overfitting despite the small amount of data. A technique like meta-learning, where the model is trained to learn quickly from small amounts of data across various tasks, is commonly used for few-shot learning.

Common Deep Learning Architectures

Deep learning has introduced several powerful neural network architectures. Each of these architectures leverages the depth and flexibility of neural networks to handle a wide range of complex tasks, from analyzing visual and auditory data to interpreting and generating human language. Their design reflects the specific nature of the data and the task at hand, showcasing the versatility and power of deep learning.

Convolutional Neural Network

A common deep learning architecture is the *convolutional neural network (CNN)*. These types of networks employ what are known as *convolutional layers* and *pooling layers* to extract hierarchical features from input data. The convolutional layer consists of a set of filters that allow the network to detect specific patterns in the data, while the pooling layer reduces the complexity of the data by retaining the most important patterns and discarding the rest. Convolutional neural networks have revolutionized image recognition and computer vision. They are specialized for processing grid-like data and are primarily used for image processing, image classification, object detection, image segmentation, and video analysis.

Real World Scenario

Automated Medical Image Diagnosis

A healthcare tech company aims to develop an automated system to detect and classify abnormalities in medical imaging. The task involves recognizing complex patterns and categorizing images based on the presence of specific features. An ideal architecture for this task is the convolutional neural network (CNN). CNNs are adept at processing grid-like data, crucial for maintaining the spatial hierarchy in medical images. Their convolutional layers excel in identifying intricate patterns, while pooling layers condense the data, preserving essential information and enhancing computational efficiency. This architecture also supports transfer learning, which is beneficial given the limited availability of labeled medical datasets. Additionally, CNNs can be trained on augmented data, bolstering their robustness to variations in medical imaging. For the deployment of a CNN-based model, the company must curate a substantial annotated dataset, preprocess images for consistency, design a tailored CNN architecture, and employ high-performance computing for training.

Recurrent Neural Network

The *recurrent neural network (RNN)* is another popular deep learning architecture. These types of networks utilize recurrent connections, which are connections that loop back on themselves, in order to maintain memory of past inputs. This recurrent nature makes RNNs well suited for sequential data, where the order of input matters, and for tasks such as time-series analysis, NLP, speech recognition, and music composition.

Long Short-Term Memory

As useful as they are, recurrent neural networks suffer from what is known as the vanishing gradient problem, a problem that makes it challenging for RNNs to handle large sequences of text, like long paragraphs or essays. To address this issue, more advanced variants of the RNN architecture, such as *long short-term memory (LSTM)* and *gated recurrent unit (GRU)*, were introduced. These architectures use gating mechanisms that allow them to handle longer sequences of data more effectively by controlling the flow of information. LSTMs and GRUs are widely used in language modeling, machine translation, speech recognition, and other tasks where understanding long-term dependencies in sequential data is crucial.

 Real World Scenario

Real-Time Stock Price Prediction

An investment firm wants to predict stock prices based on historical time-series data. The task requires understanding temporal dynamics and dependencies in the stock market. For this sequential and time-dependent data, a recurrent neural network (RNN) could be suitable due to its ability to maintain memory of past inputs. However, given the long-term dependencies typical in stock data, an LSTM (long short-term memory) network would be more appropriate. LSTMs can remember information over extended periods, which is essential for capturing the patterns that influence stock prices over time.

Transformers

Recurrent neural networks and their variants, such as LSTMs and GRUs, process input data sequentially. This inherent sequential nature makes them challenging to parallelize, meaning that increasing computational resources does not necessarily lead to a proportional speed-up in the training process. This limitation can be particularly problematic when dealing with large datasets or complex models. To address this challenge, a new type of deep learning architecture called the *transformer* was developed.

The transformer follows an encoder-decoder structure, where the encoder processes the input sequence and the decoder generates the output sequence. Both the encoder and decoder are composed of multiple layers. At the heart of the transformer is the self-attention mechanism.

Self-attention allows each element in the input data to interact with every other element, regardless of their positions in the sequence. This interaction enables the model to capture dependencies and relationships between elements, adding rich context to the input data. As a result, transformers can produce contextually relevant and coherent text, making them particularly well suited for NLP and machine translation tasks. Transformers are the foundational technology behind most *large language models (LLMs)* and LLM-based services.

 Real World Scenario

Real-Time Language Translation Service

A tech startup wants to create a near-instantaneous language translation service. The task demands understanding the context of entire sentences and paragraphs to produce accurate translations. While RNNs and LSTMs could be used here, they are less efficient due to the sequential nature in which they process inputs. A transformer is better suited for this task. Transformers process data in parallel, significantly speeding up the training process. Their use of the self-attention mechanism to weigh the influence of different words within the input data makes them an excellent choice for tasks that require an understanding of context within the input data, a capability that is essential for accurate language translation.

Generative Adversarial Networks

Another revolutionary and popular deep learning architecture is the *generative adversarial network (GAN)*. GANs consist of two neural networks—a generator and a discriminator—engaged in a competitive learning process. As the name suggests, GANs are generative models, which means they are used to create new content. In the context of image generation, the generator (also known as the artist) network within a GAN learns to gradually create images that very closely resemble real images or are virtually indistinguishable from real images based on the feedback it receives from the discriminator (also known as the art critic) network over several learning cycles. Not only are GANs useful in generating images, but they can also produce highly realistic synthetic audio, text, and video samples.

 Real World Scenario

Creating Artistic Renderings from Photographs

A mobile app development company aims to build an app that turns user photographs into artwork mimicking the styles of famous painters. A generative adversarial network is ideal for this use case due to its ability to generate new content that is indistinguishable from real data. As the generator network learns to create artistic images from photographs, the discriminator network ensures the quality of generated images by comparing them to a dataset of genuine artwork.

Autoencoders

An *autoencoder* is a deep learning architecture primarily used for unsupervised learning tasks, such as dimensionality reduction, feature learning, and data denoising. The fundamental architecture of an autoencoder consists of an *encoder* network, which is designed to encode input data into a lower-dimensional representation (latent-space representation), and a *decoder* network, which then reconstructs the original data as closely as possible from this representation. This process enables the autoencoder to learn efficient and compact representations (*encodings*) of the input data. An autoencoder variant, known as a variational autoencoder (VAE), is often used in generative modeling to generate new data points similar to the input data.

 Real World Scenario

Anomaly Detection in Network Traffic

A cybersecurity company wants to identify unusual patterns in network traffic to flag potential security threats in real time. An autoencoder could be deployed for this unsupervised machine learning task. By learning to compress and then reconstruct network traffic data, the autoencoder can learn a representation of "normal" traffic data. Reconstructions that differ significantly from the input can be flagged as anomalies, which could indicate a security incident. A variational autoencoder (VAE) could also be used if there's a need to generate new network traffic data samples for further analysis, simulation, or training.

Common Deep Learning Frameworks

Deep learning frameworks have become essential tools for developing and training deep neural networks. They provide tools and libraries that facilitate the design, training, and validation of deep learning models. Among the most prominent are the *PyTorch*, *TensorFlow*, and *Keras* frameworks, as well as several *AutoML* frameworks that simplify the process of deep learning.

PyTorch

PyTorch is an open source machine learning library developed by Facebook's AI Research lab. It is known for its flexibility, ease of use, and dynamic computational graph, which allows changes to the network architecture on the fly. PyTorch's dynamic nature makes it particularly popular for research and prototyping, as it enables a high degree of experimentation. Its straightforward syntax and integration with Python also make it very user-friendly. This integration allows for seamless compatibility with popular Python libraries and packages like NumPy. PyTorch supports GPU acceleration, which significantly speeds up computations necessary for large-scale deep learning models. This makes it highly efficient for both research and production. PyTorch also provides a rich ecosystem of tools and libraries for tasks like computer vision (torchvision), audio data processing (torchaudio), and natural language processing (torchtext).

TensorFlow and Keras

TensorFlow, developed by Google DeepMind (formerly Google Brain), is another popular deep learning framework. It offers a comprehensive, flexible ecosystem of tools, libraries, and community resources, making it suitable for both research and production. In TensorFlow, computations are represented as data flow graphs. Each node in the graph represents an instance of a mathematical operation (like addition, division, or multiplication) and each edge is a multidimensional dataset (*tensor*) on which the operations are performed. The graph is constructed by adding nodes and edges, and then the graph is executed to compute the output tensors. TensorFlow can run on multiple CPUs and GPUs and is also compatible with distributed computing, so it can handle large-scale neural networks and datasets.

With the release of TensorFlow 2.0, Keras, previously an independent high-level neural networks library, became an integral part of TensorFlow. Keras offers a simpler, more user-friendly interface for building and training deep learning models within TensorFlow.

Automated Machine Learning (AutoML)

An *AutoML* (automated machine learning) framework is a software system designed to automate many of the tasks involved in designing and deploying machine learning models such as a deep learning model. These frameworks aim to make machine learning accessible to nonexperts and to increase efficiency in ML workflows. The main objective of AutoML frameworks is to reduce or eliminate the need for specialized knowledge in machine learning and statistics, thereby democratizing the use of advanced analytics.

In a typical deep learning project, a practitioner must make several complex decisions, such as selecting the right architecture (CNN, RNN, transformer, etc.), choosing the appropriate activation functions, initializing weights, setting the learning rate, and deciding on many other hyperparameters. This process requires extensive knowledge and experience in the field of deep learning. AutoML frameworks aim to automate these decisions, making it easier to apply deep learning models to new problems, especially for those without deep expertise in the field.

Key aspects of AutoML in deep learning include:

- **Neural Architecture Search (NAS):** This involves automatically designing neural network architectures optimized for specific tasks. NAS algorithms search through a space of possible architectures and evaluate them based on their performance on a given task.

- **Hyperparameter Optimization:** AutoML frameworks use various optimization techniques to automatically select the best hyperparameters for the learning process, like learning rate, batch size, or number of layers.

- **Feature Engineering and Preprocessing:** Although deep learning models are known for their ability to automatically learn features, AutoML can further assist in preprocessing and feature engineering, particularly in selecting and transforming input data in the most effective way for the model.

- **Model Training and Validation:** AutoML tools automate the process of training models and validating their performance, often employing techniques like cross-validation to ensure that the models generalize well to new data.

- **Scalability and Efficiency:** AutoML frameworks are designed to handle large datasets and complex models efficiently, often incorporating distributed computing and optimization techniques to speed up processing.

While AutoML simplifies many aspects of model development, it's still important to have a basic understanding of machine learning principles to effectively interpret and validate the results. Examples of popular AutoML frameworks and tools include Google Cloud AutoML, H2O AutoML, Auto-Sklearn, Microsoft's Azure Automated Machine Learning, Amazon Sage-Maker Autopilot, TPOT (Tree-Based Pipeline Optimization Tool), DataRobot, and AutoKeras.

Summary

Artificial neural networks (ANNs) simulate the functionality of biological neurons, using nodes (neurons) to process input signals and produce an output signal. Inputs are weighted by importance, summed, and passed through an activation function to determine a node's output. Neural networks vary based on their topology, activation function, and training algorithm.

The topology of a network affects how it learns. Nodes are organized into layers—input, hidden, and output layers. The input layer receives signals, hidden layers perform computations, and the output layer delivers the results.

Activation functions normalize node outputs and introduce nonlinearity, which enables networks to learn complex patterns. There are various types of activation functions, each with its own unique characteristics.

Weights represent the strength of connections between neurons. Biases adjust the output of neurons by shifting them up or down. During the training process, adjustments are made to weights and biases using a process known as backpropagation.

Deep neural networks (DNNs) are advanced, multilayered neural networks that feature multiple hidden layers. They are well suited for complex and high-level feature processing, and they eliminate the need for manual feature extraction.

There are several deep neural network architectures, each with its strengths and weaknesses. Prominent architectures include convolutional neural networks (CNNs), recurrent neural networks (RNNs), long short-term memory (LSTM) networks, transformers, generative adversarial networks (GANs), and autoencoders.

Deep learning frameworks like PyTorch, TensorFlow, and Keras, along with automated machine learning (AutoML) tools, facilitate DNN development and training.

Exam Essentials

Explain the difference between the input, hidden, and output layers of a neural network.
In a neural network, the input layer receives and passes on raw data without change. The hidden layers perform complex computations and feature extraction. The output layer presents the final results of the network.

Know what an activation function is and list some of the commonly used activation functions.
Activation functions in a neural network transformed combined input signals into a single output signal, normalizing outputs to a manageable scale and introducing nonlinearity, which enables complex pattern modeling. Common activation functions include sigmoid, hyperbolic tangent, rectified linear unit, and softmax.

Explain some of the strategies used to improve the training efficiency of a neural network.
Techniques used include dropout (to prevent overfitting by randomly deactivating nodes), batch normalization (to stabilize and accelerate training by normalizing inputs), early stopping (to halt training when validation performance degrades), and learning rate schedulers (to adjust the learning rate for better convergence).

Understand what a deep neural network is and list some of the common architectures.
A deep neural network is a multilayered network with several hidden layers that enable complex, high-level feature extraction. Common architectures include convolutional neural networks (CNNs) for grid-like data, recurrent neural networks (RNNs) and long short-term memory (LSTMs) for sequential data, transformers for natural language processing, generative adversarial networks (GANs) for content generation, and autoencoders for unsupervised learning tasks like dimensionality reduction.

Review Questions

1. Jane is developing a system to classify cars in surveillance videos. Which neural network architecture should she use?

   A. LSTM

   B. GAN

   C. CNN

   D. RNN

2. Sam is training a neural network for facial recognition. To avoid overfitting, which of the following techniques should he consider?

   A. Use dropout.

   B. Add more hidden layers.

   C. Increase the learning rate.

   D. Avoid activation functions.

3. What challenge with recurrent neural networks (RNNs) is specifically addressed by long short-term memory (LSTM) networks?

   A. The vanishing gradient problem in processing long sequences of data

   B. The inability to process image data

   C. The lack of parallel processing capabilities

   D. The difficulty in handling small datasets

4. A tech company wants to create a chatbot that can understand and generate human-like responses. Which neural network architecture should they use?

   A. Autoencoder

   B. GAN

   C. Transformer

   D. CNN

5. For a multiclass classification problem, such as recognizing different types of vehicles in an image, which activation function is typically used in the output layer of the neural network?

   A. Sigmoid

   B. Hyperbolic tangent (tanh)

   C. Rectified linear unit (ReLU)

   D. Softmax

6. Melissa is building a neural network for language translation. She wants to ensure consistent performance across training batches. Which of these techniques should she use?

   A. Early stopping

   B. Batch normalization

   C. Increasing the number of batches

   D. Using batch activation functions

7. In the context of neural networks, what is the purpose of an activation function?

   A. To reduce the dimensionality of the input data

   B. To normalize the output of each node and introduce nonlinearity

   C. To increase the computational speed of the network

   D. To connect different layers of the network

8. Richard wants to use a deep learning model to identify tumors in MRI scans. Which neural network architecture should he use?

   A. RNN

   B. LSTM

   C. CNN

   D. Autoencoder

9. A neural network designed to classify emails into spam and non-spam is failing to generalize well. Which of these approaches could improve its performance on unseen data?

   A. Increasing the size of the input layer

   B. Using a threshold activation function

   C. Implementing early stopping

   D. Adding more nodes to the output layer

10. A neural network is being trained for a binary classification task. Which activation function would be most appropriate for the output node?

    A. Hyperbolic tangent (tanh)

    B. Sigmoid

    C. Rectified linear unit (ReLU)

    D. Threshold

11. Which of these is one of the primary advantages of using deep neural networks (DNNs) over simpler, shallower neural networks?

    A. DNNs require less computational power.

    B. DNNs can only process linear data.

    C. DNNs are capable of more complex, higher-level feature extraction.

    D. DNNs work only with small datasets.

12. An auto manufacturer is working on a self-driving car system that needs to process sequential sensor data. Which neural network architecture should they implement?

    A. CNN

    B. GAN

    C. Transformer

    D. LSTM

13. Which deep learning framework is known for its dynamic computational graph, which allows changes to the network architecture on the fly?

    A. TensorFlow

    B. Keras

    C. PyTorch

    D. AutoML

14. In a neural network designed for image classification, which activation function would be best to avoid the vanishing gradient problem and speed up training?

    A. Threshold activation function

    B. Sigmoid

    C. Hyperbolic tangent (tanh)

    D. Rectified linear unit (ReLU)

15. During the development of a neural network for autonomous driving, Lina and her team decide to automatically adjust the learning rate based on the model's performance on the validation data. Which of the following are they likely using?

    A. Learning rate scheduler

    B. Adaptive learning estimation

    C. Stochastic gradient descent

    D. Early learning stopping

16. A finance company is developing a fraud detection system based on transaction patterns. Which neural network architecture would be most suitable?

    A. CNN

    B. LSTM

    C. GAN

    D. Autoencoder

17. Rafa wants to train a model that is capable of categorizing animals into groups, which were not part of its training data. Which learning approach does he want to use?

    A. One-shot learning

    B. Zero-shot learning

    C. Few-shot learning

    D. Transfer learning

18. Alex is trying to improve his model's ability to capture nonlinear relationships in complex data. Which aspect of the network should he focus on tweaking?

   A. The number of nodes in the output layer

   B. The learning rate

   C. The type of activation function used

   D. The batch size during training

19. A data science team is developing a deep neural network for natural language processing. They notice that during training, the updates to the weights in the early layers are very small, slowing down the learning process. What problem is the network likely encountering?

   A. Overfitting

   B. Underfitting

   C. The vanishing gradient problem

   D. The exploding gradient problem

20. What is the primary focus of neural architecture search (NAS) in AutoML?

   A. Optimizing the learning rate and batch size

   B. Automatically designing neural network architectures for specific tasks

   C. Enhancing the scalability and efficiency of model training

   D. Conducting feature engineering and preprocessing

Chapter

11

Natural Language Processing

THE COMPTIA DATAX EXAM OBJECTIVES COVERED IN THIS CHAPTER INCLUDE:

✓ **Domain 5: Specialized Applications of Data Science**

  ▪ 5.2 Explain the use and importance of natural language processing (NLP) concepts.

Natural language processing (NLP) stands at the crossroads of computer science and linguistics, offering a fascinating glimpse into the ways machines can be taught to understand and interact with human language. This chapter delves into the core components that make NLP a transformative technology in today's digital landscape. It begins by exploring text analysis, where NLP techniques are employed for keyword extraction, matching models, sentiment analysis, and topic modeling. Next, we examine language understanding and language generation. A crucial step in the NLP process is text preparation, which involves tokenization, stemming, spelling normalization, and other similar tasks that clean and normalize text to enhance the quality of analysis. Finally, we discuss text representation, where text is transformed into a format that machines can understand, such as the vector space model and word embeddings.

Natural Language Processing

Natural language processing (NLP) is an interdisciplinary field that bridges computer science, artificial intelligence, and linguistics. Its primary aim is to enable machines to comprehend, interpret, and produce human language in a manner that is both meaningful and practical. NLP involves a range of tasks, including text analysis, language understanding, and language generation.

As you prepare for the DataX exam, you should be able to explain the use and importance of key natural language processing concepts. Make note of the techniques introduced in this chapter, how they work, and how they are used in the vast field of natural language processing.

Text Analysis

One of the fundamental tasks in natural language processing is *text analysis*. Also known as *text mining* or *text analytics*, text analysis is the process of analyzing large volumes of unstructured text in order to extract meaningful information or useful insights from it. The applications of text analysis include keyword extraction, matching models, sentiment analysis, and topic modeling.

Keyword Extraction

Keyword extraction, also known as key phrase extraction or term extraction, involves automatically identifying and extracting the most relevant words or phrases from text that represent its main content or themes. The extracted keywords or key phrases provide a concise summary of the text's subject matter and can be used for various applications. For example, extracted keywords can be used to enhance the searchability of documents in databases and search engines, enabling users to find relevant information more efficiently. This is known as *information retrieval*. Analyzing the frequency and evolution of keywords over time can reveal trends and patterns in large text corpora, such as news articles or social media posts. This process is known as *keyword trend analysis*. In digital marketing, extracted keywords are essential for search engine optimization (SEO)—optimizing web content to improve its visibility and ranking in search engine results.

Matching Models

Matching models are fundamental tools and techniques for comparing two pieces of text and assessing their similarity. They serve as the backbone for a wide range of applications that require an understanding of how well the text aligns or is duplicated. This is essential for tasks such as information retrieval, question answering, and document classification. Matching models can be broadly categorized into string matching and semantic matching.

String Matching

String matching involves comparing texts based on their lexical or syntactic similarity, often at the character or token level (see the "Tokenization" section later in this chapter). This approach is particularly useful in applications where the exact structure or composition of the text is important.

String matching algorithms, such as edit distance (discussed in a moment), are used in spell checkers to find words that are lexically similar to a misspelled word. String matching is also useful for plagiarism detection, where documents are compared at the lexical level to identify overlapping or copied content. In document clustering, string matching can be used to group together documents that have similar wording or syntactic structures.

Semantic Matching

Semantic matching involves comparing texts based on their underlying meaning rather than their surface form. This is useful in tasks where the context and semantic content of text is more important than its literal content. Deep learning models like transformers and word embeddings (discussed later in this chapter) are quite useful for semantic matching.

Semantic matching models are used in search engines to retrieve documents or web pages that are semantically related to a query, even if they don't contain the exact query terms. In question-answering systems, semantic matching helps identify answers that are semantically relevant to the posed question, regardless of lexical variations.

Sentiment Analysis

Sentiment analysis, also known as *opinion mining,* involves identifying and categorizing the opinions or emotions expressed in a piece of text. The goal is to determine the writer's or speaker's attitude (positive, negative, or neutral) toward a particular topic, product, or service. Sentiment analysis has a wide range of applications across various domains, such as business, politics, and social media.

Sentiment analysis can be performed using various techniques, one of which is known as a lexicon-based approach. With this approach the sentiment of a piece of text is determined based on the presence and combination of opinion words within the text. These opinion words are predefined words and phrases (known as an opinion lexicon) associated with positive, negative, or neutral sentiments. Another approach to sentiment analysis is the model-based approach. With this approach, supervised machine learning algorithms, such as naive Bayes, logistic regression, and neural network architectures like recurrent neural networks and transformers, are trained on labeled datasets to classify the sentiment of new text.

Topic Modeling

Topic modeling is an unsupervised machine learning technique that is used to discover the underlying thematic structure in a large collection of documents (corpus). It involves identifying "topics," which are sets of words that frequently occur together, and then assigning each document in the corpus to one or more of these topics. Topic modeling helps in understanding and organizing large datasets of textual information and can be used to do various natural language processing tasks. For example, by indexing documents based on their topics, topic modeling enhances information retrieval searches, enabling users to find relevant documents more efficiently. Similar to keyword extraction, analyzing the evolution of topics over time can reveal trends and patterns in large text corpora, such as news articles or social media posts. Topic modeling can also be used by recommender systems to recommend similar content to users based on the topics of interest in the documents they previously interacted with.

Several algorithms have been developed for topic modeling. One of the most popular and widely used is *latent Dirichlet allocation (LDA),* a probabilistic model that assumes each document is a mixture of a small number of topics and that each word in the document is attributable to one of the topics in the document. Two other common algorithms are nonnegative matrix factorization (NMF) and latent semantic analysis (LSA).

Language Understanding

Language understanding, also known as *natural language understanding (NLU),* focuses on enabling computers to comprehend and interpret human language. This involves not only recognizing the words in a sentence but also understanding their relationships, context, and the intended message or information.

In natural language processing, language understanding is essential for a wide range of applications. It is used in question-answering systems to extract answers from text based on user queries. Language understanding is used in *speech recognition* systems to transform spoken language into text for use in voice-activated virtual assistants, dictation software, and automated transcription services. Language understanding is also useful in language translation services and multilingual content management systems.

Here are some of the key components of language understanding:

- **Syntax Analysis:** This involves analyzing the grammatical structure of a sentence to understand the relationships between words. Techniques like parsing and part-of-speech tagging are used to identify nouns, verbs, adjectives, and other parts of speech, as well as the structure of phrases and sentences.

- **Semantic Analysis:** Semantic analysis aims to understand the meaning of words and sentences. This includes tasks like *word sense disambiguation* (determining the correct meaning of a word based on context) and resolving ambiguities in language.

- **Named Entity Recognition (NER):** *Named entity recognition* is the task of identifying and classifying proper nouns (names of people, places, organizations, etc.) in text, which is important for understanding the entities involved in a sentence or document. In content management systems, NER can be used for *autotagging* articles, news stories, or blog posts by extracting keywords that are contextually relevant to the content.

Language understanding is a complex and challenging area due to the inherent ambiguity and variability of human language. Some notable challenges with language understanding are:

- **Ambiguity:** Words and sentences can have multiple meanings. Determining the correct interpretation often requires context and supplementary knowledge.

- **Idiomatic Expressions:** Phrases that don't have a direct literal meaning, such as "kick the bucket," can be difficult for machines to understand.

- **Sarcasm and Irony:** Detecting sarcasm and irony requires an understanding of the speaker's intent as well as familiarity with the context of the conversation.

- **Cross-Linguistic Variability:** Different languages have different grammatical structures and idiomatic expressions, which make language understanding a challenge in multilingual contexts.

Language Generation

Language generation, also known as *natural language generation (NLG),* focuses on enabling computers to create human-like text based on specific inputs or prompts. Language generation techniques have evolved over the years from rule-based systems with limited flexibility to advanced neural network models that can generate diverse and contextually rich text. The advent of deep learning techniques such as transformers and the development of pretrained language models, in particular, has significantly improved the quality and coherence of language generation. This has opened new possibilities for the application of language generation in NLP.

Language generation is used in various applications. It is used in *question-and-answer dialogue* systems such as chatbots and virtual assistants, where language generation is used to produce natural and coherent responses to user queries or commands. Language generation is also employed in automated content creation to generate written content for websites, reports, and articles. In language translation, it is used to convert text from one language to another. This involves understanding the source language's syntax and semantics and then generating equivalent text in the target language. Language generation is also used to generate concise summaries of longer documents or articles, a task known as *text summarization*. In accessibility tools for visually impaired individuals, voice-activated assistants, and language learning apps, language generation can be used for *speech generation*, which involves converting written text into spoken language.

As with language understanding, there are some inherent challenges with language generation. They include:

- **Coherence and Consistency:** Maintaining coherence and consistency in a large amount of text output is a significant challenge. Generated text should logically flow from one sentence to the next, maintaining a clear and consistent topic or narrative. However, as the length of generated text increases, many models struggle to maintain this coherence and may produce text that is repetitive, contradictory, or off topic.

- **Control:** Controlling the content, style, and tone of the generated text is crucial for many applications. For example, a user might want to generate text that is formal, humorous, or aligned with a specific theme. Achieving this level of control is challenging because it requires the model to understand and manipulate subtle linguistic cues.

- **Evaluation:** Evaluating the quality of generated text is challenging, as it involves subjective metrics such as fluency (grammatical correctness and naturalness), relevance (appropriateness to the context or task), and coherence (logical flow and consistency).

Large Language Models (LLMs)

A *large language model (LLM)* is a deep learning model that is able to understand and generate human-like text based on the input it receives. These models are "large" due to their extensive training on vast amounts of text data, which enables them to handle a wide range of language tasks. They can predict the next word in a sentence, answer questions, summarize texts, translate languages, and even generate coherent paragraphs. LLMs have become increasingly important in natural language processing due to their ability to capture intricate patterns and nuances of human language in ways that were not possible with earlier models. Some well-known examples of LLMs include the GPT (Generative Pretrained Transformer) series, BERT (Bidirectional Encoder Representations from Transformers), and T5 (Text-to-Text Transfer Transformer).

Text Preparation

Before applying natural language processing techniques to text, it's crucial that we prepare it. This is known as text preprocessing and involves a series of steps that make the raw text data more suitable for further analysis and model training. Common text preprocessing steps include tokenization, stemming, lemmatization, removal of stop words, part-of-speech tagging, spelling normalization, and data augmentation.

Tokenization

Tokenization is the process of breaking up text data into individual units or *tokens*. It is a fundamental text processing step as it converts a stream of characters into a sequence of tokens that represent the basic elements of language syntax. For example, the text "The cow jumped over the moon" can be tokenized into individual words as "the," "cow," "jumped," "over," "the," and "moon." Tokenization is crucial for text analytics tasks like sentiment analysis, where the sentiment of each individual word is analyzed to determine the overall sentiment of the text.

Tokens are most often a single word, but they can also be a sentence, a paragraph, or any n-gram. An *n-gram* is a contiguous sequence of "n" items within text. They can be syllables, letters, words, or base pairs. The *n* in n-gram indicates the number of elements in the sequence. For instance, a 1-gram (or unigram) is a sequence with one item (typically a word), a 2-gram (or bigram) is a sequence of two items such as "hot dog," and a 3-gram (or trigram) is a sequence of three items such as "New York City."

Stemming

Stemming is the process of reducing words to their base or root form. It involves the removal of prefixes, suffixes, and pluralization. This effectively consolidates different forms of a word into a common base form. For instance, "walking," "walks," "walked," and "walker" can all be reduced to "walk." For many NLP tasks, stemming leads to accuracy improvements by shrinking the number of dimensions used by an algorithm and grouping words by concept.

Lemmatization

Lemmatization is a more advanced form of stemming that attempts to group words based on their core concept, or *lemma*. Lemmatization uses both the context surrounding a word and additional grammatical information, such as part of speech, to determine the lemma for a word. For a word such as "walking," stemming and lemmatization produce the same result—"walk." However, for a word like "meeting," which could serve as either a noun or a verb, stemming reduces it to the single root word "meet," but lemmatization produces "meet" for the verb and maintains "meeting" for the noun.

Removing Stop Words

Stop words are words that occur a lot but have very little analytic impact. Common examples of stop words include "a," "an," "and," "but," "by," "if," "it," "that," "the," and so on. Removing stop words can help NLP tasks focus on the more meaningful words in the text. This is important for tasks such as topic modeling or keyword extraction, where the objective is to identify significant words that convey the most important themes or concepts.

Part-of-Speech (POS) Tagging

Part-of-speech (POS) tagging involves identifying the grammatical part of speech (noun, verb, adjective, etc.) that each word in a sentence belongs to. It is also known as grammatical tagging or word-category disambiguation. POS tagging is essential for understanding the structure of sentences and for tasks that require a deep understanding of linguistic structure. It helps in disambiguating words that can serve as multiple parts of speech (for example, "book" can serve as a noun or a verb) and is crucial for accurate syntax and semantic analysis.

Regular Expressions

A regular expression (also known as a *regex*) is a sequence of characters that defines a search pattern. Each character in a regular expression can be either a regular character or a metacharacter. Metacharacters have special meaning, and they include $, *, +, ., ?, [",."], ^, {",."}, |, (",."), and \. Regular expressions are a powerful tool for searching, matching, and manipulating text. Let's assume we had the following text from a website `<html><body><p>Hello, <b>world</b>!</p></body></html>`. We could use regular expressions to clean it up by removing all the HTML tags in the source text. The regex pattern `<[^>]*>` will match any sequence of characters that starts with <, followed by zero or more characters that are not >, and ends with >. Applied to the source text, the result would be `Hello, world!`. Besides removing HTML tags or special characters, regular expressions can also be used to identify and extract pieces of information like dates, email addresses, phone numbers, and more from large text corpora. They are useful in several of the text preprocessing steps mentioned in this section. There are several helpful online resources for learning regular expressions. Two popular sites are RegexBuddy (`www.regular-expressions.info`) and RegexOne (`http://regexone.com`).

Spelling Normalization

Spelling normalization involves correcting spelling mistakes and eliminating variations in spelling. This process can include expanding contractions (for example, converting "don't" to "do not"), and standardizing between American and British English spelling variations. Spelling normalization is crucial for maintaining the consistency of the data and improving the performance of NLP models, especially in tasks that rely on matching text or understanding user queries.

There are several common approaches to spelling normalization. One approach is the dictionary-based approach. This involves using a predefined dictionary of correct spellings to identify and correct misspelled words in the text. Words not found in the dictionary are flagged as potential errors and replaced with the closest match from the dictionary. Regular expressions are highly effective in this context. They can be used to identify and replace words that match specific patterns. For example, a regex pattern can be created to match variations of a word and replace them with the standardized form.

Another common approach to spelling normalization is to use *fuzzy matching* algorithms, such as edit distance, to identify and cluster together words with similar spellings. *Edit distance* measures the minimum number of operations (insertions, deletions, or substitutions) required to change one word into another. Words with a small edit distance can be considered similar and potentially clustered together or replaced with a common correct form. To illustrate how this works, let's consider the misspelled word "shoose." The edit distance between "shoose" and the potential replacement "shoes" is 2, because the minimum number of operations to transform "shoose" to "shoes" is 2 (substitute the second "o" with "e" and delete the last "e").

 Real World Scenario

Spelling Normalization for an Online Retail Product Catalog

An online retail store has a vast product catalog with descriptions sourced from various suppliers. Due to manual data entry and differences in spelling conventions, the product descriptions contain inconsistencies and spelling errors. This affects search functionality, leading to poor customer experience and lost sales. To address this issue, the store aims to improve the search experience by normalizing the spelling of product descriptions using Levenshtein distance (a specific type of edit distance).

The store begins by tokenizing all product descriptions into individual words. Each word is checked against a reference dictionary. If the word is not found in the dictionary, the Levenshtein distance is calculated between the word and each entry in the dictionary. If the distance is below a predefined threshold, indicating high similarity, the misspelled word is replaced with the closest match from the dictionary. Words with no close match are flagged for manual review.

Data Augmentation (Augmenters)

Augmenters are techniques or tools used to enhance or generate additional training data from existing text data by applying transformations that preserve the meaning of the text but alter its phrasing or structure. This process is known as *data augmentation* and is crucial for improving the robustness and performance of NLP models, especially in situations where training data is scarce or lacks diversity. There are several types of augmenters, each targeting text at different levels. They include:

- **Character-Level Augmenters:** These can be used to introduce typographical errors or simulate OCR (optical character recognition) errors in text to mimic the kind of noise that real-world data often contains.

- **Word-Level Augmenters:** These can be used to insert, delete, and/or swap words at random positions within a sentence to create diversity in sentence construction. It could also involve *synonym replacement*, where words are replaced by their synonyms to create varied versions of the same sentence or the use of word embeddings (which are discussed in a moment) to find semantically similar words to replace in the text.

- **Sentence-Level Augmenters:** These can be used to rephrase an entire sentence using a technique like *back translation*, which involves translating text to another language and then back to the original language to introduce subtle variations in phrasing. More recently, generative language models such as GPT and BERT are increasingly being used as sentence-level augmenters to paraphrase or generate context-aware, human-like text from source data.

Text Representation

Text representation is a fundamental aspect of NLP. It involves converting unstructured text into a structured format that machines can understand and use to decode patterns within a language. There are several ways to represent text for natural language processing, some of which will be discussed in the following sections.

Vectorization

Vectorization, also known as *string indexing*, is the process of converting text data into numerical values or vectors so that it can be processed by analytic models. There are several techniques for vectorizing text, one of which is to use label encoding. This involves assigning a unique integer value to each unique word or token in a text corpus. For example, consider the words in the sentence "the cat jumped over the moon." Before the words can be fed to a model, they could be encoded the following way:

- "the" → 0
- "cat" → 1
- "jumped" → 2
- "over" → 3
- "moon" → 4

The entire sentence can then be represented as the vector: [0, 1, 2, 3, 0, 4].

We can also vectorize text using one-hot encoding. With this approach, each word in the vocabulary is represented as a unique vector, where the dimensionality of the vector is equal to the size of the vocabulary. The vector has all elements set to 0, except for the element corresponding to the index of the word in the vocabulary, which is set to 1. Applied to the same sentence from the previous example, each word would be represented as the following vectors:

- "the" → [1,0,0,0,0]
- "cat" → [0,1,0,0,0]
- "jumped" → [0,0,1,0,0]
- "over" → [0,0,0,1,0]
- "moon" → [0,0,0,0,1]

While label encoding and one-hot encoding are simple and intuitive, they do have several disadvantages. One-hot encoding results in high-dimensional vectors, which makes it resource intensive, especially for large vocabularies. Both approaches treat each word as an isolated entity without considering its meaning or context. This means that they are unable to capture semantic relationships between words. They are restricted to the vocabulary seen during training, making them unsuitable for handling out-of-vocabulary words.

 See Chapter 5, "Data Processing and Preparation," for more detail on label encoding and one-hot encoding.

Vector Space Model

Another approach to text representation is the use of a vector space model, such as the *document-term matrix (DTM)*. A DTM represents a corpus of text using a matrix, where each row represents a document and each column represents a token, term, or vector. The elements of the matrix represent the occurrence of tokens within each document. Vector space models operate under the *bag-of-words (BoW)* assumption, which is a simplifying assumption in NLP that treats text data as a collection (or "bag") of words without considering the order or structure of those words within a document. The core idea behind this assumption is that a body of text (such as a sentence, paragraph, or entire document) can be represented by the words it contains and their frequencies, while disregarding any grammar, syntax, or word order. The occurrence of tokens in a vector space model can be represented in three different formats: as a binary representation, a frequency count, or a float-valued weighted vector.

Binary Representation

In the binary vector space model representation, each cell in the matrix is a binary value, typically 0 or 1. A value of 1 indicates the presence of a particular word (or token) in the document, while a value of 0 indicates its absence. For example, let's assume we're working with the following three sentences (each representing a document): "Hey, diddle, diddle," "the cat and the fiddle," and "the cow jumped over the moon." The text from these three documents can be represented using a DTM similar to the one in Table 11.1.

TABLE 11.1   Binary representation of a DTM

Doc	and	cat	cow	diddle	fiddle	hey	jumped	moon	over	the
1	0	0	0	1	0	1	0	0	0	0
2	1	1	0	0	1	0	0	0	0	1
3	0	0	1	0	0	0	1	1	1	1

This binary representation is simple and can be useful for tasks where only the presence or absence of words is important. However, it does not capture the frequency or importance of words.

Frequency Count

A slight variation of the binary representation is the frequency count vector space model. Here, each cell in the model corresponds to the count of a particular word in the document (as shown in Table 11.2). This format captures more information than the binary representation, as it reflects not only the presence of words but also their frequency. However, it does not account for the relative importance of words across different documents.

TABLE 11.2   Frequency count representation of a DTM

Doc	and	cat	cow	diddle	fiddle	hey	jumped	moon	over	the
1	0	0	0	2	0	1	0	0	0	0
2	1	1	0	0	1	0	0	0	0	2
3	0	0	1	0	0	0	1	1	1	2

Float-Valued Weighted Vector

Instead of simply using word frequency, the vector space model can use a float-weighted vector to represent the perceived importance of a word within each document. A common weighting scheme is the *term frequency-inverse document frequency (TF-IDF)* of each word within a document. It highlights words that are significant in a particular document but less common in the overall corpus, providing a more nuanced understanding of the text.

TF-IDF consists of two components. The first is the *term frequency (TF)*, which measures the proportion of times a term appears in a document. It is calculated as:

$$TF(t, d) = \frac{Number\ of\ times\ term\ t\ appears\ in\ document\ d}{Number\ of\ terms\ in\ document\ d}$$

The second part of TF-IDF is the *inverse document frequency (IDF)* of a term, which measures the importance of a term across all documents. It is calculated as:

$$IDF(t, D) = \log\left(\frac{Number\ of\ documents\ in\ corpus\ D}{Number\ of\ documents\ with\ term\ t}\right)$$

The TF-IDF of a term is calculated by multiplying the TF and IDF values. For example, the TF-IDF for the word "diddle" in document 1 is calculated as:

$$\frac{2}{3} \times \log\left(\frac{3}{1}\right) = 0.32$$

Table 11.3 shows a DTM based on the TF-IDF weighting scheme. The higher the TF-IDF score for a term in a document, the more important that term is to that document within the context of the entire corpus. Conversely, the lower the TF-IDF score for a document is, the less frequent it is within the current document or the more common it is across documents in the corpus.

TABLE 11.3   Float-weighted vector representation (TF-IDF) of a DTM

Doc	and	cat	cow	diddle	fiddle	hey	jumped	moon	over	the
1	0	0	0	0.32	0	0.16	0	0	0	0
2	0.1	0.1	0	0	0.1	0	0	0	0	0.07
3	0	0	0.08	0	0	0	0.08	0.08	0.08	0.06

While useful in weighting words based on importance, TF-IDF does have some notable limitations. One of them is that it is sensitive to document length. Longer documents tend to have higher term frequencies simply due to their size, which can bias TF-IDF scores in favor of longer documents. Additionally, TF-IDF treats words as independent entities and doesn't consider the semantic relationships between words. This limits its ability to capture contextual information and word meaning. In contrast, word embeddings (discussed next) offer a robust alternative by effectively capturing and quantifying the semantic relationships between words.

Word Embeddings

Word embeddings are a powerful technique in natural language processing that represent words as dense vectors of real numbers in a high-dimensional space. In this vector space, the semantic similarity between words is captured by the distance between their corresponding vectors. Words with similar meanings tend to have vectors that are close together, while words with different meanings have vectors that are farther apart. Two popular models for generating word embeddings are Word2Vec and GloVe.

Word2Vec

Developed by a team at Google, *Word2Vec* uses neural networks to learn word associations from a large corpus of text. It can be trained using either the continuous bag of words (CBoW) method or the skip-gram method. Both approaches result in word vectors that capture semantic relationships and syntactic patterns.

Continuous Bag of Words (CBoW)

The *continuous bag of words* method aims to predict a target word based on the surrounding context words in a continuous sequence. It is called a bag-of-words model because the order of words in the context is not important. As shown in Figure 11.1, the input to the CBoW model is a set of context words, and the output is the target word that is likely to appear in the center of these context words. How many neighboring words the network uses as context words is determined by a parameter called "window size." This window extends in both the directions of the target word—that is, to its left and right.

FIGURE 11.1   The continuous bag of words (CBoW) Word2Vec method

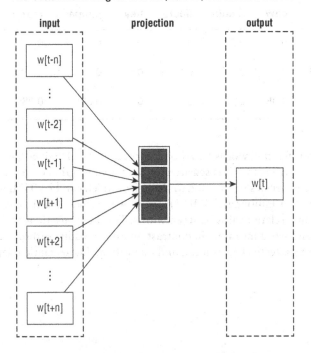

In Figure 11.1, the target word is w[t], and the inputs are the "n" (window size) context words that precede the target, w[t-1] to w[t-n], as well as the "n" words that succeed the target, w[t+1] to w[t+n].

To illustrate how the process works, let's say our training data is the input sequence "the fat cat sat on the mat" and our context window was set to 2. During the first training cycle, the model would use ["fat," "cat"] as context words to predict the probability of "the." During the next cycle, the target would shift to "fat," which means the model will now use ["the," "cat," "sat"] as the context words. As expected in the third cycle, the model will use ["the," "fat," "sat," "on"] to predict "cat." This process will continue until the target has shifted through all the words in the sequence. The interesting part is, we don't actually use the entirety of the trained model. Instead, the goal is to extract the weights of the hidden layer. These weights are the word embeddings.

Skip-Gram

Unlike the CBoW model, which predicts a target word based on its context, the *skip-gram* model works in the opposite direction: it predicts the context words given a target word. As shown in Figure 11.2, in the skip-gram model the input is a target word, and the outputs are the words that appear in the context of the target word. For example, in the sentence "the fat cat sat on the mat," if the target word is "sat" and the context window size is 2, the model will try to predict the context words ["fat," "cat," "on," "the"].

FIGURE 11.2　The skip-gram Word2Vec method

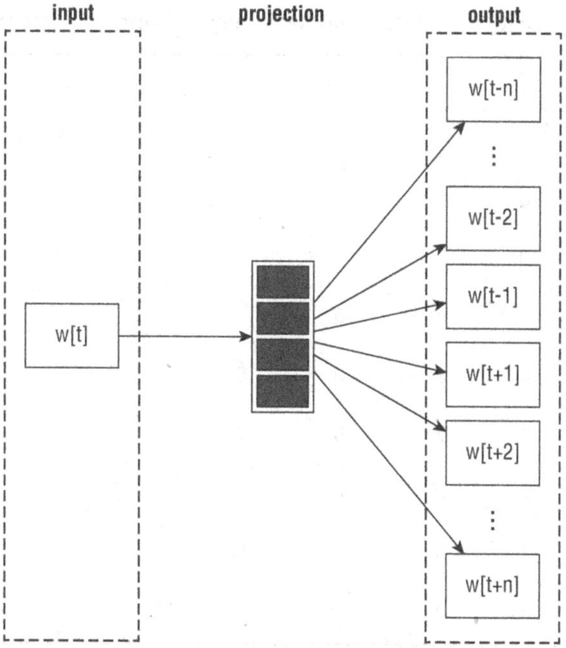

In practice, the choice between CBoW and skip-gram often depends on the specific characteristics of the data and the task at hand. CBoW is faster to train than the skip-gram because it predicts a single word based on multiple context words, rather than predicting multiple context words from a single target word. However, skip-gram is better suited for learning representations of rare words than CBoW, as it focuses on predicting the context for each target word, which allows it to capture more specific patterns related to rare words. The skip-gram model also does a better job at capturing relationships between words that are further apart in the text.

GloVe

GloVe stands for global vectors for word representation. It was developed by researchers at Stanford University. Unlike Word2Vec, which uses local context information (surrounding words) in its training process, GloVe is designed to capture both global statistics and local context in a text corpus. This is achieved by constructing a global co-occurrence matrix that tallies how often words co-occur in the corpus, and then factorizing this matrix to obtain dense word vectors. The resulting embeddings capture a rich set of linguistic relationships between words in the corpus.

To illustrate how GloVe builds the global co-occurrence matrix, let's once again assume we're working with the following three sentences (each representing a document): "Hey, diddle, diddle," "the cat and the fiddle," and "the cow jumped over the moon." GloVe iterates through the words in the corpus and builds a matrix like Table 11.4. The cells of the matrix represent the number of times word pairs occur within a specified window size in the corpus.

TABLE 11.4   Sample GloVe co-occurrence matrix

	and	cat	cow	diddle	fiddle	hey	jumped	moon	over	the
and	0									
cat	1	0								
cow	0	0	0							
diddle	0	0	0	0						
fiddle	1	0	0	0	0					
hey	0	0	0	2	0	0				
jumped	0	0	1	0	0	0	0			
moon	0	0	0	0	0	0	0	0		
over	0	0	1	0	0	0	1	1	0	
the	1	2	1	0	1	0	2	1	1	0

The rows and columns of the co-occurrence matrix in Table 11.4 are the set of unique tokens from all three documents in the corpus. The upper half of the matrix (which is not filled in) will simply be a reflection of the lower half. The co-occurrence values were generated based on a window size of 2, which extends in both directions from each word. For example, the co-occurrence of (the, cat) is 2 because "the" occurs twice in the window vicinity of "cat" within the corpus.

GloVe models have been shown to outperform Word2Vec on word analogy, word similarity, and named entity recognition tasks. Additionally, since they incorporate global statistics with local context, GloVe can capture the semantics of rare words much better than Word2Vec, even on relatively small text corpora.

Summary

Text analysis, or text mining, involves extracting meaningful information from large volumes of unstructured text. This includes keyword extraction, sentiment analysis, and topic modeling.

Natural language understanding involves comprehending the context and relationships within a sentence, whereas natural language generation enables computers to create human-like text.

Text preparation involves various preprocessing techniques to make raw text data more suitable for analysis and model training. It includes tokenization, stemming, lemmatization, removal of stop words, part-of-speech tagging, spelling normalization, and data augmentation.

Vectorization is a common method for representing text. It includes techniques such as label encoding and one-hot encoding, both of which convert words into numerical values or vectors.

The vector space model is used to represent text in a matrix format so that the occurrence and importance of words within documents is captured.

Word embeddings, such as Word2Vec and GloVe, offer a more advanced representation of text by capturing the semantic similarity between words in a high-dimensional space.

Exam Essentials

Explain the difference between string matching and semantic matching.   String matching compares texts based on lexical or syntactic similarity, focusing on exact structure or composition. Semantic matching compares texts based on underlying meaning, considering context and semantic content. String matching is used for tasks like spell checking and plagiarism detection, whereas semantic matching is used in search engines and question-answering systems.

Know what sentiment analysis is used for.   Sentiment analysis is used to identify and categorize emotions or opinions in text, determining attitudes toward topics, products, or services. It has applications in business for customer feedback analysis, in politics for public opinion tracking, and in social media for monitoring brand reputation and user sentiments.

Explain topic modeling and its use.   Topic modeling is used to discover thematic structures in large text collections, aiding in understanding and organizing textual information. It enhances information retrieval, reveals trends and patterns, and supports recommender systems by recommending content based on topics of interest.

Understand the importance and key aspects of text preparation.   Text preparation involves a series of steps used to extract meaningful information and reduce the complexity of raw text data in order to make it more suitable for NLP tasks and model training. Common text preparation steps include tokenization, stemming, lemmatization, removal of stop words, part-of-speech tagging, spelling normalization, and data augmentation.

Explain TF-IDF and its use.   TF-IDF (term frequency-inverse document frequency) is a weighting scheme used in text representation to measure the importance of a word within a document relative to its frequency across a corpus. High TF-IDF indicates a word is important and frequent in a specific document but rare across the entire corpus, whereas low TF-IDF suggests the word is either common across documents or infrequent in the document.

Understand what word embeddings are and why they are useful.   Word embeddings represent words as dense vectors in a high-dimensional space, capturing semantic similarity based on vector proximity. They are useful for encoding linguistic relationships, which enhance the performance of NLP tasks such as text classification, sentiment analysis, and language translation.

Review Questions

1. Andrezza is analyzing social media posts to determine the public's sentiment toward a new product launch. She decides to match the words used in the social media posts to a pre-defined list of words associated with positive, negative, or neutral sentiment. Andrezza is using a _____-based approach to sentiment analysis.

   A. Keyword

   B. Model

   C. Topic

   D. Lexicon

2. What is the primary purpose of text representation in natural language processing?

   A. To create visually appealing text

   B. To make text easier for models to work with

   C. To translate text from one language to another

   D. To correct the grammar and spelling in text

3. In an effort to diversify the training data for a text classification model, Christian decides to create variations of sentences by replacing words with their synonyms. For example, he wants to replace a word like "happy" with "joyful" in some instances. Which technique should Christian consider using?

   A. POS tagging

   B. Augmenters

   C. Lemmatization

   D. Sentiment analysis

4. Melinda is analyzing the quality of the text generated by a large language model. She wants to ensure that the generated text logically flows from one sentence to the next. Which challenge is Melinda trying to address?

   A. Coherence and consistency

   B. Control

   C. Evaluation

   D. Language understanding and generation

5. Which of these is a disadvantage of one-hot encoding?

   A. It is too simple to implement.

   B. It results in low-dimensional vectors.

   C. It makes it easy to capture semantic relationships.

   D. It results in high-dimensional vectors.

6. Professor Nwanganga is developing a system to improve the searchability of documents in a database. He wants to use the most relevant keywords from each document to enhance the search function. Which of these NLP tasks is Professor Nwanganga doing?

   A. Information retrieval

   B. Keyword trend analysis

   C. String matching

   D. Document clustering

7. What does the term frequency-inverse document frequency (TF-IDF) measure?

   A. The length of documents

   B. The grammar of documents

   C. The importance of words across different documents

   D. The frequency of words within a single document

8. In a text analysis project, Professor Johnson needs to identify the grammatical role of each word in a sentence to better understand its structure. She is particularly interested in identifying words that can serve as both nouns and verbs. Which text preprocessing step should Professor Johnson use?

   A. POS tagging

   B. Stemming

   C. Lemmatization

   D. Tokenization

9. As part of a customer feedback analysis project, Fred wants to understand customer attitudes toward a product. He decides to use an NLP technique that categorizes customer feedback as negative, positive, or neutral. Which technique is Fred using?

   A. Semantic matching

   B. Topic modeling

   C. Keyword extraction

   D. Sentiment analysis

10. What are word embeddings used for in natural language processing?

   A. To capture the semantic similarity between words as the distance between vectors

   B. To represent words as low-dimensional vectors

   C. To represent words as high-dimensional binary vectors

   D. To quantify the importance of words across different documents

11. Femi is working on a plagiarism detection tool. She needs to compare documents at the lexical level to identify overlapping or copied content. Which type of matching model should Femi use?

    A. Semantic matching

    B. String matching

    C. Lexile matching

    D. Document matching

12. In a content management system, Richard wants to tag articles with relevant keywords. He decides to use a technique that automatically identifies and classifies proper nouns in the text. Which technique is Richard likely using?

    A. Syntax analysis

    B. Semantic analysis

    C. Named entity recognition

    D. Language generation

13. In a machine learning project, Adaku wants to improve the robustness of her NLP model by simulating real-world data that contains typographical errors. She decides to introduce these errors into her training data. Which technique is Adaku likely using?

    A. Augmenters

    B. Word embeddings

    C. Topic modeling

    D. POS tagging

14. Which of these is the primary task of the skip-gram model?

    A. To predict a target word based on its context

    B. To predict context words given a target word

    C. To count the frequency of words in a document

    D. To represent words as binary vectors

15. Ebenezer is developing a machine learning model to predict the topic of academic papers. He wants to simplify the text data by reducing words to their base form. For example, he wants to convert "running," "runs," and "ran" to "run." Which text preprocessing technique should Ebenezer apply?

    A. Tokenization

    B. Spelling normalization

    C. Stemming

    D. POS tagging

16. What distinguishes GloVe from Word2Vec?

   A. GloVe uses only local context information in its training process.

   B. GloVe is designed to capture both global statistics and local context.

   C. GloVe represents words as binary vectors.

   D. GloVe focuses only on the frequency count of words.

17. In a research project, Professor Smith is analyzing a large corpus of scientific articles. He wants to remove common words like "the," "is," and "a," which do not contribute much to the analytic value of the text. Which text preprocessing step should Professor Smith use?

   A. Tokenization

   B. Stemming

   C. Lemmatization

   D. Removing stop words

18. Melissa is working on a speech recognition system for a voice-activated virtual assistant. She needs the system to accurately convert spoken language into text. Which aspect of natural language processing is most relevant to Melissa's project?

   A. Language understanding

   B. Language generation

   C. Named entity recognition

   D. Sentiment analysis

19. A team is developing a customer service chatbot. They want the chatbot to respond to user queries with natural and coherent responses. Which of these aspects of natural language processing is most relevant to this task?

   A. Topic modeling

   B. Language generation

   C. Sentiment analysis

   D. String matching

20. Andrew is analyzing a large dataset of research papers to identify the most relevant words or phrases that represent the main content or themes. Which text analysis task is Andrew performing?

   A. Sentiment analysis

   B. Topic modeling

   C. Keyword extraction

   D. Semantic matching

Chapter

12

Specialized Applications of Data Science

THE COMPTIA DATAX EXAM OBJECTIVES COVERED IN THIS CHAPTER INCLUDE:

✓ **Domain 5: Specialized Applications of Data Science**

- 5.1 Compare and contrast optimization concepts.
- 5.3 Explain the use and importance of computer vision concepts.

Data science encompasses a broad spectrum of applications across various domains. In this chapter, we delve into the application of data science within the specialized areas of optimization and computer vision. We start by exploring the fundamentals of numerical optimization, covering key components such as decision variables, the objective function, and constraints. We then examine both constrained and unconstrained optimization problems. Following this, we introduce the field of computer vision and highlight some of its practical applications. The chapter concludes with a detailed walk-through of the steps required to implement a computer vision system, including image acquisition, image preprocessing, and feature extraction.

Optimization

Optimization is the process of finding the best solution or outcome from a set of available alternatives, typically within certain constraints or conditions. The primary goal of numerical optimization is to identify the set of inputs or parameters that result in the optimal value of an objective function, which can represent cost, profit, efficiency, or any other measurable quantity. Optimization can be applied to a myriad of domains where it plays a crucial role in improving decision making and resource allocation.

In manufacturing, optimization techniques can be used to streamline production processes and minimize costs. This could involve optimizing production schedules, inventory levels, and resource allocation to maximize output while minimizing waste and operating expenses. Optimizing staff schedules and patient flow can help hospitals ensure that patients are seen by doctors more quickly, leading to better outcomes and higher patient satisfaction. In marketing, optimization can be used to maximize the return on investment (ROI) of marketing campaigns. This involves identifying the most effective marketing channels, targeting the right audience segments, and allocating resources efficiently to achieve the desired marketing objectives. In humanitarian operations, organizations can use optimization techniques to design the best routes for delivering aid to disaster-affected areas, ensuring that resources such as water, food, and medical services reach as many people as possible in the shortest amount of time.

In the context of machine learning and statistical modeling, optimization plays a crucial role in model training. For example, a common loss function (objective function) used by regression models is the mean squared error (MSE):

$$MSE = \frac{1}{n}\sum\left(y_i - \hat{y}_i\right)^2$$

MSE represents the average squared distance (or difference) between the predicted values of a model ($\hat{y}_i$) and the actual values in the data (y_i). During model training, optimization algorithms adjust the parameters of a model such that the value of the loss function is minimized. This is an example of what is known as unconstrained optimization, which we will discuss later in the chapter.

In general, optimization problems consist of three main components—the decision variables, the objective function, and the constraints.

As you prepare for the DataX exam, you should be able to compare and contrast concepts related to optimization. As you read through the concepts introduced in this section, make note of how they differ from each other, especially with regard to the differences between constrained and unconstrained optimization problems.

Decision Variables

Decision variables, also known as optimization variables, are the parameters in an optimization problem that can be adjusted or controlled to achieve the desired outcome. These variables are the primary focus of the optimization process, as their values determine the outcome of the objective function (discussed in the next section) and the feasibility of the solution with respect to the constraints.

Consider a simple optimization problem where a company wants to maximize its profit by deciding how many units of two products to manufacture. The decision variables in this case would be A, the number of units of the first product to manufacture, and B, the number of units of the second product to manufacture. The goal would be to find the best values for A and B that achieve the objective.

The variables, A and B, used in the previous scenario are referred to as *integer decision variables*. They must take on integer values. These types of variables are particularly relevant in scenarios where the decision variables represent countable items, such as the number of units of a product to be produced or the number of employees to assign to a task. Another type of decision variable is a binary decision variable. *Binary decision variables* are restricted to two values, typically 0 or 1. They are used in decisions that have two states, such as turning a machine on or off, or selecting a route or not. Unlike integer and binary decision variables, which can only take discrete values (specific values within a range), decision variables can also be continuous. *Continuous decision variables* are variables that can take any value within a defined range. They are often used in problems involving measurements, quantities, or any scenario where a variable can change incrementally. For example, the amount of a chemical additive in a mixture is considered a continuous variable if it can be measured precisely to any decimal.

Integer Programming

Integer programming is a type of optimization where some or all of the decision variables are restricted to take on only integer values. It is particularly useful in planning and allocation problems where fractional values do not make sense practically, such as in the earlier example of determining how many units of two products to manufacture. Integer programming problems are generally more challenging to solve than continuous optimization problems because they require finding solutions in a discrete space, which can be large and complex depending on the number of variables and constraints. This often requires specialized algorithms and computational resources, especially as the size of the problem increases.

Objective Function

The *objective function* is the function (or set of functions) that needs to be maximized or minimized to solve the optimization problem. It represents the goal of the optimization problem, such as minimizing cost, maximizing profit, or achieving the best performance.

Let's revisit the profit maximization example from the previous section. If we know that the profit from producing each unit of product A is $100 and that of product B is $150, then the objective function to maximize profit can be formulated as:

$$Maximize\ Z = 100A + 150B$$

where Z represents the total profit, and the coefficients 100 and 150 represent the profit per unit of products A and B, respectively. The goal would be to find the best values for A and B that maximize profit subject to certain conditions, which we discuss next.

Constraints

Constraints are the limitations or requirements that the solution to an optimization problem must satisfy. They can be equality constraints (e.g., the sum of decision variables must equal a certain value) or inequality constraints (e.g., a decision variable must be greater than or equal to a certain value). Constraints define the *feasible region* (solutions that satisfy the constraints) within which the optimal solution must lie.

We can further expand the profit maximization example from above to include the following constraints:

- Suppose the company has a total production capacity of 200 units. This constraint can be expressed as:

$$A + B \leq 200$$

■ Assume the company has a budget of $20,000 for production. If the production costs are $80 per unit for product A and $120 per unit for product B, the budget constraint can be formulated as:

$$80A + 120B \leq 20000$$

The quantities of products A and B produced cannot be negative, so:

$$A \geq 0, B \geq 0$$

The feasible region defined by these constraints is the set of all possible combinations of the decision variables A and B that satisfy all the constraints. Figure 12.1 shows, visually, what the feasible region (shaded area) for this problem would look like. The optimal solution to the problem is the point (or the values of A and B) within this feasible region that maximizes the profit Z.

FIGURE 12.1   The feasible region of an optimization problem

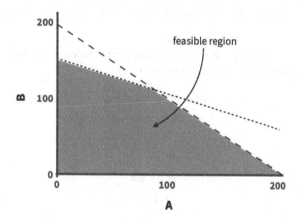

For many optimization problems, the optimal solution is often found on the edge of the feasible region defined by the constraints. These solutions are referred to as *boundary cases*. The reason why the optimal solution often lies on the boundary is that, within the interior of the feasible region, changing the decision variables usually leads to an increase in one objective while decreasing another. However, on the boundary, there are points where any small change in the decision variables would violate a constraint, making it impossible to improve one objective without worsening another. Identifying these boundary cases is a crucial aspect of solving optimization problems, as it helps narrow down the search for the optimal solution and can significantly reduce the computational effort required.

Linear vs. Nonlinear Programming

Depending on the nature of both the objective function and the constraints, optimization problems can be classified as either linear programming problems or nonlinear programming problems. *Linear programming problems* are optimization problems where both the objective function and the constraints are linear. For example:

$$Maximize\ Z = 3x + 4y$$

subject to:

$$x + 2y \le 8$$
$$3x + y \le 9$$
$$x, y \ge 0$$

These types of problems can be solved using *linear solvers* like the *simplex method*, an iterative method that efficiently navigates the corner points of the feasible region to find the optimal solution.

Nonlinear programming problems are optimization problems where either the objective function or the constraints are nonlinear. For example:

$$Maximize\ Z = x^2 + y^2$$

subject to:

$$x^2 - 2 \ge 0$$
$$x + y \le 5$$
$$x, y \ge 0$$

Nonlinear programming problems are solved using *nonlinear solvers* like gradient descent and its variants, or sequential quadratic programming (SQP). Solving nonlinear programming problems can be more challenging than linear programming problems due to the presence of multiple local optima, nonconvex feasible regions, and the complexity of the mathematical relationships.

Constrained Optimization

The optimization problems discussed so far are broadly known as *constrained optimization* problems. As the name suggests, these are optimization problems that require that we find the optimal solution of an objective function subject to a set of constraints. There are several categories of constrained optimization problems, some of which concern network topology, resource allocation, scheduling, pricing, and bundling.

Network Topology

Network topology problems involve finding the most efficient arrangement or configuration of a network, such as a telecommunications network, a transportation network, a supply chain network, or any other network consisting of nodes and connections. The goal is usually to minimize costs or maximize efficiency while satisfying constraints such as capacity limits, connectivity requirements, and quality of service.

A network is typically represented as a graph consisting of nodes (vertices) and edges (links) connecting those nodes. The *traveling salesman problem* is a classic example of a constrained optimization problem in network topology. In this problem, cities are represented as nodes, and the paths between the cities are represented as edges. The objective of the traveling salesman problem is to find the shortest possible route that visits a set of cities exactly once and returns to the starting city.

 Real World Scenario

Choosing the Best Delivery Route

A logistics company needs to plan the route for a delivery truck that must visit 10 different warehouses to pick up goods and return to the main depot. This is a network topology problem—the traveling salesman problem, to be exact. Each warehouse is a node and the routes between warehouses are edges in the network. The objective is to minimize the total distance traveled and the fuel consumption by finding the shortest route that visits each warehouse once (the constraint).

Resource Allocation

Resource allocation problems involve finding the optimal way to distribute limited resources among competing activities or projects. The constraints can include budget limitations, resource availability, and project requirements.

 Real World Scenario

Funding Environmental Conservation Projects

A government agency is responsible for allocating a limited budget to various environmental conservation projects across the country. The projects focus on different areas such as reforestation, wildlife protection, pollution control, and sustainable agriculture. Each project has an estimated cost and an expected impact score that quantifies its contribution to environmental conservation. The objective is to maximize the total impact of these projects while staying within the constraints of the available budget. This is a resource allocation problem.

Scheduling

Scheduling problems are a variant of resource allocation problems. They involve allocating resources over time to perform a collection of tasks or activities, subject to constraints like deadlines, resource availability, and task dependencies. The objective is usually to optimize criteria such as minimizing completion time or maximizing resource utilization.

 Real World Scenario

Production Scheduling

In a manufacturing plant, the production manager is faced with the challenge of scheduling the production of various products on multiple machines to meet customer demand while minimizing production costs. The plant manufactures three products: A, B, and C. Each product has a specific processing time on each machine, and each machine has a limited number of hours available for operation per day. This is a scheduling problem. The objective is to schedule the production of these products in a way that maximizes the total production output while satisfying the constraints of machine capacity and customer demand.

Pricing

Pricing problems involve determining the optimal prices for products or services to maximize revenue or profit, subject to constraints such as market demand, production costs, and competition. This can involve dynamic pricing strategies where prices are adjusted based on changing conditions.

 Real World Scenario

Airline Ticket Pricing

A budget airline is looking to optimize its ticket prices for a popular route from City A to City B. The airline has a fixed number of seats available on each flight and wants to maximize revenue while remaining competitive in the market. The pricing strategy must consider the remaining seats, time until departure, and competitor prices as constraints. The objective is to find the optimal ticket price for each flight subject to the previously listed constraints. This is a pricing problem.

Bundling

Bundling problems involve combining products or services into packages that maximize sales or profit. The constraints can include customer preferences, production costs, and inventory levels.

 Real World Scenario

Bundling Cable TV Channels

A cable TV provider wants to figure out how best to bundle packages of channels to offer to its subscribers—a classic bundling problem. The objectives are to maximize subscriber satisfaction and revenue. The constraints could include the licensing cost of each channel, the maximum number of channels in a bundle, and the need to include certain popular channels in all bundles.

Unconstrained Optimization

Unconstrained optimization refers to the process of finding the maximum or minimum of an objective function without any restrictions or constraints. In other words, there are no restrictions on the values that the decision variables can take, other than those inherently imposed by the domain of the objective function itself. Solving unconstrained optimization problems is typically achieved through mathematical techniques that involve finding the points at which the gradient (or derivative) of the objective function is zero. These points are known as stationary points, and they represent potential maxima, minima, or saddle points of the function as shown in Figure 12.2.

FIGURE 12.2 Unconstrained optimization objective function showing potential maxima, minima, and saddle points

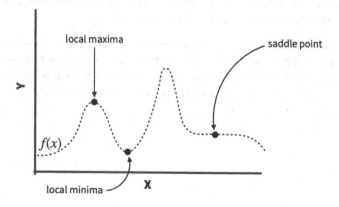

Points where the function has lower values in the immediate vicinity and the gradient is zero are known as the *local maxima*. These are potential solutions for maximization problems. Points where the function has higher values in the immediate vicinity and the gradient is zero are known as *local minima*. They are potential solutions for minimization problems. Points where the function does not have a clear maximum or minimum but still has a zero gradient are known as *saddle points*. These are not optimal solutions but are important in understanding the function's behavior.

In practice, finding the exact points where the gradient is zero can be challenging, especially for complex functions. Therefore, various iterative methods, such as gradient descent or Newton's method, are used to approximate the solution by iteratively updating the values of the decision variables until the gradient is close to zero, indicating that an optimal solution has been approached.

Unconstrained optimization is commonly applied in fields like machine learning, economics, and physics, where one might need to optimize a cost function, utility function, or energy function, respectively, without explicit constraints on the variables.

Bandit Problems

In its simplest form, the *one-armed bandit* problem illustrates a scenario where an agent must choose between multiple options with unknown probabilities of reward. It involves a single slot machine (or bandit) with one lever (or arm). When the lever is pulled, the machine provides a reward based on a certain probability distribution. The goal is to develop a strategy that maximizes the total reward over a series of lever pulls. The one-armed bandit problem falls under the umbrella of what are known as *stochastic optimization* problems. These are optimization problems that involve decision making under uncertainty.

The key challenge in the one-armed bandit problem is the trade-off between exploration (trying different actions to gather information about the reward distribution) and exploitation (using the information gathered to choose the action that is currently believed to provide the highest reward). This trade-off is analogous to some of the strategies used in unconstrained optimization to explore the search space and to exploit areas of the search space where the objective function appears to be optimal.

The one-armed bandit problem has been extended to more complex scenarios, such as the *multi-armed bandit* problem, where there are multiple levers to choose from, each with its own reward distribution. The goal is to maximize rewards over time through a sequence of actions, without explicit constraints on which machines to play or how many times.

Computer Vision

Computer vision is a field of data science that involves the use of various techniques and algorithms to enable machines to identify, process, and analyze images and videos in a manner similar to how humans perceive visual information. The field of computer vision has evolved significantly since its inception. Advancements in computational power, storage, networking, and algorithm design have enabled more sophisticated and accurate vision systems compared to those of the past. Consequently, computer vision has found applications in domains such as autonomous vehicles, facial recognition, medical imaging, augmented reality, and several others, as outlined in Table 12.1.

TABLE 12.1   Common applications of computer vision

Approach	Description	Use
Optical character recognition	Optical character recognition (OCR) involves converting images of typed, handwritten, or printed text into machine-encoded text.	It is widely used in various applications such as digitizing printed documents, automated data entry, license plate recognition, and extracting text from images for further processing or analysis.
Object detection and recognition	Object detection involves identifying the presence and location of objects within an image, whereas object recognition aims to classify the detected objects into predefined categories.	These tasks are fundamental in many applications, including surveillance, autonomous vehicles, image retrieval, and facial recognition.
Image segmentation	Image segmentation is the process of partitioning an image into multiple segments or regions, often based on certain characteristics such as color, texture, or intensity.	This is crucial in applications like medical imaging (e.g., identifying tumors), scene understanding, and object-based image analysis.
Motion analysis and object tracking	Motion analysis involves understanding the movement of objects or the camera itself within a sequence of images or video frames. Object tracking is a specific aspect of motion analysis where the goal is to monitor the trajectory of an object over time.	These techniques are essential in video surveillance, sports analysis, vehicle navigation, and human-computer interaction.

Image Acquisition

A critical step in the process of implementing a computer vision system is image acquisition. It involves capturing visual data from the environment using imaging devices such as cameras, scanners, or specialized sensors. The quality of the acquired images significantly impacts the performance of the entire system, making it essential to choose appropriate imaging hardware and settings tailored to a specific application.

In many modern computer vision systems, image acquisition goes beyond using a single sensor to capture visual data. *Sensor fusion*, a technique that combines data from multiple sensors, is increasingly employed to enhance the robustness and accuracy of image acquisition. For example, in autonomous vehicles, sensor fusion might involve integrating data from cameras, LiDAR (Light Detection and Ranging), radars, and ultrasonic sensors to create a comprehensive and detailed representation of the surrounding environment. Each sensor type has its strengths and weaknesses, and by fusing their data, the system can leverage the advantages of each sensor, leading to improved object detection, obstacle avoidance, and navigation.

Image Preprocessing

Image preprocessing is another crucial step in the process of implementing a computer vision system. It involves transforming the acquired raw image data into a format that is more suitable for subsequent analysis. This step is essential for enhancing the quality of images and ensuring that the features extracted in later stages are meaningful and reliable. Preprocessing techniques can vary widely depending on the specific requirements of the application. Some of the common methods are geometric transformations, noise reduction, contrast enhancement, normalization, color space conversion, and hole filling.

Geometric Transformations

Geometric transformations are operations that alter the spatial arrangement of pixels in an image. These transformations are used to correct or modify the geometric properties of an image, such as its position, orientation, and size. They are particularly important in applications where the position or scale of objects in an image are relevant to the task at hand. Some common geometric transformations are cropping, resizing, scaling, rotating, and flipping.

Cropping

This involves removing the outer parts of an image to focus on a specific region of interest or the elimination of an unnecessary background. Cropping is often used to highlight the important features of an image or to ensure that the input size is consistent across different images.

Resizing

Resizing is the process of changing the dimensions of an image. This is typically done to ensure that all images in a dataset have the same size, which is often a requirement for machine learning and deep learning models. Resizing can also help reduce computational load by decreasing the resolution of high-resolution images.

Scaling

Scaling involves adjusting the size of an image while maintaining its aspect ratio (the ratio of an image's width to its height). This is different from resizing, as scaling ensures that the relative dimensions of the image are preserved. Scaling can be used to normalize the size of objects within different images, making it easier for a model to detect and recognize patterns.

Rotating

Rotating an image involves changing its orientation by a certain angle. This can be useful for correcting the alignment of images. Creating rotated versions of original images can also be useful for image data augmentation, where including variations of the original data as part of the training data can help improve the robustness of a model.

Flipping

Flipping an image means reversing it along a vertical or horizontal axis. Like rotating, flipping can also be used for correcting image data and for data augmentation. When used for data augmentation, flipping can effectively increase the size of the training dataset by creating mirror images of the original data.

Noise Reduction

In the context of computer vision, noise generally refers to any random variation or distortion in an image. Noise can be introduced into image data due to various factors such as sensor imperfections, environmental conditions, or transmission errors. Noise can degrade the quality of images and negatively impact the performance of computer vision algorithms.

Spurious noise is particularly problematic or misleading in the context of a specific task or analysis. In the context of image processing, spurious noise refers to artifacts or variations in an image that are not representative of the true scene or object being imaged, and which can lead to incorrect interpretations or conclusions. For example, in a medical imaging context, spurious noise might refer to artifacts that resemble pathological features, potentially leading to misdiagnosis. A variety of noise reduction techniques can be used during image preprocessing to smooth out images and reduce the impact of spurious noise.

One common noise reduction technique is *Gaussian blurring*. This method applies a Gaussian filter to an image, which smooths out the image by averaging each pixel with its neighboring pixels. The Gaussian filter has a bell-shaped kernel that gives more weight to the central pixel and less to the surrounding ones, effectively reducing high-frequency noise and blurring the image. Gaussian blurring is particularly useful for reducing Gaussian noise, which is a common type of noise in digital images.

Another widely used noise reduction approach is *median filtering*. Median filtering is a nonlinear method that replaces each pixel value with the median value of the pixels in its neighborhood. This technique is particularly effective at removing salt-and-pepper noise, which is characterized by random occurrences of black and white pixels in an image. Unlike Gaussian blurring, median filtering preserves edges within the image, making it a preferred choice for applications where edge preservation is important.

Contrast Enhancement

The contrast of an image refers to the difference in brightness between the central objects and the background. Enhancing the contrast can make the features in an image more distinct and easier to detect. Techniques such as histogram equalization or adaptive histogram equalization are commonly used for this purpose.

Normalization

Image normalization involves scaling the pixel values of an image to a specific range, usually between 0 and 1 or −1 and 1. Image normalization ensures consistency across different images and helps in reducing the sensitivity of a computer vision system to variations in illumination or camera settings.

Color Space Conversion

For certain computer vision applications, it is sometimes beneficial to convert images from one color space to another. This conversion can simplify the analysis and processing of images by tailoring the representation of color information to the specific needs of the task at hand.

One common conversion is from the RGB (red, green, blue) color space to the HSV (hue, saturation, value) color space. The RGB color space represents colors through the combination of red, green, and blue components, which correspond to the primary colors of light. While intuitive for display purposes, the RGB color space is not always ideal for analyzing images, as it does not separate the color information (chromaticity) from the intensity information (luminance).

The HSV color space, on the other hand, represents colors in terms of their hue (the type of color), saturation (the intensity of the color), and value (the brightness of the color). This separation of chromaticity and luminance can be advantageous for tasks such as color-based object detection, segmentation, and tracking, as it allows for more intuitive and robust manipulation of color information.

Another common conversion is from RGB to grayscale. Grayscale images contain only intensity information, with no color. This conversion reduces the dimensionality of the data from three channels (RGB) to one channel (grayscale), simplifying analysis and reducing computational complexity. Grayscale conversion is particularly useful in applications where color information is not critical, such as edge detection, texture analysis, and some forms of object recognition.

Hole Filling

Hole filling is a technique used to fill in the holes or gaps within objects in a binary image. A *hole* in this context refers to a region of background pixels that is completely surrounded by foreground pixels. Holes can exist in images for various reasons. For instance, an object depicted in an image may possess internal cavities or openings that are not intrinsic parts of the object itself. A classic example of this is the letter "O," which features a hole at its center. Additionally, holes may emerge as segmentation artifacts, where imperfect segmentation algorithms produce holes within objects due to noise or other errors encountered during the segmentation process. Furthermore, in 3D scenes, *occlusions* (the partial or complete blockage of one object by another in an image or a scene) can result in the formation of holes in the 2D projection of objects.

The goal of hole filling is to identify the holes in an image and change their pixel values to match those of the foreground, effectively "filling" them. Figure 12.3 shows a binary image (A) with holes, and the same image (B) with the holes algorithmically filled.

FIGURE 12.3   Binary image with holes (A) and with the holes filled (B)

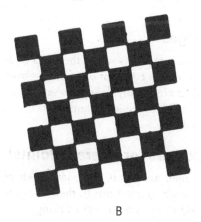

A   B

Hole filling improves the quality of images before further processing. It is a crucial image preprocessing step for a task such as image segmentation, where having complete and continuous objects is important for accurate analysis.

Feature Extraction

Feature extraction is a step in the computer vision process where the system identifies and extracts meaningful patterns, attributes, or characteristics from preprocessed images. This step transforms the visual data into a more compact and informative representation that can be used for further analysis or interpretation. Some of the common types of features that can be extracted from an image include edges, corners, blobs, ridges, and textures (as shown in Figure 12.4).

FIGURE 12.4   Feature extraction

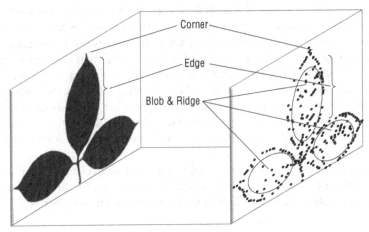

Source: ELSEVIER / https://www.sciencedirect.com/science/article/abs/pii/S0168169916300102/
Last accessed on April 30, 2024.

Edges

Edges are points where there is a boundary (or an edge) between two image regions. In general, an edge can be of almost arbitrary shape and may include junctions. In practice, edges are usually defined as sets of points in the image that have a strong gradient magnitude. Edges are important for tasks such as object detection, image segmentation, and shape analysis.

Corners (or Interest Points)

Corners are points in the image where two or more edges meet. They are often considered as points of interest due to their distinctiveness. Corners are useful for feature matching, image registration, and object tracking.

Blobs

Blobs are regions in an image that differ in properties, such as brightness or color, compared to surrounding areas. They are often used to represent objects or parts of objects in an image. Blobs are important for object recognition, segmentation, and counting tasks.

Ridges

Ridges are curved lines or elongated structures in an image where the intensity changes sharply on both sides. They are often found in natural scenes, such as the ridges of mountains in a landscape or the veins in a leaf. In medical imaging, ridges can represent blood vessels or other anatomical structures. Ridge detection is related to edge detection but focuses on capturing line-like structures.

Textures

Texture refers to the repeated patterns or structures present in an image. Texture can include fine details, such as smoothness, roughness, or patterns, and is used to identify or classify objects based on their surface properties. Texture analysis is important for tasks like material classification and terrain analysis.

Masking

Masking is the technique of selectively filtering or modifying certain parts of an image while leaving other parts unchanged. This is achieved by using a "mask," which is typically a binary or grayscale image of the same size as the original image. The mask determines which pixels in the image are affected by a particular operation.

Masking is used in various aspects of image preprocessing and feature extraction. Masking can be used to define a specific region of interest within an image, blend multiple images together, separate foreground objects from the background, highlight specific features or suppress unwanted elements in an image, or augment data by randomly masking parts of training images.

Summary

Optimization involves determining the best of the available alternatives. It is used in various domains like manufacturing, healthcare, marketing, and humanitarian operations to improve decision making and resource allocation. In machine learning, optimization is crucial for model training.

Optimization problems typically consist of decision variables and one or more objective functions. Optimization problems with a set of constraints are known as constrained optimization problems, and those without are known as unconstrained optimization problems.

The main stages of a computer vision system include image acquisition, preprocessing, feature extraction, and interpretation. Image acquisition involves capturing visual data through cameras or other imaging devices. Preprocessing techniques, such as noise reduction and image enhancement, are applied to improve the quality of the input images. Feature extraction involves identifying key attributes or patterns within the images that are relevant to the task at hand. Finally, interpretation involves making sense of the extracted features to perform tasks such as object recognition, image segmentation, or motion analysis.

Exam Essentials

Explain how decision variables, objective functions, and constraints are used in optimization. Decision variables represent parameters that can be adjusted to achieve a desired outcome. The objective function quantifies the goal of the optimization. Constraints are limitations or requirements that the solution must satisfy.

Know the difference between linear and nonlinear programming. Linear programming problems are constrained optimization problems where both the objective function and constraints are linear. Nonlinear programming problems are constrained optimization problems where either the objective function or the constraints are nonlinear.

Explain the difference between constrained and unconstrained optimization. Constrained optimization involves finding the optimal solution of an objective function subject to a set of constraints, such as equality or inequality conditions. Unconstrained optimization seeks the maximum or minimum of an objective function without any restrictions or constraints on the decision variables, except those inherent in the function's domain.

List some common applications of computer vision. Some common applications of computer vision include autonomous vehicles, facial recognition, medical imaging, augmented reality, optical character recognition, object detection and recognition, image segmentation, and motion analysis and object tracking.

Explain why image preprocessing is useful in computer vision. Image preprocessing enhances image quality and prepares data for analysis, improving the reliability of feature extraction and the performance of computer vision algorithms. It involves tasks such as geometric transformation, noise reduction, contrast enhancement, normalization, color space conversion, and hole filling.

Review Questions

1. Bola wants to remove the background from an image to focus on the main subject. Which of these geometric transformations should she apply?

   A. Scaling

   B. Cropping

   C. Rotating

   D. Flipping

2. In an optimization problem, what role do decision variables play?

   A. They represent constraints that must be satisfied.

   B. They are the parameters that can be adjusted to achieve the desired outcome.

   C. They represent the objective function to be maximized or minimized.

   D. They are fixed values that cannot be changed.

3. A company wants to digitize its historical documents for easy search and retrieval. Which computer vision approach would be most suitable for this task?

   A. Object detection and recognition

   B. Image segmentation

   C. Optical character recognition

   D. Motion analysis and object tracking

4. A remote sensing application is analyzing satellite images to classify different types of terrain. Which of these feature types is crucial for this analysis?

   A. Corners

   B. Blobs

   C. Textures

   D. Edges

5. Chidi wants to optimize his investment portfolio to maximize returns while managing risk and adhering to budget constraints. Which type of optimization problem is this?

   A. Resource allocation

   B. Scheduling

   C. Pricing

   D. Network topology

6. A radiologist is using computer vision to analyze MRI scans to identify tumors. Which of these computer vision approaches is most relevant to her task?

   A. Object detection and recognition

   B. Image segmentation

   C. Optical character recognition (OCR)

   D. Motion analysis and object tracking

7. An online advertising company wants to optimize the placement of ads on its website. The company has multiple ads to display, each with an unknown click-through rate (CTR). The goal is to maximize the total number of clicks over a given period. How does the multi-armed bandit problem apply in this scenario?

   A. It can be used to determine the exact CTR of each ad before displaying it.

   B. It helps ensure that each ad is displayed an equal number of times to ensure fairness.

   C. It helps balance the exploration of different ads and the exploitation of ads with high CTR.

   D. It helps the company focus exclusively on the ads with the highest known CTR.

8. An image analysis system needs to adjust the size of several images while maintaining their aspect ratio. Which geometric transformation should it use?

   A. Scaling

   B. Cropping

   C. Rotating

   D. Flipping

9. A customer service center operates 24/7 and needs to optimize its staffing levels to ensure that customer wait times are minimized while adhering to labor laws and budget constraints. What type of optimization problem is this?

   A. Resource allocation

   B. Scheduling

   C. Pricing

   D. Bundling

10. A traffic monitoring system needs to automatically identify and record the license plates of passing vehicles. Which of these computer vision approaches is most important for initially separating the license plate from the rest of the image?

    A. Object detection and recognition

    B. Image segmentation

    C. Optical character recognition (OCR)

    D. Motion analysis and object tracking

11. Which of these feature types is most important for shape analysis?

    A. Corners

    B. Blobs

    C. Textures

    D. Edges

12. What is the purpose of constraints in an optimization problem?

   A. To define the set of all possible solutions

   B. To eliminate the need for decision variables

   C. To maximize the value of the objective function

   D. To limit the feasible region within which the optimal solution must lie

13. A video surveillance system needs to monitor and track the movement of people in a crowded area. Which computer vision approach is most relevant for this purpose?

   A. Motion analysis and object tracking

   B. Image segmentation

   C. Optical character recognition (OCR)

   D. Object detection and recognition

14. Why is the optimal solution to many optimization problems often found on the boundary of the feasible region?

   A. Because solutions within the interior always violate constraints

   B. Because boundary solutions maximize the number of constraints violated

   C. Because boundary solutions allow for an increase in one objective without worsening another

   D. Because any small change in decision variables at the boundary would violate a constraint

15. If we know that color information is not critical for the task, which of these color space conversions should be performed before an edge detection algorithm is applied to color images?

   A. RGB to HSV

   B. RGB to Grayscale

   C. HSV to RGB

   D. Grayscale to RGB

16. An image processing application needs to focus on a specific region of interest within an image while ignoring the rest. Which of these techniques is most appropriate for defining this region?

   A. Scaling

   B. Rotating

   C. Masking

   D. Flipping

17. A computer vision system is designed to recognize and count specific objects in an image. Which feature type should the system focus on detecting?

A. Corners

B. Blobs

C. Textures

D. Edges

18. What makes nonlinear programming problems more challenging than linear programming problems?

A. The absence of any constraints.

B. The presence of multiple local optima and non-convex feasible regions.

C. The objective function and constraints are always linear.

D. The solutions are always found at the center of the feasible region.

19. A surveillance system includes data from visual cameras and infrared sensors. What advantage would sensor fusion provide in this scenario?

A. It would ensure that objects can only be detected in well-lit conditions.

B. It would enable object detection across a wide range of lighting conditions.

C. It would reduce the field of view for object detection.

D. It would increase the dependency on a single sensor type.

20. An image processing application needs to align two images of the same scene taken from different angles. Which feature type is crucial for this task?

A. Corners

B. Blobs

C. Textures

D. Edges

Appendix

Answers to Review Questions

Chapter 1: What Is Data Science?

1. B. Reference and master data management focuses on ensuring that key business data, such as patient data, is used consistently across the organization.

2. D. Conducting cost-benefit analyses allows a team to evaluate the expected costs of a project against the anticipated benefits. This provides the basis for recommending or not recommending the project.

3. B. Anomaly detection based on segmentation is useful in a manufacturing setting for identifying unusual patterns in equipment sensor data, an early warning signal of potential failure. This allows for preventive maintenance and reduces unplanned downtime.

4. D. Data architecture focuses on aligning how data is structured with business requirements. This ensures that an organization's data supports efficient operations and strategic objectives.

5. C. Data security focuses on the methods and processes used to protect data from unauthorized access, alterations, and breaches. This includes ensuring that patient information is handled respectfully and in accordance with patients' preferences.

6. D. The evaluation phase in CRISP-DM involves thoroughly assessing the performance of models to ensure that they meet the objectives of the project. Juan's task of selecting the best model based on performance fits within this phase.

7. C. Reinforcement learning is ideal for scenarios where an agent (an autonomous vehicle in this case) needs to learn to make decisions by interacting with an environment (real-time traffic conditions) while receiving feedback (rewards or penalties) to maximize overall performance.

8. A. Clustering, a popular approach in segmentation, is useful in fraud detection to analyze and categorize transaction patterns. This helps detect irregularities that deviate from normal behavior.

9. C. Semi-supervised learning is well suited for situations in which both labeled and significant amounts of unlabeled data are needed to train a model. It uses the structure of the unlabeled data along with the labeled data to improve learning accuracy.

10. B. Version control systems are essential for tracking and managing changes to code, data, and models. It can help teams track revisions and manage contributions effectively throughout the lifecycle of a data science project.

11. C. The model developed by Anna's team is primarily performing prediction, as it forecasts future inventory requirements based on patterns observed in historical data.

12. B. While the evaluation phase is primarily focused on assessing model performance, it also includes reviewing the entire project workflow to identify any issues or potential improvements.

13. C. To effectively protect sensitive data such as PII and proprietary data from unauthorized access and cyberthreats, implementing security measures like data anonymization, obfuscation, encryption, and masking is crucial.

14. B. By understanding the business processes deeply, Carmen can identify inefficiencies or repetitive tasks that are candidates for automation. This will help inform her strategy for reducing operational costs.

15. A. Dependency license management tools are specifically designed to handle the complexities associated with open source licenses in software projects. These tools, such as FOSSA, help automate the process of tracking and managing software dependencies, ensuring that each component complies with its respective legal licensing requirements.

16. D. Cost-benefit analyses help evaluate the potential costs and benefits of different solutions, which aids in prioritizing those that offer the best return on investment.

17. B. The primary purpose of documenting requirements is to provide a clear and agreed-upon guideline for all subsequent phases of the project.

18. A. Lily is in the deployment phase, which involves not only integrating the model into existing systems but also setting up continuous monitoring and adjustment mechanisms to ensure the model remains effective as new data and scenarios emerge.

19. C. Market basket analysis uses association rules to find relationships between products purchased together. It falls under the umbrella of pattern mining. Kazeem can use the information from this process to help him optimize store layout and product placement.

20. A. Multimodal machine learning is an approach to machine learning that integrates data from different types of sources or modalities, such as audio, video, and text.

Chapter 2: Mathematics and Statistical Methods

1. C. A cumulative distribution function describes the probability that a random variable takes on a value less than or equal to a given threshold by providing the cumulative probability up to that threshold.

2. B. Spearman's rank correlation coefficient quantifies the monotonic relationship between two variables, meaning it measures how well the relationship between the variables can be described using a monotonic function, where the variables move in the same direction but not necessarily at a constant rate.

3. A. The rate of change of the house price with respect to the square footage is given by the derivative of the function $f(x)$ with respect to x. The derivative of $f(x) = 2x + 3$ with respect to x is 2.

4. D. The normal (Gaussian) distribution is used to model continuous data with a symmetric distribution around the mean, making it appropriate for modeling the distribution of IQ scores for the population in question.

5. A. The rank of a matrix is the maximum number of linearly independent rows or columns in the matrix. It is an important concept in linear algebra because it provides information about the dimensionality of the vector space spanned by the rows or columns of the matrix.

6. B. The confidence level in a confidence interval indicates the probability that the interval will contain the true population parameter. A 95% confidence level means we are 95% confident that the interval contains the population mean.

7. B. Integrals measure the accumulation of quantities and can be used to calculate the area under a curve.

8. C. The student's t distribution is similar to the normal distribution but with heavier tails. It is used when the sample size is small and the population standard deviation is unknown, making it suitable for estimating the mean of a small sample from a normally distributed population.

9. D. The chi-squared test of independence is useful for testing if there is a significant association or relationship between two categorical variables. Nadine wants to test for association between product category and satisfaction level (two categorical variables).

10. B. Two vectors are considered linearly independent if neither vector can be written as a linear combination of the other. This means that the vectors have unlimited span and can be combined linearly to create new vectors pointing in any direction and of any length.

11. A. Pearson's correlation coefficient measures the linear relationship between two continuous variables, which in this case would be calorie intake and weight gain.

12. B. Emeka should use Manhattan distance, also known as the taxicab or L1 distance. It is the sum of the absolute differences between two vectors and is suitable for calculating the shortest path in a grid-like environment where movement is restricted to horizontal and vertical directions.

13. C. The central limit theorem states that for a large enough sample size, the sampling distribution of the mean will always be normally distributed, regardless of the probability distribution of the population.

14. B. Yetunde should use a two-sample t-test, also known as the independent samples t-test, because it will enable her to determine whether there is a significant difference between the means of the two independent groups.

15. D. Applying a logarithmic transformation to the values of a skewed distribution makes the distribution more symmetrical. This transformation is particularly helpful in statistical analysis and modeling when the normality assumption is required.

16. A. The discrete uniform distribution is used when each outcome in a finite set of outcomes is equally likely. It is suitable for describing the outcome of rolling a fair six-sided die, where each integer between 1 and 6 has an equal probability of occurring.

17. D. ANOVA is used to compare the means of more than two independent groups to determine if there is a significant difference among them, particularly when testing the effects of a categorical independent variable (diet) on a continuous dependent variable (average weight loss).

18. C. Enzo is using cosine distance, as it measures the angle between two vectors. It is used to compute cosine similarity, which can be used to determine how similar two songs are based on their features.

19. D. Transposing a matrix involves flipping it over its diagonal, which effectively swaps its rows and columns. This operation is essential for aligning the dimensions of matrices to ensure that mathematical operations are performed accurately.

20. B. The Poisson distribution is commonly used to model the number of events (in this case, defective products) that occur within a fixed interval of time or space, given that these events happen with a known constant mean rate (five defective products per hour) and independently of the time since the last event.

Chapter 3: Data Collection and Storage

1. D. Data sources are categorized into generated data, synthetic data, and commercial or public data. Transformed data is not a common data source.

2. C. When a user logs into a website, they generate transactional data, a type of generated data. Transactional data is generated when there is an interaction between parties. Writing a poem or reading a book are not external interactions and do not generate data. GANs generate synthetic data.

3. C. Sensors are devices that collect physical data from the world around them. A user's heart rate is a physical measure, so a wearable sensor would be the most effective option.

4. C. Sampling design, question design, and data cleaning are all key considerations when collecting survey data. These considerations ensure that the data collected is accurate and unbiased. While font size may be considered, it is not important to data quality.

5. D. A key characteristic of administrative data is that it is collected as a part of an organization's normal operations. As a result, it has a high recurrence, meaning it is generated at regular intervals over long periods of time.

6. A. Transactional data is generated when there are interactions between businesses and external users, such as customers. This differs from administrative data, which is generated only through internal operations.

7. C. Surveys are useful for collecting data about public opinion. Their relative affordability makes them easy to send out to large numbers of people. Sending surveys to diverse groups of respondents ensures that the data is representative of the larger population.

8. A. Transactional data is highly dynamic, constantly being updated with every new transaction. Administrative data tends to change less frequently, updated through organizational decisions and administrative operations.

9. C. Contrary to generated data, which describes the real world, synthetic data is artificially created to imitate the real world. Sensors and experiments would create generated data rather than synthetic data.

10. B. Data ingestion is a term that describes the complete process of data being imported, processed, and stored in a system. Storage and encryption of data are steps in the data ingestion process, and analysis occurs after data is ingested.

11. C. The purpose of transforming data is to alter the data and prepare it for later storage and analysis. Some examples of data transformations are deleting erroneous observations, converting data types, and aggregating variables into a new variable.

12. B. GPUs and TPUs are specialized hardware accelerators that can increase the processing capabilities of a system. They enable parallel processing, which allows multiple tasks to be done at the same time, and resource isolation, which separates tasks and devotes specific resources to each one.

13. A. The two main methods of data ingestion are streaming and batch. In streaming, data is processed in real time as it enters the organization. In batch, data is processed in intervals, creating a delay between when it enters the organization and when it's processed. While streaming enables quicker analysis, it is costlier than batch processing.

14. B. Customer information in a CRM is highly structured data, which is useful for conducting analysis on large volumes of data. Companies collect similar data on all customers, including name, phone number, and address, making the data structured. Text documents, images, and videos are unstructured data due to their unpredictability in storage format.

15. C. Unstructured storage is used for data that does not have a consistent schema or format. It is capable of handling diverse data types but can be more difficult to analyze due to its unpredictable nature.

16. B. JSON is a semi-structured data format that has a complex, hierarchical structure. Relational databases and data warehouses are examples of structured data. A filesystem is an example of unstructured data.

17. B. Parquet is a structured data storage format. It is highly efficient and optimized, making it a good format for working with large volumes of data. For smaller datasets, other formats are capable of handling them and Parquet is not necessary.

18. C. Data lineage is an in-depth description of data's process as it moves through a system, enabling organizations to better track and understand their data. The process of storing old data is called archiving. The refresh of data on a regular schedule is called a refresh cycle.

19. B. A refresh cycle is a regular process that updates the data within a system. By conducting refresh cycles, an organization can ensure that their data stays up to date and accurate. The cycles come at the cost of using up resources but are necessary to maintain an organization's valuable data.

20. C. Organizations must use up resources to store data in their active environments. At a certain point, old data is no longer beneficial enough to justify the cost of maintaining it. At this point, organizations archive the data by moving it to long-term storage.

Chapter 4: Data Exploration and Analysis

1. B. Discrete variables can only take on certain specific values within a given range. They typically represent countable items or events where the values are distinct and separate.

2. B. Continuous variables can take on any value within a given range, including fractions and decimals. A person cannot have a fraction of a sibling; therefore, number of siblings is a discrete variable.

3. D. Nominal variables are those that have no inherent order among their categories. Its distinguishing feature makes it the opposite of ordinal variables.

4. B. The "box" in the box plot represents the interquartile range (the middle 50 percent of the data).

5. C. A Q-Q plot, or quantile-quantile plot, is used to assess whether a dataset follows a particular theoretical distribution.

6. C. In bivariate analysis, a bar chart can be used to compare a categorical variable and a continuous variable, or two categorical variables.

7. C. In a correlation plot, a positive value near 1 indicates a strong positive correlation, meaning that as one variable increases, the other tends to increase as well.

8. C. While similar, correlation plots and heatmaps are not the same thing. Given that a heatmap is a graphical representation of data where values in a matrix are represented as colors, a correlation plot is a specific kind of heatmap.

9. B. A Sankey Diagram is a type of flow diagram that visualizes the distribution of flows or quantities from one set of values to another.

10. C. Cluster analysis aims to maximize intracluster similarity (similarity between items in the same cluster) and minimize the intercluster similarity (similarity between items in different clusters).

11. C. Principal component analysis is a dimensionality reduction technique used in multivariate analysis.

12. B. Granularity misalignment in data quality refers to the mismatch in the level of detail or specificity in data. Addressing granularity misalignment usually involves aggregating more granular data, obtaining additional data to make aggregated data more granular, or removing unnecessary or excessive detail to ensure that a consistent level of granularity is achieved throughout the dataset.

13. D. Nonlinearity arises when the relationship between the independent and dependent variables in a dataset cannot be adequately represented with a linear model.

14. D. Nonstationarity is a common data quality issue in time-series analysis where the statistical properties of a sequence of data points vary with time.

15. C. A clearer analysis could take place by evaluating just the underlying trend of the time series without the repeating seasonal pattern. Therefore, seasonality is typically resolved by removing the seasonal component.

16. B. Seasonality refers to the phenomenon of patterns in the data repeating at regular intervals, corresponding to specific seasons or times of the year.

17. C. Features are deemed insufficient only if they lack enough information to aid with accurately modeling the problem. They tend to lead to underfitting, which will result in poor model performance.

18. B. Sparsity refers to the degree to which a variable's data points are missing or are zero. Therefore, calculating the proportion of missing or zero values would help us identify the level of sparsity in a dataset.

19. C. When missing data is independent of any observed or unobserved data, it is classified as missing completely at random (MCAR). There are no systematic differences between observations with missing data and those without.

20. B. Sparse data implies that a variable itself has mostly missing values (for example, missing a majority of age values from a population surveyed), whereas missing data refers to specific data points or observations with missing values for one or more variables (for example, missing many data points from a single person who took the survey).

Chapter 5: Data Processing and Preparation

1. A. Data transformation involves converting data from one format, structure, or representation into another to fulfill specific requirements or to make it more suitable for certain tasks or analyses.

2. A. Label encoding assigns a unique integer to each category, which can imply a nonexistent ordinal relationship among categories, potentially leading to misleading results in certain algorithms.

3. C. Scaling and normalization ensure that numerical features have values on a consistent scale, preventing any single feature from having an undue influence due to its scale.

4. C. The Box-Cox transformation requires positive input values, as its formula doesn't accommodate negative numbers.

5. C. Feature engineering involves creating new, relevant variables from existing data, which can provide deeper insights during analysis. Creating a new feature by subtracting the square footage of the basement from the total square footage of a house is an example of feature engineering.

6. D. Geocoding is the process of converting addresses into geographical coordinates, which can significantly improve location-based services and operations.

7. C. An anti-join is designed to identify records in one dataset that have no corresponding matches in another.

8. A. Log transformation is useful for addressing skewness in data distribution, stabilizing variances, and handling data that spans several orders of magnitude.

9. B. Deleting missing values reduces data complexity but might result in the loss of significant data, especially if the dataset is small.

10. C. Feature extraction involves transforming high-dimensional data into a lower-dimensional form while preserving the most significant information from the original data, thus facilitating easier processing, visualization, and analysis.

11. B. Before analysis, it's imperative to convert or standardize measurements to a consistent unit to ensure compatibility and accuracy in the dataset.

12. B. This is an example of categorical inconsistency, where identical categories within a dataset are represented differently.

13. D. Undersampling reduces the number of examples in the majority class, potentially discarding valuable information that could be important for the model's learning process.

14. B. In cases of class imbalance, a model might simply predict the majority class for all inputs, achieving high accuracy while failing to correctly predict the minority class. This phenomenon is known as the accuracy paradox.

15. C. Systematic errors are consistent and follow a specific pattern, often leading to consistently misleading results if not addressed.

16. C. Binning, or discretization, involves converting continuous data into distinct categories or intervals, known as bins, for purposes like enhanced visualization or preparation for certain analysis methods.

17. D. Winsorization modifies extreme values to make them less extreme, retaining the overall data structure and size while reducing the influence of these values.

18. B. A union operation requires that each dataset has the same number of columns and that corresponding columns have compatible data types.

19. A. Class imbalance is problematic because there are fewer examples of the minority class for the algorithm to learn from, making it difficult for the model to discern the patterns that set apart the minority class from the majority class.

20. B. Linearizing data helps satisfy the assumptions of many statistical models that presume linearity, improves model performance and interpretability, and reduces complexity.

Chapter 6: Modeling and Evaluation

1. B. Binary classifiers categorize data points into one of two distinct classes.

2. B. R-squared represents the proportion of the variance for a dependent variable that's explained by an independent variable or variables in a regression model.

3. C. A/B testing is a randomized experiment that compares the impact of two variants, A and B.

4. B. BIC prefers simpler models with better fit, so a lower BIC suggests that the model strikes a better balance between complexity (number of parameters) and fit to the data.

5. B. When comparing models using AIC, the model with the lower AIC value is considered better. Thus, Model B will be the preferred model.

6. C. A high RMSE indicates poor fit, as it means the predicted values are, on average, far from the actual values. It suggests that the model may be underfitting and not capturing the underlying trends of the data.

7. B. Sensitivity is the true positive rate and has the same calculation as recall.

8. C. Occam's Razor (or the Law of Parsimony) suggests that simplicity is preferable to complexity, so a simpler model is more likely to perform better on new data.

9. A. Adjusted R-squared is used alongside R-squared because it adjusts for the number of variables in the model, only increasing if the new variables improve the model more than would be expected by chance.

10. C. Regression models establish a relationship between input features and a continuous target variable, like house prices.

11. B. Longitudinal studies involve repeated observations of the same subjects over a period of time.

12. C. An R-squared value of 0.95 indicates that 95% of the variability of the dependent variable (housing prices) around its mean is explained by the model.

13. A. Data leakage can occur when chronological data is not split chronologically, which can result in current data being included in the training data and prior data in the test.

14. C. Multiclass classifiers are used in scenarios where there are three or more potential categories.

15. C. The ROC curve visually represents the trade-off between a model's true positive rate (sensitivity) and false positive rate (1-specificity).

16. B. Sensitivity (or recall) measures the proportion of actual positive examples that are correctly identified (true positive rate). In this scenario, malignant tumors are the positive example, so if the team is concerned about correctly identifying as many malignant tumors as possible, then sensitivity/recall is the right metric to evaluate.

17. C. The main advantage of the Matthews correlation coefficient over other metrics like accuracy, precision, and recall is that it considers all four quadrants of the confusion matrix.

18. C. AUC represents the ability of a model to distinguish between positive and negative classes. A higher AUC indicates better performance, so Model A is better in this respect.

19. C. Time-series models focus on analyzing data collected over regular intervals in time.

20. B. Accuracy can be misleading when the dataset suffers from class imbalance. In this scenario, even a model that predicts every transaction as legitimate would achieve 95% accuracy.

Chapter 7: Model Validation and Deployment

1. C. Containerization supports dividing complex applications into microservices. This modularity makes it easier to separately manage and update different services like data preprocessing and inference.

2. C. For a technical audience, code documentation would be most valuable because it provides detailed explanations of the logic, parameters, and structure of the algorithms used by the model.

3. C. A residual plot displays the difference between observed and predicted values. It is ideal for assessing the goodness of fit of a model that predicts housing prices (a regression model).

4. D. Validating resource constraints specific to the deployment environment, especially in the context of edge devices or mobile applications, is important to ensure that a model continues to operate efficiently on a target device.

5. A. Benchmarking against a baseline involves comparing a new model's performance with a predefined standard to see if the value added by a new model justifies the potential increase in complexity that comes with it.

6. D. Cluster deployment offers the flexibility to dynamically scale resources up or down based on workload, which is beneficial for handling variable computational loads, such as during high-traffic events.

7. B. Precision-recall curves are crucial in scenarios like healthcare where the cost of false negatives is high, as they highlight the trade-off between precision and recall.

8. B. Benchmarking against conventional processes involves evaluating a model's performance against existing business practices to assess the real-world impact of introducing the model.

9. B. A clear pattern in the residuals, such as the variance depending on fitted values, suggests that issues like nonlinearity or heteroscedasticity may exist in the data.

10. A. Comparing a new model's performance against an existing simpler model falls under benchmarking against a baseline, which helps to determine the relative improvement or efficacy of the new model.

11. B. In a dynamic environment such as the stock market, the model's ability to adapt to market changes over time without frequent retraining is a crucial aspect of its suitability.

12. D. Code versioning enables multiple team members to work on different aspects of a project codebase simultaneously without causing conflicts.

13. B. On-premises deployment is often preferred to maintain full control over the data and to comply with security protocols.

14. B. Continuous monitoring is crucial to ensure the model performs as expected, and to identify and address issues like concept drift early.

15. D. Edge deployment is suitable for scenarios requiring real-time data processing due to its reduced latency.

16. B. A residual plot is used to assess how well a regression model fits the data by showing the residuals' distribution.

17. C. Containerization ensures that a solution runs consistently when deployed in different environments, regardless of the differences in the underlying environment.

18. B. Model validation is crucial for ensuring that a data science model meets its design specifications and satisfies the requirements it was built to address.

19. A. Model A/B testing involves running two or more models simultaneously on similar data to compare their performances. It's useful for evaluating new models or model changes in a controlled manner.

20. A. Decision tree visualizations provide a clear view of how different features lead to specific predictions. They are essential for models where explainability is important.

Chapter 8: Unsupervised Machine Learning

1. B. Content-based filtering is suitable for situations with limited user data, as it recommends items based on item characteristics rather than user-item interactions.

2. B. Principal component analysis (PCA) is a linear dimensionality reduction technique that transforms correlated features into a smaller set of uncorrelated features, retaining much of the variation in the original data.

3. A. This is a trivial rule, as it provides insight that is already well known. Buying tomato sauce with pasta is expected.

4. B. The elbow method involves plotting the total WCSS against different k values and looking for a point where the rate of decrease in WCSS sharply changes (the point of inflection).

5. B. The system is most likely using content-based filtering, by making recommendations based on item characteristics (books by the same author).

6. C. t-SNE is particularly effective for visualizing complex, high-dimensional data in lower dimensions while maintaining high-dimensional relationships.

7. A. Support measures the fraction of transactions that contain both items in the rule. This means that in this dataset 30% of all transactions include both video games and snacks.

8. B. A feature extraction technique such as principal component analysis (PCA) is effective in reducing the dimensionality of large datasets, which reduces computational complexity.

9. B. The support of 0.25 means that 25% of all transactions include both coffee and sugar; 25% of 400 transactions is 100 transactions.

10. D. Using a machine learning model to make recommendations based on a user's past interactions with items is model-based collaborative filtering.

11. C. Centroid-based clustering methods, such as k-means clustering, are known to be sensitive to outliers, which can significantly impact the calculation of cluster centers.

12. C. The system is using collaborative filtering, which bases recommendations solely on the user-item interactions matrix.

13. D. Cluster analysis can categorize network traffic activity into clusters, which helps identify outliers as anomalous behavior.

14. B. A high confidence level indicates high predictive power or accuracy. In this instance, it means that in 90% of the transactions where diapers were purchased, baby wipes were also purchased.

15. C. The platform is using content-based filtering by recommending movies with similar genres (romantic comedies) based on Xiaojing's preferences and prior history.

16. B. Agglomerative hierarchical clustering is a bottom-up approach that starts by treating each data point as a separate cluster and then iteratively merging them.

17. A. A lift value less than 1 suggests that the occurrence of the antecedent (flour) decreases the likelihood of the consequent (yeast) being purchased.

18. C. In a recommender system, the database of which items users have interacted with is known as the user-item interactions matrix.

19. A. The issue of consistently recommending popular items, while ignoring less popular but relevant content, is known as popularity bias. It is a common limitation of collaborative filtering.

20. B. A lift value greater than 1 suggests that the occurrence of the antecedent (beer) increases the likelihood of the consequent (chips) being purchased.

Chapter 9: Supervised Machine Learning

1. C. Linear regression assumes a linear relationship between the independent variables (predictors) and the dependent variable.

2. B. A key assumption of linear discriminant analysis is that the predictor variables in each class follow a Gaussian (normal) distribution.

3. B. By setting a maximum depth for the decision tree, Irene can control the complexity of the model. This approach, known as pruning, helps to prevent overfitting by limiting how deep the tree can grow, ensuring that the model remains generalizable.

4. C. Random forests is an ensemble method that addresses the issue of overfitting, which is common with decision trees. By aggregating the predictions of multiple decision trees, random forests models reduce the variance of the ensemble, thus minimizing overfitting.

5. C. Linear regression commonly uses the ordinary least squares (OLS) method to estimate the best set of coefficients. This method minimizes the sum of the squared differences between observed and predicted values.

6. C. The "zero frequency problem" in naive Bayes occurs when the model encounters a feature in the test set that it has not seen in the training set and assigns a zero probability to it.

7. B. The weighted least squares (WLS) method is an adaptation of OLS used in scenarios where different observations have different variances (heteroscedasticity).

8. B. The Durbin–Watson test is used to detect the presence of autocorrelation (correlation of error terms).

9. A. L1 regularization (LASSO regression) modifies the loss function to include a penalty that can reduce some coefficients to 0, effectively removing them from the model.

10. A. Limiting the depth of a decision tree is a form of pruning.

11. B. Regularization techniques, such as L1 or L2 regularization, are used in logistic regression to prevent overfitting.

12. B. This scenario validates the linearity assumption of linear regression, which states that the relationship between independent variables and the dependent variable should be linear.

13. A. One way to address the challenge of handling continuous data in naive Bayes is to discretize the continuous variables (e.g., binning).

14. B. Exponentiating a log-odds output converts it to odds.

15. C. If our data violates the linearity assumption, switching to a nonlinear model is an appropriate approach.

16. C. The zero frequency problem in naive Bayes occurs when the algorithm encounters a feature in the test set that it did not see in the training set.

17. B. Bob is dealing with heteroscedasticity, where the variance of residuals changes with the predictors. The weighted least squares method is specifically designed to handle this.

18. D. LDA is often preferred over QDA when the sample size is small within each class. This is because QDA is more likely to overfit with smaller sample sizes compared to LDA.

19. D. To validate the assumption of normality in the predictors, Kevin can use the Shapiro–Wilk test.

20. C. The uneven distribution of residuals across different levels of the independent variables suggests a violation of the homoscedasticity assumption in linear regression.

Chapter 10: Neural Networks and Deep Learning

1. C. CNNs are ideal for image processing and object detection in videos due to their ability to handle grid-like data such as the pixels in an image.

2. A. Dropout is a regularization technique used to prevent overfitting by randomly removing outputs between nodes during training.

3. A. LSTMs are designed to overcome the vanishing gradient problem common in traditional RNNs, particularly when dealing with long sequences of data.

4. C. Transformers, with their self-attention mechanism, are well suited for understanding and generating contextually relevant text.

5. D. The softmax activation function is used in multiclass classification problems. It converts the output logits to probabilities, which sum up to 1, making it easier to determine the most probable class.

6. B. Batch normalization stabilizes and accelerates the training process by normalizing the inputs to each layer, ensuring consistency across different training batches.

7. B. Activation functions in neural networks serve to normalize the output of nodes and introduce nonlinearity, enabling the network to learn and model complex patterns in the data.

8. C. CNNs are adept at processing and analyzing images, making them ideal for medical image analysis.

9. C. Early stopping prevents overfitting by halting the training process when the model's performance on a validation set starts to degrade.

10. B. The Sigmoid activation function outputs values between 0 and 1, making it suitable for binary classification problems where the output is often interpreted as a probability.

11. C. The deeper a neural network is, the more capable it is of extracting and learning complex patterns in data.

12. D. LSTMs are effective for learning tasks involving sequential data, such as sensor data in autonomous vehicles.

13. C. PyTorch is renowned for its flexibility and dynamic computational graph, which allows for modifications to the network during runtime. This feature makes it highly suitable for research and experimental projects.

14. D. ReLU is commonly used in deep learning networks, as it helps in mitigating the vanishing gradient problem by allowing a faster and more effective training process.

15. A. Learning rate schedulers adjust the learning rate during training, often in response to the model's performance on validation data.

16. D. Autoencoders can learn normal transaction patterns and detect anomalies or deviations.

17. B. Zero-shot learning allows a model to classify items into previously unseen classes by linking them through auxiliary information.

18. C. Activation functions introduce nonlinearity to a neural network, enabling it to capture complex patterns in the data. Adjusting the type of activation function can significantly enhance the network's ability to model nonlinear relationships.

19. C. The vanishing gradient problem occurs when the gradients become increasingly small, especially in deeper networks with many layers. This leads to very small updates in the weights of the early layers, resulting in a slow and inefficient training process.

20. B. NAS involves the automatic design of neural network architectures that are optimized for specific tasks, streamlining the process of building effective deep learning models.

Chapter 11: Natural Language Processing

1. D. The lexicon-based approach to sentiment analysis determines the sentiment of a piece of text based on the presence of opinion words (words and phrases associated with positive, negative, or neutral sentiment) within the text.

2. B. The primary purpose of text representation is to convert unstructured text into a structured format that machines (models) can understand and use.

3. B. Word-level augmenters, a type of data augmentation technique, can involve synonym replacement, where words are replaced with their synonyms to create varied versions of the same sentence.

4. A. Ensuring that generated text logically flows from one sentence to another is a challenge of coherence and consistency in language generation.

5. D. One-hot encoding results in high-dimensional vectors, which makes it resource intensive, especially for large vocabularies.

6. A. In information retrieval, extracted keywords are used to enhance the searchability of documents in databases and search engines, enabling users to find relevant information more efficiently.

7. C. TF-IDF measures the importance of a word within each document, providing a more nuanced understanding of the text by highlighting words that are significant in a particular document but less common in the overall corpus.

8. A. Part-of-speech (POS) tagging involves identifying the grammatical part of speech for each word in a sentence, which is essential for understanding the structure of sentences and for tasks that require a deep understanding of linguistic structure.

9. D. Sentiment analysis involves identifying and categorizing the opinions or emotions expressed in a piece of text to determine the writer's attitude toward a particular topic, product, or service.

10. A. Word embeddings represent words as dense vectors in a high-dimensional space, where the semantic similarity between words is captured by the distance between their corresponding vectors.

11. B. String matching involves comparing text based on its lexical or syntactic similarity, often at the character or token level. It is useful for plagiarism detection.

12. C. Named entity recognition is the task of identifying and classifying proper nouns (names of people, places, organizations, etc.) in text, which can be used for autotagging articles in content management systems.

13. A. Character-level augmenters, a type of data augmentation technique, can be used to introduce typographical errors or simulate OCR errors to mimic the kind of noise that real-world data often contains.

14. B. Unlike the continuous bag of words model, which predicts a target word based on its context, the skip-gram model works in the opposite direction. It predicts context words given a target word.

15. C. Stemming is the process of reducing words to their base or root form, which can help simplify text data analysis.

16. B. Unlike Word2Vec, which uses local context information (surrounding words) in its training process, GloVe is designed to capture both global statistics and local context in a text corpus.

17. D. Removing stop words helps focus on the more meaningful words in the text by eliminating common words that have very little analytic impact.

18. A. Language understanding is important for speech recognition systems to transform spoken language into text, as it involves recognizing words and understanding their context and relationships.

19. B. Language generation focuses on enabling computers to create human-like text based on specific inputs or prompts, which is crucial for chatbots to produce natural and coherent responses to user queries.

20. C. Keyword extraction involves automatically identifying and extracting the most relevant words or phrases from text that represent its main content or themes.

Chapter 12: Specialized Applications of Data Science

1. **B.** Cropping involves removing the outer parts of an image to focus on a specific region of interest, making it the appropriate choice for removing unnecessary background information from an image.

2. **B.** Decision variables, also known as optimization variables, are the parameters in an optimization problem that can be adjusted or controlled to achieve the desired outcome, such as maximizing profit or minimizing cost.

3. **C.** Optical character recognition (OCR) is the most suitable approach for converting images of typed, handwritten, or printed text into machine-encoded text.

4. **C.** Texture extraction is important for tasks like terrain analysis, as it involves examining the repeated patterns or structures present in an image.

5. **A.** This scenario represents a resource allocation problem, where the objective is to optimally distribute limited resources among competing activities or projects. In this case, the resource is investment capital, and the activities are the different investment options.

6. **B.** Image segmentation involves partitioning an image into multiple segments or regions, which will be useful for identifying tumors in MRI scans.

7. **C.** In this scenario, the problem can be framed as a multi-armed bandit problem where balancing exploration (testing different ads to gather information about their CTRs) and exploitation (focusing on displaying ads that currently have high CTRs) is used to maximize the total number of clicks.

8. **A.** Scaling involves adjusting the size of an image while maintaining its aspect ratio.

9. **B.** This scenario illustrates a scheduling problem, where the objective is to allocate resources over time (staff members) to perform a collection of tasks (handling customer inquiries while minimizing wait times) and adhering to constraints like labor laws and budget constraints.

10. **B.** Image segmentation is crucial in license plate recognition, as it involves partitioning the image into segments, allowing the system to isolate the license plate from the rest of the image before further processing.

11. **D.** Edges are important for shape analysis, as they define the boundaries between different regions in an image.

12. **D.** Constraints are the limitations or requirements that the solution to an optimization problem must satisfy. They define the feasible region within which the optimal solution must lie.

13. A. Motion analysis and object tracking are essential in video surveillance for understanding the movement of objects (or people) and monitoring their trajectories over time.

14. D. The optimal solution often lies on the boundary of the feasible region because, at these points, any small change in the decision variables would violate a constraint, making it impossible to improve one objective without worsening another.

15. B. Converting images from RGB to grayscale simplifies analysis by reducing the dimensionality of the data, making it suitable for applications like edge detection when color information is not critical.

16. C. Masking is used to selectively filter or modify certain parts of an image while leaving other parts unchanged. This makes it suitable for defining a specific region of interest within an image.

17. B. Blobs are regions in an image that differ in properties, such as brightness or color, compared to surrounding areas, and are often used to represent objects or parts of objects in an image. Detecting the blobs in an image is important for object recognition and counting tasks.

18. B. Nonlinear programming problems are more challenging than linear programming problems due to the presence of multiple local optima, non-convex feasible regions, and the complexity of the mathematical relationships.

19. B. By combining data from visual cameras and infrared sensors, sensor fusion would allow the surveillance system to detect objects not only in well-lit conditions but also in low-light or no-light conditions.

20. A. Corners are points where two or more edges meet and are often considered points of interest due to their distinctiveness. They are useful for feature matching and image registration.

Index

Online Test Bank

To help you study for your CompTIA DataX certification exam, register to gain one year of FREE access after activation to the online interactive test bank—included with your purchase of this book! All of the chapter review questions and the practice tests in this book are included in the online test bank so you can practice in a timed and graded setting.

Register and Access the Online Test Bank

To register your book and get access to the online test bank, follow these steps:

1. Go to www.wiley.com/go/sybextestprep. You'll see the **"How to Register Your Book for Online Access"** instructions.
2. Click "here to register" and then select your book from the list.
3. Complete the required registration information, including answering the security verification to prove book ownership. You will be emailed a pin code.
4. Follow the directions in the email or go to www.wiley.com/go/sybextestprep.
5. Find your book on that page and click the "Register or Login" link with it. Then enter the pin code you received and click the "Activate PIN" button.
6. On the Create an Account or Login page, enter your username and password, and click Login or, if you don't have an account already, create a new account.
7. At this point, you should be in the test bank site with your new test bank listed at the top of the page. If you do not see it there, please refresh the page or log out and log back in.